DATE DUE

A Configuration of the IBM System 360

Electronic Data Processing

An Introduction

IRWIN SERIES IN QUANTITATIVE ANALYSIS FOR BUSINESS

Consulting Editor

ROBERT B. FETTER *Yale University*

BOWMAN & FETTER *Analysis for Production Management* **Revised Edition**

BIERMAN, FOURAKER, & JAEDICKE *Quantitative Analysis for Business Decisions*

MARTIN *Electronic Data Processing: An Introduction* Revised Edition

BASS, BUZZELL, GREENE, LAZER, PESSEMIER, SHAWVER, SHUCHMAN, THEODORE, & WILSON *Mathematical Models and Methods in Marketing*

MORRIS *Analysis for Materials Handling Management*

FRANK, KUEHN, & MASSY *Quantitative Techniques in Marketing Analysis: Text and Readings*

HOWELL & TEICHROEW *Mathematical Analysis for Business Decisions*

MORRIS *Management Science in Action*

BOWEN *Mathematics: With Applications in Management and Economics*

BERANEK *Analysis for Financial Decisions*

McMILLAN & GONZALEZ *Systems Analysis: A Computer Approach to Decision Models*

THEODORE *Applied Mathematics: An Introduction: Mathematical Analysis for Management*

ELLIOTT & WASLEY *Business Information Processing Systems*

ELECTRONIC DATA PROCESSING

An Introduction

by E. WAINRIGHT MARTIN, JR.
Professor of Business Administration and
Director of Research Computing Center
Indiana University

REVISED EDITION
1965
RICHARD D. IRWIN, INC.
HOMEWOOD, ILLINOIS

REVISED EDITION
First Printing, March, 1965
Second Printing, September, 1965

Library of Congress Catalog Card No. 65–17692

PRINTED IN THE UNITED STATES OF AMERICA

To my "book widow,"
CHARLENE

PREFACE

This book is based upon the fundamental premise that an organization's data processing system is of crucial importance to the attainment of effective management control. The electronic computer potentially has a revolutionary impact upon data processing systems, and thus upon management control, but the full realization of this potential cannot be attained without widespread management understanding of the opportunities and problems associated with the use of this equipment.

Written specifically as a textbook for an introductory course in electronic data processing, this book was designed for the mature student, but it does not require any prior background in mechanized data processing or any mathematics beyond an ability to manipulate positive and negative decimal numbers. However, because of my conviction that (partially because of the computer) the manager of the future needs to know some mathematics, an explanation of why mathematics is important in the use of computers is included. Also, there are examples and exercises that will be familiar to students with a mathematical background.

This book has two basic objectives:

1. To provide the general manager, who does not expect to specialize in computer technology, with an understanding of the capabilities and limitations of the electronic computer, of the management considerations involved in its use, and of the impact of the computer upon the management profession.
2. To provide an introduction to this subject to those who aspire to specialize in the area of information technology.

In the attainment of the above objectives, I have attempted to provide a reasonable compromise between technical material and discussions of general implications, with major emphasis upon the concepts involved, but with enough specific material included to make the concepts meaningful. This compromise has been motivated by my feeling that general management typically suffers from too superficial a knowledge of the characteristics of electronic data processing equipment, while on the other hand data processing specialists are frequently handicapped by lack of understanding of the basic objectives of data processing and of the management problems involved in the use of computers. Since the field of electronic data processing is still young, I do not pretend to provide answers to all of these complex problems, but instead attempt to bring up the pertinent questions. Although the answers may change from time to time, the problems, like death and taxes, appear to be eternal.

This book is organized as follows: The overall impact of the computer upon our society is presented in Chapter 1. Chapter 2 is devoted to the basic objectives of data processing, to an introduction to the important concepts of *systems,* and to a breakdown of data processing into its elementary components. Chapters 3 and 4 present a concise introduction to the functions of punched card machines, the principles upon which they operate, and their use in data processing. The development of mechanized procedures is introduced, and the data recording and processing rigor required for mechanized data processing is illustrated.

It is my belief that a manager, although he may never have to write a program for a computer, needs to have a brief experience with computer programming in order to understand what computers can and cannot do, and (more importantly) what is involved in using them. Thus, Chapters 5–7 are devoted to the characteristics of the stored program and to basic programming techniques. In order to present these ideas as efficiently as possible and eliminate unnecessary complexity, the MAC (a hypothetical computer incorporating the major characteristics of many different machines) is used in Chapters 6 and 7.

The important area of *software* is discussed in Chapter 8. A symbolic programming system is described, and the basic characteristics of procedure-oriented languages are illustrated by FORTRAN. The advantages and limitations of programming languages are also discussed.

The solution of a data processing problem involves much more than the mere writing of a series of program steps. This overall process, starting with the definition of the problem and concluding with conversion of processing from the previous system to the computer, is discussed in Chapter 9. The interrelationships between the steps in this process, and their consequences, are emphasized. Chapter 10 provides some illustrations of uses of computers, with emphasis upon the creative aspects of using such equipment for data processing.

Chapter 11 discusses the characteristics of magnetic tape, and describes its use for input-output and for file processing. Chapter 12 describes random access files, discusses their use, and contrasts them with magnetic tape files. In Chapter 13, we broaden our knowledge of computers by discussing machine characteristics that are not illustrated by the MAC. Communication networks, multi-machine systems, and real-time systems are also considered in this chapter.

Systems analysis and design, which has been introduced in Chapters 2 and 9, is the subject of more concentrated discussion in Chapter 14, where basic techniques are explored and the systems approach is again emphasized. This chapter is organized around the structure provided by IBM's Study Organization Plan.

Chapters 15–17 are concerned with the management considerations associated with electronic data processing. Chapter 15 is concerned with the organization and staffing of a centralized data processing facility. Chapter 16 discusses the human relations, and organizational, administrative, and economic problems involved in installing electronic data processing machines. A case that illustrates a number of these problems is given in Appendix A.

The final chapter is concerned with the impact of the computer and its associated information technology upon management. First, there is a discussion of the common pitfalls associated with the use of the computer. Then a process of Organizational Research and Development is advocated, and concepts of the scientific method, mathematical model building, and computer simulation are discussed and illustrated. Finally, the impact of the computer upon the profession of management is considered.

I am deeply indebted to so many for help in preparing this book, and its predecessor, that it is impossible to mention everyone here. However, I would like to express special appreciation to the International Business Machines Corporation, in whose employment I received my first training and experience with computers. So much of the philosophy expressed herein and so many of the illustrations included are derived from my IBM background and experience, as well as from IBM publications, that it is impossible for me to give detailed credit for this material. However, I am particularly indebted to IBM for Exercise 7–2 and for many illustrations and examples throughout the book. I am also indebted to the editor of *Business Horizons* for permission to reproduce material used in

Chapters 1, 16, and 17, and to R. L. Ackoff as the source of some of the ideas concerning operations research and information flows expressed in Chapters 2 and 17.

Among the many who read, used, and commented upon the manuscript of the first edition, the following were especially helpful: D. R. Mason (especially Chapter 15), Van B. Thompson (especially Chapters 3 and 4), and my father, E. W. Martin, Sr.

Professor Robert B. Fetter, consulting editor of the Irwin Series in Quantitative Analysis for Business, made a number of valuable suggestions that were incorporated in this Revised Edition, and the copy editors at the Richard D. Irwin Company helped immeasurably to reduce the awkwardness in my writing.

Many teachers who used the first edition of this book have contributed valuable suggestions and comments, as have a number of students who were "subjected" to the first edition. I am specially grateful to my colleague, Professor William C. Perkins, for such suggestions, and to Mr. Paul Swadener for many helpful suggestions while carefully reading the manuscript and proofs, and for preparing the index. My deepest gratitude must be expressed to Mrs. Anna Strikis and Mrs. Patricia Wright who typed and retyped these materials with competence and good humor.

The efforts of those mentioned above have been directed toward improving the content and toward removing my errors and misstatements. Along with my thanks for their assistance, I must absolve them of blame for those inadequacies that remain, which are solely my responsibility.

Research that contributed significantly to the development of this book was supported by the Indiana University Graduate School of Business, its alumni and friends, and the Ford Foundation. Finally, I would like to express my appreciation to Deans A. M. Weimer and W. G. Pinnell for their encouragement and support, and to the Indiana University Graduate School of Business for providing secretarial and duplicating services that enabled me to test the various versions of these materials in my classes.

E. W. MARTIN, JR.

BLOOMINGTON, INDIANA
January, 1965

TABLE OF CONTENTS

1 THE IMPACT OF THE ELECTRONIC COMPUTER

FEW DEVELOPMENTS of our age have captured the imagination of the public as has the electronic computer. Almost everyone has marveled at the exploits of these so-called "giant brains" which have been reported in the newspapers and magazines and on our television screens. Much of this publicity is inaccurate and misleading, but behind the publicity is a series of accomplishments and promises of future accomplishment which indicate that the electronic computer is one of the most important developments of this century.

In testimony before a congressional subcommittee on automation in 1955, Ralph J. Cordiner, then president of General Electric Company, expressed his faith in the future of the electronic computer in the following words:

When the history of our age is written, I think it will record three profoundly important technological developments:

Nuclear energy, which tremendously increases the amount of *energy* available to do the world's work;

Automation, which greatly increases man's ability to use *tools;*

And *computers,* which multiply man's ability to do *mental* work.

Some of our engineers believe that of these three, the computer will bring the greatest benefit to man.[1]

In 1955, when these prophetic words were spoken, the computer was in its infancy, and its development since that time has been remarkable. Almost ten years later, when some 16,000 computers were in use, *Fortune* magazine editorialized:

---

[1] Quoted from testimony of Ralph J. Cordiner before the Subcommittee on Economic Stabilization of the Joint Committee on the Economic Report, October 26, 1955, p. 444 of the printed record.

Today, men who ought to know say that the computer will have an effect on human life comparable to the invention of the steam engine. If that is only half true, anybody who hopes to play a responsible part in the second half of the twentieth century had better understand as much as he can of what computers do for—and to—people.[2]

This statement may in fact be conservative. Dr. Richard W. Hamming, director of mathematics research at Bell Telephone Laboratories, points out that the first steam engines were only about ten times as effective as animal power. Steam-powered vehicles were about ten times faster than the horse and buggy. Computers, however, are up to ten million times as fast as the mechanical calculators they replace. Rather than compare the electronic computer to the steam engine which triggered the Industrial Revolution, Hamming compares it to the Darwinian and Copernican revolutions, "both of which changed man's ideas of himself and the world in which he lives."[3]

Although the major emphasis of this book is on the use of the electronic computer for business data processing, this is but one of the areas in which the impact of the computer upon our society is being felt. Since there is a tendency among businessmen to emphasize the application of the computers in the office, to the virtual exclusion of the other areas to which they have significantly contributed, this chapter will be devoted to an attempt to present an overall view of the influence which the computer is exerting upon our society.

HISTORY

The first large-scale electronic computer was the Eniac, which was completed in 1946 by the Moore School of Electrical Engineering at the University of Pennsylvania. This machine was designed primarily to perform the calculations required in the preparation of ballistics tables. Although composed of some 18,000 tubes, by modern standards the Eniac had very little flexibility, was slow, and was quite unreliable, but it was a significant step forward in computing ability and demonstrated conclusively that the electron could be harnessed to compute.

During the next few years, computers were built at various government laboratories and universities. These computers were usually

---

[2] "Onrush of the Robots," editorial in *Fortune,* March, 1964, p. 98.

[3] "New Tool, New World," special report in *Business Week,* February 29, 1964, p. 90.

"one-of-a-kind" machines, because once they had been built, the designers learned so much from their experience that they would never build another one exactly the same. However, around 1953, the Sperry Rand Univac and the IBM 701 became available on a production line basis, and dependable large-scale computers were a commercial reality. Starting from the few machines in existence in 1953, the use of computers has grown by leaps and bounds. Late in 1957, there were around 200 large-scale electronic computers and around 600 small- and intermediate-sized machines in use in the United States. By late 1959, this had grown to an estimated 400 large-scale computer systems and over 2,000 small- and intermediate-sized machines. In 1964 there were around 16,000 domestic installations involving over 100 different types of general purpose electronic computers.

Although they started slower than the United States, other countries have also made rapid strides in the use of computers. In mid-1959 it was reported that about 100 electronic computers were in use in Britain alone, and the Russians were known to be utilizing some of the most powerful computing machines in existence. By 1964 there were approximately 1,700 computers in use outside the United States, and this overseas use was expanding at a faster rate than the domestic computer market. In fact, IBM (the major producer of computers) has predicted that its overseas revenues will exceed its domestic business in a reasonable number of years (probably in the 1970s).

This rapid growth is not explained by any single use of computers —they have been widely used in both scientific computation and business data processing, they show great promise in the area of automatic control, and they are practically indispensable to our national defense and in space technology.

COMPUTERS IN SCIENCE

Computers were originally developed by scientists and engineers to aid in the solution of problems involving large amounts of computation. The classic scientific method consists of:

1. Observation of a situation under study.
2. Formation of a hypothesis to explain what was observed.
3. Further observation and experimentation to check the hypothesis.
4. Modification of the hypothesis.
5. Further observation and experimentation—and so on *ad infinitum.*

The hypotheses frequently are mathematical statements expressing relationships between observable variables. These mathematical statements are used for prediction, and the predictions are compared with the observed results. This process of using mathematical statements for prediction often involves a tremendous amount of calculation.

For example, let us consider astronomy. In astronomy, you cannot experiment; you can only observe. The motions of the various planets, comets, and stars can be represented by mathematical equations. The validity of the equations can be tested by calculating future positions of these bodies based upon these equations, and verifying (or failing to verify) these predictions on the basis of observations. Before the development of the electronic computer, many astronomers spent the major portion of their working years slaving away over hand calculators making these computations. Today, they can concern themselves instead with formulating better equations, devising equipment for obtaining more precise observations, and developing more efficient methods for solution of the equations.

Similar types of problems occur in nuclear physics, and in chemistry in the area of molecular structure. In the study of our atmosphere and its weather, extremely complicated equations involving large numbers of variables arise; and great strides have been made in the understanding of weather since the development of the electronic computer. As a matter of fact, the late John von Neumann predicted that within our lifetimes we may learn enough about weather to actually control our climate.[4]

The impact of the computer upon research is illustrated by the fact that it takes about an hour on an IBM 7094 computer to do the equivalent of a million man-hours of desk calculator work. At an hourly rate of $575 for rental of the computer, it costs just one cent for the equivalent of three man-days of desk calculator effort. One dollar buys as much calculating as a man could do in a year! Thus a scientist with a computer can solve problems that he could never even consider attempting to solve a few years ago.[5]

In many areas of scientific research, the availability of an electronic computer is an absolute necessity if a scientist wishes to pursue his interests with the most promising techniques. In certain areas of physical chemistry, for example, progress in techniques of computing eigenvalues of matrices immediately produces significant progress in

---

[4] J. von Neumann, "Can We Survive Technology?" *Fortune*, June, 1955, p. 108.

[5] "New Tool, New World," *op. cit.*, pp. 75–76.

the size of molecules that can be investigated. Thus, major universities are providing computers for their faculties and graduate students just as they provide laboratory equipment, so that scientists can effectively pursue their research. In fact, the university computing center is undoubtedly the most important single research facility on the campus.

COMPUTERS IN ENGINEERING

One approach to the design of a product so that it will meet certain specifications is for the engineer to "guess" a first design of the product (based on his past experience) , build it, and test the result. If this design is not satisfactory (and the first try usually isn't) , he can make some changes, build this new version, and test it. This process then continues until a satisfactory product is obtained. Such an approach is extremely costly in terms of time and of money, and for complex systems (aircraft, guided missiles, and atomic reactors) it is too slow and costly to be practical.

The aircraft industry provides numerous illustrations of the value of the electronic computer in design work. Indeed, it is safe to say that intercontinental ballistic missiles and space rockets could not be designed without the aid of these machines. It is simply not possible to build a multistage rocket without some assurance that it will perform properly. You must know, *before* you build it, not only that it will get off the launching pad, but also the thrust it will produce, the path it will follow, the speed it will attain, the amount of fuel it will consume, and a host of other performance factors. Likewise, in the design of a nuclear reactor, you must know before you build it that it will remain under control and will not explode.

It is not surprising that computers are desirable or necessary in the design of the fantastically complex mechanisms discussed above. But it may not be so readily apparent that the electronic computer is becoming increasingly important to the engineers who design our automobiles, dishwashers, cameras, air conditioners, and the myriad of other products which we use every day.

Mathematical Model

Rather than build a physical model of their first design, modern engineers develop sets of equations (mathematical models) that represent the performance of the product. For an electric motor, for example, these equations would involve the shape of the stator, the length of the rotor and the number of poles on it, the number of turns in the winding, the type of iron used and the shape of the magnetic circuit, and similar design parameters. To design a motor with given power and speed characteristics, an engineer would choose a combination of these design parameters. Then, using the equations, he would calculate the power and speed output given by his design. As before, if these characteristics did not meet his requirements, he would vary some of the design parameters and repeat this process. The calculations involved for one set of parameters for an electric motor would take about two days of the engineer's time if he used a slide rule. On an electronic computer these calculations take but a few seconds.

With an electronic computer available, the engineer might take a slightly different approach. Rather than choose a set of parameters for just one design and then evaluate this design, the engineer would choose parameters for many designs, and, finally, compute several hundred designs in one batch. Then he would be in a position to choose the best of these designs and to put it into production. Thus, there is a good chance that the best possible design, rather than merely a workable design, would be obtained.

Automatic Design

A method for designing transformers has been devised that actually eliminates the engineer completely.[6] In this approach the computer is given the performance figures that the design must meet, and the electronic computer simulates the method that the engineer might use: It chooses a set of design parameters, goes through the calculations to evaluate that design, and compares the design with the specifications. If the design does not meet these specifications, the machine decides which parameters to change and how much to change them. Then it repeats the process over and over until it achieves a satisfactory design.

In order to use a computer in this way, it was necessary to analyze the thinking process followed by an engineer when designing transformers so that a computational procedure could be devised to (1) Choose the starting design on the basis of the performance specifications required, and (2) Decide which design parameter to change, and how much to change it, when the trial does not meet specifications.

With a moderately fast electronic computer, the process of designing a transformer requires about 20 seconds. Not only does this

---

[6] Marshall Middleton, Jr., "Product Design by Digital Computers," *Westinghouse Engineer,* March, 1956, pp. 39–43.

release the engineer for more creative work, it also results in more efficient transformer designs from the viewpoint of economics. The computer can be "forced" to consider cost whenever it must make a design decision, and thus will produce a design that is likely to be less costly than that produced by an engineer—who considers costs only when he feels like it. More specifically, the computer can be programmed to devise its designs from standardized parts so that production economies can be realized, while the engineer is often tempted to design something new just to feel creative.

The computer has had such an important influence upon engineering that the better engineering schools have radically altered their curricula to prepare their graduates to take advantage of the computer's abilities. Computers are available to engineering students for homework problems; and leading engineering schools are experimenting with computer systems that provide communications stations so that problems may be presented directly to the computer from laboratories, classrooms, faculty offices, and eventually, perhaps, even from dormitory study halls.

COMPUTERS AND AUTOMATIC CONTROL

One of the most important developments of our age is that of self-regulating mechanisms, or automatic controls. The basic concept of automatic control (or the servomechanism) is that of the feedback loop, which is depicted in generalized form in Figure 2–1, page 25. In this diagram the block labeled Operations represents whatever it is that is to be controlled—a machine, a living organism, an organization, or a man-machine system.

In a control system the results of the operations under control are monitored and compared with the standard or planned results. If the results deviate from plans, the proper controls must be changed by the correct amount in order to bring the operations back to standard. Today, most such control loops involve one or more humans making the decisions, but in a growing number of instances in the processing industries the computer is taking over the control of entire factories through so-called "closed loop" systems in which no humans are involved.

Closed loop computer controls are being installed in increasing numbers in new oil refineries, chemical plants, paper factories, steel mills, and electric generating plants.[7] In 1961 Gulf Oil Corporation

---

[7] "Computers Start to Run the Plants," *Business Week*, November 5, 1960, pp. 50–78.

put into operation a computer controlled catalytic cracking unit in its Philadelphia refinery. In 1963 it was reported that 22 computers were in use in the paper industry, helping to control paper machines, pulp digesters, and drying equipment in the United States, Canada, France, Japan, Germany, and Italy.[8]

One of the first computer controlled factories was the Texaco Polymerization Plant at Port Arthur, Texas, where a Thompson Ramo Wooldridge Corporation R/W 300 special purpose computer receives information from about 110 sources and controls 16 flows, pressures, and temperatures.[9] The advantage of automatic control is not derived from manpower savings because this plant had already been instrumented so that it could be operated by a three-man crew. However, because of the complexity of the process being controlled, humans are able to achieve only 85 to 87 percent efficiency, while the computer should achieve above 90 percent efficiency—in addition to significantly reducing the amount of catalyst required. Incidentally, a 3 to 5 percent increase in operating efficiency can result in an increase of as much as 20 percent in the profit potential of a plant because the extra production is practically "free."

Digitizing Problem

Examining the feedback loop concept, it is apparent that in order to use the computer for process control it is necessary to convert continuous physical quantities (such as voltage, length, rotation of a shaft, and so on) into discrete numbers that the machine can use. This "digitizing" problem was solved long before closed loop control systems were perfected. For example, for several years there have been a number of installations of computers in wind tunnels where data from several hundred gauges (indicating temperature, wind velocities, pressures, and so on) are read directly into a computer, and this information is analyzed and converted to obtain the performance of the aircraft or engine under test. This information is presented to the test engineer while the test is in progress so that he can control the future course of the test on the basis of these results.

There are many such open loop computer control systems in which the computer collects and analyzes data, isolates exceptional conditions, and presents the results to an operator for decision and

---

[8] "Production Briefs," *Business Week*, August 31, 1963, p. 98.

[9] Reported in "Computer Runs Refinery Unit for Texaco," *Business Week*, April 4, 1959, pp. 44–54.

implementation. In fact, many closed loop systems are begun in this way so that operating experience can be used to obtain sufficient understanding of the process to devise procedures that the computer can use to decide how to take corrective action.

The reverse of the digitizing problem occurs at the other end of the control loop, where we must convert numbers into physical characteristics (voltage, motion of a shaft, and so on) that will control the operations involved. Examples of the solution of this phase of the problem are the several "numerically controlled" machine tools which produce complex parts, without human intervention, from a series of numbers representing the mathematical coordinates of the surfaces involved.

Of course, the major difficulties in the control loop lie in the area of decision: After determining that the operations are deviating from the standard, what action must be taken to correct the observed deviations? The more complex the system being controlled, the more difficult this question becomes, and hence even greater the desirability for a powerful computer.

SAGE System

By far the most ambitious automatic control complex in existence is the SAGE air defense system.[10] The heart of this system is a network of extremely large electronic computers into which is fed flight-plan information, reports from the Ground Observer Corps, and weather data. By means of a giant communication network, warning radar is tied directly into the computer.

When an aircraft is detected, its position is screened against the stored flight plans to determine whether or not it is a potential enemy. If it is not accounted for as friendly, the machine pictorially presents its position, direction, and speed on a cathode-ray tube map in front of the sector commander. In addition, the computer suggests a distribution of available forces to meet all of the threats. However, the human commander decides the allocation of forces (he may accept the computer's recommendations, or he may modify them in any way that he sees fit) and indicates this distribution to the computer. At this point the computer again takes over and may guide the interceptors or antiaircraft missiles to these designated targets.

This entire system is essentially an automatic control loop in which humans have a "veto power." However, it should be noted that the subprocess of guiding the interceptors to their targets

---

[10] Gilbert Burck, " 'On Line' in 'Real Time,' " *Fortune*, April 1, 1964, p. 144.

involves a closed feedback loop because deviations in the course of the interceptors must be detected and corrected, and the interceptor must react to evasive action by the enemy. Furthermore, it is obvious, if an attack comes, that the situation facing the sector commander may be so complex, and the time pressure so intense, all he could do would be to accept the computer's suggestion.

Unfortunately, the SAGE system was at least partially obsolete before it was fully installed. It was designed to cope with manned aircraft flying at about the speed of sound—but we will have to meet the threat of intercontinental ballistic missiles, for which there is no adequate warning radar or defense weapon system. However, without the experience in the problems of automatic control gained through SAGE, we would have scant hope of developing defense systems to cope with missiles, so what we have learned has probably been worth the cost.

There has been considerable discussion in the press of the growing hazards of air travel due to our lack of an adequate air traffic control system. Our already inadequate system is faced with growing congestion and faster and faster airplanes. It seems inevitable that an electronic air traffic control system, similar to SAGE, will be required long before it is actually designed and installed.

It is likewise apparent that airplanes are approaching speeds that are too fast for human control reactions. And, as we explore space, most of the direct guidance will be in the hands of computers. The astronauts will make policy decisions, maintain the equipment, react to unexpected emergencies, and observe the environment. Navigation in space, incorporating gravitational influences from the earth, sun, and moon—together with the initial velocity and rotation of the earth and motion of the target—presents mathematical problems that are unsolvable without the aid of powerful computers.

Incidentally, computers play an essential role in most modern weapons systems. Each ICBM employs a computer in its guidance system, either in the missile itself or on the ground. Modern bombers are crammed with electronic computers. And the Polaris weapons system employs several different computers in its submarine navigation, launching, and missile guidance systems.

COMPUTERS AND DATA PROCESSING

One of the major objectives of office automation is the reduction of clerical costs. Although attempts at cost reduction have sometimes fallen short of the goal, there have been some successes, especially in situations of extremely large volume. For example, the Ford Motor Company is using a large electronic computer to save several hundred thousand dollars a year in the cost of preparing its 100,000-man Detroit area payroll. In 1963, Westinghouse Electric Corporation figured that it realized a data processing cost savings of nearly 30 percent on the $16 million it spent for machine rentals and programming.[11]

Among the largest "paper-work" industries is life insurance, where large amounts of information must be maintained on each policy in force. This industry has found computers essential in halting the rising cost of paper work, and almost all large, and most medium-sized insurance companies have installed them. Computers have truly revolutionized home-office clerical operations.

Another important "paper-work industry" vitally affected by the computer is banking. In recent years hundreds of banks have installed computers for processing magnetic-ink-encoded checks. By 1962 computers were installed in 178 banks, representing about 40 percent of all commercial bank deposits. All but two of the 60 largest banks were using computers.[12]

In the early 1950s the Census Bureau employed approximately 4,500 people. In the early 1960s this government agency was utilizing computers to perform twice as much data processing work with *half* as many people. Computers also helped the Air Force Logistics Command to reduce its manpower from 212,000 in 1956 to around 146,000 in 1964. In fact, the federal government is by far the world's largest user of electronic computers, employing some 1,250 machines in 1964.[13]

Despite the instances of clerical savings described above, there are many indications that at least half of the computers installed in the mid-1960s were at best only breaking even on a cost basis, and many installations were contributing to *increased* data processing costs.

Better Information

An increase in the operative efficiency of an organization by the use of "higher quality" information promises an even larger potential savings than that achieved through increased clerical productivity. For optimal control of a complex industrial organization, management should have pertinent information for the proper

---

[11] *Ibid.*

[12] James B. Eckert and Robert R. Wyand, II, "Automation at Commercial Banks," *Federal Reserve Bulletin*, Vol. 48, No. 11 (November, 1962), pp. 1408–20.

[13] Gilbert Burck, "The Boundless Age of the Computer," *Fortune*, March, 1964, pp.101–10.

decision-maker when it is needed. However, it is much easier to talk abstractly about the need for "higher-quality" information than it is to provide it, even if an electronic data processing machine *is* available.

Perhaps the most consistently valuable application of computers in the manufacturing industries has been in the area of materials control. In a typical situation the production schedule, in terms of end items, is broken down to obtain a schedule (taking into account lead time) of parts and materials required. By maintaining up-to-date inventory information and making it available to the machine, it is possible to detect future shortages and even to write shop orders or vendor releases for the required parts and materials. The speed with which a computer can determine the effects of a schedule change can provide a monetary saving by permitting lower inventory levels; the amount of expediting and general confusion are often significantly reduced. Many of the organizations that have the materials control situation well in hand are beginning to use computers directly in the day-to-day and hour-by-hour control of production operations, an area of vast and virtually untouched potential.

Real Time Systems

Borrowing liberally from ideas developed in the SAGE system, companies are beginning to consider a "total systems" approach to their overall operations, with data gathering devices and computers interconnected by communications networks to provide computer monitoring of overall operations. In such a system the computer is in a position to acquire information covering thousands of occurrences, such as orders for products, receipts of raw materials, breakdowns of equipment, production of parts, engineering changes, and so forth. This information can be analyzed and compared with plans; and situations that require attention can be brought to the attention of the proper person in time for him to take corrective action. In many cases the computer will be in a position to suggest the most effective corrective action, or even to take action itself (for example, detecting a potential parts shortage ahead of time, rescheduling the assembly line, and initiating expediting action on the missing parts).

One of the first such "real time" operating systems is the $30-million SABRE system built for American Airlines by IBM.[14] Each American Airline ticket counter has an input-output electric typewriter that can communicate directly with a large computer system in Westchester County, New York. When a passenger calls for a

---

[14] For a description of this system see Gilbert Burck, *op. cit.*, pp. 142–43.

reservation, the agent asks for space on the desired flight for the requested date by depressing push buttons on his input-output typewriter. If the space is available, the computer indicates this fact by means of a light. If not, the computer may "suggest" alternate flights on which space *is* available.

When the agent makes the reservation, he enters the customer's name, where and when he can be reached, who will pick up the tickets, where that person can be reached, special menu requests, whether he needs a wheelchair or a rental car, etc. If the agent forgets any details, such as return-flight plans, the computer requests an explanation. If space is required on a connecting airline, the computer relays the request to the other line and, if necessary, automatically follows up the request. If schedules are changed or the customer does not pick up his tickets on time, or a flight is delayed or canceled, the computer reminds the sales agent to call the customer. If the customer cancels his reservations, the machine returns the seats to inventory.

Before take-off the machine provides the company's caterers with an estimate of the number of meals and drinks that will be needed on the flight and issues a complete list of passengers to the departure and arrival stations. Statistics on system performance, such as percent of no-shows, load factors, number of flights delayed, traffic volume between various points, etc., can be gathered and analyzed by the computer. Thus the SABRE system is indeed a tool for controlling current operations, and one that also gathers historical information as a by-product. These abilities will very likely serve as part of the conceptual prototype for other "real time" control systems in other industries.

COMPUTERS AND MANAGEMENT SCIENCE

During the past few years a great deal of effort has been applied in the area of "operations research" or "management science" in order to develop a more satisfactory understanding of some of the complex decision problems facing management. The simultaneous development of computers has interacted quite favorably with these efforts, for the mathematicians and scientists involved have developed some powerful quantitative techniques that often require computers for their application, while, at the same time, the computers have been used with some success in the process of the research itself. Although the purpose of this research is to understand and solve problems, rather than to find uses for computers, some of the most significant applications of computers have been developed in organizations with active operations research programs. Indeed, it is difficult to conceive of taking a total systems approach to data processing without also undertaking a massive research program designed to provide the necessary understanding of the factors affecting organizational performance.

Some of the mathematical models that have been developed involve tremendous amounts of computation in obtaining a solution. In this respect, the solution of these problems resembles the solution of scientific and engineering problems much more than it resembles clerical data processing operations. One of the best known of these techniques is linear programming, which has been used to decide where to locate new plants, how to ship a product from plants to warehouses, and which bid to accept in a complex situation. Linear programming has also been used in scheduling refinery production in order to obtain the most profitable mixture of output products, given the cost of the input materials; the characteristics of the refinery involved; and the prices to be obtained from the various output products.

PERT and CPM are illustrations of the application of network models to the planning and control of complex, interrelated activities such as major construction projects and research and development programs.

Simulation

Perhaps the most important development in the area of management science is the technique of computer simulation, where complicated systems are represented by mathematical and logical models that can be operated over time in the computer to test possible management decisions ahead of time. For example, a relatively simple (and readily available) inventory simulation makes it possible to test out various inventory control policies and forecasting techniques on historical demand data and to select the technique that performs best in meeting the objectives of management. Similarly, simulation models represent the machines in a job shop, and various operating policies and facilities can be tested with past or (projected) future job loads.

At least one company has developed a mathematical and logical model to represent the internal cost structure of a major division. By using an electronic computer the company can manipulate this model to forecast a complete operating budget based upon product mix, price, and marketing program. By examining several alternative combinations of these variables, management is able to reduce the area of uncertainty in making such extremely important and complicated decisions.

The industrial dynamics simulation technique, developed by Professor Jay W. Forrester at Massachusetts Institute of Technology, is designed to represent the essential, dynamic nature of entire organizations (or even industries). The objective of this type of simulation model is to obtain an understanding of the complicated interrelationships governing organizational performance and, where necessary, to redesign the system so as to produce an organization that is more successful in taking maximum advantage of the environment in which it operates.

Management Games

Many universities are using a "war games" approach in training executives to become more effective decision-makers. In this approach, teams of executives compete with each other in the operation of a hypothetical business, determining production levels, price, product research effort, and marketing expenditures. On the basis of these decisions, a balance sheet and income statement for each team is produced on an electronic computer (or by hand calculation). The same decisions must be made again for the next quarter of operations, and the computer again produces the results for these decisions. Thus in a few hours the men are able to gain experience that represents several years of actual operation of a business; and the results of the decisions are available while the decision itself is still fresh in the minds of the decision-makers. (The relationships between computers and management science will be discussed at greater length in Chapter 17.)

SPECULATIONS CONCERNING THE FUTURE

During the past few years scientists have developed uses for the electronic computer in quite "revolutionary" areas. Although some of these uses are not practical at the present, there are strong indications that most of them will have important effects within our lifetimes.

Information Explosion

One of the major problems of our technological civilization is the staggering volume of information the individual is expected to use. Sixty thousand books, 100,000 research treatises, and 1,300,000 articles are published each year throughout the world. This "information explosion" presents almost unsurmountable problems to the engineer, the scientist, the teacher, and the business executive. Who knows how much unnecessary research work is being done today because the worker is not familiar with the results obtained by others? It is obvious, then, that a large percentage of each researcher's time must be devoted to a foredoomed effort to keep abreast of the developments in his field.

The problems of information dissemination and retrieval are quite complex, involving problems in organizing and classifying the information content of documents as well as difficulties in precisely specifying the information that may be desired. Much effort is being devoted to research designed to increase our understanding of information problems, and we are only in the elementary stages of using computers to assist in coping with the information explosion.

Various government agencies (including the Department of Defense and NASA) and various scientific organizations (such as the American Society for Metals) have established computerized information retrieval systems. Each document is read and abstracted, and a list of key words is prepared which indicates its information content. This "index file" for all documents may be maintained on magnetic tape and may be searched by a computer to produce a list of those documents which are indexed under any "logical combination" of index terms. Several organizations (notably IBM and the Indiana University Aerospace Research Application Center) are attempting to provide a "current awareness" for researchers by indexing current documents and using a computer to screen them against the individual's "interest profile" to select those articles of interest to each researcher.

Language Translation

A similar but even more challenging problem is that of language translation. The possibility of using an electronic computer to translate from one language to another was demonstrated in January, 1954, when an IBM 701 was used to translate several paragraphs from Russian into English. This demonstration involved a vocabulary of only around 250 words, and employed only about eight of the estimated 90 necessary grammatical rules, but it produced a sensible output that was in proper word order and that chose between the meaning of words on the basis of context. Language scientists are devoting much work to the theoretical developments that are necessary to make automatic translation of languages feasible, but it is still a matter of conjecture as to when (or whether) these efforts will achieve success.

Heuristic Problem Solving

One of the most intriguing (and perhaps frightening) areas of this development is the use of the computer to simulate human thinking and creativity for solving so-called "ill-structured" problems. For example, a computer program (called the Logic Theorist) has been written that is designed to prove theorems in mathematical logic by simulating the processes that are used by humans in approaching similar problems.[15] Using the Logic Theorist program, a computer was able to discover proofs for 38 of the first 52 theorems in *Principia Mathematica*, which is perhaps the most influential mathematical book of this century.[16] (This, incidentally, was no mean performance, since the average beginning graduate student in mathematics would have some difficulty proving these theorems. It is interesting to note that for one of the theorems the Logic Theorist devised a proof that was more elegant and concise than the proof included in the book.) Similar programs have been devised for proving theorems in Euclidian geometry and for finding integrals of functions as taught in a course in calculus.[17]

A large-scale scientific computer has been programmed to play an amazingly good game of checkers.[18] To decide its next move the machine examines each possible move, evaluates it (looking several moves into the future), and, on the basis of a formula that evaluates each resulting board position, chooses its move. In one such version the computer has been programmed to "learn from experience" by modifying this formula on the basis of success or failure experienced in playing against human players. This has been so successful that the computer regularly beats Dr. A. L. Samuel, the creator of the program. In fact, on July 12, 1962, a match was played between the computer and Mr. Robert W. Nealey of Connecticut, a former state champion. The computer won, and Mr. Nealey commented:

---

[15] Allen Newell, J. C. Shaw, and Herbert A. Simon, "Elements of a Theory of Human Problem Solving," *Psychological Review*, Vol. 65, No. 3 (1958), pp. 151–66.

[16] A. N. Whitehead and B. Russell, *Principia Mathematica* (2d ed.; Cambridge: Cambridge University Press, 1925), Vol. I.

[17] For a description of these and other such programs see E. A. Feigenbaum and J. Feldman, *Computers and Thought* (New York: McGraw-Hill Book Co., Inc., 1964), p. 535.

[18] *Ibid.*

It is very interesting to me to note that the computer had to make several star moves in order to get the win, and that I had several opportunities to draw otherwise. . . . The machine, therefore, played a perfect ending without one misstep. In the matter of the end game, I have not had such competition from any human being since 1954, when I lost my last game.[19]

This use of a computer to solve poorly structured problems is called "heuristic" problem solving, and much research is being devoted to this area. Sufficient success is being made in this endeavor, moreover, to predict that within the near future:

1. A digital computer will be the world's chess champion, unless the rules bar it from competition.
2. A digital computer will discover and prove an important new mathematical theorem.
3. A digital computer will write music that will be accepted by critics as possessing considerable aesthetic value.
4. Most theories in psychology will take the form of computer programs or of qualitative statements about the characteristics of computer programs.[20]

The use of a computer for heuristic problem solving depends upon the development of a theory of learning and problem solving. As we reach a better understanding of how a *human being* learns, it may be feasible to develop a *machine* that can learn. Conversely, as we develop theories concerning how a human learns, we may be able to test these theories by means of a computer and observe whether or not the theory actually works. Thus the machines, though they are not real brains in any way, may lead us to a more satisfactory understanding of the human brain and, consequently, to the development of new machines or new techniques that more closely approach the capabilities of the human brain.

CONCLUSION

One obvious impact of the computer is on productivity: productivity of the scientist, the engineer, the production worker, the office worker, and the manager.

The future course of our material progress depends to a considerable extent on the productivity of our scientists and engineers. Any increase in the amount of effective work that a creative scientist

---

[19] *Ibid.*, p. 104.

[20] H. A. Simon and A. Newell, "Heuristic Problem Solving: The Next Advance in Operations Research," *Operations Research*, January–February, 1958, pp. 7–8.

or engineer can accomplish in a lifetime leads to a corresponding increase in the productivity of our production line workers, for many such productivity increases are the result of the design of better products or of more efficient machinery for production.

During recent times the productivity of the office worker, and consequently his standard of living, has lagged significantly behind that of the production worker. The advent of the electronic computer, however, should give the clerical worker the tools with which to compete effectively with the production worker, who has had the benefit of increasingly powerful machinery over a period of years.

Among the most important productivity gains are those in management, for the productivity of management determines the efficiency with which a business organization operates. This efficiency is often measured in dollars of profit or in return on investment, but it may also result in a better quality product for the same price, or the same product at a reduced price.

Thus the productivity of management has a profound influence upon the course of our economy. The operation of a modern business organization is extremely complex, and no one knows how efficiently we are operating as compared with the optimum. However, many authorities agree that, over a period of time, management productivity will increase significantly through the use of computers to obtain more effective information for management control, through the use of advanced mathematical techniques for decision making, and through implementations of the total systems approach to control of operations.

These are exacting and challenging times, for we are at the beginning of a most important technological revolution. This revolution possesses tremendous potential for increasing material welfare, but we must recognize that it also brings threats of technological unemployment both for clerical workers and for management. Frankly, we do not know how far or how fast the more esoteric developments in simulation of human thought processes will go. But it is obvious that even today many managers are technologically obsolete because they are not equipped to cope with this new technology. And it is possible that the computer may well raise difficult moral questions concerning the ultimate value of the human mind and personality.

Perhaps the most important impact of the computer during recent years has been upon management's attitudes and concepts. In order to use computers, management has been forced to adopt a systems viewpoint—to view the entire organization as an integrated system and to analyze the roles of information, of physical facilities, and of management in the performance of this system. And when one analyzes the role of management in such a system he soon discovers that the highest order of tasks for management are concerned with the modification or redesigning of the system so that it can better adapt itself to the hostile and ever changing environment in which it exists.

Furthermore, management has found by experience that computers do not by themselves solve problems—they only compute. If you know what your problem is, and if you can devise a method by which the problem can be solved by computation, then the electronic computer can be used as a very powerful tool to obtain a solution. But if you do not understand the problem, or if you cannot devise a method to solve it using arithmetic and logic, then any electronic computer is just so much excess baggage. We have found that each achievement of a so-called "giant brain" is actually the product of some man or group of men who devised the method that was utilized.

As a consequence of this need to understand complex problems in order to use computers for their solution, management's attitudes toward "management science" have changed. Most large manufacturing firms have found that money spent on product research and development pays off manyfold. Many executives are beginning to realize that research on management problems can pay off in the same way. First we must have understanding, and then we can begin to efficiently utilize the capabilities of the electronic computer. As expressed in a *Fortune* editorial:

. . . the history of science is largely the conversion of ill-structured problems to well-structured problems. Now that he has the computer, man is under greater pressure than ever to speed up this process of getting his problems into shapes that can be quantitatively solved.[21]

And at the same time that the computer has succeeded in convincing management that research on management problems is desirable, it has providentially provided tools, such as systems simulation, that have made such research more feasible.

These changes in management attitudes, combined with a realization of the increasing rate of technological change within the area of management itself, have resulted in significant changes in programs

---

[21] "Onrush of the Robots," editorial in *Fortune*, March, 1964, p. 98.

designed to educate future management. Rather than attempt to impart great masses of facts and techniques that will be obsolete soon after the student graduates, many modern programs stress the basic disciplines of economics, behavioral sciences, mathematics, and logic, and attempt to develop the student's ability to apply these analytical tools to the solution of whatever problems he may face as a manager.

Perhaps you have observed that most of the above discussion is a bit hazy and difficult to come to grips with, and this is because at this stage we know very little about the computer, what it can do, and how it does it. Much of the remainder of this book is devoted to obtaining an understanding of the computer and how it may be used. In the later chapters we will return once more to consideration of the management problems and opportunities associated with its use.

This book is devoted primarily to the use of computers in data processing. However, it is impossible to divorce data processing from science, engineering, automatic control, management science, and the use of the computer in simulating human thinking processes. For, whenever we replace a lowly clerk with a machine, we are attempting to simulate human thought processes, and when we consider providing information for improved management control, we are likely to get involved in the areas of engineering and management science. The potential of the computer is much greater than routine, paper-work mechanization, but its potential will only be attained through knowledge of the capabilities and limitations of the computer and better understanding of our problems so that we can create new techniques which use the capabilities of the computer to solve these problems.

2   FUNDAMENTALS OF

DATA PROCESSING

THE AREA of business data processing forms the major subject matter of this book. Although we will not attempt a precise definition of data processing, the term essentially refers to the gathering, recording, and manipulation of numbers and alphabetical symbols that are necessary for the proper functioning of a modern business organization. During the past few years we have witnessed an astounding growth in the size and complexity of business and government organizations which has been accompanied by an even more fantastic growth in the amount of paper-work processing that has been required. This seemingly ever growing burden of non-productive paper work has caused grave concern, and has led management to a growing awareness of the importance of data processing.

Under these circumstances it is not surprising that the development of the electronic computer was hailed with enthusiasm by those who could envision its potential in the area of data processing. After several years of experience, it is apparent that much of this potential still exists, for as yet the computer has only begun to stem the tide of paper work. One of the major reasons for the lack of more spectacular results is our lack of understanding of data processing itself.

It is widely accepted that the computers have progressed far beyond our ability to utilize them effectively. This is not intended to imply that the machines are by any means perfect, or that they are even suitable for use in all circumstances, or that there will not be fantastic improvements in the machines themselves during the next few years. This statement is merely a reflection of our lack of knowledge concerning the problems of data processing, and of the fact that our knowledge of the capabilities of the computers and the techniques necessary for their use have grown rather slowly. Thus, it is important that we consider data processing itself, and attempt to analyze why it is necessary to perform data processing.

IMPORTANCE OF DATA PROCESSING

Although it should be unnecessary to say it, perhaps the most important fundamental is that data processing is not an end in itself. Data processing is a means to an end, and unless the results of the processing are used to obtain something of value, the data processing itself is valueless. *We should not process data just to process data.*

Why, then, do we process data? Consider the following characteristics of an organization:

a) An organization is a social group, which implies that it consists of people and that there is potential intercommunication.
b) There is a collective objective of this group.
c) There is a functional division of the labor involved in attaining the objective.

The concept of a functional division of labor (or specialization) to achieve a group objective implies that there must be coordination or control of these individual efforts in order to attain the group objective. This coordination is one of the major functions of management. Coordination also implies communication, for the coordinator must be aware of the activity of the individuals involved.

Granting that communication is necessary to control an organization, the question arises: Is communication sufficient? Communication is the transmission of information (facts) from one place to another. Although, in our American civilization, we tend to glorify facts, we must always remember that without a frame of reference "facts" are merely random noise. For example, it is a fact that you are reading this piece of paper. However, depending on your frame of reference, this fact has many different meanings. To a savage who has no knowledge of reading, this fact is pure foolishness or profound magic, while to the physicist, this fact may be related to the reflection and transmission properties of light. To the physiologist, this fact is associated with the transmission of impulses along nerve pathways and with the "thought" processes which interpret these impulses. To the author, this fact means that perhaps someone is gaining an understanding of an interesting subject.

It may at first appear to be obvious that the more information everyone has and the more freely various individuals in an organization can communicate with one another, the more effectively they can work together to achieve their common goal. Thus, we might obtain the best results by using an intercom system (like that used in World War II bombers) to tie everyone in the organization together and make all information available to everyone. Upon reflection, however, it becomes apparent that, as the organization grows larger, this unlimited communication becomes unwieldy and individuals begin to interfere with each other. Furthermore, experiments have shown that even small groups can operate more effectively when their communication channels are limited and, therefore, structured.[1]

Moreover, in the complex situation presented by most modern organizations it is often necessary to take a "macroscopic" rather than a "microscopic" attitude toward facts. For example, although it may be of little significance that among the thousands of sales during a given day the 42nd dress sold was blue, the fact that 1,000 blue dresses were sold during a given period of time—as opposed to 150 pink dresses—may be of great interest. The thousands and thousands of individual occurrences are often quite meaningless until they are classified and summarized.

Thus it is apparent that effective coordination of an organization involving functional division of labor requires data processing functions other than pure communication in order to: (1) provide a frame of reference, (2) select the information to be presented to different individuals, and (3) present information in summarized form. These, incidentally, represent only a few of the reasons why data processing is required.

SERVOMECHANISM CONCEPT OF CONTROL

Coincident with the development of the electronic computer a theory of control has been created. Since one of the major purposes of management is to provide the control that enables an organization to achieve its goals, and since data processing and control are closely related, we will consider a simple representation of this servomechanism concept of control.

In the first place, the basic concept of control is applicable whether we are considering control of a living organism, a group of organisms, man-machine systems (such as a car and driver), or automatically controlled machines. In the diagram of Figure 2–1, the

---

[1] For example, see Harold Guetzkow and Herbert Simon, "The Impact of Certain Communication Nets in Task-Oriented Groups," *Management Science,* Vol. 1, No. 3–4 (April–July, 1955), pp. 233–50.

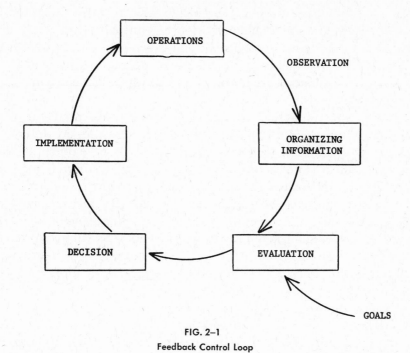

FIG. 2–1
Feedback Control Loop

block labeled Operations represents that thing (or things) which is to be controlled.

The basis for control is information concerning these operations. This information may pertain to the output of operations—for example, the quality of the product being produced. It may also be concerned with the input to the operations being controlled—in an automobile the gas gauge reports how much gasoline is in the tank. Or the information may relate to the performance of intermediate stages in the Operation process—for example, a given batch of parts may have completed the fourth step in its routing through the shop.

Control depends fundamentally upon a comparison between the results attained and the goals (or objectives) sought. There can be no concept of control without goals, objectives, expectations, or plans concerning the outcome that the operations should produce. Incidentally, these objectives must come from outside the control loop itself.

If the desired results are of any complexity, it is usually necessary to organize the raw information obtained from operations and to put it into a form that can conveniently be compared with the desired goals or plans. For example, if specified profits are the goals desired, a considerable amount of manipulation is required to determine the profit obtained based upon income and expense figures. In the usual case, the measurements of the results of operations that can conveniently be obtained are not in a form in which it is convenient to express the goals.

When the results are compared with the goals, there are two possible outcomes: they are either in agreement or they are different. If the results attained meet the goals, then the remainder of the control system is not activated; but when there is a difference, the control process involves further steps. The above discussion provides an introduction to the well-known concept of "management by exception," which involves the gathering and processing of information into a form in which it can easily be compared with plans so that only the deviations from plans need be brought to the attention of management. Since a large proportion of the information does not require management consideration, the implementation of the management-by-exception concept in the design of data processing systems not only relieves management of much tedious screening work but also makes sure that significant information will be noticed, and it allows management to concentrate upon correcting situations that require action. Of course, the success of such an approach depends upon the adequacy of the plans to detect significant deviations, which implies that more thought must be devoted to planning than is usually given.

Continuing with our discussion of the control concept, when the results of operations do not agree with the goals, then a decision (or decisions) must be made concerning necessary changes in the operations for correcting the deviations. In most organizations these decisions are made by management, but in driving a car, for example, the individual usually makes them subconsciously, manipulating the steering wheel whenever the car deviates from the center of the traffic lane.

The final step in the control loop involves implementation of this decision in order to change the operations. In driving a car, this involves turning the steering wheel, depressing the brake, or pressing on the accelerator; in an automatically controlled chemical plant, it may involve the opening or closing of valves or the adjustment of temperatures. In the business organization it usually involves a process of "order issuance," which informs everyone concerned what to do to implement the decision. For example, to increase production, schedules must be established, materials must be procured, labor must be obtained—literally hundreds of small but coordinated tasks must be performed.

In the control of a business organization it is apparent that the functions involved in organizing the information and implementation are almost exclusively data processing. As use of the management-by-exception approach becomes increasingly popular and the computer is more widely used, the area of evaluation becomes a part of data processing. And as mathematically derived decision rules are devised, the decision block is reduced to a matter of data processing. In any case it is difficult, if not impossible, to separate the feedback concept of control from data processing, for data processing is inevitably involved in some or all parts of the loop.

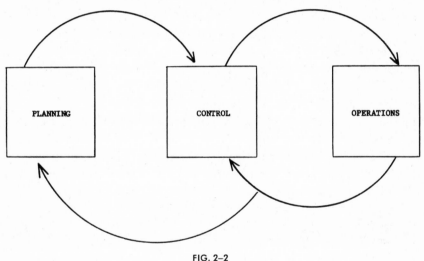

FIG. 2–2
Multilevel Control Process

It should be noted that, in the business organization, another loop is involved at the planning level where some of the information on operations is processed to evaluate the plans in the preceding loop, so that better plans can be formulated for the control of the organization. Thus we obtain Figure 2–2 as a more realistic representation of the control mechanism in an organization.

Of course, even Figure 2–2 is much too simple to represent the overall situation in the actual business organization. In the modern organization, with its various levels of management, thousands of such loops are intertwined and piled on top of each other in confusing profusion, with the decision-maker in one loop being the operations block of another loop, and so on.

However, much can be gained from an analysis of this concept of control. For example, the common thermostat on a furnace is an example of a simple feedback loop of control. The thermostat, of course, involves very little data processing and quite simple rules of decision. These rules are: (1) When the temperature exceeds a certain level (say 73 degrees) the furnace is to be turned off; (2) When the temperature falls below a certain level (say 71 degrees) the furnace is to be turned on. Thus the temperature in the house is maintained between the limits of 71 and 73 degrees.

However, consider the effect of a two-hour time lag in the operation of the thermostat. In this case, when the temperature reaches 73 degrees the furnace would continue to run full blast for two hours and then shut off, then the house would gradually cool down to 71 degrees, and two hours later the furnace would again turn on. Thus, the temperature in the house would oscillate back and forth in a quite uncomfortable manner.

We can see that the speed with which the feedback loop operates can be extremely important; therefore, if satisfactory control is to be maintained, the speed with which information can be processed may be quite important.

It is also important to notice that the information being processed in a feedback loop of control must provide the basis for detection of deviations and for the decisions necessary to correct these deviations. Here, of course, is the crucial problem involved in the design of data processing systems: What information is required for effective control of an organization? This question is most difficult to answer (in fact, we do not have adequate techniques for determining such answers), but it is frequently possible to show that the information being processed in a specific organization is not adequate for control purposes. This will be discussed further in Chapter 14.

It should be noted that at least three interrelated questions are involved in the design of a data processing system for control purposes: (1) What information should be gathered? (2) How should it be processed? (3) How much time delay can be allowed without destroying the effectiveness of the system? In a substantial proportion of situations the time question is *not* the only controlling factor. In other words, merely speeding up the processing in an existing system may produce an insignificant improvement in the effectiveness of control, and it is theoretically possible that reducing the processing delay may actually decrease the effectiveness of the system by causing it to overreact to random fluctuations.[2]

THE CONCEPT OF A SYSTEM

In the above discussion we introduced a term that represents one of the most important concepts we will encounter in this study—the concept of a *system*. In our usage system is a technical term, and does not relate directly to the word "systematic." Rather, a system is an assemblage or combination of things or parts forming a complex or unitary whole. For example, the human body is a system composed of its individual parts; a nation is a system composed of its institutions, government, and population; and an organization is a system composed of its human, physical, and financial resources.

One of the most important characteristics of systems is that they may be considered to be composed of hierarchies of *sub*systems. That is to say, the parts that form the major system may themselves be systems, and their parts may be systems, and so on. For example, the world economy can be considered as a system in which all the various national economies are subsystems. In turn, each national economy can be considered to be a system composed of its various industries. Each industry can be considered to be a system composed of the firms which make it up. And, of course, a firm can be considered to be a system composed of subsystems such as production, marketing, finance, accounting, data processing, and so on.

Value of Concept

The systems concept is a most useful device for viewing many phenomena. It is by no means a cure-all or panacea, nor does it provide a set of specific rules for solving all problems, but the systems approach provides several valuable viewpoints. First, it implicitly assumes that a system can be understood and that it should be designed to accomplish its purpose. Furthermore, systems concepts emphasize the relationships between the parts (or subsystems) and how these relationships affect the performance of the overall system. Thus the basic analytical approach is to view the system as a whole, then break it down into component subsystems and concentrate on the relationships between the subsystems. Each subsystem then can be

---

[2] For an excellent illustration, see Jay W. Forrester, "Industrial Dynamics—A Major Breakthrough for Decision Makers," *Harvard Business Review*, July–August, 1958, pp. 37–66.

analyzed by means of the same technique, breaking *it* down into its component subsystems, concentrating on the interrelationships among them, and so on.

An important tool in the analysis of systems is provided by the technique of computer simulation, in which the system is modeled so that its performance can be examined through the use of a computer. The relationships between the parts can be varied, or the characteristics of the parts can be modified and the results observed in order to evaluate the impact of such changes upon the performance of the entire system. Thus the system can be redesigned and tested in order to produce an improved system.

Organizations as Systems

There are a number of important consequences of viewing organizations in terms of systems concepts. For example, there are systems analogies between organizations and living organisms. Living organisms are self-adaptive systems in the sense that in the long processes of evolution those organisms survive that are able to successfully adapt themselves to their environment and to changes in this environment. Analogously, in order to be successful in the long run, organizations must be capable of adapting themselves to a changing (and perhaps hostile) environment. Perhaps one of the higher order tasks of management is to design the organizational system so that it can and does adapt itself to its changing environment.

When considering self-regulating systems, then, we immediately recognize the importance of the feedback concepts which we have previously discussed and illustrated. Self-regulating systems must be composed of feedback control loops combined with goal-setting mechanisms.

Finally, when we view the organization as a system, we are immediately impressed with the importance of the information subsystem. Just as the most important subsystem of a living organism is its nervous system, the most crucial subsystem of an organization is its information processing system. And the more complex and sophisticated the organism (or organization), the more important the nervous (or information processing) system becomes.

Data Processing Systems

Similarly, there are important consequences of viewing data processing in terms of the systems concept. First, and of utmost importance, the data processing system must be considered as a whole rather than as a collection of unrelated pieces. The systems approach to data processing requires the design of an integrated system that will satisfy the information needs of the organization. This may not sound particularly radical; however, when one examines the data processing area of a typical organization, one frequently discovers that this so-called "system" has grown haphazardly over the years in response to the needs and desires of hundreds of individuals and in response to the requirements of a multitude of emergencies and conditions which no longer exist. Managers typically institute recurring reports, but they seldom terminate them. Managers are promoted or fired, or even die, but their pet reports often become eternal. Similar reports, used for different purposes, are often prepared in separate parts of the organization. Files are created and maintained, but seldom referred to; and the information that is actually needed is not obtainable.

The above diatribe is intended to suggest that many data processing systems were not designed, they "just grew." They are not systems except by accident. Thus tremendous improvement can frequently be obtained by actually designing the data processing system to suit the needs of the organization. In the first place, it is usually possible to eliminate a substantial amount of the effort and expense devoted to duplication of processing or to processing information that is not being used. Even more important is the potential improvement in efficiency of operation which may be obtained by providing the proper information for adequate management control.

The change from a manual to a mechanized data processing system offers an obvious opportunity to approach data processing from a system-wide viewpoint. It is highly desirable, for instance, to capture information in "machine-processable" form as early as possible so that from this point on all manipulation and communication can be accomplished through the use of machines.

Another consequence of the systems approach to data processing is that of broadened horizons. When one really begins to consider what the pertinent subsystem is, he soon arrives at the conclusion that it is really larger than the traditional area of paper work within an organization. Rather, we should be concerned with "management information systems" which transcend customary accounting reports to provide up-to-the-minute operating information along with external information analogous to military intelligence. Rather than merely producing historical accounting reports, we should be concerned with providing for the information needs of management, whether such information comes from within the organization (financial or production data) or from the organization's environment (economic, consumer, and competitive information).

Another term, "the total systems concept," carries this reasoning one step further. The total systems concept recognizes that there are crucial interrelationships between the information system, the decision system, and the organization structure. One cannot really design an information system until one considers the types of decisions that are pertinent to the performance of the organization as well as the organizational location in which these decisions are to be made. Conversely, it is impossible to decide upon the organizational structure or the decision processes without some consideration of the realities involved in providing the necessary information.

In brief, the total systems concept suggests that we cannot separate these subsystems, and that the overall organization should be designed as a system incorporating these subsystems. This, of course, sounds a bit utopian and "blue sky," and it is; but this overall approach has been remarkably effective in military systems, such as SAGE, and in a few business organizations, and it will surely be of greater importance in the coming years.

Patterns of Information Flow

To understand the systems approach and the difficulties which must be overcome in its use, let us consider an organization's patterns of information flow. How does information flow? And how may we discover where basic information originates and how it affects each report and document?

Our first impulse is to look at the organization chart of the company involved. However, although an organization chart sometimes gives a picture of the lines of authority and responsibility and the location of decision points, the lines on the chart do not usually indicate the major paths of information flow. Most of the information flow is *across* rather than along organizational lines.

As a matter of fact, it is almost impossible to generalize concerning the detailed flow of information within organizations. We must consider an individual organization and, in order to determine the flows of information, it is usually necessary to spend a considerable effort (usually involving several man-months or even man-years) in tracing pieces of paper in their flow throughout the organization.

A simplified representation of some of the basic information flows within a manufacturing organization is presented in Figure 2–3. As can be seen from this diagram, the basic information comes in from the customers in the form of orders. When these orders reach the sales department, the information is transcribed into a document that is sent to the stock room for filling, from there to the shipping room where the material is packed, and from there one copy goes to the customer and another back to the sales department to indicate that the order has actually been shipped. Copies of this document

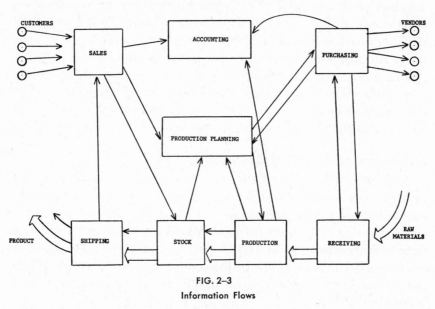

FIG. 2–3
Information Flows

also go to the accounting department, and summarized information goes to the production-planning department.

The production-planning department utilizes this sales information to determine when and in what quantities to manufacture the various products. Then it sends information to the production department in the form of production orders, and the production department notifies production-planning when production has been completed and sends the product to the stock room along with a transmittal document—a copy of which goes back to production-planning to inform them that the material is now in stock.

The production-planning department also sends information to the purchasing department, which writes orders to the vendors and sends copies of these orders to the receiving department so that when materials are received they can be identified. When the material arrives, the receiving department sends back a copy of this document to purchasing, which then notifies production-planning that the material has been received. In addition, of course, production-planning, production, and purchasing all send information into the accounting department, and information flows back and forth between the organization and its customers and vendors.

It can be seen that there is a considerable volume of common information in the areas of production scheduling, production control, timekeeping, payroll, inventory control, order writing, billing, accounts receivable, and accounting. Likewise, there are many aspects common to product development, engineering specifications, parts requirements, machine loading, material control, purchasing, stores inventory accounting, and accounts payable.

The integration of these various areas into an efficient data processing system is a difficult proposition, but the accomplishment of this integration not only can cut data processing costs but can also provide the information necessary for proper and timely control.

A Prototype Management Operation System

As another illustration of the many interrelationships between the data processing system and the management activities of planning, executing, and controlling, consider a set of basic functions that are common to most manufacturing companies.[3] There are six major functions incorporated in IBM's suggested prototype management operating system for manufacturing companies, some of which implement planning and others which implement execution and control (see Figure 2–4).

1. *Forecasting.* The beginning of a manufacturing plan is a forecast of the demand for each product so that raw materials and parts can be acquired and production schedules established. There are two basic types of information that are helpful in forecasting: historical data on parts demand and information concerning the state of the economy.

2. *Materials Planning.* After a forecast for end items is obtained, this demand must be "exploded" into a demand for the raw materials, parts, and subassemblies which compose the end items.

3. *Inventory Management.* The raw materials and parts requirements developed through materials planning must be provided at the proper time and in the proper quantity. This is the task of inventory management.

4. *Scheduling.* It is necessary to plan when and how the parts and end-items requirements, developed in previous phases, are to be produced. Then the orders must be issued to the shop at the proper time.

5. *Dispatching.* This function executes the manufacturing plan by initiating detailed action for materials, machines, tools, and manpower. Dispatching determines what each work center is to do, at each step, to complete the manufacturing schedule.

---

[3] This discussion is based on *Management Operating System for Manufacturing Industries—General Information Manual,* Form No. E20–8041, published by **IBM** Corporation, White Plains, N.Y., 1960.

6. *Operations Evaluation.* In the feedback control concept it is necessary to compare performance against standards so that corrective action can be taken when necessary. The preceding functions have provided detailed plans for use as standards in the control process, and this function maintains control by comparing actual performance with these plans and indicating significant deviations.

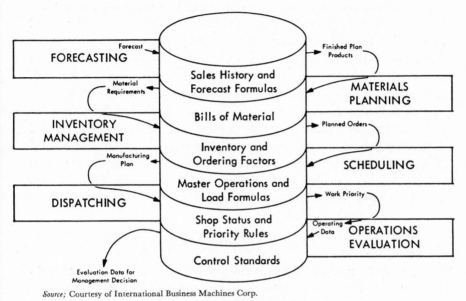

Source; Courtesy of International Business Machines Corp.

FIG. 2–4

Management Operating System

Since there are only a limited number of basic approaches to each of the six functions, the design of a data processing system for manufacturing operations can become a process of selecting a particular technique for each phase, but considering the entire process from its beginning permits the design of an integrated system.

Management Responsibility

The preceeding discussions have indicated that an important task of management is to insure that the organization is an effective system that can successfully adapt itself to its hostile and ever changing environment. We have expounded the viewpoint that the data processing system is a crucial subsystem in determining the performance of the overall organization system.

Thus we cannot escape the conclusion that the design and functioning of the data processing system is of vital concern to management; it is not the domain of the lowly clerk or the machine. Management must decide what information is necessary to control the operations of a business organization. This does not imply that management should not *use* technical assistance in designing data processing and organizational systems, but it insists that it is the responsibility of management to set the objectives for these specialists and to make sure that the objectives are properly attained.

Again, let us emphasize that the attitude of management toward the use of the information and the participation of management in the establishment of the objectives of the data processing system are vital, necessary ingredients for effective data processing and, consequently, for effective management control.

In much of the remainder of this book the tools and the means for efficiently accomplishing data processing will be discussed. We will become involved in a study of powerful and glamorous machines and the techniques that are required for their use. However, we must diligently guard against the temptation to ignore the basic objectives to which data processing must contribute.

BASIC TERMINOLOGY

The previous discussion was primarily concerned with the establishment of a frame of reference for considering data processing. Now let us discuss some of the basic terms that are used to describe data processing.

The fundamental unit of raw material of data processing is the *transaction,* which is a complete unit of information for an occurrence. For example, the sale of an item to a customer, the removal of an item from inventory, the payment of an account, the work of one man on one particular job, and the ordering of a quantity of a specific raw material all give rise to transactions.

Two basic types of information are necessary to describe a complete transaction. Of course, there must be *quantitative* information telling "how much" or "how many." But most of the information contained in a transaction is usually included for the purpose of *identification.* This type of information denotes the type of transaction, tells who or what was involved, and describes the pertinent characteristics of the transaction for the data processing which is to follow. For example, in the sale of a single item the quantitative information in the transaction consists of the quantity sold and the total dollar amount of the sale. The identifying information may include the item number, the date, the salesman who made the sale, the customer who bought the item, and the terms of the sale.

Data processing thus starts with transactions, any one of which may affect many of the end products of the data processing system. It is imperative, then, that the transaction include the information necessary to associate the quantitative information in the proper relationship with other transactions in order to produce all of the required end products.

Data processing may be roughly divided into four major functions: data *recording*, data *transmission*, data *manipulation*, and *report or document preparation*. Let us consider further subdivisions of these four major functions.

Recording

The importance and the complexity of the data recording function is frequently overlooked. In order to properly record a given transaction it may be necessary to perform each of the following:

Identify the particular transaction so that it can be distinguished from other transactions;

Audit the information contained in the transaction to determine that it is consistent and accurately represents the occurrence itself;

Edit the information to eliminate that which is extraneous in further processing;

Assign codes to the transaction which will be used to control some of the further processing of the information;

Transcribe the information into a form where a human or a machine can process the transaction during the data manipulation phase; and, finally,

Verify that this entire procedure has been accomplished without error.

It may be desirable to elaborate upon the subject of coding. Basically, coding accomplishes two purposes: classification and condensation. For example, John Robert Smith, Jr., may be referred to as J. R. Smith, Jr., J. Robert Smith, Jr., John R. Smith, Jr., Jack Smith, Bob Smith, and so on ad infinitum. Humans, and machines especially, have a difficult time recognizing that all of these variations refer to the same person. However, if we assign this man the employee number 97621, then we have classified all of these representations into a specific and concise way of referring to this employee in our data processing.

Incidentally, the advantage of conciseness that is associated with coding necessarly introduces a corresponding disadvantage of "lack of redundancy," which makes errors much more serious. For example, "John R. Smrth, Jr.," would probably be interpreted properly by anyone reading it, but the man-number "97261" (instead of 97621) not only fails to signal that a mistake has occurred but gives no clue as to the correct information. Thus, verification assumes even greater importance when coding is involved.

The design of a coding system is inextricably related to the data manipulation that is to be performed to produce the results desired from the data processing system. It is desirable that two transactions that are identical with respect to subsequent processing be assigned the same code, yet it is impossible for data processing manipulation to provide an analysis with a finer breakdown than that which is provided in the coding system.

The above discussion of the aspects of data recording does not imply that each is necessarily a separate step in the process or that each is involved in recording all types of transactions. For example, where the accuracy of each transaction is not crucial to the use of the information, verification may be deemphasized. And in some automatic data gathering systems the entire recording function may be performed by machines communicating with other machines.

Data Transmission

The difficulty and complexity of data transmission can vary from that of moving a piece of paper from one desk to another to that of instantaneous electronic communication from one continent to another. The method of data transmission chosen will depend upon the time requirements imposed by the system, the accuracy which must be maintained, and the economics of the particular communications facility.

Engineering developments in the transmission of information in machine-processable form have come thick and fast in recent years. It is now possible to connect a wide variety of devices by means of telephone or telegraph circuits, the only major considerations being the accuracy, reliability, and cost of the facilities used. Punched cards, punched paper tape, and magnetic tape may be transmitted from one location and reproduced in another; and, if desirable, the transmitted information may be entered directly into a computer for immediate processing and the results automatically returned to the remote location. We do not imply, however, that the design of such a data processing system is a simple task or that such spectacular communications facilities are always required (or even desirable) in a data processing system.

Manipulation

Data manipulation can be complex and difficult to categorize, but it is roughly classifiable according to the following subfunctions:

Arrangement of the information into the proper sequence so that it can be associated with file information and/or conveniently processed;

Reference to file information, which must be associated with the current information;

A *logical function,* which consists of a precise determination of the procedure or subprocedure to be followed in the processing of a particular transaction or group of transactions;

The *arithmetic functions* of addition, subtraction, multiplication, and division; and

The *updating* of the file information to reflect the effect of the transaction being processed.

As an example of the influence of arrangement, suppose we are concerned with reflecting the result of 1,000 transactions upon 200 accounts. Several approaches might be used. The straightforward approach would be to place the transactions in a stack, pick up the first one, find the record for the account which it affects, post the transaction, and then repeat this process with each succeeding transaction. Another approach involves the preliminary step of arranging the transactions in sequence according to account number. Then all the transactions affecting a given account are together and the account record must be located only once. A third approach would be to sort the transactions as in the previous approach and then to total the transactions for each account, thus posting only this summarized total rather than the individual transactions.

When most of us think of sorting or arrangement the first thing that comes to mind is arranging a hand of cards. A common way of doing this is by looking at the whole group, picking out the first card of a suit, then the second, then the third, and so forth. Another approach is building the hand by successively looking at cards and inserting each in its proper place. Both of these techniques are satisfactory when only a few cards are involved, but neither is practical if there are thousands of cards. In succeeding portions of this book we will discuss practical mechanizable methods of sorting when large numbers of transactions are involved. We will also investigate approaches to data processing that do *not* involve sorting or arrangement of transactions.

Much to the surprise of most people who have experience in manual data processing, the logical function mentioned above is of considerable complexity and requires a great proportion of the effort when data processing is mechanized. In most cases, humans perform these logical functions without conscious effort—while machines require that a special effort be expended in this area. Humans find these logical choices much less difficult than arithmetic, while for machines choices are difficult and arithmetic is easy. Thus a computer engaged in data processing may spend 75 percent of its time performing logical functions, while a human, doing the same job, would spend 75 percent of his time calculating.

Report Preparation

In addition to the arrangement of the information and the physical printing necessary in report or document preparation, other important characteristics must be considered. In the first place, the reports or documents must be available when they are needed; they must contain all the information necessary for the use to which they are to be put; and they must be presented in a form that is understandable and usable with a minimum of further analysis. (But of course these considerations influence the *entire* process of data processing; the recording, transmission, and manipulation of the data, as well as the preparation of the reports.)

One must recognize that we are talking about making information available for effective use and are not merely discussing formal, periodic reports. It may be desirable to have the information available, but unprinted, until someone wants it, and then to produce it in visual or auditory form. Thus we return to the fundamental question: What are the information requirements and how can they best be satisfied?

SUMMARY

The achievement of adequate management control so that the objectives of the organization may be effectively attained is the basic motivation for data processing. This implies that the data processing system is an important management consideration, for efficient control is impossible without a suitable data processing system.

The data processing complex of an organization must be considered as a system, and this system should be designed to eliminate duplication and waste while providing the information needed for control purposes at the required place and time and in a usable form.

The raw materials for data processing consist of transactions. The basic functions of data processing are recording, transmission, manipulation, and report preparation. Each of these functions involves several subfunctions and many considerations.

The motivation discussed above and the functions described apply to data processing without regard to the tools used for its accomplishment. The *objective* is the important thing—the *tools* are secondary. If we lose sight of these objectives and have a data processing system that cannot contribute to adequate performance of the organization, then the most elaborate and powerful tools are useless.

EXERCISES

2.1 Describe the feedback concept of control. Discuss its implications for data processing.

2.2 What is a system? Why is the concept of a system important to a manager?

2.3 What are the objectives of data processing?

2.4 Discuss the advantages of the systems approach to data processing.

2.5 How can you determine the data flows within a specific organization?

2.6 What is a transaction, and what two basic types of information must be included?

2.7 Describe each of the four major data processing functions.

2.8 Why do we code information for data processing?

2.9 Describe the logical function in data manipulation. Why is this function of importance?

2.10 How does your instructor determine your grade? Relate this process to the major functions of data processing described in Exercise 2.7.

SUPPLEMENTAL READINGS

CANNING, RICHARD G. *Electronic Data Processing for Business and Industry.* New York: John Wiley & Sons, Inc., 1956.
    Chapter 2 includes a good discussion of the motivation for data processing and information flows within an organization.

CHAPIN, NED. *An Introduction to Automatic Computers.* Princeton, N.J.: D. Van Nostrand Co., Inc., 1955.
    Chapters 3 and 4 contain a discussion of feedback control systems and their relationship to data processing.

CHURCHMAN, C. W.; ACKOFF, R. L.; AND ARNOFF E. L. *Introduction to Operations Research.* New York: John Wiley & Sons, Inc., 1957.
    Chapter 2 presents an excellent analysis of information flows in a manufacturing organization.

GALLAGHER, JAMES D. *Management Information Systems and the Computer.* New York: American Management Association, Inc., 1961.
    The first chapter of this little book discusses management information systems, data processing, and the computer.

Introduction to Data Processing. Haskins and Sells (a public accounting firm), 1957.

The first 59 pages of this little book present an excellent introduction to the basic operations involved in data processing.

JOHNSON, R. A.; KAST, F. E.; AND ROSENZWEIG, J. E. *The Theory and Management of Systems.* New York: McGraw-Hill Book Co., Inc., 1963.

Chapter 1 provides an excellent introduction to systems concepts and their impact upon management thinking.

KOZMETSKY, G., AND KIRCHER, P. *Electronic Computers and Management Control.* New York: McGraw-Hill Book Co., Inc., 1956.

Chapter 8 includes a discussion of feedback and its importance in management control. Chapter 9 discusses the systems approach to data processing.

MALCOLM, D. G., AND ROWE, A. J. *Management Control Systems.* New York: John Wiley & Sons, Inc., 1960.

This is the proceedings of a symposium held at the System Development Corporation. It contains a number of papers on the relationships between data processing systems and management control.

Management Operating System for Manufacturing Industries—General Information Manual (Form E20–8041). International Business Machines Corporation, White Plains, N.Y.

A description of the concepts of a management operating system and the various techniques involved in each phase.

3 PUNCHED CARD
DATA PROCESSING

ALTHOUGH WE MUST NEVER lose sight of the basic motivation for data processing presented in Chapter 2, this book is primarily concerned with the *mechanization* of data processing. But before studying the use of electronic computers for data processing, it is desirable that we discuss the use of punched card machines (frequently referred to as *unit record* equipment).

Punched cards are of great importance in their own right, for they are powerful data processing tools and have achieved widespread popularity. Also, most of the computers now in use have been installed in organizations in which data processing has become highly mechanized through the use of unit record equipment, and the computers have been combined with these punched card systems so that both types of machines are usually utilized together within the same organization.

Many problems that must be solved to use computers are the same problems that must be solved when data processing is mechanized— by any method—so a study of punched card data processing provides a valuable background for the study of electronic data processing. Furthermore, the various data processing functions discussed in Chapter 2 are performed by separate punched card machines while the same computer equipment may be used for everything. Thus a study of punched cards allows us to become more familiar with the individual data processing functions.

THE PUNCHED CARD

Basic to the punched card method, of course, is the ubiquitous punched card itself. Few among us have not had contact with punched cards, for they are in general use as government checks, defense bonds, soap coupons, gasoline credit slips, student registration cards, Christmas Club coupons, utility bills, and insurance renewal notices; while business employees handle them in the form of internal documents, such as time cards, labor tickets, requisitions, inventory-picking tickets, and so on.

Basically, the punched card is a piece of high-quality paper 7⅜ inches long and 3¼ inches wide (the size of the old-style United States dollar bill) on which information is recorded by means of holes punched in specified positions on the card. One corner of the card is usually clipped so that the cards can be easily replaced in the proper orientation if they are accidentally dropped.

Information Representation

There are two major manufacturers of punched card equipment in the United States: the International Business Machines Corporation and the Sperry Rand Corporation. Although their cards are the same size and shape, they may be distinguished from one another by the fact that the IBM cards are punched with rectangular holes while the holes in the Sperry Rand cards are round. As can be seen in Figures 3–1 and 3–2, the digits zero through 9, the letters A through Z, and several special characters may be represented in each system by means of vertical combinations of holes. Each character requires one "column" of the card, so the amount of information that may be recorded on any single card is limited by the standard number of columns available.

The IBM card includes 12 horizontal rows and 80 vertical col-

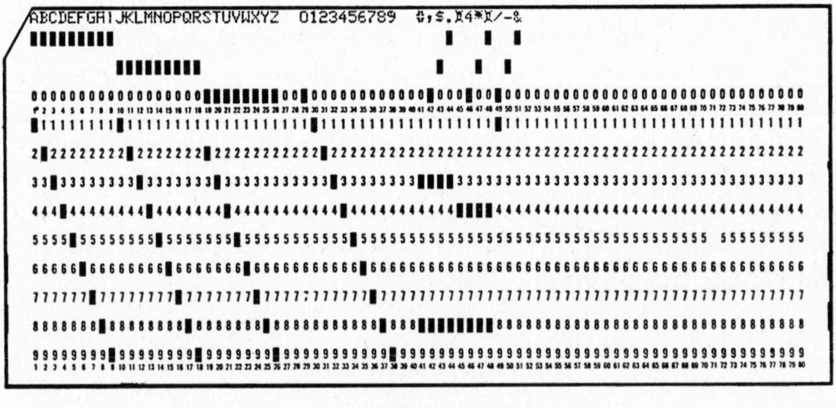

FIG. 3–1
IBM Card

umns. Each row of the card has a specific designation. The top row is
called the 12 (or Y) row and the next row is the 11 (or X) row.
These two rows are used primarily to record holes that control
the operation of the machines or as "zone" punches for recording
alphabetic information. The third row represents the number zero,
the fourth represents the number 1, and so on, till we reach the
bottom row, which represents the number 9. As can be seen from
Figure 3–1, each numeric digit can be represented in any column by
a single punch in the row associated with that digit.

Alphabetic information is represented by means of a zone punch
(X, Y, or zero) combined with a numeric punch (1 through 9) in a

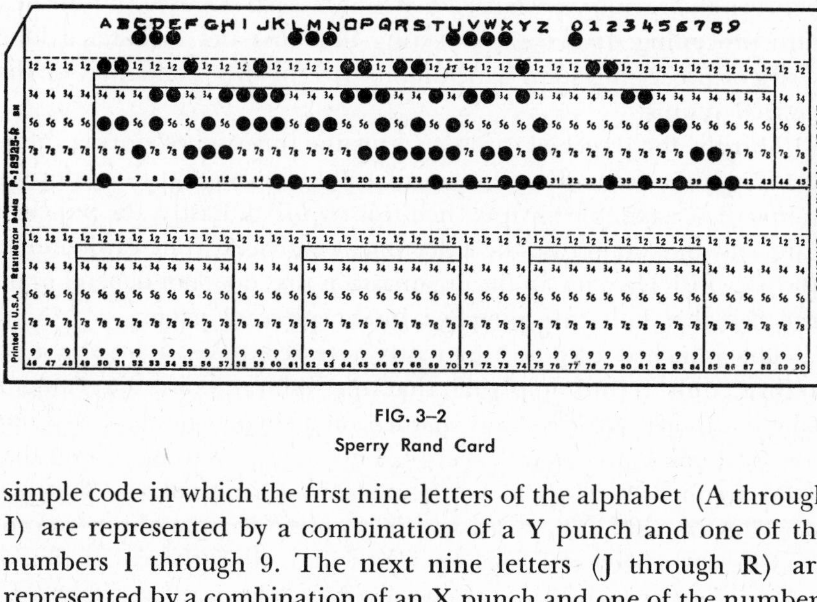

FIG. 3–2
Sperry Rand Card

simple code in which the first nine letters of the alphabet (A through
I) are represented by a combination of a Y punch and one of the
numbers 1 through 9. The next nine letters (J through R) are
represented by a combination of an X punch and one of the numbers
1 through 9. The last eight letters (S through Z) are represented by a
combination of a zero punch and one of the numbers 2 through 9.

The special symbols are represented by various combinations of
one, two, or three punches within one column.

The Sperry Rand card has 90 columns of information, 45 columns
arranged along the upper half of the card and 45 on the lower
half of the card (see Figure 3–2). There are six rows in each of
these sections; the odd numbers are represented by a single hole in
the proper row and the even numbers are represented by two holes.
The punching combinations for alphabetic characters are as shown
in Figure 3–2, and while these combinations do not appear to follow

any particular rule this causes little difficulty because we seldom attempt to read information directly from the holes themselves.

What the Punched Card Does

The punched card serves a variety of uses in a punched card data processing system. First, it is an input media which enters information into the machines (which cannot read ordinary written material) in a form which they *can* accept. The card also provides an output from these machines. In other words, the punched card is the principal media through which men communicate with the machines.

Secondly, the punched card is a common communication media between the various specialized machines which are used in punched card processing. It is the connecting link that ties together a long series of processing steps which culminate in the production of the desired results.

Thirdly, the punched card performs the function of storing information in the form of machine-processable files so that this information will be available for use when it is required. Lastly, the punched card may in certain cases be a document (a check, time card, and so forth) which has a use in the organization that does not depend upon the fact that holes are punched in the piece of paper.

The punched card is frequently referred to as a *mobile unit record,* unit record implying that the information concerning a single transaction is usually recorded on a single card (there is one and only one transaction per card). This concept is so important that IBM frequently refers to "unit record" rather than to "punched card" equipment. The word mobile implies that these unit records may be rearranged and reprocessed at will to allow the transaction to be incorporated into the various reports which it affects. Thus, by recording the information once on a punched card, it may be posted to different accounts, ledgers, or reports by a mechanized process without additional human effort and without the transcription errors so prevalent in manual data processing. This concept of mobility is of such great importance that a rule of thumb is frequently applied which states that the information should be used in at least three different postings in order to qualify as a good punched card application.

Card Format

One of the basic requirements associated with mechanized data processing is that information to be entered into the machines be recorded in a rigid format. The information is identified to the machine as a man-number or a dollar amount by means of its position alone. That is to say (in terms of punched cards) that the column or columns in which a number is recorded is the only means by which the machine can identify the information; hence this location becomes the key to meaningful processing. Thus each type of transaction is recorded on cards of a specific format so that each unit of information occupies the same position on all cards for a particular type of transaction.

Fields

A group of card columns (usually adjacent) that is assigned to a particular unit of information (such as a name, hourly rate, description, unit cost, or tax class) is called a *field*. In designing the format of the punched card the 80 or 90 columns may be grouped together to form fields in any way that seems desirable—subject to the restriction that the total number of columns in all the fields may not exceed the number of columns available on the card.

Enough columns must be allowed in each field to permit recording the largest number or the longest group of alphabetic characters that may occur among the units of information that are to be recorded in that field. For example, if price may range from 25¢ to $850.00 a five-digit field must be assigned to price; if the price could go as high as $1,000.00, a six-digit field would be required. Note that the decimal point is not usually punched, so it does not require a card column. Numeric fields are customarily justified to the right, and zeros are inserted to the left of small numbers to completely fill the columns allocated. Thus, in a five-digit field, 745 would be recorded 00745. Alphabetic fields are customarily justified to the left, and unused columns to the right are left blank.

Card Design

One of the important preliminary steps in utilizing punched card equipment for data processing is that of designing the cards that are involved. Several considerations are involved in allocating the card columns among the various pieces of information: the total amount of information to be recorded, the sequence in which the fields should appear on the cards, and the relationship of the location of a specific field on one card form to the location of the same field on another card form. As we will see when we discuss the accounting machine, it is not necessary that there be any relationship between the sequence of fields on the card and the position of the information on the reports that are printed—fields on the left-hand side of the card may be printed on the right-hand side of the reports, and conversely.

As can be seen from Figure 3–3, once the allocation of the fields is made, special forms may be printed designating the uses to which each field is put. The different cards that enter into the processing usually have different formats and may be made of different colors of paper or identified by different corner cuts or by horizontal stripes of various colors. The machines do not detect color nor do they read the information printed on the card, but the different colors and the different printed formats are used to reduce the chance of confusing the people who may be working with the cards.

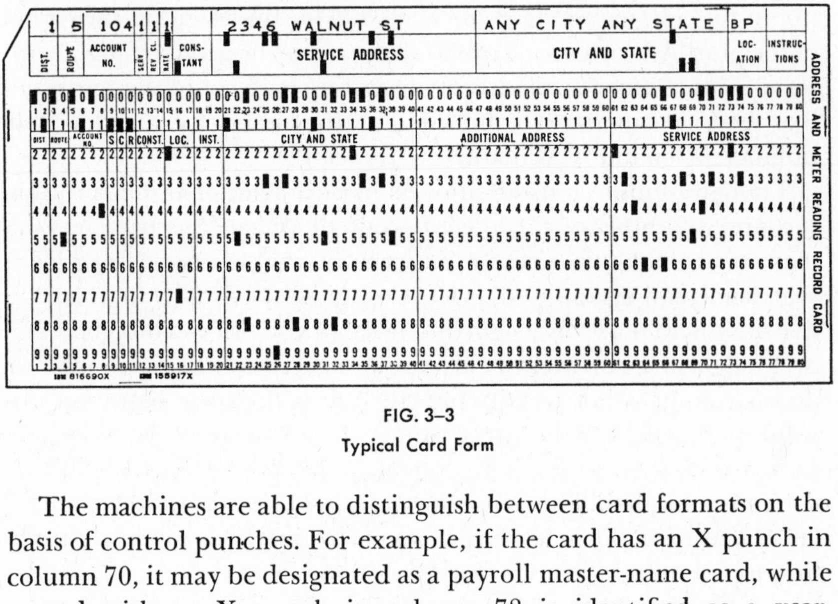

FIG. 3–3
Typical Card Form

The machines are able to distinguish between card formats on the basis of control punches. For example, if the card has an X punch in column 70, it may be designated as a payroll master-name card, while a card with an X punch in column 78 is identified as a year-to-date earnings card.[1] These control punches do not require an extra card column, for they may be over numeric fields. In such cases the combination of a zone and numeric punch is not interpreted by the machines as an alphabetic character because no letter can appear in a numeric field. How these control punches are used to enable the machine to handle cards with different formats in different ways will be discussed later in the section on selectors.

---

[1] As discussed above, an X punch is a punch in the second-from-the-top row of the card. This is not to be confused with the letter X, which is a zero punch combined with a 7 punch.

Good card design is of great importance to the successful use of punched card machines. In the first place, all the information that will be needed (even some time in the future) should be included in the original design, for the card form is difficult to change and it is costly and inconvenient to add information to cards that have already been punched. Secondly, poor card design may significantly increase the complexity of the processing procedures and may even cause the capabilities of the machines to be exceeded.

Because of the limited space and time that we can devote to the subject of punched card data processing, the following discussion will be based upon the equipment of only one manufacturer. We have chosen to discuss the IBM equipment because about 90 percent of the punched card equipment in use in the United States is of this type. However, even though the individual machines of the different manufacturers vary considerably in details of operation and in the combination of functions they perform, the basic functions performed are, fortunately, almost identical. Thus the capabilities that are present in an installation of Sperry Rand equipment are roughly equivalent to those in a similar installation of IBM equipment.

RECORDING METHODS

The first step in the punched card process is that of recording the information in a form which can be processed—that is, punching the information into cards. There are a variety of methods by which cards may be punched, and, in many situations, several different methods are used within the same punched card procedure or even to record information on the same card.

Key Punching

The most commonly used punching method, called *key punching,* involves the use of a manually operated machine with a keyboard resembling that of an electric typewriter both in appearance and in operation. Since no distinction is made between the upper case and lower case characters on punched card equipment, it is possible to superimpose a ten-key numeric keyboard upon the normal alphabetic keyboard, distinguishing one from the other by means of the shift key (see Figure 3–4). Cards are automatically fed into this machine one at a time, and are punched column by column as the keys are depressed. By means of a previously prepared program card (which is wrapped around a program drum and moves in synchronization with the cards being punched) skipping between fields, ejection of the card, assignment of the keyboard to alphabetic or numeric status for each card field, and duplication of fields from one card into the following cards may be automatically controlled (see Figure 3–5). Some models of the key punch can simultaneously print all or part of the information along the top of the card as it is being punched.

FIG. 3–4

Keyboard

Recording by means of key strokes is basic not only to punched card data processing but also to most other methods of mechanized data processing, including electronic data processing. This is essentially a manual step, and frequently represents a substantial percent of the total cost of the entire data processing procedure. Therefore it is important that key punching be accomplished as efficiently as possible. It is customary to perform the functions of editing and coding before key punching so that the key punch operator can concentrate on recording the information accurately and efficiently.

Moreover, the arrangement of the form from which the information is punched should be correlated with the sequence of fields on the card form so that the information appears in the order in which it is to be punched with a minimum of skipping around. Because of the design of the keyboard on the key punch, it is desirable that the operator be right handed; and it is generally conceded that women perform this operation more efficiently than men.

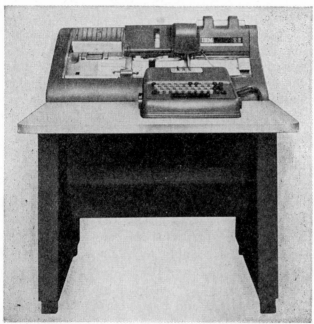

Source: Courtesy International Business Machines Corp.

FIG. 3–5
Key Punch Machine

The Sperry Rand key punch does not punch the card column by column as does the IBM key punch. As the keys are operated, the information is stored within the machine, and after the card is completed, all the holes are punched simultaneously when a trip bar is depressed. This method of operation has two advantages: not only can the keyboard be operated slightly faster than with the IBM key punch, but keying errors which are detected by the operator may be corrected before the holes are actually punched so that the card itself is not destroyed. However, as will be seen in a later section, these advantages must be balanced against IBM's advantages in the area of verification.

Prepunching

Another widely used method of recording information is by *prepunching* the cards. A number of duplicates of a master card may be prepared by *gang punching,* or an entire file of cards may be duplicated by a machine process called *reproducing* (see the subsequent discussion on these subjects). Then the information so recorded can be introduced into the punched card procedure by simply choosing the proper prepunched card. Prepunching is frequently combined with key punching or some other method of recording so that the constant information is prepunched and variable information pertaining to the transaction is entered by some other method. For example, in a payroll procedure the time cards may be prepunched with man-number, department number, shift code, hourly rate and other information peculiar to the man, and the total hours worked may be entered into the card by key punching.

Mark Sensing

Another useful method for entering small quantities of information into a card is by means of *mark sensing.* With a special pencil or pen conductive marks may be made in designated spots on the punched card, and these marks may be converted into punches at a speed of 100 cards per minute by the use of the *mark-sensing reproducer* (available only from IBM). As can be seen from Figure 3–6, for each column to be punched there must be a column of marking areas on the card, and a mark corresponding to the desired hole must be made in each such column. Since alphabetic informa-

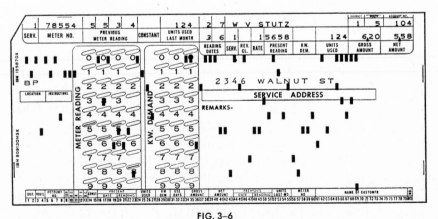

FIG. 3–6
Mark Sense Card

tion requires two holes per column and the alphabetic code is not easily remembered, the use of mark sensing is usually restricted to the recording of numeric information. Similar equipment, operating on a photoelectric principle, is available from Sperry Rand.

Many of the most prevalent errors involved in marking cards, such as failure to mark a digit or to make a readable mark, are detected by the machine. These errors cause the machine to stop, and the operator must isolate the card and correct the error. If these stoppages become frequent, the operation becomes inefficient, so it is apparent that the marking must be done with care. Mark sensing, then, can be effectively used only when the persons recording the information can be motivated to take the care necessary to do it properly. Since the possibility of confusion increases rapidly with the number of columns to be marked, it is most effective when only a few columns must be marked on each card.

Key punching from written material is much faster than placing the marks on mark-sense cards, so it is not usually efficient for someone to read from a document and mark the cards. Mark sensing is most efficient when the marking can be done at the point where the information originates and by a person who can perform the marking as a by-product of his major work without adversely affecting his working efficiency. An example of an excellent mark-sensing application is that of utility meter reading, where the mark-sense cards become the meter book and the meter reader marks the card as he is reading the meter dials.

Other Punching Methods

A widely used method of punching—that of duplicating information from one card to another when using the key punch—has already been mentioned. Occasionally a modified conductor's punch, aligned by means of minute *finder holes,* is used for recording small amounts of information in the Sperry Rand system. Also, IBM produces Port-A-Punch cards in which some of the punching positions are prescored and may be punched out by use of a pencil point or a special tool in a manner similar to a punchboard.

A wide variety of devices are available that produce machine-processable information as a by-product of their major function. For example, there are electric typewriters that produce standard punched cards containing selected portions of the information that is typed. Certain production-recording equipment produces information in punched card form. And toll road equipment is in use that weighs and counts the axles of each vehicle and produces a punched card that is used as a ticket.

A multitude of adding machines, typewriters, bookkeeping machines, and production recorders produce selected by-product information in the form of punched paper tape. The information in these paper tapes can be automatically transmitted over teletype or telephone lines, then converted by a card machine into punched cards or be fed directly into a computer. Needless to say, the format of the paper tape must be carefully integrated into the data processing system.

Although key punching is undoubtedly the basic method of recording information in punched card form, it should again be emphasized that in a mechanized system the recording function is of utmost importance and that ingenuity in the choice of recording techniques may pay handsome dividends.

VERIFICATION

Not only is recording of information important from the standpoint of costs, it is also crucial from the standpoint of accuracy. Although the machines can and do make mistakes, their accuracy is phenomenal when compared with that of humans. On the other hand, machines do not have judgment: although they may be programmed to perform specific tests that may *detect* errors, they cannot sense that a number is wrong in the same way that a human might sense an error.

Errors in recording can best be rectified when the source documents are available to provide the correct information. After the mechanized processing begins, the source documents and the cards prepared from them go their separate ways, and correction of these recording errors becomes much more difficult for it also involves locating the source document. Furthermore, once the processing reaches the mechanized stage, interruption to correct errors may cause grave disruption and drastically reduce the efficiency of the overall process.

Therefore it is extremely important that the information which enters a mechanized system be as accurate as possible. It is usually worthwhile to go to considerable effort and expense to reduce the incidence of transcription and recording errors before reaching the machine-processing stage. Thus verification is an important preliminary step in a mechanized data processing procedure, and there are several methods that may be used singly or in combination for verifying the accuracy of recording.

Key Verification

Key verification is quite similar to key punching except that a verifier is used instead of a key punch. In outward appearance the two machines are almost identical, but in place of a punching mechanism the verifier has a sensing device that reads the holes in the card column and compares them with the key that is depressed by the operator. If the holes do not agree with the key that the verifier operator has depressed, this indicates that the card was mispunched or that the verifier operator has depressed the wrong key. In this case the machine keyboard locks, a red light goes on, and the verifier operator then has two opportunities to depress the proper key. If the verifier operator made the mistake, she can release the card and continue verification by depressing the correct key. Since the card column being verified is covered by the mechanism and the card cannot be spaced without indicating an error, if the card has been mispunched the operator cannot release it without indicating an error (unless she can guess what is punched in the column). If the card is in error, a notch is punched in the top of the card in the column in which the error occurred. If no errors are detected, the machine places a notch in the right edge of the card as it is ejected from the machine so that the cards which are in error may be easily located.

After punching, the cards, along with the documents from which they were punched, are taken to a verifier and are verified by a different operator. Frequently, only a portion of the information that was punched must be key-verified, for the accuracy of certain information (such as alphabetic descriptions) may be of little importance in the subsequent processing, or some of the information may be verified by other methods. As with the key punch, format control, skipping of fields, designation of alphabetic and numeric status, and feeding and ejection of the cards is automatically controlled by use of a program card.

Cards found to be in error must be returned to a key punch, along with the source documents from which they were punched, for repunching. The duplicating feature of the key punch may be used to repunch the correct portions of the cards. Since the verifier operator has a chance to correct her errors without damaging the cards involved, verification may be performed faster than key punching.

In the Sperry Rand system the key punch machine is also used as a key verifier. The card is simply displaced vertically about one-sixteenth of an inch, and the card is then repunched. After this process the correct information will be represented by oval-shaped holes. The cards are then run through a machine (called a verifier) which detects the round holes and inserts a finder card in front of each card containing an error.

Then the error cards must be returned to a key punch operator, the source documents from which they were punched must be found, and the cards must be repunched. You may have noticed that in this system not only the errors arising in key punching but also those made in the process of verification require repunching of the cards.

Visual Verification

One of the *least* effective verification methods is visual verification. After the cards have been punched they may be printed (one line for each card) on a punched card accounting machine, then this printed list can be visually compared with the original source documents. This comparison is best accomplished by using two persons, one reading aloud to the other, but it is neither a popular nor effective method: its cost is higher than that of key verification (if there is enough verifying to keep a machine busy) and it is substantially inferior to key verification in detecting errors. (Incidentally, the holes themselves are seldom visually read for verification.)

Batch Totals

Batch totals, obtained by running the cards through the accounting machine, may be compared with totals obtained independently from the source documents, thus providing another effective verification method. In this method the source documents are delivered to the key punch operator in batches, accompanied by an adding machine tape totaling one or more fields of information. After the cards are punched they may be listed on the accounting machine to provide totals to compare with the adding machine totals. If these totals agree there is an excellent probability that this field (or fields) of the cards is correctly punched, since compensating errors are highly unlikely. If the totals, however, do not agree, there is either a key punching or an adding machine error (or errors) in the batch which must be located by comparing the adding machine tape item by item with the list prepared on the accounting machine.

The number of cards that should be included in a batch is

determined by the expected error rate, for if there are one or more errors in each batch the situation reduces to sight verification. For this method to be used effectively the batches must be small enough so that most of them will contain no punching errors.

This method of verification is frequently used because the batch totals may also be used to establish overall controls on the entire data processing procedure, for these totals may be accumulated again at later stages in the processing to verify that all of the proper cards have been processed at that stage. This is an extremely important technique in the overall control of accuracy of mechanized data processing systems.

Self-Checking Numbers

One of the most interesting methods of verification involves the use of so-called *self-checking numbers*—along with a special device on the IBM key punch. This method cannot be used to check the accuracy of quantitative information—it is used only with identifying information because it involves the modification of the number itself by the addition of a *check digit*.

The check digit is computed by applying some rule to the original digits of the number so that most of the usual mistakes will give numbers for which a different check digit would be computed. One method of computing a check digit involves multiplying every other digit of the original number by 2 and adding these values to the remaining digits of the number. The units digit of the result is then subtracted from 10 to obtain the check digit.[2]

To illustrate the process, let us compute the check digit for the number 72546. The alternate digits are first multiplied by 2:

$$2(7) = 14 \qquad 2(5) = 10 \qquad 2(6) = 12$$

Then the remaining digits (2 and 4) are included and the *digits* are added:

$$
\begin{array}{ccc}
14 & 10 & 12 \\
\downarrow & \downarrow & \downarrow \\
\end{array}
$$
$$(1 + 4) + 2 + (1 + 0) + 4 + (1 + 2) = 15$$

The 5 is subtracted from 10 to give a check digit of 5, and the number becomes 725465.

---

[2] Two other variations of self-checking numbers are explained in the booklet *Account Numbering System,* Form G1196, published by Burroughs Corporation.

As the digits of the self-checking number are being punched, a special device on the key punch repeats the above calculation. When the check digit is punched, it is automatically compared with the computed check digit to detect punching errors. Suppose the second and third figures in the above number were reversed and that the number was punched as 752465. The check digit computation would be as follows:

$$2(7) = 14 \qquad 2(2) = 4 \qquad 2(6) = 12$$
$$(1 + 4) + 5 + (4) + 4 + (1 + 2) = 21$$
$$10 - 1 = 9 \text{ check digit}$$

Thus, when the digit 5 is punched, the machine expects a 9, so an error would be indicated.

The check digit must be computed and added to the number before it is assigned to the item it is to identify. For example, the number 725465 would be assigned to a man as a man-number when he first becomes an employee. He would not have to be aware that it is a self-checking number, so the last digit has no special significance to him. But whenever the number is key-punched it may be automatically checked for accuracy. The check digit may originally be computed by a punched card calculator or it may be generated by use of the self-checking number device on the key punch.

You may have noted that the other methods of verification only check the accuracy of the key punching and do not verify in the sense that this word was used in our discussion of the recording function in Chapter 2. However, the above method of verification also detects errors of original coding and transcription, for it makes no difference to the equipment whether the inconsistency in the number came from a key punching error, or in assigning the number, or in transcribing it onto the source document. Thus, at the "expense" of an extra key stroke and an extra card column, it is possible to provide excellent verification of identifying information simply by precomputing check digits and treating them as integral parts of the identifying numbers.

The use of self-checking numbers is not restricted to punched card systems, for they are frequently used as account numbers in banking systems—and could profitably be used by mail order houses as catalog numbers so that transcription errors by the customer in ordering could be easily detected. They may be used in punched card systems for man-numbers which must be written on labor tickets, for item identification numbers in inventory control procedures, and for customer account numbers in accounts receivable procedures.

SORTING

After the cards have been punched and verified, the next step in a typical punched card procedure is *sorting* to arrange them in the proper sequence for further processing. Indeed, much of the power of the punched card method is due to the ability to rapidly and inexpensively arrange the punched cards in sequence according to

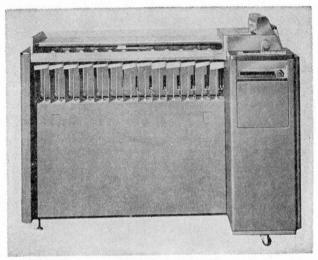

Source: Courtesy International Business Machines Corp.

Fig. 3–7
Punched Card Sorter

any field (or group of fields) on the card. This field (or fields) is called the *sorting key*. For example, in a payroll procedure, punched card labor tickets might first be sorted by man-number in order to group all the cards for each man for pay computation. Later in the procedure the cards might be sorted in job number sequence, and thus grouped by job number, so that the total cost for each job could easily be determined.

The sorter has one card-feeding mechanism and 13 output card stackers (called pockets) —12 for the 12 possible punching positions (or rows) —and the reject pocket is for cards that are blank (see Figure 3–7) . On each pass of the cards the machine examines a single column and routes each card into the output pocket that corresponds to the punch in that column. Thus, if that column is punched with a hole in row 7, the card is placed in the 7 pocket.

Depressing certain buttons causes any row of the card to be ignored in this process. If, for example, we wished to extract all cards with a 7 punch in column 20 (without disturbing the sequence of the other cards), we could depress the buttons that blank out all rows

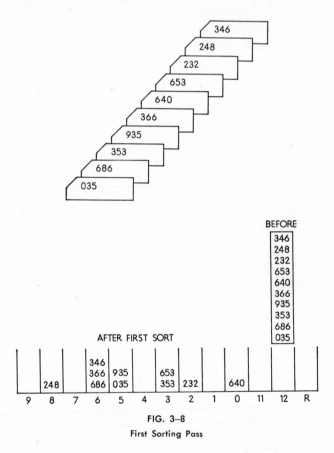

FIG. 3–8

First Sorting Pass

except the 7 row. Then, when sorting column 20, cards containing a 7 would be placed in the 7 pocket and the other cards would be placed in the reject pocket.

Sorting is accomplished by repeatedly passing the cards through the machine, setting it on a different column during each pass. The *reverse digit* method is usually used to sort numeric information. On the first pass the machine is set to sort on the column corresponding to the low-order digit of the sorting field. On succeeding passes the machine is set to sort on each column of the field, proceeding to the left column by column. After completion of each pass the cards are removed from the pockets and recombined so that the zeros are first, 1s next, the 2s next, and so on through the 9s.

As an illustration of sorting, suppose we wish to sort the cards whose identifying numbers (the sorting key) are shown in Figure 3–8. Placing these cards face down in the feed hopper of the sorter produces the "before" situation shown in Figure 3–8. Sorting on the units digit of the key places the first card (035) in the 5 pocket, the second card (686) in the pocket, the third card (353) in the 3 pocket, the fourth card (935) on top of the 035 in the 5 pocket, the fifth card (366) on top of 686 in the 6 pocket, and so on, as shown in

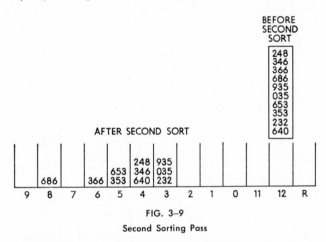

FIG. 3–9

Second Sorting Pass

Figure 3–8. The cards are removed (face down) by taking the cards from the zero pocket first, placing the cards from the 1 pocket face down on top of these, then the cards from the 2 pocket, and so on, till the cards from the 9 pocket have been placed on top of the rest. When these cards are replaced in the feed hopper they are arranged as shown in the "before" of Figure 3–9. Notice that they are in order according to the units digit of the sorting key.

On the second pass we set the sorter to sort on the 10s position of the sorting key. As shown in Figure 3–9, the first card (640) falls in the 4 pocket, the second card (232) falls in the 3 pocket, the third card (353) falls in the 5 pocket, the fourth card (653) falls on top of the 353 in the 5 pocket, the fifth card (035) falls on top of the 232 in the 3 pocket, and so on. When these cards are removed (face down, starting with the zero pocket and working to the left) and placed in the feed hopper, they are arranged as shown in the "before" portion of Figure 3–10. Notice that they are in sequence according to the two right-hand digits of the sorting key.

The result of the third sort is shown in Figure 3–10. Notice that since 46 precedes 53, the *346* card falls into the 3 pocket before the

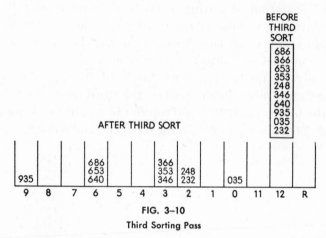

FIG. 3–10

Third Sorting Pass

353 card. Similarly, the *353* card precedes the *366* card because 53 precedes 66 as the result of the previous sortings.

After the cards are properly removed from the sorter pockets and combined, they are in sequence according to the three-digit sorting key shown in Figure 3–11.

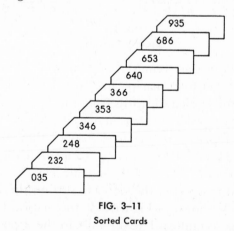

FIG. 3–11

Sorted Cards

This illustration indicates that, for numeric sorting, the cards must be run through the sorter once for each column of the sorting key field—a three-column numeric field requires three passes through the machine while a seven-column numeric field requires seven passes.

For large sorting jobs it is sometimes convenient to split the work among several sorters by using the technique of *block sorting*. In this method the cards are first sorted according to the high-order digit of the key field, thus separating the cards into ten separate groups, each of which can be sorted individually by the preceding method. At the conclusion of the process the separately sorted decks[3] must be recombined in the proper sequence.

Alphabetic sorting requires that the cards be passed through the sorter twice for each column of the key field. The first pass arranges the cards according to the numeric punch: the As and Js are placed in the 1 pocket, the Bs, Ks, and Ss are placed in the 2 pocket, etc. The second pass then ignores the numeric punch and arranges the cards by zone, so that the A through I cards fall in the 12 pocket, the J through R cards fall in the X pocket, and the S through Z cards fall in the zero pocket.

Various models of the sorter operate at from 450 to 2,000 cards per minute per pass. Since a considerable amount of card handling is involved in the sorting process, the machines actually operate substantially below their rated speeds. It is not unusual for one person to operate as many as three 650-card-per-minute machines simultaneously. A large punched card installation is likely to have several high-speed sorters and to keep them operating most of the time.

AUXILIARY EQUIPMENT

The basic steps involved in most punched card procedures include punching, verifying, sorting, file reference, report preparation, and file updating. File reference is accomplished by means of the *collator,* and the remaining steps are accomplished by means of the *accounting machine* and the *summary punch.* However, between these major steps there may be a number of intermediate processing steps, some of which will be discussed in this section.

Reproducing

Reproducing is the process of making a duplicate of an original deck of punched cards, thus preparing a single copy of each old card by duplicating some or all of the information punched in the original card. A machine, called the reproducer, performs this operation (and

---

[3] Naturally, any stack of data cards is usually referred to as a deck.

FIG. 3–12
Control Panel

several others, including mark sensing) at the speed of 100 cards per minute.

Like most other IBM machines, the reproducer is controlled through the use of a removable panel (called a *control panel*) containing holes into which the ends of special wires may be inserted

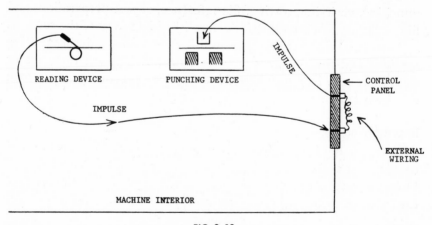

FIG. 3–13
Control Panel Wires Transmit Impulses

to provide paths for electrical impulses which, in this case, transfer the information from one card to another (see Figures 3–12, 3–13, and 3–14). The newer Sperry Rand machines also utilize this method of control, but many of the others use removable *wiring*

FIG. 3–14
Control Panel Being Inserted into Machine

units by means of which physical force is applied from one part of the machine to another to perform the functions desired.

Punched cards are read by passing them between a brass roller and a set of wire brushes, one brush for each of the columns of the card. The card serves as an insulator, but the brush makes contact with the roller where there is a hole and current is able to flow (see Figure

3–15). Everything within the machine is synchronized with the movement of the card.

Figure 3–16 shows a diagram of the reproducer. The original deck is placed in the left-hand feed and blank cards are placed in the right-hand feed. The movement of both decks of cards is synchro-

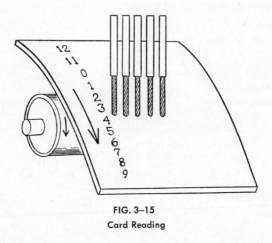

FIG. 3–15
Card Reading

nized so that cards are passing each of the three sets of reading brushes and the punch dies simultaneously. Thus when the 1 row of a card is under the reproducing brushes, it is being read at both the comparing and punch brushes, and the 1 row is under the punching dies at the punching station.

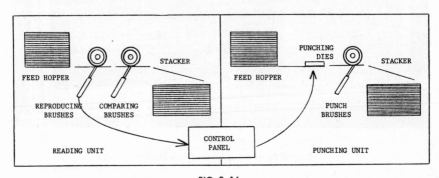

FIG. 3–16
Diagram of Reproducer

The control panel of the reproducer includes a set of holes (frequently called *hubs*) for each of the reading stations, one hole for each card column for each reading station. There is also a set of holes which are connected to the punching mechanism, one hole for each of the 80 columns which may be punched. By inserting one end of a wire into the hub corresponding to a column of a card being read by the reproducing brushes, and the other end of the wire into a hub corresponding to a punching magnet, a hole that is read causes the machine to punch a corresponding hole in the card that is under the punch dies. Then, as each card of the original deck passes under the reproducing brushes, the information in the columns wired to punch is punched into the corresponding card under the punch mechanism.

Gang Punching

The reproducer is also used in *gang punching,* which is the process of making a large number of duplicates of a single "master" card. This is accomplished by placing the master card, followed by the proper number of blank cards, into the punch feed of the machine. By means of wiring from the punch brushes through the control panel to the punching dies (refer to Figure 3–16) the original card is duplicated into the first blank card, and this card then moves to the punch brushes where it is duplicated into the next card, and so on. It is possible to interrupt this process for one card cycle so that master cards may be interspersed between groups of cards into which the master information is to be duplicated.

Interpreting

Whenever it is necessary for people to read directly from cards, a machine called an *interpreter* may be used to print information that has been punched into a card on the face of that same card. Although key-punched information may also be printed along the top of the card, sometimes this information is not located in the best place when cards are to be used for documents or for reference. Furthermore, information may have been punched by some other method, such as reproducing, gang punching, or by the calculator. In these cases, the cards may be interpreted before they become part of a file or are used as documents.

FILE REFERENCE

One of the major functions performed by punched card machines is that of file reference. Transaction cards must be associated with information maintained in punched card files so that this combined information may be processed and the file information updated. This function of file reference can sometimes be accomplished by sorting, but it is usually performed by means of the *collator*.

The Collator

The collator (see Figure 3–17) is one of the most versatile punched card machines, performing such operations as sequence checking, selecting, matching, merging, and various combinations of these operations. As can be seen from Figure 3–18, the collator has

Source: Courtesy of International Business Machines Corp.

FIG. 3–17

The Collator

two input feeds and four output pockets. Its basic function is that of comparison, and it feeds cards and ejects them into the desired pocket on the basis of these comparisons. Cards from the primary feed may go into pockets 1 or 2 while those in the secondary feed may go into pockets 2, 3, or 4.

Merging

The collator is frequently used to combine two different files—in the same sequence according to the control field—into a single file in that same sequence. This is called *merging,* and may be used to insert transaction cards in their proper place in a file for subsequent processing with the file cards.

In the merging operation the card read at the primary reading brushes is compared with the one read at the secondary reading brushes, and the card with the smaller number is dropped into pocket 2. Then the next card is compared with the one that was larger, and the process is repeated. By experimenting with different numbers in the collator diagram, it can readily be seen that this process works

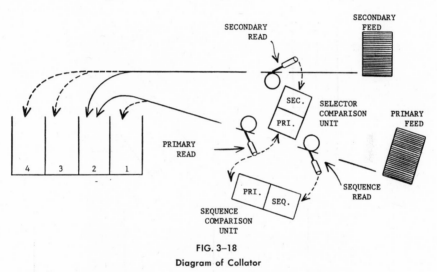

FIG. 3–18
Diagram of Collator

properly only when the two files are in *correct sequence.* This is an important characteristic of collator operations in which two decks of cards are involved.

Matching

Another basic collator operation is that of *matching,* in which the cards in the primary and the secondary feeds are compared. Those that are equal are dropped side by side into pockets 2 and 3, while secondary cards for which there is no matching primary card are placed in pocket 4, and primary cards for which there is no matching secondary card are dropped into pocket 1 (see the example in Figure 3–19).

Match-Merging

The matching and merging operations may be combined so that the cards that match are merged together rather than placed side by side. This operation is typically used for file reference. For example, in a punched card payroll procedure, a master payroll file is maintained (in man-number sequence) containing a card for each worker. When the time cards are returned from the timekeeper, they may be sorted in man-number sequence. If they are then match-merged with the payroll master file (with the payroll master cards in the primary feed), unmatched primary cards represent workers whose time cards are missing while unmatched secondary cards

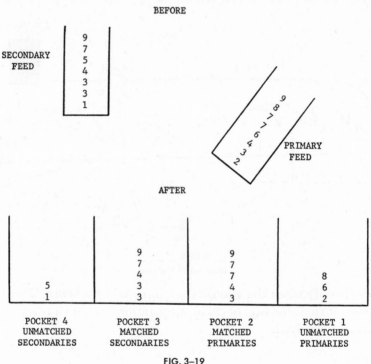

FIG. 3–19

Example of Matching

represent time cards for which there is no payroll master card. Both of these situations would have to be investigated and the proper corrections made. The merged master cards and time cards would then be processed in the payroll calculation.

The collator can be used for several other processing operations. For example, by storing a number A in the sequence unit and a number B in the selector comparison unit, and comparing them with the card read at the primary reading brushes, it is possible to select from a file of cards those cards in which the number in a given field lies between the numbers A and B. Proceeding at a speed of 240 cards per minute, this operation might be used to select for further processing those accounts in an accounts receivable file that are between four and six weeks overdue.

REPORT PREPARATION AND FILE UPDATING

After the file cards and the transaction cards have been associated by the collator, the next step in punched card processing is that of *report preparation,* which is frequently combined with the step of *file updating.* Report preparation is performed with various models of the accounting machine. This type of machine adds and subtracts, takes totals, prints, controls the spacing of the forms being printed upon, and (in conjunction with the reproducer) *summary punches* into new cards for file updating purposes.

The Accounting Machine

The two most popular models of *accounting machines* (see Figure 3–20) can print a line for each card at a speed of 100 or 150 lines per

FIG. 3–20

Accounting Machine

minute. Through the wiring of the control panel it is possible to eliminate part of the information on the card and to rearrange the sequence in which the information is printed across the page so that it need have no relationship to the sequence in which it appears on the card. However, the continuous forms which are fed through the machines can only space upward, and cards must be arranged in the proper sequence so that the information will print on the desired line of the form. That is to say, if card A precedes card B through the machine, then card B cannot print above card A on the form. If they both print on the same line, then all cards between the two either must *not print* or *must also print* on that line.

Most accounting machines have from 80 to 120 counter positions, grouped to form counters of various sizes, which may be used for adding and subtracting fields from the cards to accumulate totals. Thus each accounting machine may be thought of as containing several adding machines, each of which may be associated with a particular field of the cards.

Group Control

One of the most important capabilities of the accounting machine is its ability to pause between cards and take a total at the proper time. This capability, known as *group control,* depends upon the fact that the cards are in sequence before they are placed in the accounting machine. The process of sorting not only arranges the cards in sequence but also associates them in groups, for all those cards which contain the same number will be together in the deck (see below).

$$
\begin{array}{ll}
\left.\begin{array}{l}103\\103\\103\end{array}\right\}\text{First Group} & \left.\begin{array}{l}119\\119\end{array}\right\}\text{Third Group}\\[2ex]
117\ \ \text{Second Group} & \left.\begin{array}{l}123\\123\\123\end{array}\right\}\text{Fourth Group}
\end{array}
$$

As is shown in Figures 3–21 and 3–22, the accounting machine contains two sets of reading brushes and a comparing mechanism which emits an impulse when the two numbers being compared are

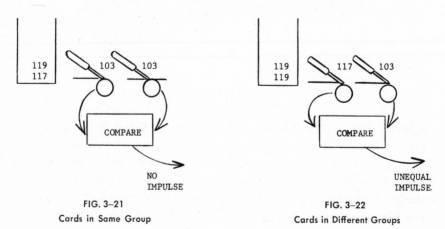

FIG. 3–21	FIG. 3–22
Cards in Same Group	Cards in Different Groups

unequal. Wiring from both sets of reading brushes into the comparing mechanism makes it possible to compare each card with its successor. If the two are equal, then the second card is a member of the same group as the first, but if they are not equal, the first card is the final card in its group, and the machine may be directed to print a total and clear the counter.

The accounting machine can handle three separate sets of comparisons at the same time, enabling it to handle three different classes of

LABOR COST REPORT			
Department Number	Job Number	Hours	Cost
21	1234	20	45 23
	1234	69	147 82
	1234	5	12 70
		94*	205 75*
	1265	105	224 40
	1265	243	517 82
	1265	90	203 00
	1265	175	386 07
		613*	1331 29*
	1342	73	150 20
	1342	65	143 56
	1342	38	81 93
		176*	375 69*
		883**	1912 73**
23	1234	55	125 64
	------	----	------

FIG. 3–23

Detail Printed Report

totals (called *minor, intermediate,* and *major*). For example, if we wish to produce a labor distribution report from a deck of cards which contains a department number, job number, hours worked and labor costs, we would first sort the cards on the job number field and then sort them according to department number. By using the job number as the minor control and the department number as the intermediate control, a report of hours and cost by job within the department can be produced (see Figure 3–23). Notice that each intermediate total (identified by **) is the sum of the minor totals (identified by *) in that department.

The relationship between sorting and the use of the accounting machine is extremely important. The minor control is associated with the finest breakdown on the report, the intermediate control gives totals of minor totals, and the major control gives totals of intermediate totals. To arrange the cards in proper sequence we must first sort on the minor control field, then on the intermediate control field, and finally on the major control field.

Detail Printing and Group Printing

On the report in Figure 3–23 there is a line for each card and a line for each total. Such a report is called a *detail printed* or *listed report*. It is also possible to produce a report in which only identifying information and the totals are printed (see Figure 3–24). Such a report is said to be *group printed* or *tabulated*.

LABOR COST REPORT			
Department Number	Job Number	Hours	Cost
21	1234	94	205:75
	1265	613	1331:29
	1342	176	375:69
		883 *	1912:73 *
23	1234	182	387:50
	------	----	-------

FIG. 3–24
Group Printed Report

Counters

By means of control panel wiring, each counter must be given four basic directions: (1) what field of the card to add (or subtract); (2) which cards to add, subtract, or ignore; (3) when to take a total and/or clear; (4) where on the report to print the total. Thus, great flexibility is provided in the results that may be obtained through the use of counters.

As was mentioned previously, counters may be of several different sizes. On most machines there are counters with two, four, six, and eight positions. It is possible to couple two (or more) counters together to form a larger counter. A six-position counter and a four-position counter may be coupled to form a ten-position counter.

The size of the counter required is related to the number of digits in the largest total that is to be accumulated in that counter. If negative totals may be produced, it is necessary to provide one more counter position than there are digits in the largest total. Also, a separate counter must be provided for each class of total that is produced on the report. In the Labor Cost Report (shown above) four counters would be required: one for the Job (minor) total of hours, one for the Department (intermediate) total of hours, one for the Job (minor) total of cost, and one for the Department (intermediate) total of cost. Assuming that neither hours nor cost could be negative and that the numbers shown in Figures 3–23 and 3–24 have as many digits as any which will occur, four-position counters would be adequate for the two Hours totals and six-position counters would do for the two Cost totals. However, if the Department (intermediate) totals of Cost could be in the tens of thousands of dollars, an eight-position counter would be required for this total.

Summary Punching

By means of a cable, a reproducer may be connected to the accounting machine to *summary punch* new cards containing information from the accounting machine counters during accounting machine total cycles. In this process blank cards are inserted into the punch feed of the reproducer. By control panel wiring, it is possible to pause before the counters are cleared during a total cycle and cause the reproducer to punch a card containing information from some or all of the accounting machine counters. All information to be summary-punched, including identifying information, must be in the accounting machine counters.

Summary punching may be used to combine information from transaction cards with information from file cards to produce updated file cards, which may become the new file or which may be merged back into the file to update it before the next processing cycle.

Selectors

Punched card machines are both flexible and versatile. The *selector,* which is used in most of the machines, contributes greatly to the flexibility of this equipment. Basically, the selector enables the machines to distinguish between two kinds of cards and to handle them differently.

A selector is a relay that acts like a switch in a railroad track: it routes electricity along one of two possible paths, a *normal* path and a *transferred* path. The path chosen when the card is at the second reading station is determined by whether the pickup of the selector has been actuated by a pulse of electricity produced when an X punch was read when the card was at the first reading station.

On the control panel a selector appears as shown in Figure 3–25. The upper hub of the selector is the *pickup,* which controls the internal connection between the common, normal, and transferred hubs. If an X impulse reaches the pickup hub when a card is at the first reading station, then there is an internal connection between the common and transferred hubs when the card is at the second reading station, and there is no connection between the common and normal hubs. However, if an X impulse does not reach the pickup, then the internal connection is between the common and normal hubs when the card is at the second reading station, and there is no connection

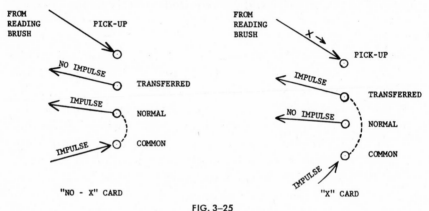

FIG. 3–25
Normal and Transferred Selectors

between the common and transferred hubs. Note that there is *never* any electrical connection between the pickup hub and any of the other hubs—the pickup merely controls the connection between the other hubs.

For example, suppose that in using the accounting machine we wish to add a field from a *sales* card and subtract that field on a *returns* card to arrive at a net sales figure. In the first place, the machine must be able to distinguish between the two types of cards, and this is accomplished by including an X punch in a specific column of all of the returns cards and specifying that an X may *not* appear in that column of any of the sales cards. Thus, all returns cards might be distinguished by an X punch in column 56.

To add the sales cards and subtract the returns cards we:

1. Take a wire on the control panel from the column 56 reading brush (at the first reading station) to the selector pickup;

2. Take a wire from a source which produces an impulse on each card to the common hub of the selector;

3. Take a wire from the normal hub of the selector to the add hub of the counter; and

4. Take a wire from the transferred hub of the selector to the subtract hub of the counter.

Then, on the cards which do not have an X in column 56 (the sales cards), the connection is between common and normal, and the counter is told to add; while on those cards with an X in column 56 (the returns cards) the connection is between common and transferred, and the counter is told to subtract (see Figure 3–26).

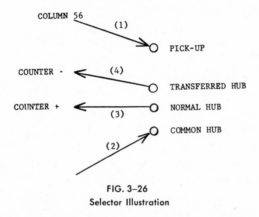

FIG. 3–26
Selector Illustration

Selectors may also be used to route impulses so that a field will print in one column of the form for an X card and in another column on a no-X card; or so that one field on an X card will print in the same place as another field on a no-X card; or so that an X card will not print at all; or so that spacing will not take place after an X card, and so on. Multiple-point selectors exist so that several columns of the card can be controlled by means of the same pickup. For example, if we wish to print columns 1 through 5 from an X-50 card in the same area of the form as columns 76 through 80 of a card that has no X in column 50, we would wire as shown in Figure 3–27.

The selector allows punched card machines to perform elementary "logical" or decision making functions. As we will see later, these functions are performed in computers by means of "branching" instructions. Obviously the selector is an extremely useful device on a punched card machine, but there are only a limited number of selectors on any machine, which places a limitation on the ability of the machine to handle further complications.

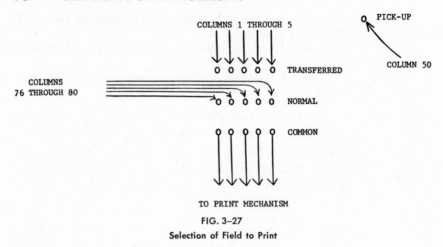

FIG. 3–27
Selection of Field to Print

Forms Control

To avoid the problems involved in separate feeding of forms, it is customary to use continuous forms with the accounting machines. Of course, it is possible to produce multiple copies by using carbon paper or special, chemically treated paper.

Spacing and skipping may be controlled to handle most of the types of forms that are in common use. For example, payroll checks and earnings statement may be printed on the accounting machine, and invoices can be prepared containing a heading section and a body section with the invoice total printed on the bottom line of the form. Such invoices present interesting forms control problems, for it is possible to have more lines on an invoice than can appear on a single page. In this case, the machine can be controlled so as to number the pages and skip the heading of the following form and print the remaining lines in the body of the form.

The Calculator

In some punched card data processing procedures it is necessary to multiply and/or divide. The ordinary punched-card accounting machine can add and subtract but it does not multiply and divide. Punched card machines that can perform all four arithmetic operations are called *calculators*. These machines usually read several fields from a card, perform a number of calculating steps to produce answers, and punch these answers into the same card. Depending upon the model of the machine and the complexity of the problem, these machines operate at between 20 and 150 cards per minute.

Although most of these punched card calculators employ electronic circuits to perform their computations, they are not included in the category of electronic computers. The punched card calculator and the electronic computer are distinguished from one another primarily by the means through which they are controlled, and secondarily by the fact that the electronic computer frequently includes means of input and output other than the punched card. In later chapters we will discuss how the electronic computers are controlled.

The punched card calculator, like the other punched card machines, is controlled by means of a wired control panel. These control panels contain a series of rows of program hubs which emit impulses one row at a time, starting with the first row and proceeding to the last one. By wiring these impulses to other sets of hubs on the control panel it is possible to select each factor that enters into the calculation, to determine what arithmetic operation is to be performed, or to place a result in the proper position to be punched into the card. In various models of the calculators from 12 to over 100 rows of program hubs are available, so calculations involving over 100 steps may be accomplished on one pass of the cards through the latter type of machine.

Example

Suppose we wish to use the IBM 604 calculator to: (1) read the three-digit numbers K, S, and T from a card; (2) calculate $(K + S) \times T = P$; and (3) punch the result P into the card. We would first break this calculation down into simple steps by prepar-

OP. NO.	OPERATION	FACTOR STORAGE 1	2	3	4	MULTI.-QUOT.	COUNTER	GENERAL STORAGE		
R	Read	K xxx	S xxx			T xxx	K xxx			
1	Add K	R.O.					K xxx			
2	Add S		R.O.				K+S xxxx			
3	Store & Reset						Read Out & Reset	K+S xxxx		
4	Mult. (K+S)T						(K+S)T xxxxxxx	R.O.		
5										

FIG. 3–28

Calculator Planning Chart

ing a planning chart (see Figure 3–28). In the line corresponding to READ, we assign K to factor storage unit 1, S to factor storage unit 2, and T (by which we will multiply) to the multiplier-quotient unit.

This chart would then be translated into wires on two control panels, one devoted to reading and punching the card and the other to the calculations. The first will not be illustrated, but the entering of K, S, and T into factor storage (in step R) and the punching of the result from the counter would be wired on that control panel.

In Figure 3–29 (which is not a geometrically accurate representation of the 604 control panel), the wires for each program step correspond to one line on the planning chart. On program step 1, wire A reads out factor storage 1, and wire B causes the counter to add. On program step 2, wire C causes factor storage 2 to read out, and wire D causes the counter to add. On step 3, wire E reads K + S out of the counter and resets it to zero, and wire F causes K + S

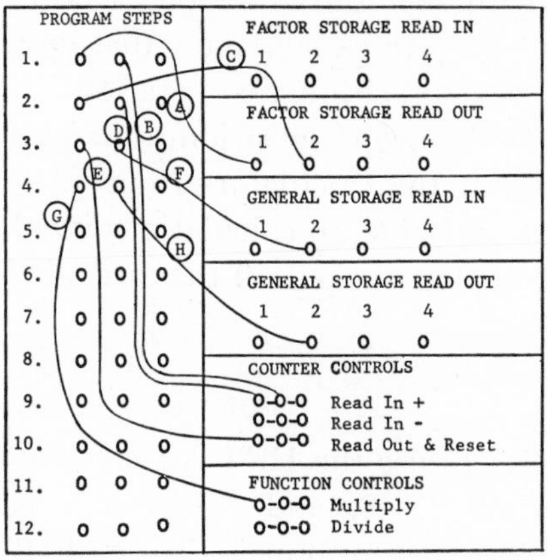

FIG. 3–29

to enter general storage 2. Then, in step 4, wire G causes the machine to multiply the contents of the multiplier-quotient register by the sum K + S, which is designated by wire H, and the result appears in the counter, from which it will be punched into the card.

Punched card calculators are used in payroll computations, in invoicing applications to multiply quantity by price, in computing parts and material requirements based upon a production schedule, and in any other punched card applications which involve multiplication or division. In some applications the cards are passed through the calculator several times to perform (and check) all the calculations involved.

The Printing Calculator

The Sperry Rand Univac 1004 is controlled by a wired control panel like other punched card machines, yet it possesses many of the capabilities of the small data processing computers that we will discuss in later chapters. This machine combines the printing ability of the accounting machine with the calculating ability of the punched card calculator.

Depending upon the number of columns read and the amount of processing required on each card, the Univac 1004 can read around 300 to 400 cards per minute. It can print alphabetic information at 300 lines per minute, and models are available that can punch cards at a maximum of 200 cards per minute. Since it costs about the same as an accounting machine (that prints at 150 lines per minute) plus an electronic calculator (that processes 150 cards per minute), the Univac 1004 provides attractive data processing capability for its cost.

SUMMARY

The punched card is used to record information in machine-processable form. Such information is identified to the machines by the card format and the field in which the information is located.

The basic steps in most punched card procedures involve:

1. Recording the transaction information in the cards;
2. Verifying the accuracy of recording;
3. Sorting the cards according to one or more identifying fields;
4. Associating the transaction cards with file records through use of the collator;
5. Preparing a report and updating the file through use of the accounting machine and summary punch.

In most cases, the efficiency of the use of punched cards depends upon repeating steps 3 through 5 several times so that the information is used in several sequences to prepare a number of results.

It is obvious that any single punched card machine is of little use by itself; they are designed to be used together to perform the various functions involved in data processing. However, the number and types of machines required in any given installation are determined by the type and volume of work to be done. Although the machines discussed above are considered basic, there are other punched card machines that can be included in an installation to perform specialized functions.

A typical, medium-sized, punched card installation might include five key punches, three verifiers, three 650-card-per-minute sorters, three reproducers, two accounting machines, one collator, and one interpreter. On a one-shift basis, the total rental for this type of installation would be approximately $2,000 per month. For additional hours that any piece of equipment is operated on a second shift, additional rental is charged (at a rate substantially less than the first-shift rate). The equipment may also be purchased at a price ranging from about 45 to 60 months' rental.

An electromechanical punched card calculator could be added to the above installation for slightly less than $300 per month, while an electronic calculator could be added for around $600 per month.

EXERCISES

3.1 Define each of the following terms:

A field	Reproducing	Listing
A self-checking number	Matching	Group printing
Interpreting	Merging	An X punch
Gang punching	Summary punching	

3.2 Describe the functions performed by the accounting machine.

3.3 Describe group control on the accounting machine and discuss what it accomplishes.

3.4 What is a selector and what does it do?

3.5 Describe three ways that information may be recorded in punched cards.

3.6 Which is faster, key punching or mark-sense recording?

3.7 Explain why the accuracy of recording is even more important for mechanized data processing than it is for manual systems.

3.8 Describe three methods of verification used in punched card work.

3.9 How is mark-sense information verified?

3.10 What are the basic steps involved in the typical punched card procedure?

3.11 *a*) If we wish to sort cards on a five-digit numeric field, how many passes through the sorter would be required?

b) If there are 10,000 cards in part (*a*), how many cards would be processed through the machine?

c) If the sorter operates at an effective speed of 600 cards per minute, how long would it take to complete this sort?

3.12 *a*) If no collator were available, how could two decks of cards be merged?

b) Could this same technique be used to match-merge two decks of cards? Why?

3.13 A rate-master computation deck (containing rate, hours, and rate times hours), a sorter, a collator, and a gang punch can be used to multiply rate by hours to compute gross pay in a payroll procedure. Can you suggest how this might be accomplished?

3.14 Suppose we wish to add all cards except those with an X in column 75 into a counter. Draw a diagram showing how the selector would be wired to accomplish this.

3.15 Suppose we wish to add those cards into a counter that have an X in column 75 unless they also have an X in column 60 in which case we wish to subtract the card. Cards with neither an X in 75 nor in 60, and those with an X in 60 but not in 75, are to be ignored. Draw a diagram showing selector wiring. (*Hint:* Use at least two selectors.)

SUPPLEMENTAL READINGS

Functional Wiring Principles (Form 224–6275–0). International Business Machines Corporation, 590 Madison Avenue, N.Y.

An excellent general presentation of the way that the various functions of the IBM machines are accomplished, with emphasis on the basic principles of the control panel wiring involved.

Functions of Remington Rand Univac Data-Automation System (Form U 1363). Remington Rand Univac Division of Sperry Rand Corporation, 315 Fourth Avenue, N.Y.

A brief presentation of each of the major Sperry Rand punched card machines and the functions they perform.

IBM Accounting Machine Functions (Form 22–8208–2). International Business Machines Corporation, 590 Madison Avenue, N.Y.

A brief presentation of each of the major IBM punched card machines and the functions they perform.

4   A PUNCHED CARD
APPLICATION

IN CHAPTER 3 the basic considerations involved in punched card data processing and the capabilities of the most common punched card machines were discussed. The objectives in this chapter are (1) To illustrate how these capabilities may be utilized in a data processing system and (2) To obtain an understanding of the considerations involved in designing a mechanized system.

To accomplish the first objective, an example of a punched-card payroll procedure will be presented. Unfortunately, however, such a presentation may not fully attain the second objective, for in this study of end results it is not always possible to adequately reconstruct the somewhat devious process by which these end results were created. For this reason an exercise is included which should at least raise *some* of the problems that must be faced in such a process.

PAYROLL APPLICATION

To illustrate how punched card equipment may be used for data processing, a simple payroll application will be discussed. This example will be simplified in at least two ways. In the first place, the payroll will be on an hourly basis—with none of the complications involved in job rates or incentives. Secondly, only a few of the many reports that must be produced from payroll records will be considered.

The first step in the design of a data processing procedure is that of determining the desired results. In this example we wish to produce a payroll register, a check and earnings statement for each employee, and a labor cost report. Although the final forms of these reports are shown in Figures 4–1, 4–2, and 4–3, it should be understood that only

ACME MANUFACTURING COMPANY
Acme City, Ohio

268

PAY TO THE ORDER OF _____ J. P. BURDELL

PAY _____

Dollars Cents **70 58

Date 3-7-65

ACME CITY BANK
Acme City, Ohio

J. L. Jones
Treasurer

ACME MANUFACTURING CO.
Acme City, Ohio

Social Security No. 254 33 4218

J. P. BURDELL

Hours	O.T.Prem	Reg.Earn.	Total Earn.	Dept.No.	Man No.	Period Ending
43 0	1 5	86 00	89 00	23	2715	3 7 65

WH Tax	FICA	State		Year-to-Date	
10 30	2 23	1 89	13 42-	3425 70	Earnings
Voluntary Deductions		5 00		483 37	W. H. Tax
			70 58 Net Pay		

Statement
of
Earnings & Deductions

FIG. 4–1 Check and Earnings Statement

PAYROLL REGISTER

Employee Dept.	Number	Social Security No.	Hours Worked	Rate	Earnings Regular	Overtime	Total	Deductions W.H. Tax	FICA	State	Other	Net Pay	Year to Date W.H.Tax	FICA	State	Earnings
1	433	143652407	40 0	2 100	84 00		84 00	16 00	2 35	1 68	6 75	57 22	235 50	38 25	25 90	1177 50

Fig. 4–2 Payroll Register

their general information content would be known at the start, and the development of their exact formats would depend to a certain extent upon processing considerations. The approximations with which we start would be repeatedly modified to produce the reports shown. The card forms and procedures, which will be discussed later, are also presented in their final form.

LABOR COST REPORT						
Job Number	Work Order Number	Dept.	Current Week		Total	
			Hours	Amount	Hours	Amount
143	2047	1	15	30	25	168	342	75
		5	7	15	32	78	172	98
		13	62	148	16	359	824	50
		37	22	53	43	204	475	83
			106*	247	16*	809*	1816	06*
	2881	3	19	41	12	253	540	77
		5	56	212	77	803	1836	28
		12	12	26	07	48	104	00
		13	92	198	95	241	516	26
		34	24	53	40	105	218	83
			203*	532	31*	1450*	3216	14*
	3456	10	18	39	50	63	143	23
		11	44	102	25	105	221	11
		12	7	15	16	27	56	10
		22	15	33	42	45	99	63
		29	26	61	05	63	131	17
		30	14	29	20	40	86	05
		35	31	66	88	31	74	00

FIG. 4–3

Labor Cost Report

It is worth remarking again that we are considering only a few of the reports that are desired (or required) from a payroll system. Other reports might include deduction registers, employee earnings records, analyses of overtime by departments, attendance analyses, W-2 forms for each employee, social security reports, and income tax reports for federal and state governments.

The next step in designing a procedure is to determine just where the information required for the output results may be obtained. In this case the information comes from the employee's time card, from labor tickets which record the time worked on each job, and from file information concerning the employee, his deductions, and his payment history.

Card Forms

Our next step is to consider the card forms which are required. We must determine the number of different card forms that should be involved, decide what information must be included on each card form, and assign each field to specific columns on each card form. The size of each field is determined by the largest number that will be recorded there, but the determination of the arrangement of the fields is complicated by three considerations:

1. *The Relationship of the Cards to the Source Document.* Cards should be designed to correspond to the document from which they are key-punched (and vice versa) so that the key punch operator can punch from the document with a minimum of skipping around.

2. *The Relationship of the Cards to Each Other.* The same types of information should be located in the same columns of different card forms. This is particularly important if the different forms are to be combined and sorted on that field.

3. *The Relationship of the Cards to the Required Reports.* In order to reduce the number of selectors used, information that is to be printed in the same column of a report should be located (whenever possible) in the corresponding columns of the cards involved. (This does not imply that information that is to be printed on the left side of a *report* should be punched on the left side of the *card,* for control panel wiring will easily perform this type of rearrangement.)

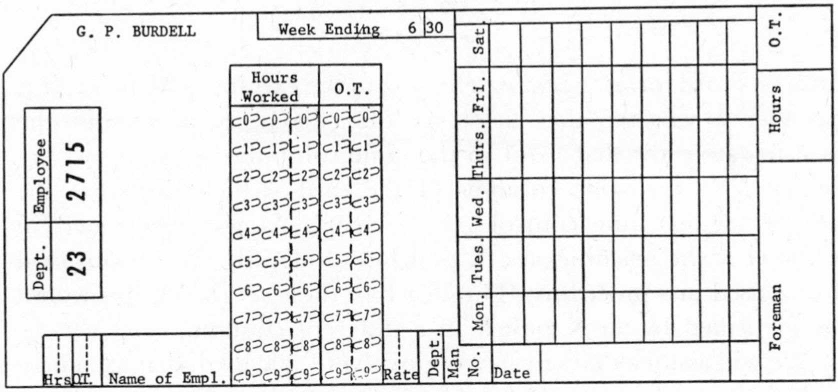

FIG. 4–4

Time Card

In our illustration the time card will be a punched card in which total hours worked will be entered by means of mark sensing. The time card, shown in Figure 4–4, will be prepunched with department number, employee name, hourly rate, and date, while regular hours and overtime premium hours will be mark-sense punched. The labor ticket is a dual card, that is, a card designed so that information may be written on its face and subsequently key-punched into the same card. As can be seen in Figure 4–5, this card form provides separate locations in which to write department number, employee number, job number, work order number, operation code, hours, and date. These may then be key-punched in the same card and verified.

Four additional card forms are involved in our payroll processing: the payroll master card, the current earnings card, deduction cards, and the year-to-date earnings card (see Figure 4–6). Notice that department number and man-number are aligned in the same columns

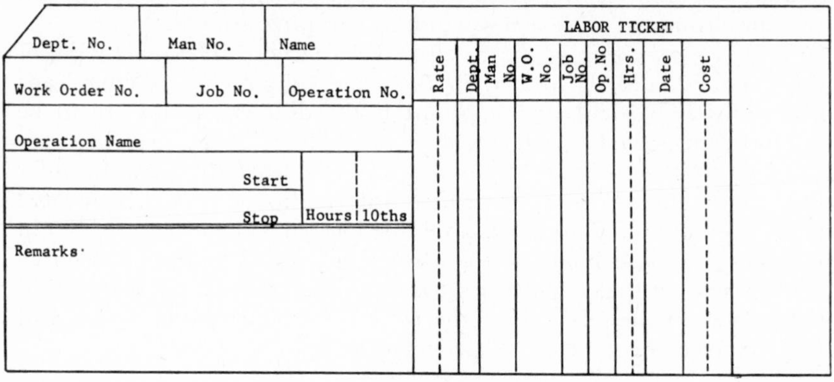

FIG. 4–5
Labor Ticket

on all six card forms. Also, by referring to the earnings statement, it is possible to observe that fields on the current earnings and the year-to-date cards that print in the same columns of this report are punched in the same columns of the card—which simplifies the accounting machine control panel wiring. As was mentioned in Chapter 3, the machines use X punches to identify the various card forms used in a procedure. Thus, each of these six card forms would be identified by an X punch in a different column.

We will assume that our payroll involves 1,500 men, that each man works on an average of 1.2 jobs per day, and that each has three voluntary deductions. Checks, covering the previous week's earnings, are prepared and distributed weekly.

Flow Charting

The next step in our process is to design the procedural steps that will be followed in processing the payroll. Punched card procedures are usually expressed in flow chart form, using a number of standard symbols (which are found in the flow-charting template available from the machine manufacturers) to visually represent the various machine operations, cards, documents, and reports. These symbols are shown on page 90.

Although brief descriptions may be written inside the symbols, it is usually necessary to number at least some of the processing steps so

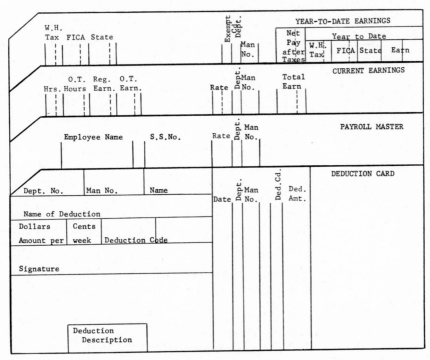

FIG. 4–6
Additional Card Forms

that they can be described in greater detail. However, it is surprising how effective a flow chart, with but a few words inside the symbols, can be in presenting the fundamentals of a punched card procedure.

Payroll Procedure

Labor tickets, recording the individual worker's performance of an operation on a particular job, are filled out at the time the work is performed and are turned in to the machine accounting department on a daily basis. These cards may be key-punched and verified as they are turned in during the week. The time cards, recording attendance time during the week, are marked by the timekeepers and turned in

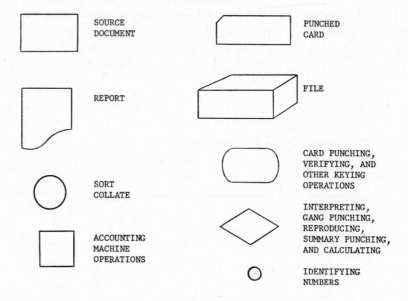

SOURCE DOCUMENT

PUNCHED CARD

REPORT

FILE

SORT COLLATE

CARD PUNCHING, VERIFYING, AND OTHER KEYING OPERATIONS

ACCOUNTING MACHINE OPERATIONS

INTERPRETING, GANG PUNCHING, REPRODUCING, SUMMARY PUNCHING, AND CALCULATING

IDENTIFYING NUMBERS

to the machine accounting department at the end of the week. The payroll is then processed according to the procedure shown in Figure 4–7. The following comments refer to the numbered steps of this procedure.

1. Match-merge (on man-number and department) the time cards and the labor tickets. Unmatched cards will have to be investigated and the reason for this determined.

2. The accounting machine adds total attendance time from each man's time card and subtracts job time as each of the job cards is read. If the result is not zero, the difference is printed (along with the department and man-number) so that differences can be investigated and corrected.

3. The employee's rate from his time card is gang-punched into the job cards which follow so that the hours can be multiplied by rate (step 8). In the following step the time cards and job cards are separated by sorting on the column containing the identifying X punch (while blanking out the other rows) so that one type of card is placed in the X pocket and the other type in the reject pocket. The time cards are reproduced and filed (they are legal records), and the current earnings cards, thus prepared, are used for further processing.

4. This step calculates regular earnings, overtime earnings, and total earnings and punches them into the current earnings card. A second pass through the calculator may be required to check these calculations. Before gross-to-net calculations can be made, it is necessary to insert the year-to-date cards by match-merging, investigating any unmatched cards.

5. This pass calculates federal and state withholding taxes and Old Age, Survivors, and Disability Insurance to produce net pay before vol-

untary deductions. Exemption code and year-to-date earnings from the year-to-date card are used in this calculation. A second pass through the calculator may be necessary to check these calculations. Before preparing the payroll register, it is necessary to merge the payroll master cards and the voluntary deduction cards so that complete information is available on each employee.

6. Only one line is printed for each man on the payroll register. This is accomplished by accumulating totals and suppressing spacing so that all of the cards for an employee print on the same line.

7. The checks and earnings statements are printed simultaneously side by side. At the same time, new year-to-date cards are summary-punched for use next week. The new year-to-date cards must be run through the accounting machine again so that their total can be compared with the payroll register total in order to check the accuracy of the summary-punching operation.

8. This portion of the procedure is concerned with the distribution of labor costs. In this calculator operation, rate is multiplied by hours for each card to obtain the labor cost. This simple calculation may be checked on the same run in which the calculation is performed.

9. In the labor cost report, the minor control is on department number, the intermediate control on work order number, and the major control on job number. Thus we must sort first on work-order number, then on job number. Since the cards are already in department-number order when they come to this step, it is unnecessary to sort first on this field.

10. The labor cost report contains total hours and cost as well as the current week's figures. Thus, before preparing this report, we must merge in the balance-forward summary cards that were produced last week (in step 11).

11. The labor cost report is tabulated and new balance-forward cost cards are summary-punched and filed for use next week. It should be noted that this report would strain the counter capacity of the 80-counter IBM 402, since counters must be provided for summary punching identifying information as well as for accumulating three totals for each of four columns on the report. Fortunately, the IBM 407 has at least 120 counter positions.

Time and Cost Determination

Frequently there are several alternative procedural arrangements that would accomplish essentially the same results, but in order to choose between them it is necessary to estimate the time and cost for each alternative. Furthermore, to decide whether or not to acquire punched card equipment, or (if it is already available) to mechanize a given application, it is necessary to determine the costs involved in doing the job through the use of punched cards.

Let us consider how the time figures shown for the steps in our procedure were arrived at. In the first place, we must know the rated

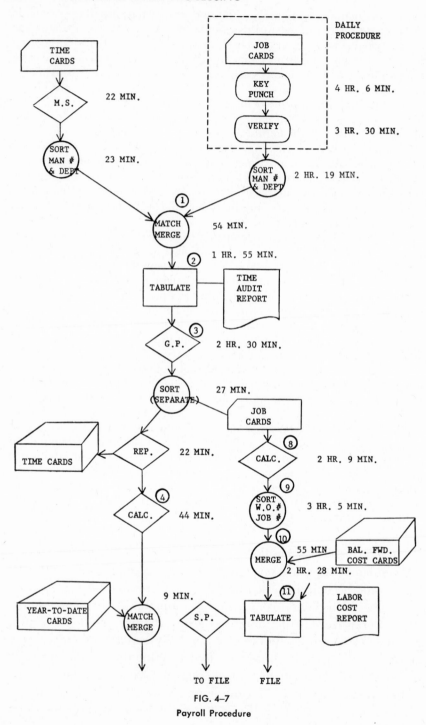

FIG. 4–7

Payroll Procedure

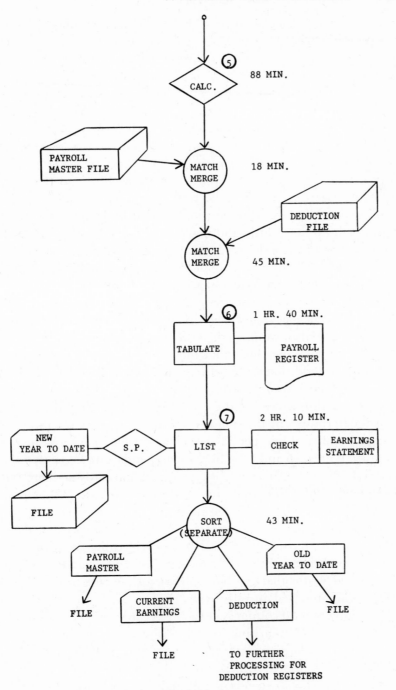

FIG. 4–7 (cont.)

speeds of the equipment involved. For example, we assumed that our illustration included a calculator and reproducer that operate at 100 cards per minute, an accounting machine that operates at 150 cycles per minute whether printing, accumulating, or totaling (except that it takes 1.2 seconds for each summary punch cycle), a sorter that operates at 650 cards per minute, and a collator that operates at a maximum of 240 cards per minute in each feed.

There are several methods that might be used to estimate the amount of time required for each step in a procedure. For example, we might use a standard setup time for each machine and an effective operating rate to determine the time for each step. Since our estimates will at best be crude, we will use a less sophisticated approach in which setup time, card handling time, machine and operator error time, etc., are all combined into a figure representing the overall efficiency at which the machines will be operated. This figure, of course, will vary from one installation to another.

The above illustration also assumed that the sorter was operated at 60 percent efficiency and the other equipment at 70 percent efficiency. We also assumed that the key punch operator averaged 10,000 key strokes per hour and the verifier 12,000 key strokes per hour, with an additional second required to feed and eject each card on each of these two machines.

We must also determine the card volume through each machine. This is determined by the number of men on the payroll and by the average number of jobs per day per man. Since we have assumed that there are 1,500 men and 1.2 jobs per man per day, we know that there will be 1,500 time cards per week and 1,800 job cards per day. Now, starting with the mark-sense punching of the time cards, 1,500 cards divided by 70 percent of 100 cards per minute gives about 22 minutes. The time to sort these cards on man-number and department number (6 columns) is $6 \times 1,500$ divided by $.60 \times 650$, which comes to slightly more than 23 minutes. Incidentally, IBM furnishes a plastic calculator that can be used like a slide rule to perform the calculations involved in estimating time.

Assuming that 20 columns on each job card must be key-punched and verified, the punching time in hours would be $1,800 \times 20$ divided by 10,000 plus 1,800 seconds for card feeding—or 4 hours and 6 minutes. Similarly, verifying will require $1,800 \times 20$ divided by 12,000 plus 1,800 seconds—or a total of 3 hours and 30 minutes. Some additional time will be required to repunch cards that are in error. The time to sort the 9,000 job cards at the end of the week is

$6 \times 9,000$ divided by $.60 \times 650$—about 2 hours and 19 minutes.

Timing the collator operations requires more specific knowledge of the collator's operation than was given in Chapter 3, for we must know when the two feeds operate simultaneously and when they operate separately. At step one, 9,000 job cards and 1,500 time cards will be involved, but the time cards will fall into a pocket simultaneously with the first job card for that man, so we need only allow time for 9,000 cards at 240 cards per minute at 70 percent efficiency, giving approximately 54 minutes.

In addition to the 10,500 cards involved in step 2, a total is required for each man, giving 12,000 machine cycles for the report.[1] Thus the time required is 12,000 divided by $.70 \times 150$, or slightly less than 1 hour and 55 minutes. To separate the time cards from the job cards requires only one pass, so the time required is given by 10,500 divided by $.60 \times 650$, which comes to slightly less than 27 minutes.

In the payroll side of the procedure, 1,500 cards are involved in reproducing the time cards and in the calculation of item 4, but the calculation involves two passes through the machine. Then we merge in 1,500 year-to-date cards, but the cards involved feed simultaneously, so the time required is 1,500 divided by $.70 \times 240$, which is slightly less than 9 minutes. After step 5, we merge in 1,500 payroll master cards, which would fall simultaneously with the year-to-date cards, so the time necessary is the 18 minutes required for a single feed operation with 3,000 cards.

The merge step preceding step 6 involves 4,500 cards in each feed. The situation here is more complex, for the only simultaneous feeding obtained would be the current earnings card and the first deduction card for each man, so 7,500 card-feed cycles are required. Thus, the time is 7,500 divided by $.70 \times 240$, which equals about 45 minutes.

In step 6 a total is required for each man, so 10,500 cycles would be needed, which takes 1 hour and 40 minutes. Step 7 requires the same time plus time for 1,500 summary punch cycles, at 1.2 seconds each, for a total of 2 hours and 10 minutes. Since the identifying X punches are in different card columns, the separation shown in the last sort operation cannot be accomplished in one pass. On the first pass, requiring 23 minutes, we would pull out the 4,500 deduction cards.

---

[1] In the interest of simplicity we have purposely ignored the fact that total cycles do not involve card handling or operator error and should therefore probably be timed at a higher efficiency figure than card cycles.

Thus the next pass to extract the payroll master cards would involve only 4,500 cards and require 12 minutes. The final pass of 3,000 cards would separate the current earnings and the old year-to-date cards, and could be accomplished in 8 minutes, for a total of 43 minutes.

Returning to the procedure for preparing the labor cost report, we note that 9,000 job cards are involved in steps 8 and 9. Step 9 requires sorting 9,000 cards on 8 columns. In step 10 the balance-forward cards will fall simultaneously with the first current card, so they will require no extra time (except in cases where there is no activity on the work order in a department that had previously worked on it, and we will assume that this occurs infrequently). Thus the merge requires 54 minutes, and we will allow an extra minute for inactive work orders.

In order to time step 11, we must estimate the number of summary-punch and total cycles. This estimate, in a given situation, would be based on an analysis of experience, but we will assume that there is an average of 5 departments working on each work order, 6 work orders for each job, and 50 active jobs. Thus we would have $5 \times 6 \times 50$ minor totals and summary cards, 6×50 intermediate totals, and 50 major totals. Therefore we have 10,500 cards, 1,850 totals, and 1,500 summary punch cycles, which require a total of 2 hours and 28 minutes.

Scheduling

Translating the individual machine times into a schedule for machine operation, it appears that Monday would be devoted to key punching and verifying the job cards for Friday's work (which can be partially overlapped) and to sorting the entire 9,000 job cards. The time necessary to mark-sense punch and sort the time cards is relatively insignificant. On Tuesday, we could overlap steps 1, 2, and 3 and perform them in around $3\frac{1}{2}$ or 4 hours. However, we must allow sufficient time to reconcile any discrepancies noted in the time-audit report, so we will allow Tuesday for performing these functions and for separating the job cards from the time cards.

Considering the main payroll processing, it appears possible to complete the payroll on Wednesday, and the payroll checks could be available for distribution Thursday morning. This, however, does not leave any time for such emergencies as machine downtime or operator errors. Thus we probably should not plan to distribute the checks until Thursday afternoon or some time Friday (since weekly payrolls are traditionally paid on Friday).

The labor cost report should also be available some time Thursday, especially if some block sorting were done to overlap part of the sorting with the printing of the report.

It should be noted that the above discussion on scheduling ignores machine conflicts which may arise as a result of other applications for which the machines may be used. The fitting together of schedules for several procedures is an involved process, but it must be planned and adhered to if the punched card installation is to operate efficiently and produce its reports on time. The efficiency of scheduling and the due dates of reports also influence the total amount of punched card equipment required for the installation. Since much accounting work seems to be concentrated at the end of the month, either some reports must be substantially delayed or excess equipment must be provided which will be idle during slack periods of the month. This problem is sometimes handled economically by overtime, extra shift operations or by using service bureau facilities during these peak-load periods.

In estimating the total cost of a procedure it is customary to estimate the cost per hour for operating each of the different machines. This cost must include the machine rental, the operator cost, and usually an overhead cost. Then the total time involved for each machine may be multiplied by the cost per hour for that machine, and these figures accumulated to estimate the total cost of the procedure. If these costs compare favorably with the present costs of performing the work, or if intangible factors are involved which make mechanization desirable, it may be advantageous to convert to the use of punched cards.

If it is decided to mechanize the application, much work must be done before reports can be actually prepared on punched card equipment. Control panels must be wired, operating procedures must be written, card and report forms must be ordered, additional punched card equipment may have to be installed, and personnel outside the machine accounting department may have to be trained in new procedures. Then, once the changeover starts, a substantial period of time is necessary to iron out the bugs that will arise and to complete the conversion. It is therefore obvious that several months may be required for planning and converting to a mechanized procedure of even moderate complexity.

SALES ANALYSIS PROBLEM

As was mentioned at the beginning of this chapter, it is difficult to obtain an understanding of how a procedure was created by studying the end product. The primary purpose of this exercise, therefore, is to raise questions and force you to deduce the answers. It may be that you will not be able to answer all the questions satisfactorily because of your rather incomplete knowledge of the equipment and its use. But don't give up; postulate a reasonable answer and go on with the rest of the problem. Indeed, an awareness of the type of questions that must be faced is frequently more important than the answers themselves. According to Charles Kettering, "It isn't the things you don't know that get you into trouble, it's the things you know for sure that are not so."

The following illustration is from the area of sales analysis, which is usually integrated with inventory control, invoicing, and accounts

Daily	*Monthly*
Invoice register	Sales by product
Product class report	Sales by location
	Sales by salesman (with year-to-date amounts)

DAILY SALES BY CLASS Report 2	
Class	Amount
1	106601
2	98493
3	117380
4	62175
5	141918
6	110021
7	97550
8	107190
9	118083
	959411*

FIG. 4–8

Daily Sales-by-Class Report

receivable for efficient mechanization. But in order to restrict the scope of the problem, the output requirements are specified and the input has been set up so as to isolate the application from others with which it would normally be associated. Thus we have eliminated unnecessary complexity in order to concentrate upon obtaining a basic understanding of how the punched card machines are used for data processing.

The General Manufacturing Company manufactures casters of various sizes and shapes and sells them throughout the country. We will assume that this company has an installation of punched card

				MONTHLY			
Sales by Product Report 3							
Product							
Cl.	Item	Description	Quantity	Amount		Cost	
1	210	Square Shank Rg 1	40000	14765	54	13437	54
	1426	Square Shank Rg 2	205	1476	31	1344	52
	2735	Square Shank Rg 3	1473	19437	24	17655	54
			41678	35679	09*	32437	60*
2	610	Caster 10/22	9	141	50	150	75
	2011	Caster 10/32	4765	9655	40	8613	42
	6314	Caster Red 14/52-	451	10571	20	9544	67*
				914376	50	549176	43

FIG. 4–9

Sales-by-Product Report

machines which includes all the equipment described in the previous illustration (except the calculator) and that they wish to produce two daily reports: a sales-by-class report (Figure 4–8) and an invoice register (not shown) that has one line for each sales analysis card and includes all the card's information. In addition, they wish to produce the three end-of-month sales analysis reports shown in Figures 4–9, 4–10, and 4–11.

An analysis of the source documents and reports has been made, yielding the following average volume figures:

				MONTHLY			
Sales by Location Report 4							
Location		Pr.					
St.	City	Cl.	Quantity	Amount		Cost	
29	1	1	4007	4176	52	2075	43
		2	275	549	76	275	97
		5	7643	3919	87	2715	43
			11925*	8646	15*	5066	83*
	2	2	4310	4975	37	2197	61
		5	510	1041	00	971	67
		6	204	465	87	401	19
		7	120	305	40	255	20
40		1	21	47	50	29	75
		2	470	397	50	298	40
			491*	445	00*	328	15*
	State	Totals	74343**	40419	75**	29547	53**

FIG. 4–10

Sales-by-Location Report

MONTHLY

Sales by Salesman
Report 5

Sales Br.	Sales Man	PR. Cl.	Current Month Amount		Current Month Cost		Year to Date Amount		Year to Date Cost	
1	1	1	143	27	98	00	4133	33	3142	20
		2	2100	00	1000	05	19742	76	9176	50
		6	3201	20	2107	62	21734	12	10147	61
			5444	47 *	3205	67 *	45610	21 *	22466	31 *
	2	1	104	37	89	42				
			24845	97 **	15486	27 **	114476	10 **	97239	10 **
2	3		-----	--	-----	--	-----	--	-----	--

FIG. 4–11
Sales-by-Salesman Report

GENERAL MANUFACTURING CO.
Podunk, Indiana

Invoice No. 12351 Date: 10/31/60
Branch 10 Salesman 24

To: Local Furniture Co.
2314 S. Ferry Street
Crawfordsville, Mo.

City	State	Customer
15	23	14765

Quantity	Item	Description	Unit Price	Amount	Cost
15	17203	Caster Rnd	$1.62	$ 24.30	$ 19.50
5	21103	Caster Ball Brng	1.77	8.85	6.67
50	32103	Caster S.S 10/22	2.69	134.50	103.60
20	54107	Caster Brass 14/52	4.98	99.60	81.68
			Total	$267.25	

FIG. 4–12
Invoice

Invoices per day	100	States	40
Items per invoice	10	Cities per state	40
Working days per month	22	Product classes per city	2.5
Product classes	9	Product classes per salesman	4
Items	3,000	Salesmen	110
		Branches	12

We will assume that the billing department types invoices from orders which have been stamped with a serial invoice number (Figure 4–12). Note that the cost column would not appear on the copy of the invoice that is sent to the customer.

At the end of each day an adding machine tape of the invoice totals is run. Then the invoices, in consecutive number sequence, are sent to the machine accounting department accompanied by the adding machine tapes.

EXERCISES

4.1   Design the card form (or forms) for the preceding application. What fields are required and how large should they be? Note that the reports show only typical figures, and not neccessarily the maximum size figures that can be expected. You may have to make reasonable assumptions concerning the maximum sizes of the numbers in order to design the card(s).

4.2   Devise a daily procedure to produce the cards, invoice register, and product class report.

4.3   Devise a procedure to produce the end-of-month reports.

4.4   Making the same timing assumptions as in the previous illustration, estimate the time required for each machine operation in the two procedures. About how many working days would be required for the production of the monthly reports?

4.5   Which of the monthly reports would be prepared first? Why?

4.6   The foregoing has assumed that the cost amount on the invoice is entered manually by cost clerks before the invoice is sent to the machine accounting department. If this cost figure were not entered on this invoice, and a punched card calculator were available, what modification in the daily procedure could be used to enter costs automatically into the sales analysis reports and to check price and the extended amount?

4.7   How many counter positions will be required to produce the sales-by-salesman report? What information will be contained in the summary cards produced with this report? How many summary cards will be produced each month?

4.8   What would happen if several cards were lost during the monthly procedure? How could this loss be detected? How could the error be corrected?

5 BASIC CONCEPTS OF ELECTRONIC COMPUTERS

DATA PROCESSING ITSELF and the use of punched card equipment for data processing were discussed in previous chapters. All of this, however, has been only a preliminary to the major purpose of this book: obtaining an understanding of the electronic computer and its use in data processing. This chapter introduces the basic ideas associated with the electronic computers themselves and it is concerned with the questions: What is an electronic computer? and What are its capabilities?

In the first place, the term *electronic computer* has been applied to two basically different types of machines, digital computers and analog computers. The *digital computer* operates on numbers— adding, subtracting, multiplying, and dividing with them like a hand calculator or an adding machine, or just as we learned to do in grade school. On the other hand, the *analog computer* does not compute directly with numbers; it manipulates some physical quantity, such as voltage or length or shaft rotation, which (to a certain degree of accuracy) *represents* the numbers that are being computed. For example, a slide rule calculates by the analog principle—multiplying by combining two lengths.

In other words, the analog computer utilizes an *analogous* physical situation for the purpose of computing; and the digital computer computes with *digits*. Although the analog computer is simpler and more convenient than the digital computer for certain engineering and scientific problems, the accuracy of these machines is limited (by physical considerations) to approximately one-tenth of 1 percent. Thus they are not satisfactory for most data processing purposes, and we will confine our discussion to the digital machines.

GENERAL CHARACTERISTICS OF COMPUTERS

Many different types of digital computers have been built, ranging in cost from a few thousand to several million dollars. Though they vary greatly in size, speed, and details of their operations, most of them have the same basic logical structure, and the diagram in Figure 5–1 is representative of the entire class of digital computers. The heavy arrows in Figure 5–1 represent flows of data and the single arrows indicate implementation of control functions. Let us consider each block of this diagram.

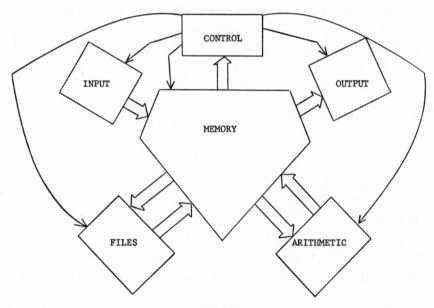

FIG. 5–1

General Diagram of a Computer

Input

If a machine is to process information, that information must be made available to the machine in a form it can utilize. Information in the form of written symbols like those you are now reading is not directly usable in a computer. As was seen in the discussion of punched card equipment, machine information takes the form of electrical pulses, with different combinations of pulses representing different characters in a manner similar to the familiar Morse code, which uses combinations of dots and dashes (short and long pulses).

Although great progress has been made in the development of optical or magnetic ink devices that will read printed material and translate each character into the corresponding pulse code, most computer inputs are presented in a form that directly produces the pulse code itself. Many such devices are available for use as inputs to electronic computers. Among them are punched cards, punched paper tape, magnetic tape, and various types of keyboards. One or more of these devices may be used to enter information into a computer, and the speed with which the information is entered can range (depending on the devices used) from a manual speed of a few characters per second up to hundreds of thousands of characters per second on magnetic tape.

In Chapter 3 it was shown that information may be recorded in punched cards in many ways, including key punching, prepunching, and mark sensing, and as the output of various information-recording and -processing devices. Likewise, punched paper tape and magnetic tape may be generated by the use of key-driven equipment (similar in operation to the key punch) or by other information-recording and -processing devices. Thus, the function of recording information for entry into an electronic computer is similar to that of recording for punched card data processing, and the same basic considerations are involved.

Memory

From the input device or devices, the information is entered into the heart of the machine, which is the information storage section (or *memory*). Although the memory of an electronic computer serves many purposes, it is sufficient at this point to note that the complexity of the problems that can easily be handled by a machine and the speed with which they can be handled are basically determined by the size and the speed of the memory of the machine.

The memory of a machine serves many of the same purposes as the memory of a human, but the machine memory is more analogous to the memory of a reference book than to the memory of the human brain. For a machine to be able to recall information, it is necessary that it be told the location (or page) in the memory where the information is stored.

For this reason, the memory of a machine may be divided into cells called *words*. Each word consists of a certain number of digits or characters, and each of these cells is identified by a number called the *address* of that word, usually starting with zero and continuing sequentially to the highest number required. For example, if the memory of the machine contains 4,000 ten-digit words (or storage for 40,000 digits of information), they will be numbered from 0000 to 3999.

The average time necessary for a machine to recall information from a single memory cell is termed the *average access time* of the memory. There are several different electronic and magnetic principles that can be employed to provide memory with rapid access, including rapidly rotating *magnetic drums,* small bead-like *magnetic cores,* and *thin film* magnetizable dots.

Although they differ greatly in the engineering details of their method of operation, the major difference between these methods of memory, from the standpoint of the user of the machine, is their speed. The magnetic *drum* memory has an average access time ranging from approximately 1 millisecond (1 millisecond represents $\frac{1}{1,000}$ of a second) to around 20 milliseconds; magnetic *core* memory has an average access time of from 1 to 50 microseconds (a microsecond is $\frac{1}{1,000,000}$ of a second); while the average access time of *thin film* memory is measured in hundreds of nanoseconds (a nanosecond is $\frac{1}{1,000,000,000}$ of a second). The capacity of the main memory ranges from around 1,000 characters for a small machine to around 100,000 characters for a large machine, with millions of characters of supplementary (but slower) directly addressable memory available on some machines.

Files

As was mentioned in Chapter 2, one of the functions of data processing is reference to files of information, and this is accomplished within machines (as shown by the diagram in Figure 5–1) by having machine-processable files available for many (but not all) of the machines.

There are two basic types of files that can be referred to by computers: *sequential* and *random* access files. The sequential file usually consists of reels of magnetic tape, on which the first record in the file must be read before the second, which must be read before the third, etc. Magnetic tape has the advantages of low cost and almost unlimited capacity. One reel of tape may hold millions of information characters, and any number of reels may be used.

The random access files are characterized by an ability to skip around within the file and to extract information with no particular regard to the sequence in which the extraction is performed. Large capacity magnetic drums, magnetic card files, and magnetic disc memories are some of the devices used for random access memory. They range in capacity from a few hundred thousand characters for the magnetic drums to billions of characters for the magnetic card files, and their access times will range from around 15 milliseconds for the drums to around one-half second for the magnetic card files.

Machine files are actually a type of memory and are distinguished from the working memory, discussed in the previous section, by several characteristics. In the first place, file memory is usually larger than working memory, and access to file memory is much slower than to working memory. Secondly, information in the file memory cannot be processed without first bringing it into the working memory. In this respect, file memory resembles an input device. It should be noted at this point that magnetic tapes, for example, can be used either for input or file memory, and for output as well.

Arithmetic

With the transaction information entered into the memory from the input devices, and the file information entered from the files, the computer is in a position to manipulate the information and perform its arithmetic and logical operations. These operations are performed in the arithmetic section of the machine, one operation at a time, with intermediate results being stored in the memory, which in this case is used as scratch paper. Thus, the arithmetic section will perform the operations of addition, subtraction, multiplication, division, and certain simple logical operations such as comparing two numbers for equality. Depending upon the size and cost of the machine, the speed of arithmetic will range from a few hundred operations per second up to several million operations per second, where each operation is typically performed on a machine *word*.

Output

When the processing is completed, it is again necessary for the machine to communicate with the outside world and produce information in a form that humans can use. This is accomplished through various output devices, such as electric typewriters, line printers, TV tube displays, punched cards, magnetic tapes, and punched paper tapes. The last three of these can be processed further on auxiliary equipment to produce printed copy or they can be re-entered into the machine for further processing. These output devices will range in speed from about 10 characters per second for the electric typewriter to several thousand 120-character lines per minute for direct-printed output—or to hundreds of thousands of characters per second on magnetic tape (which can be printed on a line printer in a separate operation).

Control

To recapitulate, variable information is read from the input devices into the memory, where it is combined with file information and manipulated back and forth between the memory and the arithmetic section to produce the desired results, which are then communicated to humans (or to other machines) by output devices. All of these processes can take place with fantastic speed. Still, we have not yet seen the true power of the electronic computer, for although it is impressive that a machine can perform thousands of calculations in a second, the truly amazing aspect is that they can perform the particular operations in the specified sequence to produce the results that are required. The outstanding capability of the electronic computer is best explained in terms of the remaining block, the block labeled *control*.

As is indicated by Figure 5–1, information is taken from the memory section of the machine into the control section, and, on the basis of this information, all of the functions of the machine are controlled. The control section tells the input devices what information to enter into the memory and when to enter it; it tells the memory where to place this information; it tells the arithmetic section what operations to perform, where in memory to find the information, and where to store the results; it locates the file information and stores it in the memory; and finally, it controls the output devices and determines what information is printed or written. All of this is accomplished by the *stored program*, the fundamental idea associated with the electronic computer.

THE STORED PROGRAM

Stored program refers to storing within the memory of the machine the program or procedure which the machine will follow to accomplish the desired processing. Thus the memory not only collects the information to be processed and associates it with other information (even serving as scratch paper), it also tells the machine what to do. The procedure to be followed must be broken down into a series of elementary operations that are performable by the particular machine, and each of these basic operations is represented by an instruction stored in the memory of the machine. When the machine is in operation the first instruction is taken to the control section, interpreted, and the operation called for is carried out. Then the next instruction is taken to the control section, interpreted, and executed; the third instruction is taken to the control section, interpreted, and executed; and so on through the procedure. When the last instruction has been completed, the machine returns to the first instruction and the same procedure is repeated (but with new input information) to process another transaction.

Instructions

Each instruction includes two basic types of information. The first type is embodied in the *operation code,* which tells the machine what function it is to perform. For example, the code 70 may tell the machine to read a card, the code 60 may tell the machine to add, the code 19 may tell it to multiply, and so forth. The other type of information required (the *address*) designates the location (or locations) in the memory where the data to be manipulated can be found, or where to store results that have already been produced. A particular machine will have from 20 to more than 100 different operation codes available for use, depending upon the design of the logic of the machine and its variety of input and output units. The address section of the instruction can refer to any of the locations available in the memory. Of course, each of the instructions is *also* stored in a memory location and is therefore associated with its own address location.

At this point it would be desirable to present an illustration of a typical computer program, but unfortunately this is not feasible. A computer program consists only of a list of code numbers which tell the machine what operations to perform, and these codes are quite incomprehensible to the beginner. Furthermore, a typical computer program is long and complex, involving hundreds or even thousands of individual instructions. Without such material as written descriptions and/or flow charts, a typical computer program is very difficult for a human (as opposed to the computer) to understand: even the man who wrote it may later find it difficult to read.

However, a simple illustration of a small portion of a program *can* be presented, initially using words rather than codes to describe the operations. Most machine programs, incidentally, are written in a form similar to this and are later translated into machine codes.

Suppose we have computed gross pay and the total of the voluntary and mandatory deductions for an employee and have stored them in memory. We would like to subtract the deductions total from gross pay to obtain and store net pay in memory. But we must be more specific; we must specify exactly where in memory each of these numbers is to be found and where net pay is to be stored. Suppose that gross pay is in location 1450, the sum of the deductions is in 1451, and we wish to store net pay in 1452. This portion of the program would involve three steps:

1. Insert into the arithmetic unit the number in location 1450.
2. Subtract the number in location 1451 from the contents of the arithmetic unit.
3. Store the contents of the arithmetic unit in location 1452.

Each of these instructions must also be located in memory, let us say, in locations 1000, 1001, and 1002.

If the operation code for entering a number into the arithmetic unit is 65, the code for subtracting a number from the contents of the arithmetic unit is 16, and the code for storing the result in memory is 20, then the program might appear as follows:

Location of Instruction	Operation Code	Address
1000	65	1450
1001	16	1451
1002	20	1452

The program would accomplish the following:

$$\text{Gross Pay} - \text{Deductions} = \text{Net Pay}$$
$$1450 \qquad\quad 1451 \qquad\quad 1452$$

After the first instruction is executed, the arithmetic unit contains Gross Pay; after the second instruction is executed, it contains Net Pay; and after the third instruction is completed, Net Pay is stored in location 1452 (replacing the previous contents of this memory word).

This is a good place to introduce some necessary terminology. Two numbers are associated with each memory word: the *address* of the word and the *contents* of the word. In the above example, 1450 is the address of gross pay, and the contents of location 1450 is gross pay. Similarly, the contents of location 1000 is the instruction 65 1450, while the location of the instruction 65 1450 is 1000. We must also notice that the address 1450 is a part of this instruction because the instruction performs an operation involving gross pay (the contents of 1450).

Yes-or-No Decisions

One of the most powerful capabilities of the electronic computer is its ability to make simple yes-or-no decisions. This *logical* function is accomplished by the use of so-called *branching* instructions which decide, on the basis of the answer to a specific question that can be answered by either a yes or a no, where in memory to go for the next instruction (see the accompanying illustration).

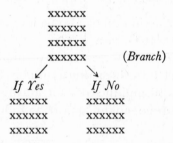

Typical branching questions are—Are these two numbers equal? Did the card have an X in column 75? Have we reached the end of this magnetic tape?—and each can be answered by yes or no. On the basis of the answer, the machine determines which set of instructions to execute next.

This branching ability enables the computer to handle data processing situations in which exceptions occur, for the exceptions can be isolated by means of these questions and the proper procedures for handling the exceptions can be executed. Thus the normal data processing program appears as in Figure 5–2. On the basis of the particular transaction being processed, the proper path through this maze of instructions is chosen. The first transaction may follow the path from A to B to C to E to L; the second transaction from A to G to F to I to K; the third from A to B to D to L; the fourth from A to G to H to J to K; the fifth from A to G to F to I to L; and so on. It should be noted that the machines make these yes-or-no decisions at the same speed at which they compute.

Let us examine this decision making ability of the electronic computer further. Notice that the machines do not actually make decisions in the normal sense of the word; they *follow* decisions that were made when the program was designed. In other words, someone must decide what exceptions can arise, someone must devise a set of

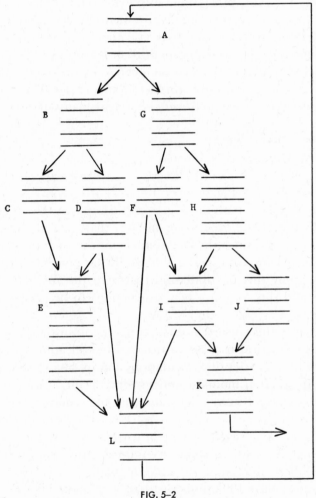

FIG. 5–2
Structure of a Typical Program

yes-or-no questions adequate to distinguish one exception from another, and someone must also determine the exact procedure that can be used to process each exception. *Then* the machine can follow through this maze of decisions and procedures rapidly and accurately. However, if an exception arises that was not planned for in the program, the computer is completely helpless; it will either stop or it will process the transaction incorrectly.

In Chapter 2 we discussed the logical function in data manipulation which involves the precise determination of the procedural steps to be followed in the processing of a transaction. In the use of computers for data processing, this logical function may be performed through the use of branching instructions. From the standpoint of the person who must devise the computer program, the establishment of the logical framework of the problem is usually the most important part of the job—so much so that he tends to view the entire program in terms of its branch points rather than in terms of the program steps that perform the actual manipulation.

Instruction Modification

The late John von Neumann (a famous and versatile "mathematician's mathematician," who created the mathematical theory of games) was one of the pioneer thinkers who contributed to the logical development of the electronic computer. He is generally credited with having originated the idea that since the instructions are numbers, and since the electronic computer is quite talented at manipulating numbers, perhaps it would be possible for the computer to apply this manipulating power to the instructions in its program and thus produce new instructions to be executed by the machine.

Apparently this concept is difficult for the uninitiated to visualize and put to practical use, yet instruction modification is used quite routinely in both scientific calculations and in data processing applications. Instruction modification is so important in the use of computers that special instructions and machine components (such as indirect addressing and index registers) have been devised to accomplish the same results with less arithmetic and manipulation.

Although instruction modification is used in many other ways—so that the following example does not do justice to its capabilities—let us say that we have 100 numbers stored in memory and that we want to obtain their total. This could be accomplished by using 101 instructions, one instruction to add each of the numbers into the accumulator and the 101st to store the results.

However, if the numbers were stored in sequential memory locations, we might write an instruction which would add the first number into the accumulator, then instructions that would add 1 to the address in this instruction (making it refer to the next number) , and then would go back and repeat this process of instruction execution and modification until the entire 100 numbers were totaled.[1] This program of instruction modification involves only about 10 instructions instead of the 101 required with the direct approach.

Does the computer exhibit any creativity in the process of instruction modification? Is the machine actually *creating* its own instructions? Again, since a human is performing all the creative work of this process, the answer is no. The person who designs the program must write the instructions that determine how the machine will manipulate the instructions that are being modified, and the human must plan each possible outcome of this modification so that the machine will perform the operations that will produce the desired results. Thus the computer merely follows (though at a superhuman pace) the procedure that a thinking human devised for it.

Universality

Theoretically, any electronic computer can solve any computation problem; this is why they are called universal automatic computers. A small, inexpensive computer (again theoretically) can be used to solve any problem that the largest, most expensive computer can solve, since both of them have the same general structure and capabilities. However, the amount of *time* required with the small machine may make its use impractical for some problems, just as many problems routinely solved by computers are impractical to solve by hand.

The fundamental economic question in the use of computers is not "How much does the machine cost?" or even "How fast is it?" but *"How much does it cost to solve a specific set of problems using a particular machine?"* Many different computing machines are available, which vary in reliability and cost, and each basic model can be obtained in differing configurations. Thus there are many different mixtures of input and output devices and speeds, memory size and speed, order structure and arithmetic speed, and file storage devices. For any particular set of problems, one of these different computers will be best, yet no single machine configuration is best for *all* types of problems.

---

[1] As we will see later, the most difficult part of this process is getting it stopped at the proper place.

SUMMARY

The basic components of an electronic computer are input devices, memory devices, an arithmetic and logical unit, output devices, and the control section. Many computers also include storage devices which make file information available for machine reference and processing.

The characteristic of the electronic computer that distinguishes it from the punched card calculator and other calculating machines is the manner in which computers are controlled. The stored program, which provides a powerful method of automatic control, is the most important concept associated with the computer; and an understanding of the stored program and its use provides an understanding of the electronic computer's capabilities and limitations.

As an illustration of the importance of the stored program, suppose we had a desk calculator that would do an addition, subtraction, multiplication, or division in one-millionth of a second. This super-calculator would still operate at about the same speed as an ordinary machine, for without the stored program it would still be tied to the speed at which a human operator could push the buttons telling it what to do.

The stored program, through its logical capabilities of branching and instruction modification, also allows elementary decisions to be incorporated into an automatic procedure. And the stored program gives these machines great flexibility, for a computer can be changed from one job to another simply by entering a new program into its memory. For example, to change from computing the solution of a set of simultaneous linear equations to the processing of inventory records it is only necessary to feed the inventory program into the memory through the input device and place inventory information in the input mechanism.

The electronic computer has the following important capabilities:

1. It can follow long and complicated procedures, even those involving large numbers of exceptions.
2. Through its memory and its access to files, it can organize all the information necessary for processing.
3. It can perform arithmetic.
4. It can do all of this with amazing speed and heretofore unobtainable accuracy.

On the other hand, in order to use a computer, we must completely pre-think the procedure and express it in great detail. It is not possible in a data processing situation to tell the computer to "use your own judgment," or "come and ask me if something comes up that you don't know how to handle." Not only must we figure out how to answer all the questions beforehand, we must know what the questions are going to be before they actually arise.

The machines, therefore, are utterly dependent upon humans. Rather than giant brains, they are large, fast morons, for they do just what they are told without question. Thus computers may be the quickest and most efficient method yet "devised" for turning out *wrong* answers, for if they are fed incorrect information or an inadequate program they will obligingly produce wrong answers, and at the same fantastic speed with which they produce correct results.

Besides requiring a large volume of processing to justify its use, a computer can be used to solve only those problems that involve much repetition, for writing a computer program is many times harder than computing the answer. The necessary repetition usually arises in data processing because many transactions must be processed. But in scientific computation, a single problem, such as solving a set of simultaneous linear equations, may involve performing the same elementary sequences of operations over and over with the coefficients of the unknowns. Thus, a computer may be efficiently used to solve one, or a small number, of such problems.

EXERCISES

5.1   What is the typical basic structure of an electronic computer?

5.2   What are the various functions performed by the memory of a computer?

5.3   How are computers controlled?

5.4   What is a *word?* Distinguish between the *address* and the *contents* of a memory location.

5.5   Distinguish between the working memory and file memory of a computer.

5.6   What is branching? Why is branching important?

5.7   Is there any "best" computer? Explain the answer.

5.8   What are the capabilities of the computer?

5.9   What are the limitations of the computer?

5.10 Can a computer think? Defend your answer. In Chapter 1 it is reported that a computer can prove mathematical theorems. Is this thinking? What do we mean by the word *think?*

5.11 All computers have the same basic capabilities: they can add, subtract, multiply, divide, and branch. Can all computers be used to solve the same problems? How do computers differ?

SUPPLEMENTAL READINGS

BELL, WILLIAM D. *A Management Guide to Electronic Computers.* New York: McGraw-Hill Book Co., Inc., 1957.

Chapter 2 introduces the basic concepts associated with electronic computers.

CHAPIN, NED. *An Introduction to Automatic Computers.* Princeton, N.J.: D. Van Nostrand Co., Inc., 1957.

Chapter 2 poses the question "What is an Electronic Computer?"

LAURIE, EDWARD J. *Computers and How They Work.* Cincinnati: South-Western Publishing Co., 1963.

Chapter 2 describes and pictures the basic components of computers.

6 BASIC PROGRAMMING
CONCEPTS (I)

TO OBTAIN a realistic understanding of the capabilities and limitations of the electronic computer—as well as the management problems involved in the use of a computer for data processing—it is necessary to progress beyond the stage of vague generalities and to study in some detail how the computer is programmed. This does not mean that the major objective of this book is to develop programmers—it is simply an expression of the conviction that anyone who makes decisions concerning computers, or who works with computers in any way, needs to understand what is involved in programming.

To understand computer programming, then, it seems we would have to study the operating details of an actual computer. Although all machines differ in many respects, there is a sufficiently large core of basic similarities so that we can learn the basic concepts we need to know by using any one of a number of computers for our example. And, after learning one machine, the task of learning to use any other is relatively simple.

However, there are excellent reasons why we *do not* choose to use an existing machine for our illustration. First, we prefer to combine elements of several machines so as to obtain greater breadth. Secondly, each actual machine incorporates a considerable number of details that would only introduce complications we prefer to avoid at this stage. By avoiding these possibly confusing nonessentials we are able to make more efficient use of our time and energy, and at the same time obtain a more comprehensive understanding of computers in general. Finally, new computers are being introduced so rapidly that the lead time required in book publication and student graduation may make detailed knowledge of any *specific* machine out of date by the time it could be useful to most students.

THE MAC COMPUTER

Our machine, which we will call the MAC (Martin's Automatic Computer), will be representative of "intermediate" electronic data processing machines: it is intermediate in size, speed, and cost. In its simplest configuration, which we will study in this chapter, the MAC would rent for about $3,500 per month, on a single-shift basis, or sell for about $175,000. Performing around 4,000 operations per second, the basic MAC has only punched card input and punched card and printer output facilities and would operate in conjunction with the standard punched card key punches, sorters, reproducers, and collators to provide a complete data processing installation.

The MAC, however, is also a "building block" machine and can readily be augmented with more memory and additional input-output devices and automatic files in order to significantly increase its processing capabilities (and its cost) and reduce its dependence upon punched card equipment. In this chapter we will restrict our consideration to the basic MAC, with limited input and output, and will leave consideration of the expanded machine to later chapters, where we will also discuss some possible variations among different machines.

Character Codes

Information is not written in the memory of a digital computer in the same way that we would write it on a piece of paper. In all digital computers information is recorded in coded form by some combination of elements (called *bits*) which have but two possible states, usually designated by 0 and 1. For example, in the punched card we use a 12-bit code for alphabetic or numeric information in which the absence of a hole (in a row) corresponds to a zero bit and the presence of a hole represents a 1 bit. In this code each numeric digit is represented by a combination of 11 zero bits and a single 1 bit, while an alphabetic character is represented by a combination of 10 zero bits and two 1 bits.

Such codes must be used because computers are constructed of binary elements—elements that have exactly two states, such as "off" and "on." Each such element can represent a *bit* of information. The 12-bit code used by the punched card is inefficient because it requires

12 binary elements to represent each digit of information, and we will soon see that we can get by with far fewer than 12 bits. This raises the question: How many bits are required to represent the digits 0 through 9? Since each character represented must have a distinct combination of bits, this question reduces to: How many different combinations can be constructed from a single bit, or 2 bits, or 3 bits, or 4 bits, etc.?

It is customary to represent the on condition of an element by 1 and the off condition by 0. Then a single bit gives two combinations, 0 and 1. Two bits give four combinations: 00, 01, 10, and 11. If we add a third bit there are eight possible combinations, since each of the above can be combined with both a 1 and a 0 to obtain the following combinations:

	Previous Combinations			
	00	01	10	11
Adding a 0 on left 000	001	010	011
Adding a 1 on left 100	101	110	111

This illustrates the fact that each time we add a bit we double the number of combinations, so that n bits give 2^n combinations.

Since $2^3 = 8$, and there are 10 digits, three bits are not enough to represent the numeric digits. However, $2^4 = 16$, so four bits are more than enough to represent the ten digits. The question then becomes: Which 10 of the 16 possible combinations shall we use, and which of these combinations shall be assigned to each of the digits 0 through 9? Perhaps the most common assignment of combinations to numbers (and the one used in the MAC computer) is the *binary-coded-decimal* (or BCD) representation, which uses four bits, with values corresponding to 8, 4, 2, and 1 to represent the digits 0 through 9. In BCD the digits 0 through 9 are represented as shown in Figure 6–1.

An important variation of BCD is the *excess-three* BCD notation, in which 3 is added to the digit before it is expressed in BCD form (see Figure 6–2). The excess-three notation has a valuable property for subtraction, since the nines' complement of any digit may be obtained by substituting zeros for ones and ones for zeros in the bit representation.

A two-out-of-five representation, used by several machines, is also shown in Figure 6–2. This representation has self-checking properties, since the dropping or the adding of a one bit results in an invalid representation (a combination that does not correspond to any digit). It should be observed that the BCD representation has little self-checking capability, for the dropping of a one bit *always* results in another valid number, and the addition of a one bit *may* result in a valid number.

Bit Positions

	8	4	2	1
Zero	0	0	0	0
One	0	0	0	1
Two	0	0	1	0
Three	0	0	1	1
Four	0	1	0	0
Five	0	1	0	1
Six	0	1	1	0
Seven	0	1	1	1
Eight	1	0	0	0
Nine	1	0	0	1

FIG. 6–1
Binary-Coded-Decimal Notation

With the bit values 8, 4, 2, 1 used in the BCD code we could represent the number 13 by the combination 1101 and the number 15 by the combination 1111. This is as far as we can go with only four bits, but we can add another bit to the left with value 16 (doubling the 8) so that 10110 would represent the number 22. By adding further bits to the left (doubling the value each time) we can express any number, no matter how large, in *binary* notation.[1] As its name implies, binary-coded-decimal represents each decimal digit *separately* in binary notation.

The number of bits required for representing numeric information is minimized when the numbers are converted to the pure binary system. However, numbers cannot be translated digit by digit

---

[1] For a further discussion of binary notation see Appendix B.

into this notation, so a considerable amount of computation is required to make the conversion. Thus most computers designed for data processing use one of the notations discussed above. However, several machines are designed to operate on numbers in either pure binary or binary-coded-decimal form, depending upon which is the most convenient. In these machines binary representation is used to store instructions, and it can be used for data in suitable circumstances.

If we wish to represent both the numeric digits and the alphabet, we must have 36 different characters. Since $2^5 = 32$, five bits are too

	Excess Three				Two-Out-of-Five				
	8	4	2	1	0	1	2	3	6
Zero	0	0	1	1	0	1	1	0	0
One	0	1	0	0	1	1	0	0	0
Two	0	1	0	1	1	0	1	0	0
Three	0	1	1	0	1	0	0	1	0
Four	0	1	1	1	0	1	0	1	0
Five	1	0	0	0	0	0	1	1	0
Six	1	0	0	1	1	0	0	0	1
Seven	1	0	1	0	0	1	0	0	1
Eight	1	0	1	1	0	0	1	0	1
Nine	1	1	0	0	0	0	0	1	1

FIG. 6–2
Other Notations

few, so six bits are required. And since $2^6 = 64$, with a six-bit code we have enough combinations to handle any reasonable number of special characters in addition to the alphabet and numeric digits.

Several popular alpha-numeric codes are based on the logic of the punched card code, using four bits (binary-coded-decimal or excess-three representation) to represent the numeric punch and the other two bits (four combinations) to represent the no-zone, 12-zone, 11-zone, and zero-zone possibilities.

Since errors are not detected by these codes, a seventh bit position is frequently added to the code to make it self-checking. This bit, called a *redundancy* or *parity* bit, is added so as to make the total of one bits in each valid character an even number (or in some machines, odd), so that if a single bit is changed an invalid character results.

Like several other machines, the MAC uses an eight-bit (two-digit) code to represent alphabetic information. For example, in this code JONES would be represented as 71 76 75 65 82 when stored in the memory of the MAC.

Memory

The memory of the basic MAC computer is composed of 2,000 ten-digit (and sign) words. As discussed above, one such word can

Courtesy of International Business Machines Corp.

FIG. 6–3
Magnetic Core Plane

also store five alphabetic characters. In order to operate at a speed of thousands of operations per second, the MAC uses a *magnetic core* memory which provides an access time of a few microseconds.[2]

---

[2] A microsecond is one-millionth of a second. Since a second is one million microseconds and since light (and electricity) travels at 186,000 miles per second, light travels about 1,000 feet in one microsecond.

A magnetic core is a doughnut-shaped ring, less than 1/10 of
in outside diameter,[3] made of a magnetizable ceramic r
These small beads, each of which can remember one "bit ʋ⸱ ⸱⸱⸱
formation, are strung on lattices of wires, as illustrated in Figure
6–3.

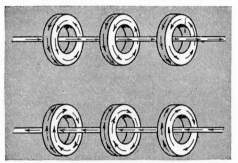

Courtesy of International Business Machines Corp.

FIG. 6–4
Polarity of Magnetic Cores

As you may have seen demonstrated in elementary physics, a
current sent through a wire that is coiled around a piece of iron will
magnetize the iron, and the direction of the magnetization depends
upon the direction of the current through the wire. Similarly, if the
magnetic core is wrapped around the wire and a sufficiently strong

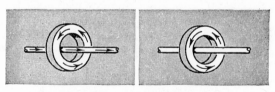

Current is applied   Current is removed;
                            Core remains magnetized
Courtesy of International Business Machines Corp.

FIG. 6–5
Magnetizing a Core

current is sent through the wire, a magnetic flux is generated in the
core. As shown in Figure 6–4, the direction (or polarity) of the magnetization depends upon the direction of the current in the wire. The
magnetization remains after the current is no longer present (see Figure 6–5) , and the direction of the magnetization can be changed (the

---

[3] Some magnetic cores are almost unbelievably small—no larger than the period
produced by an ordinary typewriter.

core "flipped") by a pulse of current in the opposite direction (see Figure 6–6). Thus one direction of magnetization can be used to represent a zero bit and the other direction can represent a 1 bit.

Magnetic cores have one additional property that enables computers to conveniently select the particular core in which to record a bit of information. If the core is magnetized in one direction, a suitably strong current is required to cause it to flip to the opposite

Current is applied   Core is magnetized   Current is reversed; the core reverses its magnetic state

Courtesy of International Business Machines Corp.

FIG. 6–6
Reversing a Core

state. If the current required to flip a core is denoted by I, then a current of $\frac{1}{2}$I will not affect the cores. Thus we are able to record a bit of information where we desire by selecting one horizontal wire and one vertical wire, then sending half the required current through each of these wires. As shown in Figures 6–7 and 6–8, only

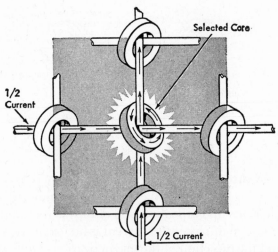

Selected Core

1/2 Current

1/2 Current

Courtesy of International Business Machines Corp.

FIG. 6–7
Selecting a Core

the core at the intersection of these two wires will have a current sufficient to flip the core, so a bit will be recorded in this core—and nowhere else—in a core plane containing thousands of individual cores.

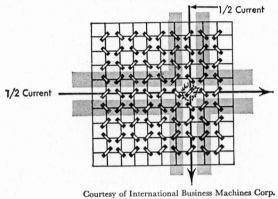

Courtesy of International Business Machines Corp.

FIG. 6–8

Magnetic Core Plane

To read information from a magnetic core memory, another wire is threaded through all of the cores in a plane.[4] When a core flips, a current is generated in this wire, as shown in Figure 6–9. Thus, to read out a core, current is sent through the proper pair of wires to

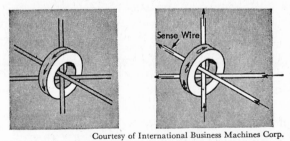

Courtesy of International Business Machines Corp.

FIG. 6–9

Core Sense Wires

record a 0. If the core flips, a pulse on the read-out wire indicates that a 1 was present in the core. If it does not flip, there is no pulse available on the read-out wire, and a 0 was present. This process always sets the core to the 0 state, destroying the information stored,

---

[4] Actually, in order to make it possible to more easily select an entire word from memory, a fourth wire (called an *inhibit wire*) is also threaded through all the cores in a plane. Thus each core has four wires passing through it.

whence all such memories are constructed so that the information is automatically rewritten to be held for later reference.

Since in binary-coded-decimal form each digit requires 4 bits, a 10-digit word requires 40 cores plus those bits required for the sign. In the MAC we will use 2 bits for the sign, so 42 cores are required to

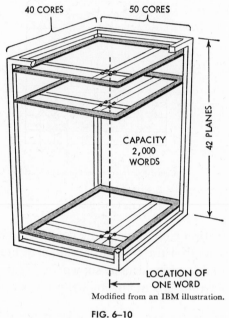

40 CORES 50 CORES

42 PLANES

CAPACITY
2,000
WORDS

LOCATION OF
ONE WORD

Modified from an IBM illustration.

FIG. 6–10
MAC Memory Array

represent a word in memory. The memory is physically arranged in 42 planes of 40 by 50 cores each, with 1 bit of each word in each plane (as shown in Figure 6–10).

Input-Output

The input and output of the basic MAC consists of punched cards and a line printer. The card reader-punch on the MAC has a Read feed by which the information on punched cards may be read (transferred into the magnetic core memory) at a maximum rate of 600 cards per minute. It also has a separate punch feed which allows the machine to punch information from the memory into blank cards at a maximum rate of 200 cards per minute. Notice that the machine cannot punch into the cards which are read without manually moving the cards from one feed to the other.

A printer, similar to MAC's, is shown in Figure 6–11. The

printing mechanism is composed of a rapidly revolving linked chain with characters engraved on its outer surface. There are 120 hammers behind the paper, one for each printing position. At the instant the proper character on the chain is positioned in front of the column of the form where it is to be printed, the hammer strikes the paper from behind, forcing it against the ribbon and the character, thus printing the character (see Figure 6–12). This printer can print on

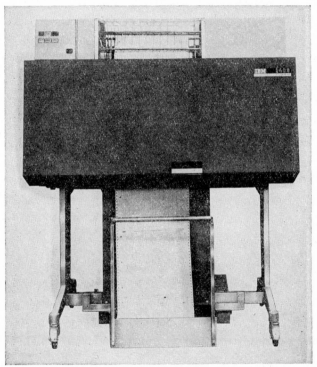

Courtesy of International Business Machines Corp.

FIG. 6–11
Line Printer

continuous forms at a maximum rate of 600 120-character lines per minute. Spacing and skipping of the form is controlled by an automatic carriage that responds to information in the memory of the MAC.

Both the input and the output of this machine are "buffered," which means that the operations of reading, computing, punching, and printing can be overlapped. In other words, the machine can print the results of one calculation while calculating on a card that has just been read, and, at the same time, physically read a third card.

The MAC's wired control panels, similar to those in punched card machines, are used to rearrange the format of the input cards as they are read, the output cards as they are punched, and the output information as it is printed so as to allow the most efficient processing within the machine. These control panels also assist in the process of

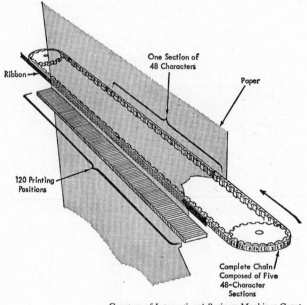

Courtesy of International Business Machines Corp.

FIG. 6–12

Chain Printing Mechanism

translating to and from the two-digit code in which alphabetic information is stored in memory.[5]

Basic Instruction Format

Each MAC instruction requires 10 digits, and therefore fits quite snugly into a single word (see below). Since each instruction must be stored in the machine memory it must have a definite location, and that location is the address of the instruction. It should be noted that this is not a part of the instruction; it is a number, associated with the instruction, that tells where the instruction is to be stored in the machine memory.

---

[5] Many machines do not have such control panels. However, programming is simplified if data rearrangement can be accomplished by a control panel rather than programmed. In a later chapter we will discuss machines without input-output control panels.

In the instruction itself the first two digits form the operation code, which tells the machine what operation to perform—addition, subtraction, multiplication, division, storing, reading a card, punching a card, shifting a number left, etc. The data address tells the machine where to find the information that is to be manipulated in this operation (or where to store the result of an operation). In operations that do not require a reference to memory the data address may provide other necessary information, such as how many positions to shift the A register or where to go for the next instruction. The

Address of Introduction	Operation Code	Data Address	Special Indicators	
xxxx	xx	xxxx	xxxx	±

remaining four digits of the instruction are used for special modifications of the basic operations. (A discussion of these last four digits would confuse the issue at this stage, so we will postpone their consideration until we have obtained an understanding of the basic machine operations.)

Internal Information Flow

Although a computer consists of many physical components—wire, transistors, germanium diodes, resistors, capacitors, etc.—the machine is rather simple to the user. The user is concerned only with the input and output, the memory, and a few registers which are required to manipulate the information being processed. Figure 6–13 shows the internal registers of the MAC computer and the paths between them along which numbers can be transferred.[6] These registers are used to analyze instructions and to perform arithmetic operations. Composed of magnetic cores like the main memory, the special uses of registers distinguish them from the regular memory of the machine.

The M register and the A register are used in the arithmetic operations of the machine. Both are 10-digit registers and both have a sign. For some purposes, the two registers act together in a coordinated manner, but they can also be used independently. All numbers that are transferred from the memory into the A or M registers must pass through and appear in the memory register, which also

---

[6] When we study the use of the final four digits of the instruction, it will be necessary to augment this diagram, but to do so now might be confusing.

holds a 10-digit number and its sign. It should be noted that this register is not available to the programmer, but a knowledge of its existence is helpful in understanding how the machine works, for it stores the word taken from memory while it is being acted upon by the arithmetic unit.

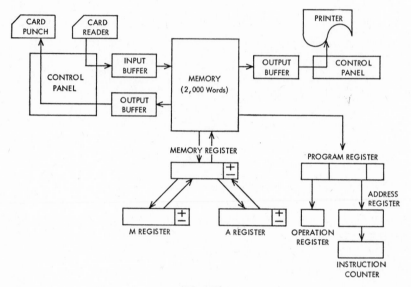

FIG. 6–13

Registers of the MAC

The A register does not calculate, it only stores the results of calculations. The calculation is accomplished by a one-digit adder (see Figure 6–14) which takes one factor from the memory register, the other from the A register, and places the result in the A register. Again, the one-digit adder is not available to the programmer of the machine—knowledge of the adder simply helps us understand why the machine operates as it does.

The lower right-hand portion of Figure 6–13 represents the control portion of the MAC in which instructions are interpreted and the components of the machine are made to perform their proper function at the correct time. As each instruction is executed, it is transferred from the memory into the program register, where it is broken down into its basic segments. The operation code is then transferred to the two-digit operation register, where its decoding sets up circuits to perform the proper operation.

The data address is transferred to the address register and the circuits are set up to transfer information from that memory address to the memory register—or from the memory register to that memory address. After the arithmetic operation is completed, a 1 is automatically added to the instruction counter (containing the location of the instruction just executed) and the circuitry is set up to transfer the next instruction into the program register.

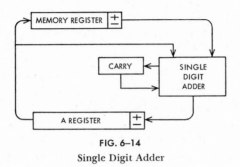

FIG. 6–14
Single Digit Adder

Thus the machine executes instructions that are sequentially located in memory[7] unless special instructions are executed which interrupt this sequence. The execution of each instruction requires two separate activities: *obtaining* the instruction and *executing* it. This is why the speed of the memory is of such great importance, for each instruction execution requires two memory accesses, one to get the instruction and another to obtain (or store) the data.

PROGRAMMING THE MAC

To understand what an electronic computer can do, what it cannot do, and what is involved in preparing a problem for machine solution, we will have to study machine programming. Roughly speaking, programming refers to the process of breaking the problem down into a sequence of steps which the machine can follow, and expressing these steps in specific instructions which the machine can perform.[8] To understand what is involved in programming, it is therefore necessary to understand the basic operations that the machine can perform. This provides the raw materials with which we

---

[7] When 1 is added to 1999 in the instruction counter, the result is 0000. Thus the machine considers location 0000 to be the successor of location 1999. If an instruction is executed in location 1999, the next instruction would come from location 0000.

[8] The second part of this process, writing the machine instructions, is known as *coding*.

must work. However, the task of assembling these elementary operations in the sequence that will most efficiently accomplish the desired result involves an extremely complex synthesizing process. In the following pages we will discuss many operations of the MAC and attempt to provide some ideas and techniques that will be useful in this creative synthesizing process.

As we prepare a program, we will write it on a programming form (see Figure 6–15) which includes space for the location of the instruction, the operation code, and the data address. In addition, the

Location	Operation Code	Data Address	M Register	A Register	Remarks

FIG. 6–15

MAC Programming Form

programming form provides an area for the M register and the A register which may be filled in to follow through an example and to show the exact numbers that will be present in these registers after each instruction has been executed (for a specific example). There is also space for remarks which describe what each small group of instructions is designed to accomplish. These remarks are most helpful in reading a program that has been set aside for a few hours.[9]

In order to program the machine we must have more than a hazy idea of what the instructions accomplish. The machine will do exactly what it is told, so you must know exactly what to tell it or

---

[9] When we consider the final four digits of the instruction we will add some more columns to the programming form.

the program may not accomplish your intention. It is not necessary to memorize the operation code numbers; you may use the operation abbreviations when first writing the program and fill in the operation codes later, but you must *clearly understand* what each operation code accomplishes.

It should be noted that the MAC computes with signed numbers; it handles these positive and negative numbers automatically, according to the proper rules of arithmetic.[10] Therefore, it behooves us to know these rules of arithmetic so that we will know what to expect from the machine.

Add, Subtract, and Store Operations

The illustrations in this section will be presented in a form similar to the programming form. The first line of each illustration indicates the contents of the memory word referred to by the data address of the instruction, the contents of the M register, and the contents of the A register, all *before* the instruction is executed. The second line gives the instruction and the results obtained from that instruction, showing the new (changed or unchanged) contents of the memory location, the M register, and the A register. Since these operations are the same no matter where the instruction is located in memory, the location of the instruction need not be given. Note that each illustration is entirely independent of those preceding and following it.

65 RAA (Reset and Add to A Register). This operation code resets the A register to plus zero and then adds the contents of the data address location (with its sign) into the A register. This oper-

---

[10] For those whose arithmetic is a bit rusty, four rules may be used to add and subtract signed numbers. (1) The sum of two positive numbers is a positive number. (2) The sum of two negative numbers is a negative number. (3) The sum of a positive and a negative number is obtained as follows: (*a*) Ignore the signs of the two numbers; (*b*) subtract the smaller number from the larger; (*c*) give this result the sign of the larger of the two numbers. (4) In order to subtract one number from another, change the sign of the number to be subtracted and add the resulting two numbers.

In the following illustrations, the signs inside the parentheses denote the algebraic signs of the numbers, while the plus and minus signs between the parentheses denote the operations of addition or subtraction.

$(+5) + (+7) = +12$	(Rule 1)
$(-7) + (-5) = -12$	(Rule 2)
$(+7) + (-5) = +2$	(Rule 3)
$(-7) + (+5) = -2$	(Rule 3)
$(+7) - (-5) = (+7) + (+5) = +12$	(Rules 4 and 1)
$(-7) - (+5) = (-7) + (-5) = -12$	(Rules 4 and 2)
$(+7) - (+5) = (+7) + (-5) = +2$	(Rules 4 and 3)
$(-7) - (-5) = (-7) + (+5) = -2$	(Rules 4 and 3)

ation code is illustrated in Examples 6–1 and 6–2 in the following table.

15 ADA (Add to A Register). This operation code causes the contents of the data address location to be added to the contents of the A register. Notice in Examples 6–1 through 6–5 that the M register is not affected by the Reset-Add and Add operations, and that these operations obey the rules of signs.

When we add two 10-digit numbers together we may obtain an overflow carry to produce an 11-digit number. As is illustrated in Example 6–6, if such an overflow occurs in the A register, the resulting 1 is lost. However, the occurrence of such an overflow sets the *overflow circuit,* which affects the operation of the Branch on Overflow instruction (which will be discussed under *Branching* later in this chapter).

20 STA (Store A Register). This operation code causes the contents of the A register, with its sign, to be stored in the location specified by the data address of the instruction. The contents of the A register remain undisturbed. This operation is illustrated in Example 6–7.

Example Number	Operation	Contents of Data Address Location	M Register	A Register
6–1	RAA	0000012345 + 0000012345 +	5555555555 + 5555555555 +	4444444444 + 0000012345 +
6–2	RAA	0000012345 − 0000012345 −	5555555555 + 5555555555 +	4444444444 + 0000012345 −
6–3	ADA	0000022222 + 0000022222 +	0000077777 + 0000077777 +	0000044444 + 0000066666 +
6–4	ADA	0000022222 − 0000022222 −	0000077777 + 0000077777 +	0000044444 + 0000022222 +
6–5	ADA	0000066666 − 0000066666 −	0000077777 + 0000077777 +	0000044444 + 0000022222 −
6–6	ADA	6000000000 − 6000000000 −	0000000000 + 0000000000 +	7000000000 − *3000000000 −
6–7	STA	0123456789 + 0000055555 −	2222222222 − 2222222222 −	0000055555 − 0000055555 −

* Overflow circuit set.

As our first illustration of how these instructions may be combined to accomplish useful results, suppose we wish to add two numbers that are in memory and to store the result in memory. To be specific, suppose that the two numbers to be added are stored in memory locations 0100 and 0101, and we wish to place their sum in location 0102. Notice that at this point we are not concerned with the two specific numbers—whatever the contents of these two memory locations may be, we wish to find their sum and place it in location 0102. In the usual situation these numbers will change with each transaction that is processed. Therefore, the program can process the various transactions one after another. In other words, the program of a machine corresponds to an algebraic formula, and the various values of the different symbols of this formula are inserted for each transaction.

However, in order to visualize what is going on within the machine, let us suppose that the contents of 0100 are 0000001111+ and the contents of 0101 are 0000002222+. The following program (shown as on a programming form) will produce the desired result. Since none of these program steps affect the contents of the M register, its contents will be unchanged by this portion of the program.

Location	Operation	Data Address	M Register	A Register
1005	RAA	0100	unchanged	0000011111+
1006	ADA	0101	unchanged	0000033333+
1007	STA	0102	unchanged	0000033333+

As a result of the above program steps, the number 0000003333+ appears in location 0102, replacing its previous contents. Locations 0100 and 0101 are unchanged. It is important to observe that *each storage location is cleared only when new information is entered:* the same information may be read out of storage over and over without being affected, but the previous information is lost when a new number is entered (or stored) in the location.

In the above illustration we arbitrarily decided to allocate memory locations 1005, 1006, and 1007 to this small portion of the program. Any of the memory locations that are not used for some other purpose might have been used to store these instructions. In the usual case their location would be determined by the location of the instructions preceding this portion of the program, since the machine obtains its instructions sequentially.

66 RSA (Reset and Subtract from A Register). This operation code resets the A register to plus zero and subtracts the contents of the data address location from the A register. Notice in Examples 6–8 and 6–9 that this results in entering the number from the memory into the A register with its sign changed.

16 SUA (Subtract from A Register). This operation code causes the contents of the data address location to be subtracted from the A register. Example 6–10 shows the result of subtracting a larger number from a smaller to produce a negative result, while Example 6–11 shows that subtracting a negative number can produce a positive result. As shown in Example 6–12, overflows can also occur in subtraction. In this case, of course, the overflow circuit would also be set.

It should also be noted that the MAC computer usually produces a plus zero as the result of an addition or subtraction, as shown in Example 6–13, but that in some circumstances a zero with a minus sign can result, as in Example 6–12. Although it may seem downright discouraging, such subtleties may be very important when writing a program for a computer. *A good programmer knows what will happen under every conceivable circumstance.*

So far we have been concerned with instructions that affect only the A register. The following two instructions enter and remove information from the M register. In addition to enabling us to effectively utilize the M register, they are also useful for transferring information from one part of memory to another.

69 LDM (Load M Register). This operation code causes the contents of the data address location of the instruction to be placed, with its sign, in the M register.

24 STM (Store M Register). This operation causes the contents of the M register, and its sign, to be stored in the location specified by the data address of the instruction.

These last two instructions are illustrated in Examples 6–14 and 6–15.

Input and Output Instructions

Since the reading and punching of cards and printing are mechanical processes, they are much slower than the electronic processes involved in computing. Thus it is highly desirable that these mechanical processes be handled in a way that will allow computation to proceed with minimum delay. Devices, called *buffers,* are used to overlap the card reading, calculation, printing, and punching. An input buffer is a memory device that receives information at the

Example Number	Operation	Contents of Data Address Location	M Register	A Register
6–8		0123456789+	9876543210−	0005678999−
	RSA	0123456789+	9876543210−	0123456789−
6–9		0123456789−	0000011111+	0005678999−
	RSA	0123456789−	0000011111+	0123456789+
6–10		0000044444+	0000011111+	0000033333+
	SUA	0000044444+	0000011111+	0000011111−
6–11		0000044444−	0000022222+	0000033333−
	SUA	0000044444−	0000022222+	0000011111+
6–12		7000000000+	0000022222+	3000000000−
	SUA	7000000000+	0000022222+	*0000000000−
6–13		7000000000−	0000022222+	7000000000−
	SUA	7000000000−	0000022222+	0000000000+
6–14		0000033333+	0000077777−	0000066666+
	LDM	0000033333+	0000033333+	0000066666+
6–15		0000033333+	0000077777−	0000066666+
	STM	0000077777−	0000077777−	0000066666+

* Overflow circuit set.

speed at which the input device operates and assembles it so that it may be transferred into main memory at the speed at which information can be recorded in memory. Thus the addressable memory of the machine is not tied up with card reading except for the time required to transfer the contents of the buffer into the memory. Similarly, an output buffer accepts information from memory at the speed at which memory can operate and doles this information out at the speed that the output device requires. In the MAC an area of core memory that is not addressable by the program provides three 20-word buffers: one for card reading, one for punching, and one for printing.

One might wonder why there is a 20-word buffer when the card has only 80 columns. In the first place, each alphabetic column requires 2 digits of storage, so a completely alphabetic card would require 16 words (160 positions) of storage. The other 4 words are provided for additional flexibility in grouping the information into words and in handling control punches in the cards. Note that the printer can print 120 positions on a line. If this were all alphabetic, 24 words (240 positions) would be required! Therefore, since the buffer has only 200 positions, we can print a maximum of 100 characters on a completely alphabetic line.

As a card is read the wiring of the control panel determines which field of the card will be entered into any particular word of the 20 available buffer words, and, as a card is punched, the wiring of the control panel determines in which field each of the 20 output words is punched. Thus the control panel allows information to be rearranged or eliminated as the cards are read or punched (see Figure 6–16).

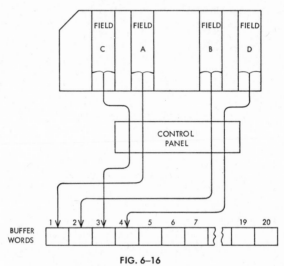

FIG. 6–16
Control Panel Rearranges Input

Similarly, information may be rearranged as it is printed. Several 80-position selectors on the card units (and 120 position selectors on the printer) allow different formats of cards (and printed lines) to be handled easily. On input, these selectors are controlled by punches in the card, but on output they are controlled by control digits in the last word of the output buffer (as will be discussed later). Since we are primarily interested in the characteristics of the stored program, further details of control panel wiring will not be discussed.

After the card has physically passed the reading brushes and its information has been assembled in the Read buffer, the contents of the buffer may quickly be transferred into main memory—at the speed at which magnetic core memory operates—by the following operation.

70 RDC (Read Card). This operation code causes the machine to read cards by a two-step process. First, the contents of the 20-

word Read buffer are transferred into a block of 20 consecutive words in memory, beginning with the word designated by the data address of the instruction. Secondly, the next card is fed under the reading brushes and the information read is entered into buffer storage to await the next Read Card instruction.

The execution of the machine instructions is delayed only during the first portion of this process, and computing may take place during all or part of the time that the second step of the process is taking place. Thus, of the 100 milliseconds that are required to physically read a card, around 95 milliseconds are available for computation without slowing the card-feeding speed below 600 cards per minute. Of course, if another Read instruction is encountered before the completion of the second step of this process, an interlock delays the execution of the second Read instruction until the card has been read and the buffer completely filled. Programming, therefore, cannot get ahead of the card reading and cannot cause part of the card to go unread.

Of all the instructions in the basic MAC, Read Card is unique because it is the only instruction that can alter more than one word of memory. Even if only one or two words are actually read from a card, the entire 20-word block of input storage will be replaced by the contents of the Read buffer, which will contain one or two words of data, and the remaining words will be zeros. Thus unused words in the input block (into which a card is read) cannot be used for storing instructions, for they are erased each time a card is read.

An additional complication is encountered when we begin reading into a block in the upper portion of memory so high that there are less than 20 words remaining. In such a case the remaining words "wrap around" into the lower portion of memory. For example, if we give a Read Card instruction with a data address of 1997, the first word of the buffer will be entered into location 1997, the second word into location 1998, the third word into location 1999, the fourth word into location 0000, the fifth word into location 0001, and the twentieth word will be entered into location 0016.

In order to enter the program into the memory of the machine, certain cards may be designated as *load* cards by means of a 12 (or Y) punch in a specified column. When a load card is read, the control panel wiring is ignored so that the card is read column by column into the first eight words of the buffer, and the MAC takes its next instruction from the location given by the data address, which is the first word of the card that was read. This condition will be more fully discussed in subsequent sections on branching and on loading the program.

If the card feed runs out of cards the machine stops when the next Read Card instruction is executed. At this time there are still several cards to be processed. The operator can place more cards in the feed and press the start button. The Read Card instruction will be executed and processing will continue. On the other hand, if there are no further cards to be placed in the feed, the operator presses the End of File button on the card reader to finish the processing and set the Card End of File indicator that can be tested by a branch instruction to determine when processing has been completed.

71 PCD (Punch Card). This operation code causes a card to be punched by a two-step process. First, the machine transfers a 20-word block of storage, starting with the word designated by the data address of the instruction, to the output buffer. Secondly, the card is punched with the information in buffer storage. Of the 300 milliseconds required to punch a card, only about 5 milliseconds are necessary to perform the first part of this operation. During the second part of the operation about 295 milliseconds are available, during which other instructions may be executed.

As in the Read Card instruction, if a data address in the upper 19 words of memory is used, the punch block will wrap around into the lower portion of memory. Unlike the operation of the Read Card instruction, punching from a block of storage does not alter the contents of that block, so unused words in that portion of memory can be used for other purposes and the control panel wiring can eliminate punching the extraneous information into the card.

As was mentioned in connection with the Read Card instruction, although buffers allow overlapping of reading, computing, and punching, they do not physically speed up the punching of cards beyond the rate of 200 cards per minute. For example, if the computing time required between two separate punch instructions is less than 295 milliseconds, the programming will be delayed until the completion of punching of the current card before transferring the information for the following card into the punch buffer.

72 PRT (Print). This operation code causes a line to be printed by a two-step process. First, the machine transfers a 20-word block of storage, starting with the word designated by the data address of the instruction to the output buffer. Secondly, the line is printed with the information in buffer storage. Of the 100 milliseconds required to print a line, only about 5 milliseconds are necessary to perform the first part of this operation. During the second part of the operation, about 95 milliseconds are available for executing other instructions.

As in the above instructions, if a data address in the upper 19 words of memory is used, the print block will wrap around into the lower portion of memory. Printing from a block of storage does not alter the contents of that block, so unused words in that portion of memory can be used for other purposes. The control panel wiring can eliminate printing of the extraneous information.

In order to present an example of a complete computer program we need one more instruction.

40 BRU (Branch Unconditionally). When this operation is executed, the data address of the instruction is inserted into the instruction counter, replacing its contents. The instruction thus alters the sequence of the program steps so that the next instruction is taken from the location given by the data address instead of from the next sequential location.

An Example

As an example of an extremely simple but nevertheless complete program, let us consider a situation where we have a deck of punched cards, each containing two numbers (designated A and B). From each of these cards we would like to print a line with A, B, and their sum, C. In this problem we must read a card, compute the sum of A and B and store it for printing, print the line, and return to the beginning of the program.

Whenever we begin planning a program, we must decide what steps must be accomplished and the sequence they must follow to produce the desired results. This planning is best done by means of a *block diagram*. Although in the simple problems which we will use for exercises it may appear that a block diagram is superfluous, in any particular program—requiring hundreds of separate instructions —the situation is almost impossibly confusing unless such a diagram is prepared before programming is started. As a matter of fact, in a complicated situation the development of a satisfactory block diagram may be more difficult and time consuming than the subsequent writing of the program itself. Furthermore, it is usually necessary to explain a program to others (or for them to be able to read what you have done), and a block diagram is the best means of transmitting the basic logic of the approach that has been taken. Figure 6–17 shows how a block diagram of this illustration might appear.

Notice that an arrow leads from block 3 to block 1, indicating that after the first line is printed we read the second card, and after the second card is completed we read the third, and so on. Thus, no matter how many cards we have to compute, the machine will continue to feed them and process them until the machine either runs out of cards or the operator pushes the stop button.

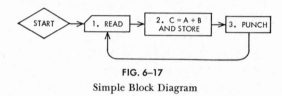

FIG. 6-17
Simple Block Diagram

As in all programs, so with our example: we must allocate the memory to the various functions it will serve. We must decide what area to use for input and output storage, and where to locate the instructions. In the program which follows we have arbitrarily decided to read the cards and print the results from the same block; that is, from location 1951 to 1970. We have also decided to store the instructions in sequential locations beginning with 0100. We will assume that, by control panel wiring, factor A is entered into the first word of the buffer and factor B is entered into the second word. Likewise, we will print A from the first word of the buffer, B from the second word, and their sum, C, from the third word. From the above we may deduce that A is located in 1951, B in 1952 and C must be stored in 1953. For illustrative purposes, we will let A = 0000000005 + and B = 0000000007+.

Location	Operation	Data Address	M Register	A Register	Remarks
0100	RDC	1951	0000000000+	0000000000+	Read
0101	RAA	1951	0000000000+	0000000005+	Compute
0102	ADA	1952	0000000000+	0000000012+	C
0103	STA	1953	0000000000+	0000000012+	Store
0104	PRT	1951	0000000000+	0000000012+	Print
0105	BRU	0100	0000000000+	0000000012+	Return

It is obvious that several arbitrary decisions were made when the above program was written. For example, B could have been added before A, or we could have used the same input area and another area for output. It should be noted that if we were accumulating results from several cards in the output area, it would be necessary to use a separate block from which to print.

Since the above program is so short, it will operate at the maximum input-output speed, so there is little chance that we could write an inefficient program for this problem even if we tried. However, in the usual practical problem there are many possible variations that will accomplish the desired result, some of which may be more efficient, or more elegant, than others. A really creative programmer will succeed in producing an efficient program, not one which merely *works*. Frequently, improvements in a program will require changes in the block diagram or even in the overall procedure involving several machine runs.

Multiplication and Shifting

In the preceding operations the M register and the A register have operated completely independently; however, they will work together in many of the operations in this section. One reason for this is the fact that the product of two 10-digit numbers can be a 20-digit number. In multiplication the first (lower) factor is called the *multiplier,* the second (upper) factor is called the *multiplicand,* and the result is called the *product.*

19 MPY (Multiply). This operation causes the multiplicand (obtained from the data address location) to be multiplied by the multiplier (which must be in the M register) to form a 20-digit product which appears with the proper sign in the M register and the A register, replacing the previous contents of these registers. The high-order 10 positions of the 20-digit product appear in the M register, replacing the multiplier, while the low order 10 positions of the product replace the previous contents of the A register. The signs of both the M and the A register are the same as the sign of the product.[11]

It should be noted that it usually requires two program steps to accomplish a multiplication: one to place the multiplier in the M register and the second to perform the multiplication. If we wish to multiply A (located in 0100) by B (located in 0101) and store the result, C, in 0102, the program in the example below would be satisfactory (supposing that 0000000027+ is in 0100 and that 0000000062+ is in 0101).

---

[11] The sign rule in multiplication is simple. The product of two numbers with the same sign is positive; the product of two numbers with unlike signs is negative.

Location	Operation	Data Address	M Register	A Register
0976	LDM	0100	0000000027+	unchanged
0977	MPY	0101	0000000000+	0000001674+
0978	STA	0102	0000000000+	0000001674+

If the numbers multiplied in the example above had been 2700000000+ and 6200000000+, the result appearing in the M register would have been 1674000000+, and the A register would contain 0000000000+. If the numbers had been 0012345678− and 0094271365+, the result in the M register would have been 0000116384− and the A register would contain 3916910470−. In this latter case, it would have required both a Store M register and a Store A register instruction to save the entire result. The contents of the M register (with its sign) might have been stored in 0102, while the contents of the A register (with its sign) might have been stored in 0103.

It may interest you to know that the MAC multiplies by repeated addition, one multiplier digit at a time, starting with the high-order position of the M register. First the multiplicand is placed in the memory register and the A register is cleared. Then the M register and the A register are coupled and shifted left one position, thus shifting the high order digit out of the M register and into a special storage position, where it is analyzed, and the multiplicand is added from the memory register into the A register the number of times indicated by the digit being analyzed. (Any carries that occur in this addition process are added to the low-order position of the M register which has been cleared by the left shift.)

The M register and the A register are then shifted one more place to the left, with the upper position of the A register being shifted into the lower position of the M register. The next digit is analyzed, the multiplicand is added into the A register the proper number of times, and overflows are added to the M register. After ten such shifts, all 10 digits of the multiplier have been analyzed and the partial product obtained from the high-order digit has been shifted 9 places into the M register. This process is illustrated in detail in Figure 6–18. In this example the multiplier is 2700000004+, the multiplicand is 6200000000+, and the resulting product is 16740000024800000000+.

We ordinarily multiply by starting with the right-hand digit of the

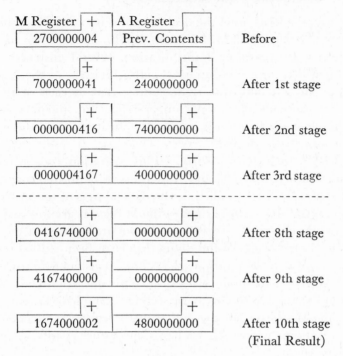

M Register │ + │	A Register │ │	
2700000004	Prev. Contents	Before

+	+	
7000000041	2400000000	After 1st stage

+	+	
0000000416	7400000000	After 2nd stage

+	+	
0000004167	4000000000	After 3rd stage

- -

+	+	
0416740000	0000000000	After 8th stage

+	+	
4167400000	0000000000	After 9th stage

+	+	
1674000002	4800000000	After 10th stage (Final Result)

FIG. 6–18

Example of How the MAC Multiplies

multiplier and proceeding to the left. In some parts of Europe, however, everyone multiplies by starting with the left-most digit and proceeding to the right—pretty much as does the MAC. The two procedures give equivalent results, as shown below.

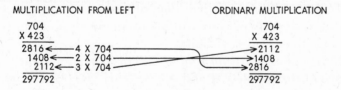

MULTIPLICATION FROM LEFT   ORDINARY MULTIPLICATION

```
    704                                704
  X 423                              X 423
  2816 ←——4 X 704————————————————→2112
  1408 ←——2 X 704————————————————→1408
  2112 ←——3 X 704————————————————→2816
297792                             297792
```

The time required to multiply depends upon the number of additions, which is determined by the sum of the digits in the M register. For example, a multiplier of 195 would require $1 + 9 + 5 = 15$ additions, while a multiplier of 1020000000 would require only $1 + 2 = 3$ additions. Therefore, to achieve maximum speed, the factor whose digits will average to the smallest sum should be used in the M register as the multiplier.

Although we have so far ignored its influence in the arithmetic operations, the location of the decimal point is extremely important. In order to properly align the decimal point and to drop or round unnecessary figures after multiplication, several instructions are available which shift the coupled M and A registers, or the A register alone, to the left or to the right. Notice that in each of these instructions the data address no longer refers to a memory location (since no memory location is involved), but it indicates the number of positions to be shifted.

30 LRS (Long Right Shift). This operation code causes the contents of the coupled M and A registers to be shifted to the right the number of places specified by the data address of the instruction. All numbers shifted off the right of the M register are inserted in the upper positions of the A register, and zeros are inserted at the left of the M register to replace the digits that have been shifted away. A shift of more than 19 positions clears both registers to zeros. A data address of zero will produce no shift. This operation code is illustrated in Example 6–16. As can be seen in Example 6–17, neither the sign of the M register nor the sign of the A register is affected by the shift operations, which can lead to some weird results when these two signs differ.

35 LLS (Long Left Shift). This operation code causes the contents of the coupled M and A registers to be shifted to the left the number of places specified by the data address of the instruction. All numbers shifted off the left end of the M register are lost, digits are shifted from the high-order positions of the A register into the low-order positions of the M register, and zeros are inserted at the right end of the A register to replace numbers that are shifted to the left. Again, a shift of more than 19 positions sets the registers to zeros, and a data address of zero will result in no shift. Example 6–18 illustrates the Long Left Shift.

31 LSR (Long Shift and Round). This operation code causes the contents of the coupled M and A registers to be shifted right, as in the Long Right Shift. However, to compensate for the digits thus dropped, a 5 is added (with a plus sign if the A register is positive and a minus sign if the A register is negative) to the number in the last position that was dropped because of the shift. Thus, if the highest-order digit dropped is a 5, or greater, an overflow increases the resulting units digit by 1; if the highest-order digit lost is 4 or less, no overflow will occur and the units position of the result will not be affected. Examples 6–19 and 6–20 illustrate the Long Shift and Round instruction.

Example Number	Operation	Data Address	M Register	A Register
6–16	LRS	0003	0000012345 − 0000000012 −	0345436724 − 3450345436 −
6–17	LRS	0003	0000012345 − 0000000012 −	0345436724 + 3450345436 +
6–18	LLS	0007	6789012345 + 3459876543 +	9876543211 + 2110000000 +
6–19	LSR	0005	0057233119 − 0000000572 −	0023447632 − 3311900234 −
6–20	LSR	0005	0000000027 + 0000000000 +	3425961234 + 0002734260 +
6–21	ARS	0003	0000012345 − 0000012345 −	0345436724 − 0000345436 −
6–22	ALS	0007	6789012345 + 6789012345 +	9976543211 + 2110000000 +
6–23	ASR	0005	0057233119 − 0057233119 −	0023447632 − 0000000234 −

The following three instructions shift the A register alone and do not affect the contents of the M register.

32 ARS (A Register Right Shift). This operation code causes the contents of the A register to be shifted to the right the number of places specified by the data address of the instruction. It is similar to the Long Right Shift instruction, except that only the A register is affected. This instruction is illustrated in Example 6–21, which is similar to Example 6–16.

33 ALS (A Register Left Shift). This operation code causes the contents of the A register to be shifted to the left the number of places specified by the data address of the instruction. It is similar to the Long Left Shift, except that it affects only the A register. This instruction is illustrated by Example 6–22, which is similar to Example 6–18.

34 ASR (A Register Shift and Round). This operation code causes the contents of the A register to be shifted right the number of places specified by the data address of the instruction. As in the Long Shift and Round instruction, to compensate for the digits thus dropped, a 5 is added (with a plus sign if the A register is positive and a minus sign if the A register is negative) to the number in the last position dropped because of the shift. This operation is illustrated in Example 6–23, which is similar to Example 6–19.

Multiplication with Decimals

The MAC computes as though the decimal point in the numbers were at the extreme right. In other words, it handles numbers as though they were integers, and we must make allowance in our program for the proper placing of the decimal point. Notice in the following discussion that the decimal point never explicitly appears in the memory of the machine, but we must know where the decimal should appear in each number, and we must program the machine so that the results will appear in the desired form.

Let us consider an example of multiplication with decimals. Suppose that we have a number of cards in which are punched the numbers A and B. A has the form xxx.xx and B has the form x.xxx. We would like to find their product, C, and punch it into a card, saving only two decimal places. In this discussion, the number of x's involved denotes the maximum size that the numbers can assume. For example, xxx.xx represents any number between 000.00 and 999.99.

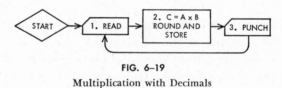

FIG. 6–19

Multiplication with Decimals

The placement of a decimal point in multiplication is quite simple: the maximum number of figures in a result is the sum of the maximum number of figures that can be in each of the factors, and the decimal point is placed by counting the total number of digits to the right of the decimal point in the two factors and placing the decimal point the resulting number of places from the right end of the answer. Thus, A × B would have the form xxxx.xxxxx. Again, this symbolism only indicates that the resulting number will be between 0000.00000 and 9999.99999. Thus, we see that this result must be rounded by dropping three positions.

If we desire to punch A, B, and C into the output card, the block diagram shown in Figure 6–19 would be satisfactory. Assume that we wire the control panel so that A enters the first word of the buffer and B enters the second word of the buffer, and that we wire the output part of the control panel so that A is punched from the first word, B is punched from the second word, and C is punched from the third word of the output buffer. One satisfactory program for this problem is shown below as Example 6–24. For purposes of illustration, let A = 23.46 and B = 1.225. Again, note that although we include the decimal points on our program form for our own convenience, they do not appear in the memory or the registers of the machine.

Example 6–24

Location	Operation	Data Address	M Register	A Register
0001	RDC	1951		
0002	LDM	1952	0000001.225+	
0003	MPY	1951	0000000000+	00028.73850+
0004	LSR	0003	0000000000+	00000028.74+
0005	STA	1953	0000000000+	00000028.74+
0006	PCD	1951	0000000000+	00000028.74+
0007	BRU	0001	0000000000+	00000028.74+

Since we know that the size of the product cannot exceed 9 significant digits, we could have used the A register Shift and Round in step four in Example 6–24 instead of the Long Shift and Round instruction.

Division

Among the arithmetic operations, division is by far the most troublesome to both the mathematician and the computer programmer. The mathematician must always guard against the possibility of dividing by zero.[12] The machine programmer must likewise guard against this possibility, but he must also be certain that the size of the result of a division does not exceed the limits specified by the design of the machine. Specifically, any quotient that has more than 10 digits is essentially equivalent to infinity to the MAC.

---

[12] As an example of the difficulties that may arise, there is a well-known "proof" that two equals one.

(1) Let	$a = b$	
(2)	$a^2 = ab$	(multiplying both sides by a)
(3)	$a^2 - b^2 = ab - b^2$	(subtracting b^2 from both sides)
(4)	$(a - b)(a + b) = b(a - b)$	(factoring both sides)
(5)	$a + b = b$	(cancelling the factor $a - b$)
(6)	$b + b = b$	(substituting b for a)
(7)	$2b = b$	
(8)	$2 = 1$	(dividing both sides by b)

Of course, in step 5, when we cancelled the factor $(a - b)$, we were actually dividing by $(a - b)$, and, since $a = b$, we were dividing by zero.

14 DIV (Divide). This operation code causes a 20-digit dividend—whose upper 10 positions are located in the M register and whose lower 10 positions are in the A register—to be divided by a 10-digit divisor whose location is given by the data address of the instruction. The resulting quotient appears in the A register (with its proper sign) and the remainder appears in the M register (also with its proper sign).[13] If the A and M registers have different signs before division, the sign of the A register is taken as the sign of the dividend.

In order to prevent the development of a quotient of more than 10 positions, *the portion of the dividend that is located in the M register must be smaller than the divisor* in absolute value. If this rule is violated, or if division by zero is attempted, a quotient overflow will occur, the A and the M registers will be set to zero, and the quotient overflow indicator will be set. This indicator can be tested by a Branch instruction, which will be discussed later in this chapter, and corrective action can be taken or the machine can be stopped.

Notice in Example 6–25 that the MAC does not automatically add zeros to obtain more decimal places in the quotient—it merely leaves the remainder in the M register so that it can be used. Example 6–26 illustrates that the signs of the remainder and the quotient can be different, while Example 6–27 must be worked out by long division, using a 20-digit quotient and a 10-digit divisor (note that if the nine zeros are cancelled off the end of the two numbers, the resulting remainder will be incorrect). Example 6–28 shows how a violation of the rule that the divisor must exceed the portion of the dividend in the M register leads to a quotient overflow condition.

One of the interesting aspects of division is that it is easy to determine the number of *decimal places* that will be found in the quotient, but it is difficult to determine the exact number of *figures* in the quotient. The number of decimals in the quotient may be found by subtracting the number of decimal places in the divisor from the number of decimal places in the dividend. This is equivalent to the rule for marking off the decimal place in the process of long division. However we must remember that the MAC does not

---

[13] The rule for determining signs in division is as follows: (1) The quotient is positive if the divisor and the dividend have the same sign; the quotient is negative if the divisor and the dividend have different signs. (2) The remainder always has the sign of the dividend.

For example, −21 divided by −5 gives a quotient of +4 and a remainder of −1. This may be checked by verifying that −5 times +4 plus −1 equals −21, since A divided by B equals C, with a remainder of R, if and only if A is equal to B times C plus R. Likewise, +21 divided by −5 equals −4 with a remainder of +1.

Example Number	Operation	Contents of Data Address Location	M Register	A Register
6–25		0000000050 +	0000000000 +	0000000627 +
	DIV	0000000050 +	0000000027 +	0000000012 +
6–26		0000000050 −	0000000000 +	0000062730 +
	DIV	0000000050 −	0000000030 +	0000001254 −
6–27		9000000000 +	4570000000 +	0000000000 +
	DIV	9000000000 +	7000000000 +	5077777777 +
6–28		0000000002 +	0000000004 +	4000000000 +
	DIV	0000000002 +	0000000000 +	*0000000000 +

* Quotient overflow indicator set.

automatically add zeros at the right of the dividend, and if we wish more quotient decimal places than this rule produces (or if this rule produces a negative result), it is necessary to insert zeros at the right by shifting the A and M registers to the left before division.

For example, if we wish to divide A = xxxxxx.xx by B = xxxx.xx and produce a quotient, C, rounded to three decimal places, it will be necessary to add zeros to the dividend before dividing. In order to determine how many zeros to add, it is convenient to set up the problem just as you would set it up to divide out by hand:

$$\text{xxxx.xx} \overline{)\, \text{xxxxxx.xx}_{\wedge}0000 } \quad \text{xxx.xxxx}$$

In order to round to three positions, we must produce four, so we must add four zeros to the dividend before dividing. If A is located in 0100, B is located in 0101, and we wish to store C in 0102, the program shown in Example 6–29 below will suffice. In this example, we let A = 140.00 and B = 65.24.

Note that in this example we had to make sure that the M register was cleared to zeros before dividing. This was done in step two by loading the M register from location 1999, which is shown (by the last line in the illustration) to contain ten zeros. These zeros are an important part of the program, and we provide for placing them in location 1999 by writing them on the programming form. They are placed in memory in the same way (and at the same time) that we insert the instructions themselves in the proper locations of memory of the machine—which will be discussed when we describe loading the program.

Example 6–29

Location	Operation	Data Address	M Register	A Register
1001	RAA	0100	0000000005+	00000140.00+
1002	LDM	1999	0000000000+	00000140.00+
1003	LLS	0004	0000000000+	0140.000000+
1004	DIV	0101	0000001484+	000002.1459+
1005	ASR	0001	0000001484+	0000002.146+
1006	STA	0102	0000001484+	0000002.146+
1999	00	00000000+		

Perhaps the basic difficulty with the division process is illustrated by the fact that without additional information we do not know that the result, C, will have only the six figures indicated in the above analysis—the program in Example 6–29 could actually cause a quotient overflow. We must remember that the notation xxxx.xx merely indicates a number between 0000.00 and 9,999.99. If the number B were 0000.32 and the number A were 400,000.00, after shifting left four positions the two left-most positions of A (namely 40) are in the M register, which would exceed the divisor, and a quotient overflow would occur.

In other words, to determine the maximum size of a quotient it is not sufficient to simultaneously consider the maximum divisor and the maximum dividend. We may consider the maximum dividend with the minimum divisor to get an upper limit on the size of the quotient. However, this approach may also be misleading, for the maximum dividend may never occur with the minimum divisor.

This problem is akin to the one we faced in the design of cards, when we had to decide how many digits to include in a given field. Sometimes we have additional information concerning the size of the numbers with which we are working that enables us to determine that the numbers obtained will never be large enough to overflow the A register (or a certain field size). If we have no such additional information, it is necessary to be extremely careful in programming the machine. Occasionally it is necessary to do a division in two steps (utilizing the remainder) to handle cases where a quotient of more than 10 digits might conceivably arise.

In data processing work we are extremely fortunate because we usually have considerable additional information concerning the size of the numbers that can arise. However, in scientific or engineering calculations, which often involve tens of thousands of steps, the scientist frequently knows the size of the numbers he is putting into the calculations and the size of the numbers he will receive as answers, but he often has meager knowledge of the size of the intermediate results obtained in the process of these thousands of computations. In order to handle such situations conveniently, machines designed as scientific computers frequently utilize special circuitry or automatic programming techniques that enable them to operate with "floating decimal" numbers.[14]

An Illustration

In order to illustrate the analytical process of designing a program (and to illustrate some further considerations involved in programming), let us consider the following simple problem. We wish to read cards containing four numbers, and for each card punch a card containing these numbers and their average. In writing this program we will not be concerned with the format of the cards—this is taken care of in wiring the control panel. We will assume that the control panel is wired so that the data will be inserted in the input buffer in the following form:

Word 1.	xxx.xx	1st number (A)
Word 2.	xxx.x	2nd number (B)
Word 3.	xxx.x	3rd number (C)
Word 4.	xxx.xx	4th number (D)

The control panel is wired so that the output must be provided to the output buffer as shown above, with the average of these numbers (rounded to two decimal places) placed as shown below:

| Word 5. | xxx.xx | average |

The initial block diagram for this problem appears to be straightforward and is shown below.

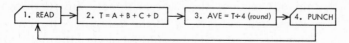

However, when we start to write the program for the second block we run into difficulties because the decimal points do not line up in the

---

[14] Floating decimal notation is discussed in Appendix C.

four numbers. Numbers B and C have one digit to the right of the decimal, while A and D have two digits to the right of the decimal. One way to handle this is to add B and C, shift this sum one place to the left, and then add A and D. Thus we might revise the block diagram as shown below.

This is a simple illustration of the fact that the block diagram may have to be revised when you run into difficulties in writing the program. And the more complicated the program, the more likely that such revisions will be required.

Now, T has the form xxxx.xx. We wish to divide this by 4 and produce a result with three figures after the decimal point, so that we can round. Thus we have the following situation, and we need to shift left one position before dividing:

$$\begin{array}{r} \text{xxx.xxx} \\ \hline 4\,\big|\,\overline{\text{xxxx.xx0}} \end{array}$$

How do we divide by 4? We simply store a 4 in memory as a part of the program, and divide by it as shown in step nine of the program in Example 6–30.

The Read instruction data address of 1900 and the control panel wiring locate the input information as follows. A is in 1900, B is in 1901, C is in 1902, and D is in 1903. If we are to punch from 1900, then the average must be placed in 1904 (to correspond to the fifth word of the output buffer).

Note again that the constants 0 and 4, stored in locations 1999 and 1998, are as much a part of this program as the instructions located in words 0100 through 0112.

BRANCHING INSTRUCTIONS

In the previous sections the basic arithmetic instructions of the MAC were discussed. Frankly, were the computers merely able to perform arithmetic rapidly, they would be of very limited usefulness to the scientist and engineer, and of little interest to those concerned with business data processing. In the following sections some of the logical and decision making capabilities which make these machines such powerful tools for calculation and data processing will be considered.

Example 6–30

Location	Operation	Data Address	M Register	A Register	Remarks
0100	RDC	1900			1. Read
0101	RAA	1901		xxx.x	2. Add B
0102	ADA	1902		xxx.x	B + C
0103	ALS	0001		xxx.x0	
0104	ADA	1900		xxxx.xx	3. Add A
0105	ADA	1903		xxxx.xx	Add D
0106	ALS	0001		xxxx.xx0	4. Shift left
0107	LDM	1999	0000000000		Clear M Reg.
0108	DIV	1998	Remainder	xxx.xxx	Divide
0109	ASR	0001		xxx.xx	Round
0110	STA	1904			Store Average
0111	PCD	1900			5. Punch
0112	BRU	0100			Return to Start
1999	0000000000+				Constant Zero
1998	0000000004+				Constant 4

Among the most important characteristics of the electronic computer is its ability to follow simple yes-or-no decisions. This capability is obtained through the use of branching instructions. Each of these instructions asks a question which can be answered either yes or no. If the answer is no, the normal sequence of instructions is followed by the machine. However, if the answer is yes, the machine executes an alternate sequence of instructions. Thus it is possible to follow different procedures, depending upon the answer to this question.

All of the MAC branching instructions operate in essentially the same way. If the answer to the yes-or-no question is no, the instruction sequence proceeds in the usual way, and the next instruction is taken from the next location in memory If the answer is yes, the location of the next instruction is given by the data address. Thus, if the answer is yes, the Branch instruction operates in the same way as the Branch Unconditionally instruction, with which we are already familiar.

46 BMA (Branch on Minus in the A Register). This instruction causes the MAC to examine the sign of the A register. If the sign is minus, the next instruction is taken from the location given by the data address. If its sign is plus, the next instruction is taken from the next sequential location in memory. The numbers in the A register are ignored. Note that it is possible for the A register sign to be negative while it contains only zeros.

As an illustration of the use of branching instructions, suppose we are using the MAC to maintain finished goods inventory records. We will only consider a small part of the program, and assume that the item number, the on-hand balance for the item, the order number, and the amount ordered are available in the memory. We wish to check to see if there is enough on hand, and if so, to ship it. If not, we wish to go to a back-order procedure. This situation might be handled as shown in the partial block diagram in Figure 6–20. Notice

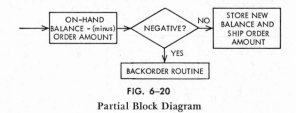

FIG. 6–20

Partial Block Diagram

that diamond-shaped blocks are used to indicate decision points in our block diagrams.

Let us assume that the on-hand balance (98, for example) is in location 1200, the order amount (35, for example) is in location 1201; and we wish to store the new balance (if not negative) in 1200. Also assume that we have decided to place the first word of the backorder routine in location 0200. Then we might write the pro-

Example 6–31

Location	Operation	Data Address	M Register	A Register
0100	RAA	1200		0000000098+
0101	SUA	1201		0000000063+
0102	BMA	(0200)*		0000000063+
0103	STA	1200		0000000063+

*See page 4 of program.

gram shown in Example 6–31. Notice that the data address of the BMA instruction is circled. This indicates to someone reading the program that the instruction to be executed may not be the next instruction written on the programming form. If the program is lengthy, it is helpful to indicate (as shown by the asterisk) where the instruction referred to by this address may be found.

It should be observed in Example 6–31 that if the on-hand balance were 20 and the order amount were 35, then the instruction in location 0103 would not be executed; the machine instead would go to location 0200 and execute the backorder routine.

45 BZA (Branch on Zero in the A Register). This operation code causes the machine to examine the entire A register. If the A register is zero, the next instruction is taken from the location specified by the data address. If any number other than zero is in the A register, the next instruction is taken from the next sequential location in memory. The A register sign is not considered in this instruction.

End-of-File Detection

When we discussed the Read Card instruction we indicated that when there are no more cards to be processed the operator terminates the job by depressing the End-of-File button on the card reader. Depressing this button turns on the End-of-File Card indicator *after* the last card has been read. This indicator can be interrogated by the following instruction.

49 BEC (Branch End-of-File Card). This operation code examines the End-of-File Card indicator. If this indicator is on, it is turned off and the next instruction is taken from the location given by the data address. If this indicator is not on, the next instruction is taken from the next sequential location in memory.

In our previous programs we have not used the Branch End-of-File Card instruction because the machine automatically stops when it attempts to read another card (execute a Read Card instruction) *after* the last card has been read. However, if we wish to take special action after all cards have been processed, this instruction is most useful (as will be illustrated in the following section).

In order to stop the machine when we wish, we need the following instruction.

01 HLT (Halt). This instruction causes the machine to stop. The data address of this instruction has no influence on the machine's operation, but may be observed on the control console of the machine and used to indicate which Halt instruction caused the machine to stop.

Programming Group Control

A frequent problem in data processing is that of determining whether the transaction just read pertains to the same man-number, account number, or item number as the previous transaction. This situation (which is handled so simply and neatly by group control on the punched card accounting machine) must be handled by programming in an electronic computer.

For example, suppose we wish to use the MAC to prepare a summary report of total hours worked on each job as though the MAC were a punched card accounting machine. We have a set of punched card labor tickets containing job number and hours which we wish to summarize by job number. As we will see later, it is possible to take other approaches to this problem, but when using the MAC in the same way that we use the accounting machine, our first step would be to sort these cards into job number sequence, thus grouping together all the cards pertaining to each job. Then we would process these cards through the MAC and print a line for each job containing job number and total hours.

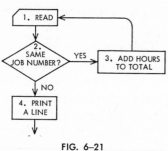

FIG. 6–21

Initial Partial Block Diagram

Here, for the first time, we are faced with a problem for which the block diagram is not immediately obvious, although the basic approach is relatively straightforward. For each card that is read, we must ask the question: Is this card for the same job? If the answer is yes, then we should add these hours to the total. If the answer is no, we should print a line for the job that was just processed. This partial block diagram is shown in Figure 6–21.

In this situation it is apparent that we can ask if this is the same job number by subtracting the job number of the card just read from the previous job number and using the *Branch on Zero in the A Register* (BZA) instruction. Although we would like to maintain the total hours in the A register, this is impossible because we must also use the A register to determine whether this is the same job number. Thus it is necessary to use a memory location (say 1971) to perform the functions of a punched card counter by reset adding the contents of 1971 into the A register, adding hours from the current card, and storing the result back in 1971, where it will be available for printing. This process is illustrated diagramatically in Figure 6–22. Note that because we are accumulating hours from several cards we are unable to print from the card input area.

What do we do after we print the total? Our first temptation is to take an arrow back to block 1, but upon analysis we find that this would cause the first card of each group to be ignored. We wish to process this card, but we do not wish to do it by going to block 3, since this would add the hours from the first card of the new group to the total hours for the previous group. Thus we are led merely to store the job number (in 1970) for printing and to store hours from the card (in 1971) to start the new group. Incidentally, storing the

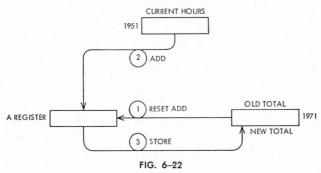

FIG. 6–22

Accumulating Totals in Memory

new job number makes it available for comparison when we read the next card.

One question still remains: How do we get started? If we start with block 1 on the first card, there is no previous job number to compare with, and we would progress along the "no" branch and print an extraneous line. A more desirable solution would be achieved by starting as shown in the diagram of Figure 6–23.

Finally, we must recognize that the block diagram in Figure 6–23 will not print the total for the last job number. After the last card has been read and processed, the machine attempts to read another card. Since there are no more cards, the machine stops without printing the total. This can be avoided by inserting a block after block 3 that asks: Is this End-of-File? This is shown in Figure 6–24, along with a rearrangement and renumbering of the blocks so that the diagram is simpler and more understandable.

A possible program for this problem is given in Example 6–32. For

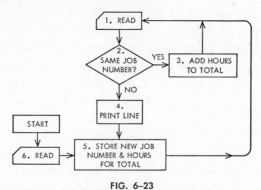

FIG. 6-23
Intermediate Block Diagram

illustrative purposes, we assume two input cards. The first card has job number 123 (wired through the control panel into the first word of the input buffer) and 32.4 hours (placed in input word 2); the second card also has job number 123 but with 16.3 hours. We have arbitrarily allocated memory so that we start our program in location 0101, and we use the block 1950 through 1969 for input and the block from 1970 through 1989 for output storage.

As we write this program, everything is relatively routine until we reach the sixth instruction. At this point we do not know what to use

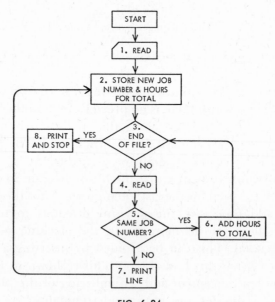

FIG. 6-24
Block Diagram for Group Control

Example 6–32

Location	Operation	Data Address	M Register	A Register	Remarks
0101	RDC	1950	0000000123+		1. Read
0102	LDM	1950	0000000123+		2. Store Job No.
0103	STM	1970	0000000123+		and Hours for
0104	LDM	1951	000000032.4+		Total
0105	STM	1971	000000032.4+		
0106	BEC	⟨0117⟩	000000032.4+		3. End-of-File?
0107	RDC	1950	000000032.4+		4. Read
0108	RAA	1950	000000032.4+	0000000123+	5. Same Job No.?
0109	SUA	1970	000000032.4+	0000000000+	
0110	BZA	⟨0113⟩	000000032.4+	0000000000+	
0111	PRT	1970			7. Print
0112	BRU	⟨0102⟩			Go to 0102
0113	RAA	1971	000000032.4+	000000032.4+	6. Add Hours to
0114	ADA	1951	000000032.4+	000000048.7+	Total
0115	STA	1971	000000032.4+	000000048.7+	
0116	BRU	⟨0106⟩	000000032.4+	000000048.7+	Go to 0106
0117	PRT	1977			8. Print
0118	HLT	0001			Stop

for the data address of the Branch on End-of-File Card (BEC) instruction, for we must decide where to locate the ending instructions of the program. This can be an arbitrary decision, for it makes little difference where it is located. However, if we wish to make the program as compact as possible so that it will fit in a small block of memory, it is possible to leave out this data address and proceed with writing the rest of the program. When we complete this process we know that location 0117 can be used to start the terminating steps of the program, so we go back and insert 0117 as the data address of the instruction located in 0106. A similar comment applies to the instruction in location 0110. Again, the circled addresses indicate possible deviations in the sequence of execution of the instructions as compared with the sequence in which they are written on the programming form.

The above illustration can be generalized to provide both an intermediate and a minor total on the report. Suppose the cards contain department number as well as job number and hours. If we sort the cards first on job number and then on department number, we can produce a report with a total for each job, and then a total of the hours for each job in each department (as shown in Chapter 3 in Figure 3–24). For simplicity, let us modify this so that the department number is repeated on each minor total line, and let us also eliminate the cost column.

One block diagram (of many possible ones) for this program is shown in Figure 6–25. It should be noted that this block diagram was

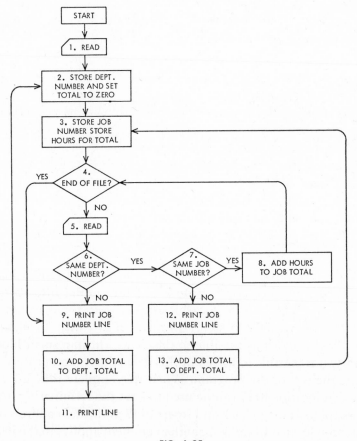

FIG. 6–25
Two-Level Group Control

not just written down as it is but represents the result of considerable trial and error. Such a block diagram should be tested with a sequence of transaction cards to see if it handles each condition properly.

The End of File test is worth a little discussion. When the last card is read it is processed as part of the old group or as the first card of a new group. Then, before reading a new card, we Branch on End-of-File Card, skip the Read Card instruction, print a job total and department total, and go back to block 2. Blocks 2 and 3 store information from the last card (which will never be used), and when we reach block 4 the End-of-File indicator is off, so the machine stops when it attempts to read the next card. Thus we do not need a Halt instruction, and can use blocks 9, 10, and 11 as our End-of-File routine instead of writing them again with a Halt instruction following them.

Overflow Detection

As mentioned in our discussion of the Add and Subtract instructions, an overflow out of the upper position of the A register is lost, except that it turns on the overflow indicator. Subsequent overflows after the indicator is turned on do not affect the indicator (unless in the meantime it has been turned off).

47 BOV (*Branch on Overflow*). This operation code causes the machine to examine the overflow indicator. If the overflow indicator is *on*, the Branch on Overflow instruction causes the next instruction to be taken from the location given by the data address, and it also turns off the overflow indicator. If the overflow indicator is *off*, the next instruction is taken from the next sequential memory location.

An overflow may occur inadvertently because of errors in the program logic or input data, or it may be a normally expected event used by the programmer in the logical design of his program. If one wishes to be aware of each overflow that occurs, it is obvious that a Branch on Overflow instruction should be given after each addition that could cause an overflow. Otherwise, more than one overflow might occur between branching instructions.

For example, if in the illustration shown in Figure 6–24 and Example 6–32 we want to make sure that the total hours never exceed a ten-digit number, we could insert a block between blocks 6 and 3 in Figure 6–24 that would ask the question: Overflow? The "yes" branch would lead to some type of exception routine and the "no" branch would lead to block 3. In the program in Example 6–32 we would merely need to insert a single Branch on Overflow (BOV) instruction after the instruction in location 0114 (or, for that matter, after the instruction in location 0115) with a data address designating the beginning of the exception routine.

As was mentioned in connection with the description of the Divide instruction, a quotient overflow sets a quotient overflow indicator similar to the overflow indicator discussed above.

48 BQO (Branch on Quotient Overflow). This operation code causes the machine to examine the quotient overflow indicator. If the quotient overflow indicator is on, the Branch on Quotient Overflow instruction causes the next instruction to be taken from the location given by the data address, and it also resets the quotient overflow indicator. If the quotient overflow indicator is off, the next instruction is taken from the next sequential location in memory.

Loading the Program

As we consider the use of a computer in which the instructions to be executed are stored in the memory of the machine, the question naturally arises of how these instructions and the necessary constants are entered into the memory. The process of entering the program into the memory of a machine is called *loading* the program. A simple method of loading the MAC involves the use of single-word load cards, illustrated in Figure 6–26.

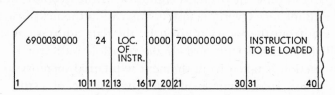

FIG. 6–26

Single-Word Load Card

When the program written on the planning chart is presented to the key punch operator she inserts single-word load cards into the key punch. These cards are prepunched as follows:

Columns 1 through 10 are punched with 6900030000;

Columns 11 and 12 are punched 24;

Columns 17 through 20 are punched 0000;

Columns 21 through 30 are prepunched with 7000000000.

For each line on the coding sheet the key punch operator produces a load card which contains (in addition to the prepunched information) the memory location of the instruction to be entered, which she punches into columns 13 through 16, and the instruction to be loaded, which is punched into columns 31 through 40. All of these cards are identified as load cards by a Y punch in a specified column (for example, column 1).

Of course, the program-drum card of the key punch controls the skipping of the cards, so that when the card is fed into the machine it immediately skips to column 13, and after column 16 has been punched, the card automatically skips to column 31.

After the cards for a program have been key-punched, they are placed in the read-feed of the machine, and the load button on the console of the MAC is depressed. This button causes the machine to read one card into locations 0000 through 0019 and to go to location 0000 for the next instruction. The Y punch in column 1, desig-

Location	Operation	Data Address	Indicator	M Register
0000	LDM	0003	0000	Instruction to be loaded
0001	STM	XXXX	0000	Instruction to be loaded
0002	RDC	0000	0000	
0003	Instruction to be loaded			

FIG. 6–27

Single-Card Loading Routine

nating a load card, causes this card to be read into memory column by column; that is to say that column 1 of the card is read into the first position of the first buffer word, column 2 goes into the second position, and so on through column 80, which goes into the low-order position of the eighth word of the buffer.

Now let us examine what is in memory at this time. Consider Figure 6–27, where this information is presented as on a programming form. It is apparent that we have a small program in memory. The first instruction (in location 0000) loads the M register with the instruction which was punched in columns 31 through 40 of the load card just read. The next instruction in the program (located in 0001) stores the instruction to be loaded from the M register into the proper word of memory as indicated by the key punch operator when she punched the location of the instruction into columns 13 through 16. Finally, the instruction in word 0002 reads the next card, and, since it is a load card (and the Read Card instruction also branches on a load card), the program branches and returns to 0000 for the next instruction. This sequence is repeated until every instruction in the program has been loaded.

A transfer card, prepunched with 40YYYY0000 in columns 1 through 10, can be added as the last card of the program deck. When this card is read and the machine executes the instruction in columns 1 through 10, a BRU instruction is executed whose data address is YYYY. Of course, YYYY specifies the location of the first instruction of the program that is to be executed. Thus input data cards can follow the program deck, and the machine immediately executes the program that has just been loaded.

The single-word loading routine described above is simple and convenient for checking out programs. However, to conserve punched-

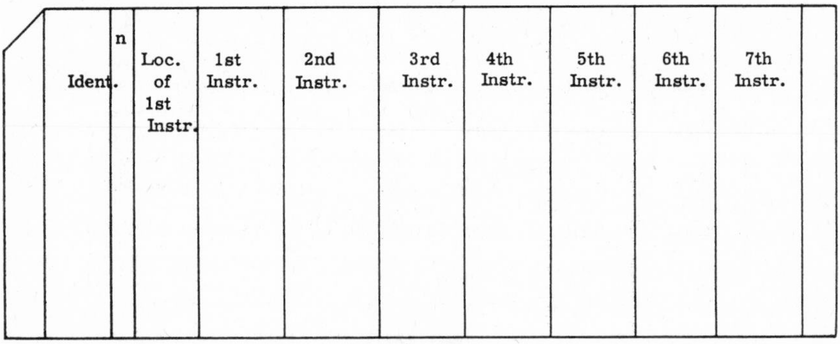

	n	Loc. of 1st Instr.	1st Instr.	2nd Instr.	3rd Instr.	4th Instr.	5th Instr.	6th Instr.	7th Instr.	
Ident.										

FIG. 6–28
Multiple-Word Load Card

card file storage space and machine loading time it is desirable to have routines which load several instructions from each card. A card form for a routine that will load up to seven words from each card is illustrated in Figure 6–28, where n is the number of instructions $(n \leqq 7)$ to be loaded from the card. Loading routines exist which read such cards as input data and move the instructions contained in them into the proper locations of memory. Of course, such a loading routine would have to be entered into the memory of the MAC through use of single-card loaders before the program itself could be loaded.

As was mentioned previously, programs are originally punched into single-card loaders, and the errors in the program are detected and corrected in this form. After the program is ready to be used in a routine fashion, it can be condensed into seven instructions per card by means of automatic conversion routines which read the single card loaders into the MAC and punch out loading cards in the condensed form.

Control Words

In punched card equipment, X punches are used to distinguish one type of card from another and (with the use of selectors) to process them differently. In the MAC, alphabetic characters translate into two-digit numbers, and for all characters involving an X-zone punch (J through R and the X punch itself) the left-hand digit is a 7. Thus, if there is an X punch in a column that is treated as alphabetic information, it will be translated into a two-digit number whose left-hand digit is 7. And if there is no X punch in the column, the left-hand digit will *not* be a 7.

When several different types of cards are used in a given procedure, each column that might have a distinguishing X punch may be wired into a position of a single alphabetic input word (usually the twentieth) called the *control word*. Likewise, through control panel wiring, 7s in the proper positions of an output word may be used to make X punches in the output cards.

We have already mentioned that the Xs in the card may also be used to control selectors, which vary the control panel wiring upon entry, so that the information on each card form is entered into the most convenient positions of the input storage words. Likewise, the 7s in the proper position of word 20 of output storage (which can be translated into Xs in the card) can also be used to vary the format of the output. Thus, in effect, a separate control panel is available for each type of input and output card. This ability to vary the format on input and output reduces the amount of rearrangement of information that must be programmed.

In order to determine the type of card that has been read, and to branch to the proper part of the program to handle this type of card, the control word is entered into the A register, shifted left, and then right, to eliminate all digits of the control word except the position in which a 7 would indicate an X. Then we subtract a 7 and use a Branch on Zero in the A register to test whether or not this position is zero.[15]

Suppose, for example, we have cards in our procedure that may be

---

[15] After we have studied the use of the indicator positions of the instruction, this shifting back and forth (to eliminate the other digits of the control word) will not be necessary.

punched with Xs in columns 40, 50, and 75. We may set the control word up as indicated in Figure 6–29, where the position designated by A indicates an X in column 50, the B position indicates an X in column 75, and the C position indicates an X in column 40. Then, if we read a card with an X in column 75 but no X in 40 or 50, this control word would have a 7 in the B position and *other* than a 7 in the A and C positions. If, on the other hand, the card had an X in column 40 and an X in column 50, the control word would have 7s in the A and C positions.

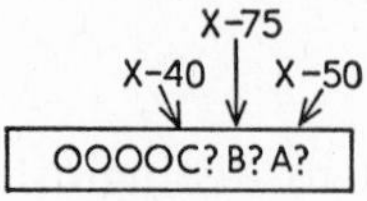

X–75
X–40   X–50
|OOOOC?B?A?|

FIG. 6–29
Control Word

SUMMARY

At this point we complete our detailed study of the *basic* operation codes available in the MAC computer. Because they will allow us to perform any procedure that we *can* perform with this machine, these instructions are complete in themselves. Later, however, in connection with the discussion of the use of the last four digits of the instruction, we will consider some further operation codes that make it easier to perform some of the operations described in the next chapter.

Also, it should be noted that we have been relatively restrained in our choice of operations for the MAC, for we could easily have added a number of obvious operations to our repertoire. For example, we could have introduced a Branch on Plus or a Branch on Nonzero instruction; and we could have had instructions that would add into the M register and subtract from it, and instructions that would branch on the M register. Many machines have such instructions, making it easier to write certain programs. They also sometimes allow the programmer to use fewer instructions and thus produce more efficient programs. However, in our situation they would simply add to the number of operations that need to be learned and remembered, and thus add to our already considerable burdens in this respect.

The basic motivation for our discussion of the MAC instructions and their use has been to obtain an understanding of the stored program, its capabilities and limitations, and the considerations involved in programming. In addition to the machine instructions themselves, we have found that we must concentrate a substantial portion of our attention upon the logical problems associated with analyzing the situation and expressing it in terms of a block diagram.

EXERCISES

In the following problems, the first line indicates the contents of the registers before the instruction is executed. In the second line, fill in the contents of the registers as they would be after the indicated instruction has been executed.

Exercise Number	Operation	Contents of Data Address Location	M Register	A Register
6.1	66-RSA	0000000044 −	0000000009 +	0000066666 +
6.2	15-ADA	0000000066 −	0000000099 −	0000000077 +
6.3	16-SUA	0000000066 +	0000000099 −	0000000077 +
6.4	16-SUA	0000000066 −	0000000099 +	0000000077 +
6.5	16-SUA	0000000066 +	0000000099 +	0000000055 +
6.6	15-ADA	0000000066 +	0000000099 −	0000000066 −
6.7	15-ADA	0006666666 +	0000000099 +	9997777777 +
6.8	69-LDM	0000000066 −	0000000099 +	0000000055 +
6.9	24-STM	0000000066 −	0000000099 −	0000000055 +
6.10	19-MPY	0000000008 +	0000000006 −	0000000055 +
6.11	19-MPY	0000008000 −	0000060000 −	0000000055 +
6.12	19-MPY	8000000000 +	6000000000 −	0000000000 +
6.13	14-DIV	0000000003 +	0000000000 +	0000000007 +
6.14	14-DIV	0000000003 −	0000000000 +	0000000007 +
6.15	14-DIV	0000000003 +	0000000000 −	7000000000 −
6.16	14-DIV	3000000000 +	0700000000 +	0000000002 +
6.17	14-DIV	3000000000 −	7000000000 −	0020000000 −
6.18	14-DIV	3000000000 −	0000000700 −	0000000002 +

Exercise Number	Operation	Data Address	M Register	A Register
6.19	35-LLS	0015	2222222222 +	3333333333 +
6.20	30-LRS	0003	2222222222 −	3333333333 +
6.21	31-LSR	0007	0000012345 −	6789012345 −
6.22	31-LSR	0007	0000012345 +	4321012345 −
6.23	32-ARS	0015	2222222222 +	3333333333 +
6.24	33-ALS	0003	2222222222 +	3333333333 −
6.25	34-ASR	0007	0000012345 −	6789012345 −

In the following exercises, prepare a block diagram and write a program to accomplish the desired results. You may use operation abbreviations rather than the numeric operation codes when writing these programs.

6.26 We have a group of time cards in which are punched man-number, regular hours, and overtime hours. The control panel is wired so that these are entered into the buffer in the following form:

Man-Number	00000xxxxx	Word 1
Regular Hours	0000000xx.x	Word 2
Overtime Hours	00000000x.x	Word 3

For each such card we wish to punch a card containing man-number and total hours. The control panel is wired so that we must punch the information from the buffer in the following form:

Word 1	00000xxxxx	Man-Number
Word 2	0000000xx.x	Total Hours

At what speed would this program cause the MAC to read cards?

6.27 Suppose that the input cards in Exercise 6.26 also contain the regular hourly rate, and that the control panel is wired so as to place it in the fourth word of the input buffer in the form x.xx. For each such card we wish to print a line with man-number, regular hours, and regular pay (regular hours times regular hourly rate, rounded to the nearest cent). The control panel is wired so that we must print the information from the buffer in the following form:

Word 1	00000xxxxx	Man-Number
Word 2	0000000xx.x	Regular Hours
Word 3	00000xxx.xx	Regular Pay

6.28   Given the input cards in Exercise 6.27, and assuming that we pay time and a half for overtime, we wish to print a line for each man containing his man-number, regular hours, overtime hours, and total gross pay. The control panel is wired so that we must print the information from the buffer in the following form:

Word 1	00000xxxxx	Man-Number
Word 2	0000000xx.x	Regular Hours
Word 3	00000000x.x	Overtime Hours
Word 4	00000xxx.xx	Gross Pay

(*Hint:* It will help to store in memory, as a part of the program itself, the constant 1.5. Then gross pay is regular rate times the sum of regular hours and 1.5 times overtime hours.)

6.29   Modify the program in Exercise 6.28 so as also to accumulate gross pay from all the cards in some memory location and print this total at the conclusion of the machine run. (It will be desirable to make sure that this location is cleared to zero before the first card is read.)

6.30   We have a group of cards in which are punched item number, total dollar sales of the item during the first month, total dollar sales of the item during the second month, and total dollar sales of the item during the third month. The control panel is wired so as to enter this information into the input buffer in the following form:

Item Number	0000xxxxxx	Word 1
Sales 1st Month	000xx,xxx.xx	Word 2
Sales 2nd Month	000xx,xxx.xx	Word 3
Sales 3rd Month	000xx,xxx.xx	Word 4

For each item, we wish to punch a card containing item number, average dollar sales for the three months, and percent of the total three-month sales of this item that was sold in each of the three months. You may assume that some of each item was sold. Round these percent calculations to the nearest tenth of a percent.

The control panel is wired so that we must punch the information from the buffer in the following form:

Word 1	0000xxxxxx	Item Number
Word 2	000xx,xxx.xx	Average Sales
Word 3	000000xxx.x	% First Month
Word 4	000000xxx.x	% Second Month
Word 5	000000xxx.x	% Third Month

6.31   Read cards containing an identification number and two quantities, A and B. The control panel is wired so that this information enters the buffer in the following way:

Identification	xxxxxx	Word 1
Quantity A	xxx.xx	Word 2
Quantity B	xxx.xx	Word 3

If A = B, ignore the card. If otherwise, punch an output card in which the identification is punched from word 1 of the buffer and the larger of A and B is punched from word 2 or the buffer.

6.32 Read cards containing an identification number and three quantities: A, B, and C. The control panel is wired so that the information enters the buffer in the following way:

Identification	xxxxxx	Word 1
Quantity A	xxx.xx	Word 2
Quantity B	xxx.xx	Word 3
Quantity C	xxx.xx	Word 4

Punch a card in which the identification is punched from word 1 of the buffer; the largest of A, B, and C is punched from word 2; the middle-sized of A, B, and C is punched from word 3; and the smallest of A, B, and C is punched from word 4.

6.33 Three different types of cards are involved in a MAC procedure: balance cards (X-75), sales cards (X-43), and returns cards (X-50). Prepare a *partial* block diagram that will read a card and direct the program to the balance card routine if the card is a balance card; to the sales card routine if the card is a sales card; and to the returns card routine if the card is a returns card. In this diagram you may use such general questions as: Is this an X-75 card? Do not write the program, but answer the following questions:

  a) What would happen if a card without an X punch came along?
  b) What would happen if a card came along that had an X in 75 and an X in 50?
  c) In what sequence should the questions be asked? Why?
  d) Modify the block diagram to assure that the machine would stop for all possible mistakes, such as those in (*a*) and (*b*).

6.34 Consider cards containing man-number and hours worked. The control panel is wired:

Man-Number	00000xxxxx	Word 1
Hours	0000000xx.x	Word 2

We wish to add up the hours for all these cards and print the total from word 1 of the output buffer.

6.35 Consider the following problem (similar to that of Exercise 6.27). The control panel is wired as shown below:

Man-Number	00000xxxxx	Word 1
Regular Hours	0000000xx.x	Word 2
Regular Rate	0000000x.xx	Word 3

In this problem we may have *several* such cards for each man. Assuming that the cards are sorted in man-number sequence, for each man print one line with the following information:

Word 1	00000xxxxx	Man-Number
Word 2	0000000xx.x	Total Hours
Word 3	00000xxx.xx	Total Pay

Note: Do not neglect to print the information for the last man.

6.36 Modify Exercise 6.35 so as to accumulate total hours and total pay for the entire group of cards. After all the cards are processed, print these totals from buffer words 1 and 2, respectively.

7 BASIC PROGRAMMING CONCEPTS (II)

THE INSTRUCTIONS studied in the previous chapter are adequate for expressing almost any problem that can be solved by the basic MAC. However, we have not yet discussed several important ways in which these basic instructions can be employed. In particular, we have not considered the important concept of instruction modification. In this chapter we will examine some additional programming techniques and introduce some further MAC instructions that, although not absolutely necessary, certainly simplify the programming of many problems and increase speed by reducing the number of instructions that must be executed.

LOOPING

In all of our previous programs we have obtained the repetition that is necessary to justify the use of a computer by returning to the beginning of the program and executing it over again. Thus all our programs could have been considered to be repetitive loops. This concept of looping is an important one in computer programming, and is frequently incorporated in the body of a program to provide subloops within the overall loop of the program.

Count-Controlled Loops

Of course, the most interesting thing about a loop is: How do we get out of it? One important way of determining when to exit from a loop is by planning to execute the loop a specified number of times. Then the program can count the repetitions in order to determine when to terminate the looping process.

In general, a count-controlled loop involves four types of processes, as illustrated in Figure 7–1. The (*a*) and (*b*) versions of this figure are but two possible variations of a general count-controlled loop, for it is possible to rearrange the sequence of the three blocks within the loop in a variety of ways as long as the initialization, modification, and testing are coordinated to achieve the desired results; i.e., to exit from the loop after the proper number of repetitions.

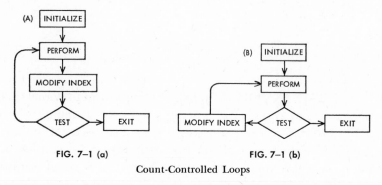

FIG. 7–1 (a)   **FIG. 7–1 (b)**

Count-Controlled Loops

In Figure 7–1 the block labeled Perform is intended to indicate the procedure that we intend to execute repeatedly in the looping process. This block, of course, can indicate a short—or a long and complicated—procedure, depending upon the type of program with which we are concerned.

The block labeled Modify Index denotes the counting process which determines the number of times that the loop has been executed. The block labeled Test works together with the modification block to determine when the proper number of repetitions has been achieved, and it signals the exit from the loop at that time. Of course, if the end of the process has not been reached the test block returns the program to perform the procedure again.

The first block, Initialize, sets up (or resets) the routine to begin the counting process, and it frequently is used to reset to zero words that are used to accumulate totals within the loop and to set up the conditions that are used to test for exit from the loop.

The above discussion has attempted to present the general ideas involved in count-controlled loops, but we may have raised some questions which we have not yet answered. Also, it may not be apparent how we can write a MAC program to accomplish what we have been describing. Let us therefore consider a simple example which will illustrate our concepts.

Suppose that we would like to use the MAC as a modified reproducer to produce a number of duplicates of each of the cards that is read. To be specific, we would like to read a deck of cards, each card containing item number, price, and a number, n. Assuming that n is greater than zero, we would like to punch n duplicates of each of the cards that is read. The control panel is wired to enter the information in the form shown below:

		Input	Output
Item Number	xxxxxx	Word 1	Word 1
Price	xxx.xx	Word 2	Word 2
n	xx	Word 3	

A possible block diagram for this problem is shown in Figure 7–2, which is very similar to Figure 7–1 (b). The block labeled Read and the block which sets $i = 1$ are the initialization portion of the program. The block labeled Punch corresponds to the Perform block in Figure 7–1 (b); block "$i = n$?" corresponds to the Test block; and the block "$i = i + 1$" corresponds to the Modify Index block. Incidentally, the notation "$i = i + 1$" deserves some explanation, for it is obvious that this equality cannot be satisfied for any value of i. However, in our block diagramming conventions, this notation indicates that we substitute $i + 1$ for i in the memory location or register where i is stored.

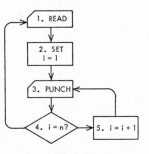

FIG. 7–2

Looping Example
(Counting Upward)

A program corresponding to Figure 7–2 is shown below in Example 7–1. It should be noted that in this program we are using the A register to hold the count "i" and that we are increasing it by 1 each time we punch a card. In more complex programs the A register is used for calculations, in which case this count would have to be stored in some memory location to avoid destroying it when another number is entered into the A register. In order to initialize the loop and to add 1 to i each time around it, a 1 is stored in location 1999 as a part of the program. As you recall from previous illustrations, many programs include such constants.

After examining the above program carefully, you might notice that it is rather awkward to ask "Is $i = n$?" In the first place, we have to subtract n from i in order to accomplish this; and secondly, we must reconstruct i so that it can be increased by 1. The instructions in locations 0004, 0006, and 0007 are employed in this process.

Example 7–1

Location	Operation	Data Address	Indicator	A Register	Remarks
0001	RDC	1950	0000		1. Read
0002	RAA	1999	0000	0000000001	2. Set i = 1
0003	PCD	1970	0000		3. Punch
0004	SUA	1952	0000	1 − n	4. Subtract n
0005	BZA	(0001)	0000		Zero?
0006	ADA	1952	0000	0000000001	5. Add n back
0007	ADA	1999	0000	0000000002	Add 1
0008	BRU	(0003)	0000		Return to Punch
1999	00	0000	0001		Constant

Since it is quite easy to branch on zero, we might start with $i = n$ and subtract 1 each time around the loop so that we will complete the process when $i = 0$. A block diagram for this approach is shown in Figure 7–3, which is similar in form to Figure 7–1 (a). The program for this approach is shown in Example 7–2. Contrasting the two programs, we note that the program in Example 7–1 involves six instructions in the counting loop while the program in Example 7–2 involves only four instructions in this loop. Thus it is frequently more efficient and elegant to count downward rather than upward in a count-controlled loop.

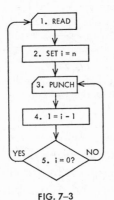

FIG. 7–3

Looping Example
(Counting Downward)

The major difficulty in writing programs involving count-controlled loops is in making sure that the loop will be executed the correct number of times.[1] We frequently find that our first approach to writing such a loop will be "off" by one execution. It is a good idea to test the block diagram before writing the program by following it through, say, with n = 3, and checking to make sure that the loop is performed the proper number of times. In the block diagram in Figure 7–3, for example, we start with $i = 3$, punch the first card, then reduce

---

[1] This is the reason we used a different sequence of the blocks Perform, Modify Index, and Test in Figure 7–3 than we did in Figure 7–2. Had we initialized by setting $i = n − 1$, Figure 7–3 would have had the same form as Figure 7–2.

Example 7–2

Location	Operation	Data Address	Indicator	A Register	Remarks
0001	RDC	1950	0000		1. Read
0002	RAA	1952	0000	n	2. Set i = n
0003	PCD	1950	0000		3. Punch
0004	SUA	1999	0000	n − 1	4. i = i − 1
0005	BZA	(0001)	0000		5. Test i = 0?
0006	BRU	(0003)	0000		Return to Punch
1999	00	0000	0001		Constant

i to 2. Since 2 is not equal to zero (written $2 \neq 0$), we punch the second card. Then we reduce i to 1, and since $1 \neq 0$, we punch the third card. Finally, we reduce i to zero and return to read the next card after punching three cards.

Condition-Controlled Loops

Instead of controlling the exit from a loop on the basis of the number of times the loop has been executed, it is possible to control the exit on the basis of a condition that has arisen in the procedure that is being performed. The general approach to a condition-controlled loop is illustrated in Figure 7–4.

You may recognize that the group control illustration (discussed previously) is an example of a condition-controlled loop. Specifically, examining Figure 6–24 we note that blocks 4 and 6 correspond to the Perform block while block 5 is the Test block, and block 2 is the Initialization block. The condition that controls the exit from the loop is the detection of a new job number. Incidentally, the end-of-file test (block 3) is another condition controlling the entire program as a loop.

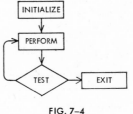

FIG. 7–4
Condition-Controlled Loop

A Square Root Program*

Although the MAC computer has instructions which add, subtract, multiply, and divide, it has no operation that takes the square root of a number. Few digital computers have such an operation, which

---

* Starred sections may be skipped without destroying continuity.

illustrates one of the difficulties involved in using a computer for solving mathematical problems. In order to solve a mathematical problem, the problem must be translated into an arithmetical problem—one that can be solved by addition, subtraction, multiplication, and division. This process of translating from a mathematical to a numerical problem is called *numerical analysis.*

As an illustration of how this may be done—and also of a condition-controlled loop—consider the following problem: Suppose we have a number N of the form xxxxxx+ in the A register and wish to compute the square root of N (denoted $\sqrt{N}$) to the nearest whole number and leave it in the A register.

There are a number of methods that can be used to compute the square root of a number, including the one we learned in grade school. In this illustration we will use Newton's iterative method, which takes any approximation to the square root (denoted by x_i) and obtains from it a better approximation to the square root (denoted by x_{i+1}) by the following formula:

$$x_{i+1} = \tfrac{1}{2}\,(x_i + N/x_i)\,.$$

Suppose for a moment that x_i is a close approximation to the square root of N, but is slightly larger than the actual square root. Then, N/x_i is also a fair approximation of the square root of N, since N equals $(\sqrt{N})^2$, and $(\sqrt{N})^2 \div x_i$ is approximately $\sqrt{N}$. However, if x_i is larger than $\sqrt{N}$, N/x_i is smaller than the actual square root of N. Thus the *average* of the approximations, x_i and N/x_i should be closer to the square root of N than either by itself.

A block diagram[2] for using Newton's method in the problem described above is shown in Figure 7–5. To determine when the process has produced an approximation that is sufficiently accurate, we can test the difference between x_i and N/x_i, and terminate the procedure whenever this difference is smaller than .05. You should note that the first approximation used is $x_i = \tfrac{1}{2}\,N$, which is greater than the square root of N whenever N is greater than 4 (which we assume will always be the case).

It can be shown that if the first approximation is greater than $\sqrt{N}$, then all of these approximations (x_i) are greater than $\sqrt{N}$. Thus x_i is always greater than $T_i = N/x_i$, so $S_i = x_i - T_i$ is always positive,

---

[2] The symbol $<$ is read as "less than." Thus block 4 is read: "Is S_i less than .05?" The symbol $>$ means "greater than," while $\leq$ means "less than or equal to" and $\geq$ means "greater than or equal to."

and we can test for end-of-loop (block 4) by subtracting .05 from S_i and branching on minus.

In Example 7–3 we arbitrarily start the program in location 1000. In addition to the instructions themselves, we need three temporary storage locations (for N, x_i, and T_i) and two constants. You may note in the instruction located in 1017 that we temporarily store $x_i + T_i$ in location 1028, where we have already stored x_i. This is legitimate because we do not need the value of x_i again until it is re-computed and stored in 1028, and by that time we are through with the value of $x_i + T_i$. In most of our previous programs we have stored our constants in the upper locations of memory, but we decided

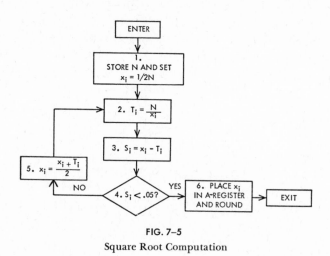

FIG. 7–5
Square Root Computation

to fit this program into a compact block and therefore stored them right after the last instruction of the program. Since we do not know where in memory we wish to go after finding the square root, we have used question marks in the data address of the BRU instruction in location 1025.

INSTRUCTION MODIFICATION

One of the most powerful characteristics of the stored program electronic data processing machine is its ability to operate on its own instructions and thus modify or synthesize instructions that it will execute later on in the program. This capability is frequently combined with the concept of looping so that instructions are modified for each execution of the loop.

Example 7–3

Location	Operation	Data Address	M Register	A Register	Remarks
1000	STA	1026			1. Store N
1001	LDM	1027	0000000005+		Set $x_i = N/2$
1002	MPY	1026		.5N = xxxxxx.x	
1003	ALS	0001		xxxxxx.x0	
1004	STA	1028			Store x_i
1005	RAA	1026		xxxxxx	2. Compute
1006	LDM	1030	0000000000	0000xxxxxx	$T_i = N/x_i$
1007	LLS	0005	x	xxxxx00000	
1008	DIV	1028	Remainder	0xxxxxx.xxx	
1009	ASR	0001		xxxxxx.xx	
1010	STA	1029			Store T_i
1011	RAA	1028		xxxxxx.xx	3. $S_i = x_i - T_i$
1012	SUA	1029		S_i = xxxxxx.xx	
1013	SUA	1027			4. $S_i - .05$
1014	BMA	⟨1023⟩			$S_i < .05$?
1015	RAA	1028		xxxxxx.xx	5. $x_i + T_i$
1016	ADA	1029		xxxxxx.xx	
1017	STA	1028			
1018	LDM	1027	0000000005		$.5(x_i + T_i)$
1019	MPY	1028		xxxxxx.xxx	
1020	ASR	0001		xxxxxx.xx	
1021	STA	1028			Store x_i
1022	BRU	⟨1005⟩			Return to 2
1023	RAA	1028		xxxxxx.xx	6. Round $\sqrt{N}$
1024	ASR	0002		xxxxxx	
1025	BRU	⟨????⟩			Exit
1026	N = xxxxxx				Storage of N
1027	0000000005				Constant 5
1028	x_i = xxxxxx.xx				Storage of x_i
1029	T_i = xxxxxx.xx				Storage of T_i
1030	0000000000				Constant Zero

As an illustration of how instruction modification can be used, consider a situation in which we have information stored in memory which we would like to punch into cards. Specifically, suppose we have accumulated in memory a set of labor cost balances for 500 job numbers. These balances are located so that the cost for job number 1 is accumulated in storage location 0001, the cost for job number 2 in storage location 0002, and so on. In other words, for any job number between 1 and 500 the memory location corresponding to the job number has been used to accumulate total cost. Our problem is to get this information out of memory and into cards, each card containing a job number and the balance for that job.

A written description scarcely conveys the true flavor of the process of developing such a program, for the development involves preparing an initial block diagram, beginning to write a program from this block diagram, discovering that the program would be more efficient if the block diagram were modified, modifying the block diagram, and repeating this process (usually several times). We might begin by noticing that starting with job number 1, increasing the job number by 1 each time we punch a card, and stopping when the job number reaches 500 is very similar to our first example in looping (see Figure 7–2). Thus our initial approach to a block diagram might be similar to the diagram shown in Figure 7–6.

Now the question arises: How can we store the proper balance for punching into each card? This appears to involve instruction modification, and one logical way to approach such a problem is to start to write the main loop of the program in a rough form, ignoring, for the moment, such details as the locations in which the instructions are stored and the specific data addresses corresponding to some of the instructions. Assuming that we intend to punch the job number from 1970 and the balance from 1971, we would write block 2 of Figure 7–6 as:

> LDM (Job No.)
> STM 1971.

For the first job we would load the M register from 0001 and store it for punching. For the next card we would load the M register from 0002 and store it for punching. For the next card we would load the M register from 0003 and store it for punching, and so on. Thus we need to increase the data address of the Load M Register instruction by 1 each time around the loop. Also, part of our initialization should start the LDM instruction with a data address of 0001. Thus we might arrive at the block diagram shown in Figure 7–7. The hexagonal shape of blocks 2 and 7 indicates that these blocks involve instruction modification.

In the program in Example 7–4 we include the constant

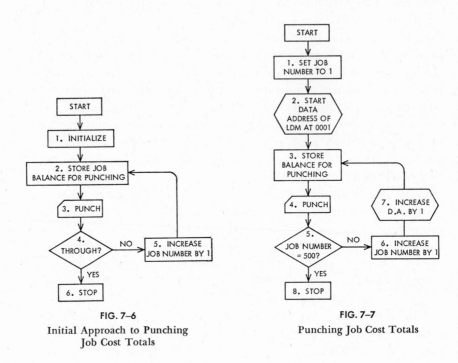

FIG. 7–6

Initial Approach to Punching
Job Cost Totals

FIG. 7–7

Punching Job Cost Totals

6900010000, which is the instruction LDM 0001, since operation code 69 says to load the M register. Block 2 inserts this constant into location 1004 where it is *executed* as an instruction in block 3. We set up the output area to punch the job number from 1970 and the balance from 1971, so we store the balance in 1971 (in the step located in 1005) and punch the card.

Then, starting with the instruction located in 1007, we subtract 500 from the job number and branch on zero. This leaves the job number − 500 in the A register. By adding 501 to this result we cancel out the −500 and add one more, a tricky way of increasing the job number by one with a single instruction (located in 1010).

To add 1 to the data address of the instruction in location 1004, we place this instruction in the A register, add 0000010000 to it, and store the result back in 1004. (Note that addresses that are modified are written enclosed in parentheses to indicate that they change during the execution of the program.)

Example 7–4

Location	Operation	Data Address	M Register	A Register	Remarks
1000	LDM	1999	0000000001		1. Set Job No.
1001	STM	1970			to 1
1002	LDM	1998	6900010000		2. Set LDM instruction
1003	STM	1004			to LDM 0001
1004	LDM	(0001)	Balance		3. Store Balance
1005	STM	1971			for punching
1006	PCD	1970			4. Punch
1007	RAA	1970		0000000001	5. Is Job No. = 500?
1008	SUA	1997		0000000499 −	
1009	BZA	(1016)			
1010	ADA	1996		0000000002 +	6. Increase Job No.
1011	STA	1970			by 1
1012	RAA	1004		6900010000	7. Increase Data Address
1013	ADA	1995		6900020000	by 1
1014	STA	1004			
1015	BRU	(1004)			Return to 3
1016	HLT	0001			8. Stop
1995	0000010000				Constant 1 for Data Address
1996	0000000501				Constant 501
1997	0000000500				Constant 500
1998	6900010000				Constant LDM 0001
1999	0000000001				Constant 1

It is fairly obvious that we could terminate our looping procedure with the question: Is the Data Address of the LDM instruction equal to 0500?—instead of with block 5 in Figure 7–7. To program this question we would subtract the constant 6905000000 from the instruction in location 1004 and branch on zero. Then we could reverse the order of blocks 6 and 7, and add the constant 6905010000 to this result to increase this data address by 1.

Generalized Memory Punch*

The above illustration may be generalized by making the particular block of memory to be punched into cards depend upon the contents of a card that is read. Specifically, we wish to read a card containing B and n, and punch n cards, each containing an address (starting with B) and the contents of that memory location. The first card should contain the number B; the second card should contain the number B + 1 and the contents of location B + 1, and so forth till we reach memory location B + n − 1. In the following, B will be assumed to be a four-digit number greater than 100, and n will be a four-digit number less than 1900. Consequently, we may use the first 100 positions of memory for our program. In the following discussion we will denote the ith location, whose contents are punched, by B_i.

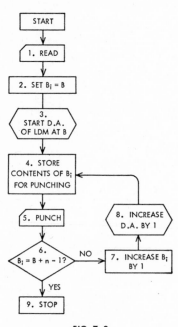

FIG. 7–8

Initial Diagram for Punching a
Block of Memory

Translating the block diagram in Figure 7–7 into our new notation, we obtain the block diagram shown in Figure 7–8. Notice in block 6 that we terminate our loop when B_i equals B + n − 1, since at that time we will have punched n cards (including the one from location B).

When we begin to program this problem we find it is basically the same as Example 7–4 except that in the initialization process we must create test constants corresponding to the 500 and 501 located in 1997 and 1996. Thus we need an additional block:

$$\boxed{\begin{array}{c} \text{Create Test} \\ \text{Constants} \\ K_1 = B + n \\ K_2 = B + n - 1 \end{array}}$$

Also, we must create our beginning LDM instruction by shifting B left 4 places and adding the constant 6900000000 to it to obtain the instruction LDM (B) 0000 to begin with. Thus we have the block diagram shown in Figure 7–9. This program will be left as an exercise for the reader (see Exercise 7.6).

Inventory Cost Illustration

Suppose we have 500 different items in inventory and have the amount of each of these items stored in the computer memory so that the amount for the first item (denoted A_1) is in location 0001, the amount for the second item (A_2) is in location 0002, and so on. Similarly, the unit costs of these items are stored so that the unit cost for the first item (denoted C_1) is in location 0501, the unit cost for the second item (C_2) is in 0502, and so on. This memory allocation is indicated below:

Memory Location	Contents	Memory Location	Contents
0001	A_1 = Amount of item 1	0501	C_1 = Unit cost of item 1
0002	A_2 = Amount of item 2	0502	C_2 = Unit cost of item 2
0003	A_3 = Amount of item 3	0503	C_3 = Unit cost of item 3
. . . . .	. . . .	. . . . .	. . . .
0500	A_{500} = Amount of item 500	1000	C_{500} = Unit cost of item 500

To determine the total cost of this inventory of 500 items we would add the cost of item 1 times the amount of item 1, the cost of item 2 times the amount of item 2, and so on. In symbols, Total Cost, T, is:

$$T = C_1A_1 + C_2A_2 + \cdots + C_{499}A_{499} + C_{500}A_{500}.$$

Let us write a program to compute this total cost and punch it into an output card.

Since we will be using the A and M register for multiplication, we must accumulate total cost in some memory location (say 1970) from which it can be punched. We recognize that we must repeatedly multiply C_i by A_i and add it to the partial sum T_i, so we would start with a block diagram similar to the one shown in Figure 7–10.

To proceed further, we would begin to scratch out a rough program corresponding to blocks 2 and 3, and would start with:

```
LDM    0501
MPY    0001
ADA    1970
STA    1970
```

Then the next time around the loop we would expect to execute:

$$
\begin{array}{ll}
\text{LDM} & 0502 \\
\text{MPY} & 0002 \\
\text{ADA} & 1970 \\
\text{STA} & 1970
\end{array}
$$

Thus we wish to increase the data address of both the LDM instruction and the MPY instruction by 1 each time around the loop. We also recognize that in initialization we must set the instructions to start with LDM 0501 and MPY 0001. Also, in order to prevent

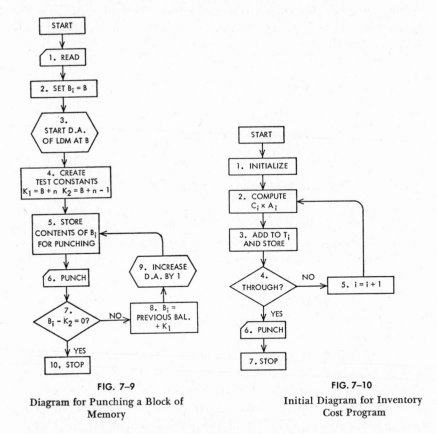

FIG. 7–9

Diagram for Punching a Block of
Memory

FIG. 7–10

Initial Diagram for Inventory
Cost Program

adding the previous contents of 1970 to Total Cost T, we should set 1970 to zero during the initialization.

How do we determine when to terminate the loop? We are through when the data address of the LDM instruction reaches 1000, or when the data address of the MPY instruction reaches 0500. The above discussion gives rise to the block diagram in Figure 7–11.

Example 7–5

Location	Operation	Data Address	M Register	A Register	Remarks
1001	LDM	1999	0000000000		1. Set T = 0
1002	STM	1970			
1003	LDM	1998	6905010000		2. Store starting LDM
1004	STM	1007			
1005	LDM	1997	1900010000		Store starting MPY
1006	STM	1008			
1007	LDM	(0501)	C_1		3. Compute C_iA_i
1008	MPY	(0001)		C_1A_1	
1009	ADA	1970		$0 + C_1A_1$	4. Add to T
1010	STA	1970			and store
1011	RAA	1008		1900010000	5. Have we reached
1012	SUA	1996		0004990000 −	MPY 0500?
1013	BZA	(1019)			
1014	ADA	1995		1900020000	6. Add 1 to Data Address
1015	STA	1008			of MPY instruction
1016	ADA	1994		6905020000	7. Add 1 to Data Address
1017	STA	1007			of LDM instruction
1018	BRU	(1007)			Return to 3
1019	PCD	1970			8. Punch
1020	HLT	0001			9. Stop
1999	0000000000+				Constant zero
1998	6905010000+				Constant LDM 0501
1997	1900010000+				Constant MPY 0001
1996	1905000000+				Test Constant 190500
1995	1905010000+				Constant 190501
1994	5005000000+				Constant 500500

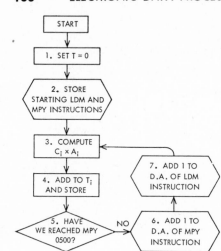

FIG. 7–11

Diagram for Inventory Cost Program

In the program in Example 7–5 the first 6 instructions and the first 3 constants provide the initialization. Note that the data address of the STM instructions in location 1004 and 1006 cannot be filled in until we recognize that the program for block 3 begins in location 1007.

When we reach block 5 (the instruction located in 1011) we subtract the constant 1905000000 from the Multiply instruction in 1008 and branch on zero to see if its data address has reached 500. If not, we add 1905010000 to the result of the subtraction to create the Multiply instruction with its data address increased by 1. Then we really get subtle and add the constant 5005000000 to this instruction to create our LDM instruction, with a data address 500 larger than the data address of the MPY instruction.

Vector Multiplication*

Those who have been exposed to Linear Algebra may have recognized that the above illustration is an example of the general mathematical operation of vector multiplication, with the cost vector being multiplied by the amount vector to obtain the scalar total cost. Of course, there is no mathematical reason that these vectors *have* to represent unit cost and amount, nor must they be stored beginning in locations 0501 and 0001, respectively, nor must each involve 500 numbers. As in our illustration of punching a block from memory, the above illustration can be generalized to a problem in which the vector **a** is stored in sequential locations in memory, beginning with location A, and the vector **c** is stored in sequential memory locations beginning with C. Both vectors *must* involve the same number n of memory locations. We could write a program that will read a card containing A (in the first input word), C (in the second input word), and n (in word 3), compute the vector product, T, and punch it in the output card, then stop.

Actually, the resulting program would be quite similar to Example 7–5, except that the initialization would be more complicated because it would have to create the constants located in 1994 through 1998 from the information read from the card and other "skeleton" constants. For example, the beginning MPY instruction would have

Memory Location	Contents
A	a_1
A + 1	a_2
.	.
.	.
.	.
A + n − 1	a_n

Memory Location	Contents
C	c_1
C + 1	c_2
.	.
.	.
.	.
C + n − 1	c_n

A as its data address and could be created by shifting A left four places and adding 1900000000. The creation of the testing and modifying constants would involve n as well as A and B. Again, this program will be left as an exercise (see Exercise 7.7).

INDEX REGISTERS

Because of the fundamental importance of looping and instruction modification in the use of electronic computers, many machines have special provisions that simplify the programming required for these operations and, at the same time, speed up the processes by reducing the number of nonproductive instructions required. In such machines, one or more special registers (called *index registers*) are provided for this purpose. The same size as the address register, index registers may be added to, subtracted from, and branched on, much the same as the A register. In addition, for any "tagged" instructions the contents of an index register is added to (or subtracted from) the data address of the instruction before that instruction is executed and without changing the instruction as it is stored in memory.

The MAC computer includes three index registers, which are related to the other registers of the MAC as shown in Figure 7–12. Note that for simplicity Figure 7–12 does not portray the M or the A registers, for these registers are not related to the index registers. Figure 7–12 indicates that there are two paths that the data address of an instruction may take to reach the address register. For an instruction that is not tagged, the data address goes directly to the address register. However, for a tagged instruction, the dotted lines indicate that the data address is added to the contents of an index register before being placed in the address register.

In order to tag an instruction, we use one of the indicator positions of the instruction which we have so far ignored in our discussion of

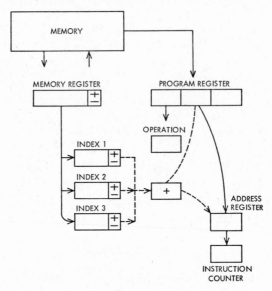

FIG. 7–12

Index Registers on the MAC

the MAC computer. Specifically, the left-most position of these indicator positions is used for the index tag (as shown below).

Operation Code	Data Address	Index Tag
xx	xxxx	x xxx

A zero in this position indicates that the instruction is not tagged, and therefore the contents of the index registers do not influence the data address of the instruction. This of course corresponds to what we have previously learned about the operation of the MAC instructions and is also illustrated in Example 7–6, which shows the instruction as it is written, the contents of the three index registers, and the instruction as it is executed. One, 2 or 3 in the index tag position causes the contents of the designated index register to be added to the data address of the instruction before it is executed. As can be seen from the diagram in Figure 7–12, this does not affect the instruction as it is stored in memory; it affects only its interpretation after it has been placed in the program register.

Consider Example 7-7. Here, the index tag is 1, so the contents of index register 1 (0100+) is added to the data address, 0420, and the "effective address" of the executed instruction is 0520. Similarly, in Example 7-8 the index tag is a 2, so the contents of index register 2 (0050−) is added to the data address (0420) to obtain the effective address, 0370 (0420 − 0050 = 0370).

Example	Instruction Written				I_1	I_2	I_3	Instruction Executed
7-6	ADA	0420	0	xxx	0100+	0050−	1832+	ADA 0420
7-7	ADA	0420	1	xxx	0100+	0050−	1832+	ADA 0520
7-8	ADA	0420	2	xxx	0100+	0050−	1832+	ADA 0370
7-9	ADA	0420	3	xxx	0100+	0050−	1832+	ADA 0252
7-10	BMA	1402	1	xxx	0100+	0050−	1832+	BMA 1502
7-11	STA	1402	3	xxx	0100+	0050−	1832−	STA 1570

In Example 7-9 the index tag is 3, so the contents of index register 3 (1832+) is added to the data address (0420) before the instruction is executed. However, 1832 + 0420 = 2252, which is not a legitimate memory address, since our version of the MAC has only 2,000 words of memory. Whenever the result of such a combination is greater than or equal to 2,000, a suitable multiple of 2,000 is automatically subtracted from the result to produce an address between 0000 and 1999. Thus 2000 is subtracted from 2252 to produce the effective address of 0252.

Example 7-10 shows that data addresses of branching instructions may be modified by means of the index registers, and even data addresses of shift instructions can be similarly modified. Example 7-11 illustrates that when the effective address would be negative as the result of an indexing operation, a suitable multiple of 2,000 is automatically added to the result to produce a positive address between 0000 and 1999. Here 1402 − 1832 = −0430, but 2000 is added to this to produce the effective address of 1570.

For each of the three index registers the MAC computer has seven instructions: Reset-Add, Reset-Subtract, Add, Subtract, Store, Branch on Zero, and Branch on Minus. Our operation abbreviations will be of the form XXi, where i designates 1,2, or 3. For example,

RA1 designates Reset-Add into index register 1; RA3 indicates the instruction Reset-Add into index register 3. Since the index register contains only four positions—while the memory words contain ten —the Add, Subtract, and Store instructions are concerned with the low-order four positions of the memory word (except as we will explain later on in this chapter in our discussion of Partial Word Operations). Three operation codes are given for each of the following operations. The first code is for index register 1, the second code is for index register 2, and the third code is for index register 3.

RAi 02, 03, 04 (Reset and Add to Index Register i). This operation code resets index register i to zero, and then adds the contents of the data address location (with its sign) into index register i.

ADi 05, 06, 07 (Add to Index Register i). This operation code causes the contents of the data address location to be added to the contents of index register i.

RSi 08, 09, 10 (Reset and Subtract from Index Register i). This operation code resets index register i to zero and subtracts the contents of the data address location from index register i. This results in entering four positions of the number from memory into the index register with the sign changed.

SUi 11, 12, 13 (Subtract from Index Register i). This operation code causes the contents of the data address location to be subtracted from the contents of index register i.

As mentioned before, only four positions of the number in memory are considered in these operations; and, with this restriction, the rules of signs are obeyed so that results are similar to those obtained in the A register.

STi 21, 22, 23 (Store Index Register i). This operation causes the contents of index register i (with its sign) to be stored in the location specified by the data address of the instruction. Zeros are inserted in the other six positions of the memory word (unless the Partial Word Indicators are used).

BZi 36, 37, 38 (Branch on Zero in Index Register i). This operation code causes the machine to examine index register i. If this index register is zero, the next instruction is taken from the location specified by the data address. If any number other than zero is in the index register, the next instruction is taken from the next sequential location in memory. It should be noted that the index register sign is not considered in this instruction.

BMi 41, 42, 43 (Branch on Minus in Index Register i). This instruction causes the MAC to examine the sign of index register i. If this sign is minus, the next instruction is taken from the location given by the data address. If the sign is plus, the next instruction is taken from the next sequential location in memory. The contents of the index register are ignored.

Example

As our first example of the use of index registers, consider the first illustration in our discussion of looping, in which we read a card containing the number *n* and wished to punch *n* duplicates of this card. Unfortunately, this example is too simple to exhibit the full power of the index register, for we would use the block diagram in Figure 7–3 and merely substitute an index register for the A register in the program in Example 7–2. If the A register were being used for some other purpose in the program, then the use of the index register for controlling exit from the loop would be advantageous.

As a better example of the use of index registers, let us consider the first example under Instruction Modification, in which memory locations 0001 through 0500 contain a set of labor cost totals for the job numbers 1 through 500. We wish to punch 500 cards, each containing a job number and the total cost for that job.

A block diagram for this problem

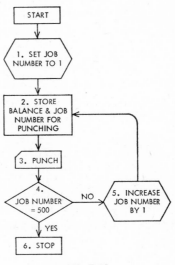

FIG. 7–13
Punching Job Cost Totals

is given in Figure 7–7. The use of index registers enables us to combine blocks 1 and 2 and blocks 6 and 7 to obtain the diagram shown in Figure 7–13. As in Instruction Modification, indexing blocks also are hexagonal in shape. Note in Example 7–12 that the programming form has been revised to include the indicator positions of the instruction and the contents of the index registers.

The program in Example 7–12 is relatively straightforward. The LDM instruction in location 1001 is tagged for index register 1, and increasing the job number (in index register 1) by 1 also increases

Example 7–12

Block Number	Location	Operation	Data Address	Indicator	I_1	I_2	I_3	M Register	A Register
1	1000	RA1	1999	0000	0001				
2	1001	LDM	(0000)	1000				Balance	
	1002	STM	1971	0000					
	1003	ST1	1970	0000					
3	1004	PCD	1970	0000					
4	1005	SU1	1998	0000	0499 −				
	1006	BZ1	1009	0000					
5	1007	AD1	1997	0000	0002 +				
	1008	BRU	1001	0000					
6	1009	HLT	0001	0000					
	1999	00	0000	0001					
	1998	00	0000	0500					
	1997	00	0000	0501					

the data address of the LDM instruction. Since the job number is maintained in the index register rather than in memory, it must be stored by the instruction in location 1003 before punching.

Testing whether the job number has reached 500 is accomplished by subtracting 500 from the index register and branching on zero in the index register (accomplished by the instructions in locations 1005 and 1006). The index register is restored to the job number, and a 1 is added to it at the same time by adding 501 to the (negative) contents of the index register.

Now we may obtain an indication of the power of the index register. A comparison of the program in Example 7–4 with the program in Example 7–12 is presented in the table below.

	Without Index Registers	With Index Registers
Initialization	4	1
Loop	12	8
Constants	5	3

Inventory Cost Illustration Revisited

As an illustration of the use of an index register in a situation where we modify two instructions in the same loop, consider the inventory cost illustration where we have inventory amounts (A_i) stored in locations 0001 through 0500, and the corresponding unit costs (C_i) stored in locations 0501 through 1000. We wish to determine the total cost of this inventory by multiplying each amount A_i by its cost C_i, totaling these products, and punching the result, T.

$$T = C_1A_1 + C_2A_2 + C_3A_3 + \ldots + C_{500}A_{500}$$

A block diagram for this program (without index registers) is shown in Figure 7–11. If we use an index register we can replace block 2 by a block that sets the index register to 1. Block 5 of Figure 7–11 becomes: Is the index register equal to 500? We can also replace blocks 6 and 7 of Figure 7–11 with a single block that increases the index register by 1. Thus we obtain the block diagram shown in Figure 7–14.

After some experience in programming with index registers we recognize that it is inconvenient to determine if the index register is 500 but convenient to determine if it is 0. By using the fact that the index register can handle negative numbers, and by changing the data addresses of the instructions that are being modified to refer to the last memory position referred to in the loop, we can count upward to zero by use of negative numbers. In this case we would change block 2 of Figure 7–14 to read: Set I.R. to −499, and we would change block 5 to read: I.R. = 0?

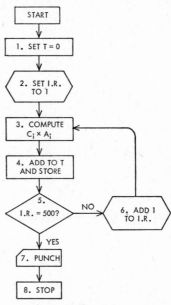

FIG. 7–14
Inventory Cost Program Using
Index Registers

The program corresponding to this final block diagram is shown in Example 7–13. When the LDM 1000 and MPY 0500 instructions are executed the first time around the loop (with the index register equal to −499) they multiply the cost in 0501 by the amount in 0001. When the index register finally becomes zero, these instructions

Example 7–13

Block Number	Location	Operation	Data Address	Indicator	I_1	I_2	I_3	M Register	A Register
1	1001	LDM	1999	0000				0000000000+	
	1002	STM	1970	0000					
2	1003	RA1	1998	0000	0499−				
3	1004	LDM	(1000)	1000	0499−			C_i	
	1005	MPY	(0500)	1000	0499−				$C_i{\cdot}A_i$
4	1006	ADA	1970	0000					$T + C_i{\cdot}A_i$
	1007	STA	1970	0000					
5	1008	BZ1	⟨1011⟩	0000					
6	1009	AD1	1997	0000	0498−				
	1010	BRU	⟨1004⟩	0000					
7	1011	PCD	1970	0000					
8	1012	HLT	0001	0000					
	1999	00	0000	0000+					
	1998	00	0000	0499−					
	1997	00	0000	0001+					

multiply the cost in 1000 by the amount in 0500, and the loop should be terminated.

In the table below, the program given in Example 7–5 is contrasted with the above program. As you can see, the use of an index register results in considerable simplification, fewer required memory locations, fewer executed instructions, and consequently faster operation.

	Without Index Registers	With Index Registers
Initialization	6	3
Loop	12	7
Constants	6	3

INDIRECT ADDRESSING

As an adjunct to (or a substitute for) index registers, computers frequently use *indirect addressing*. In indirect addressing the data address of a tagged instruction does not refer to the location of data; it *specifies* the memory location at which the actual data address will be found.

In the MAC computer the indirect address tag is placed in the third position (from the right) of the instruction, as shown below. A "one" in this position causes the MAC to go to the location given

| Operation
Code
xx | Data
Address
xxxx | Indicators
x x xx (Indirect Address Tag), |

by the data address of the instruction, and to take the low-order four positions of that location as the effective data address of the tagged instruction. Indirect addressing is illustrated in Example 7–14, where the instruction written in memory is ADA from location 1000. However, since this instruction is tagged for indirect addressing, we go to location 1000 (which contains 0000000107 +) and substitute the 0107 into the address register before the instruction is executed. Thus the instruction executed would be ADA 0107.

In Example 7–15 there is a negative number in the memory location referred to in indirect addressing. The minus sign is ignored when this number is substituted into the address register. Example 7–16 shows that the upper six positions of the memory location are ignored when the lower four positions are inserted into the address register as the result of indirect addressing.

Example Number	Instruction in Memory	Contents of Memory Location 1000	I_1	I_2	I_3	Instruction Executed
7–14	ADA 1000 0100	0000000107 +	0040+	0100−	0500+	ADA 0107
7–15	ADA 1000 0100	0000000107 −	0040+	0100−	0500+	ADA 0107
7–16	ADA 1000 0100	1476321407 +	0040+	0100−	0500+	ADA 1407
7–17	ADA 1000 1100	1476321407 +	0040+	0100−	0500+	ADA 1447

How do the index registers and indirect addressing interact with each other? In the MAC the contents of the indirect address are first obtained, and then this new address is modified by means of the tagged index register. Thus, in Example 7–17, the machine goes to location 1000 to obtain the data address, 1407; then the contents of index register 1 is added to this address before the instruction is executed.

Although we will not study any further types of indirect addressing, an indirect address tag of 2 could be used to specify that the data address positions (rather than the low-order four positions) of the word designated should be used as the effective address of the instruction. A 3 could be used to specify that the tagged index register be applied to the data address before the word containing the indirect address is obtained; and other digits could be used to indicate other variations of indirect addressing that might be desirable for certain types of operations.

Indirect addressing is quite useful whenever a single address, which is being modified, is referred to several times within the same loop. In this case, we can modify this address in all of the instructions in which it is used by modifying the single word in memory and using its location as the indirect address of the several instructions. The use of indirect addressing, combined with the index registers, greatly simplifies the initialization portion of the general vector multiplication problem posed in Exercise 7–7. The use of indirect addressing will be illustrated in the next section in Example 7–19.

TABLE LOOK-UP

When utilizing computers, it is frequently necessary to refer to information stored in memory under circumstances in which it is impossible for the programmer (at the time the program is written) to know where the information is stored, for this depends upon the transaction itself. For example, let us consider the following situation.

Suppose we have 50,000 cards in random sequence, each containing a job number and a number of hours worked on that job. Just as in the example in the section on Programming Group Control, we would like to obtain from these cards a total of the hours worked on each of the 500 jobs, except that we would prefer not to sort the cards. Assuming that the job numbers range from 001 to 500, we could assign memory in the following way:

Use storage location 0001 to accumulate the hours for job number 001;
Use storage location 0002 to accumulate the hours for job number 002;
. . . .
Use storage location 0500 to accumulate the hours for job number 500.

Assuming that these 500 memory locations contain zeros as the result of the initialization, our first approximation of a block dia-

gram might appear as in Figure 7–15. In the following discussion we
will assume that the control panel is wired so that "Job Number"
enters word 1 and "Hours Worked" enters word 2 of the input
buffer.

If we attempted to write a program for this without using either
indirect addressing or the index registers, we would discover that we

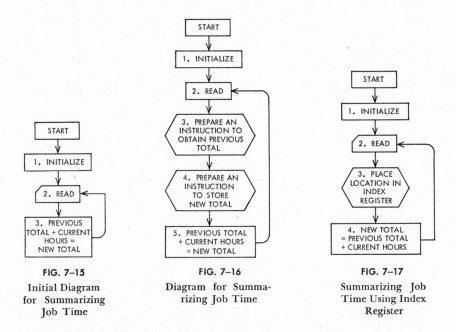

FIG. 7–15	FIG. 7–16	FIG. 7–17
Initial Diagram for Summarizing Job Time	Diagram for Summarizing Job Time	Summarizing Job Time Using Index Register

must construct an instruction to obtain the previous total from
among the 500 possible totals stored in the memory, and construct another instruction to store the result back in the proper
memory location. Thus we are led to reason that we would need a
Reset Add instruction whose data address is the same as the job
number to obtain the previous total, and a Store A Register instruction with this same data address to return the new total to storage.
We would finally arrive at a block diagram similar to the one in
Figure 7–16.

If we use an index register, the block diagram would be simplified
to the form shown in Figure 7–17. With the omission of initialization, the program corresponding to this block diagram is shown in
Example 7–18.

If we use indirect addressing, the block diagram reduces to that
shown in Figure 7–15, and the program (omitting the initialization)

is given in Example 7–19. Since location 1950 contains the job number, the RAA 1950 instruction tagged for indirect addressing is executed with job number as its data address, thus obtaining the balance for that job number. Similarly, the STA 1950 instruction tagged for indirect addressing is executed with job number as its data address, thus storing the total back where it belongs in memory.

Because of the way identifying codes are designed, it is frequently inconvenient, or impossible, to assign the memory location as the corresponding code number—as was done in the previous example. Most identifying codes contain more digits than the memory address allows, and codes usually are rather sparsely distributed over their

Example 7–18

Location	Operation	Data Address	Indicator
1000	RDC	1950	0000
1001	RA1	1950	0000
1002	RAA	(0000)	1000
1003	ADA	1951	0000
1004	STA	(0000)	1000
1005	BRU	(1000)	0000

range of values. For example, the item numbers identifying the parts in a production control system might contain seven digits, which allows for 9,999,999 different parts. However, there may be only 15,000 parts in the system, in which case only 15,000 of these parts numbers would be used. Likewise, there may be a five-digit job number and only 400 active jobs.

How can we handle such situations? In the first place, we might attempt to devise a formula for computing a memory location from the identifying number. For example, if the 400 job numbers ranged from 45027 to 45426, we could subtract 45027 from each to obtain memory locations ranging from 0000 to 0399. Unfortunately, because the identifying numbers may be widely scattered, it is usually impractical to attempt to find a usable formula.

In such cases we must store a table in memory, including both the identifying number (called the *argument*) and the information desired (called the *function*). The telephone book is an example of such a table, where the *name* is the argument and the *telephone number* is the function. A table may have more than one function for the same argument. In the telephone book, for example, both address and telephone number are associated with the name.

The telephone book illustrates another important characteristic of usable tables, for our ability to find a telephone number depends upon the fact that the names are in alphabetical order. For example, if you know a telephone number, can you easily find the person's name? Not from the telephone book. But if you had a book in telephone number order, you could easily refer to it to find in whose name a number is listed, and where the phone is located.

Thus, for ease of reference, tables are arranged in the computer

Example 7–19

Location	Operation	Data Address	Indicator
1000	RDC	1950	0000
1001	RAA	(1950)	0100
1002	ADA	1951	0000
1003	STA	(1950)	0100
1004	BRU	1000	0000

memory in sequence according to the argument. Usually the arguments are stored in one block of memory, and the functions are stored in a separate block of memory a specified number of locations away. For example, if job numbers are stored in locations 0001 to 0400, the corresponding hourly totals might be stored in locations 0401 to 0800. The job number whose corresponding total is being sought is called the *search argument*. To locate the total for a given search argument, we first find the location of this job number in the table and then add 400 to this location to obtain the location of its total.

How, then, can we write a program to find the argument that is stored in memory? One approach would be to start at the beginning of the table and examine each argument in sequence until an argument greater than, or equal to, the search argument is found. This might be accomplished through the use of the block diagram shown in Figure 7–18. Here, the notation "arg (i) " means the table argument stored in memory location i.

Using index registers, the MAC program for the above block diagram would require the execution of perhaps five instructions each time around the loop until the argument is found. If the table contained 400 entries, this would mean an average of 5 (200) = 1,000 instructions executed. A few machines have a special instruction that automatically performs a Table Look-up by means of a sequential search. If the MAC had such an instruction, the search argument would be placed in the M register before executing the TLU instruction whose data address would specify the location of the first argument of the table. As a result of this instruction, the memory location of the first table argument greater than or equal to the search argument would be inserted into index register 3, and the argument and table value could easily be obtained.

It should be emphasized that the block diagram in Figure 7–18 presents an inefficient approach to programming a table look-up. In

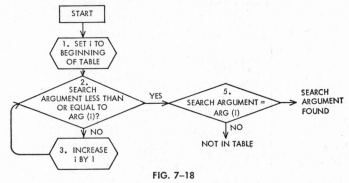

FIG. 7–18

Table Look-Up by Sequential Search

machines that do not have an automatic Table Look-up instruction, a so-called *binary search* is frequently programmed. The basic idea of the binary search is first to look at the middle of the table and then decide which way to go; then look halfway to the end, in the proper direction, and again decide which way to go. This process is continued, each time halving the length of the step.

The program for a binary search (using index registers) might execute ten instructions every time around the loop, but for a 400-entry table we would have to go around the loop only about nine times, thus executing about $10(9) = 90$ instructions. For machines that can execute instructions almost as rapidly as the automatic Table Look-up can scan memory, the binary search may be as fast for large tables as an automatic Table Look-up instruction.

PARTIAL WORD OPERATIONS

Frequently it is desirable to be able to manipulate certain portions of a memory word without affecting the remainder of the word. For example, we might have a man-number in the upper six positions of a word and the rate for that man in the lower four positions of the same word. This is called *packing;* and it is frequently used to increase the speed of magnetic tape input and output.

Packing (and *unpacking*) can be accomplished by *shifting.* For example, if we have man-number xxxxxx in location 0100, and rate yy.yy in location 0102, and we wish to "pack" them together and store them in location 0500, we could use the following sequence of program steps:

Operation Code	Data Address		A Register
RAA	0101	0000	0000xxxxxx+
ALS	0004	0000	xxxxxx0000+
ADA	0102	0000	xxxxxxyy.yy+
STA	0500	0000	xxxxxxyy.yy+

Similarly, instructions could easily be written that would reverse this process and "unpack" the man-number and rate, both stored together in location 0500.

To avoid the awkwardness, bother, and time involved in packing and unpacking, the positions of each memory word are numbered from left to right, starting with zero and proceeding through 9, as shown below. The right-most two positions of the MAC instruction

Memory Word: x x x x x x x x x x

Position: 0 1 2 3 4 5 6 7 8 9

are used as partial word indicators. If the partial word indicators are AB, the instruction refers to the portion of the memory location starting with position A and proceeding to the right until the position *just to the left of position B is reached.* A zero in position B is interpreted as a 10, so an instruction in which these indicator positions are 00 refers to the entire word.

Notice in the illustrations that follow that the partial word indicators refer to the *positions of the memory word* and not to the register involved, for the low-order positions of these registers are always used. In Example 7–20, the number 054 in positions 0 through 2 of memory location 1000 is added into the A register. Example 7–21 indicates that the sign of the memory location goes along with the portion of the word that is used, so 054— is added. In Example 7–22, the indicator position is 70, and the 0 refers to 10, so positions 7, 8, and 9 of the memory location are used. The number 4607 in positions 3, 4, 5, and 6 of the memory location is used in Example 7–23.

The remainder of the examples illustrate the use of the partial word indicators in Store operations. In Example 7–24, positions 1 and 2 of the memory location are replaced by the low-order two positions of the A register. Example 7–25 illustrates the fact that in a

Example Number	Instruction	Contents of Memory Location 1000	A Register
7–20	ADA 1000 0003	0544607305+ 0544607305+	0000000124+ 0000000178+
7–21	ADA 1000 0003	0544607305− 0544607305−	0000000124+ 0000000070+
7–22	ADA 1000 0070	0244607305+ 0244607305+	0000000124+ 0000000429+
7–23	ADA 1000 0037	0244607305+ 0244607305+	0000000124+ 0000004731+
7–24	STA 1000 0013	0244607305+ 0894607305+	0123456789+ 0123456789+
7–25	STA 1000 0006	0244607305+ 4567897305−	0123456789− 0123456789−
7–26	STA 1000 0077	0244607305+ 0244607305−	0123456789− 0123456789−

store operation the sign of the A register is substituted for the sign of the memory location, even though only a portion of the memory word is replaced. Finally, Example 7–26 illustrates the fact that if the partial word indicators are the same (and not 0), no positions of the memory location are affected; but the sign position may still be changed.

When partial word indicators are used in instructions that operate upon the index registers, they operate just as they do with the A register. Thus the information placed into the index register need *not* come from the low-order four positions of the memory word. Likewise, information stored from an index register may be placed where desired in a memory word.

You may recall that in our discussion of control words we said that we could eliminate the shifting involved in isolating the digit that indicates an X by using the indicator positions of the instruction. Suppose, for example, that a 7 in position 2 of the control word in location 1989 indicates an X in column 75. Then we would obtain this position in the A register by executing the instruction:

RAA 1989 0023

It is obvious that most fields that arise in data processing applications of the computer are not exactly ten digits in length (or any *other* fixed length). If it were necessary to use a full word for each data field, the efficiency of utilization of memory for storing data would be substantially reduced. The use of partial word indicators for field definition within words makes it convenient to pack more than one field into a word, thus increasing the efficiency of utilization of memory and (perhaps more importantly) of magnetic-tape or random-access file memory.

SWITCHES (OR VARIABLE CONNECTORS)

When block diagrams become large and complicated, *connectors* can make it possible to conveniently spread the diagram over several pages—or can avoid complicating the diagram with too many long flow-path arrows. A connector is simply a small circle that contains a symbol (usually a number). An arrow leading to such a symbol denotes that the indicated path is resumed where this symbol, with an arrow leading away from it, is repeated. This is illustrated in Figure 7–19, where connector 1 on page 1 leads to the connector on page 3.

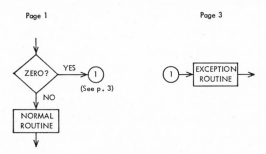

FIG. 7–19

Illustration of a Connector

A *variable* connector (or *switch*) is an extension of the above concept. Frequently a condition detected at one place in a program requires that modification be made at one or more places in the program that may be executed later. The "remembering" of these conditions is accomplished by the use of switches (or variable connectors), analogous to the switches which control traffic on a railroad.

Switches and variable connectors are denoted by the following symbols in the block diagram. It should be noted that of the two or

VARIABLE CONNECTOR

more possible paths away from the symbol, one and *only* one path can be active at any time. This is controlled elsewhere in the program by setting the switch or connector to the desired position, as illustrated in Figure 7–20.

To illustrate the use of switches we will imagine a file of cards which contains a number of cards for each man-number, grouped together in man-number sequence. This group of cards will contain an X-79 card for some man-numbers somewhere in the group. We want to process the file for each man-number group, processing all the cards, up to and including the X-79 card (if one is present), ignoring all cards in the group after the X-79 card has been reached.

A block diagram for this problem[3] is given in Figure 7–20. In this figure, cards for a given man-number are read and processed until an X-79 card is detected. At this time the switch is set to the transferred position (the variable connector is set to A_2), so that subsequent cards are simply checked to see if the man-number has been changed, and if not, they are ignored. When the man-number *does* change, this switch is reset to the normal position (the variable connector A is reset to A_1), and the first card and all following cards are processed until an X-79 card is again detected. The switch is set to the normal position at the start of the program so that the first card will be processed properly.

One way to program this switching function is through the use of the Branch Unconditional instruction. Assuming that the Read instruction of block 6 is located in 0001, and that the first instruc-

---

[3] Other block diagrams could handle this problem, some of which would not involve the use of switches or variable connectors. Note that end-of-file considerations have been omitted from these diagrams for purposes of simplicity.

tion of block 3 is located in 0100, we could store the constant 4001000000+ in location 0500, the constant 4000010000+ in location 0501, and write programs for blocks 2 and 5 (as shown below in Example 7–27). You should notice that the resulting BRU (40) instruction in location 0150 is the switch (or variable connector).[4]

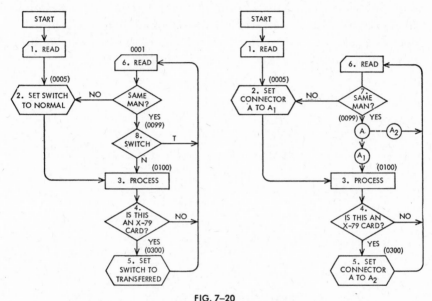

FIG. 7–20

Illustration of Switch and Variable Connector

Some machines have a special *sense register* that can be used to simplify the programming of switches. Special instructions can be used to set each position of this sense register to 0 or to 1, and other instructions can branch on 0 in each position. Thus block 2 of Figure 7–20 could be accomplished by a single instruction that would set position 1 of the sense register to 1. Block 5 would consist of an instruction that would set position 1 of the same register to 0. The switch itself would be an instruction that would branch to 0001 on zero in position 1 of the sense register; otherwise it would proceed to the next instruction (in location 0100).

SUBROUTINES

The early users of computers quickly noticed that certain sequences of program steps recurred so often that writing them over

---

[4] The numbers in parentheses in the block diagram indicate the beginning memory location of the blocks.

and over appeared to be wasteful. It is possible to write portions of programs that occur repeatedly in a form in which they may be incorporated into any program in which that sequence of steps may be required. These "building blocks," known as *subroutines,* are of substantial value in reducing the effort involved in programming, and sometimes in reducing the amount of memory required. For example, whenever we wish to perform a Table Look-up with a machine that does not have this instruction, we may simply incorporate into our program a subroutine that performs a binary search.

Example 7–27

Location	Operation	Data	Indicator	Remarks
0005	LDM	0500	0000	2. Set switch to
0006	STM	0099	0000	Normal
0007	BRU	(0100)	0000	
0300	LDM	0501	0000	5. Set switch to
0301	STM	0099	0000	Transferred
0302	BRU	(0001)	0000	
0099	BRU	(xxxx)	0000	8. Switch
0500	40	0100	0000	Constant
0501	40	0001	0000	Constant

We will see later that the processes of reading a record from magnetic tapes, checking for end-of-file and error conditions, and rewinding and alternating tape units involve sequences of instructions that are basically the same in many programs, and thus may be written as subroutines. In the area of scientific computing, the same mathematical operations frequently reappear within the same program or in different programs. Subroutines for computing the square root, the logarithm, the sine or the cosine of an angle, or for floating decimal point arithmetic have found widespread use in computational programs.

There are two basic varieties of subroutines: the *open* (in-line) routine and the *closed* (off-line or linked) routine. The open subroutine is inserted directly into the sequence of the main program, as shown in Figure 7–21. The closed subroutine is designed to be used several times within a single program but is stored only once in the memory of the machine.

A subroutine is similar to a machine instruction in that the programmer must understand precisely what the subroutine does in order to incorporate it into his program. Consider, for example, the

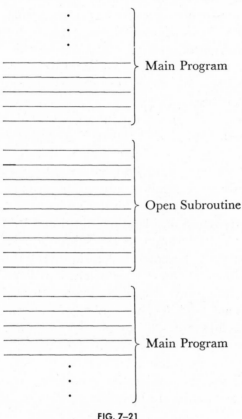

FIG. 7–21

Program with an Open Subroutine

program for computing the square root which we developed in Example 7–3. The programmer must know that this subroutine takes the number N of the form xxxxxx located in the A register, computes its square root to the nearest whole number, and places this result in the A register. In this process the previous contents of the M register are destroyed. Thus, if the contents of the M register will be needed later, they must be stored *before* entering the subroutine.

Note that this subroutine might have been designed to store the previous contents of the M register before using it—and to restore the M register to its previous value before returning to the main program. In this case the programmer would not have to worry about preserving the contents of this register. Thus, either the subroutine or the programmer can have the responsibility for preserving the contents of registers (the M register, the A register, or the index registers) which the subroutine uses. Moreover, as with a machine instruction, the programmer must understand what happens under any "pathological" conditions that may arise, such as attempting to take the square root of a negative number. In this case our square root program would terminate the iterative process on the first iteration (since $S_i - .05$ would be negative) and give the negative number, $\frac{1}{2}N$, as the answer.

All the above information about the input data and the subroutine, the results produced, the registers whose contents are destroyed, what happens under error conditions, the amount of memory required, etc., must be made available to the user of the subroutine through a detailed subroutine write-up. Without this write-up the subroutine is practically useless.

Another important consideration illustrated by the program in Example 7–3 is the location of the subroutine in memory. This program is written to be stored in locations 1000 through 1030. But what if we wished to insert it into locations 0426 through 0456? Actually, this subroutine should be written to correspond to locations 0000 through 0030. Then it could easily be relocated by adding a constant (in this case 426) to each location and address in the subroutine *except* the addresses of the shift instructions (which are absolute addresses and should be so identified). As we will see in Chapter 8, this process of relocation of the subroutine can easily be handled by the machine itself in the process of "assembling" the program.

Now suppose we had a program that involved the calculation of many square roots (say 40). This square root routine requires 31 memory locations, and if we insert it 40 times we will use up $40 \times 31 = 1240$ memory locations. Instead, we would use it as a closed (off-line or linked) routine, as illustrated in Figure 7–22, and execute it 40 different times in the course of our program, each time returning to a different location for the next program step. The use of such a closed subroutine can be indicated in the block diagram by noting the words "Call square root subroutine" in the blocks where it is employed.

Many machines have a Branch and Return instruction that greatly simplifies linkage of closed subroutines.

44 BRR (Branch and Return). This is an unconditional branch instruction. In addition, it inserts the contents of the instruction counter (the address of the BRR instruction) into index register 3.

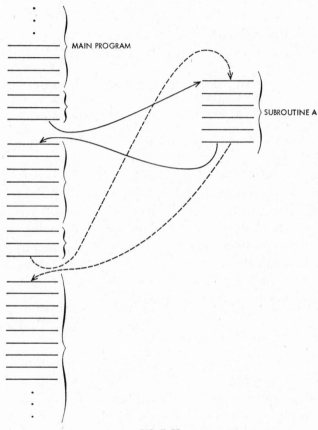

FIG. 7–22

Closed (or off-line) Routine

If we branch to the beginning of a subroutine by means of a Branch and Return instruction, we can then return to the next instruction in our main program with a BRU 0001 instruction tagged for index register 3.

Actually, many subroutines operate upon several words of data rather than just one. A standard method of linking such subroutines is to store this data (in the sequence specified by the subroutine write-up) right after the Branch and Return instruction, as is shown below for three data words.

> *BRR Instruction*
> Data D$_1$
> Data D$_2$
> Data D$_3$
> *Next Instruction of Main Program*

In this case the subroutine could obtain each data word by tagging addresses for index register 3 as shown below:

RAA	0001	3000	would obtain D$_1$
RAA	0002	3000	would obtain D$_2$
RAA	0003	3000	would obtain D$_3$.

The return to the main program would be handled by the instruction BRU 0004 3000.

As may have been inferred from the above discussion, the use of subroutines is a very powerful technique. Actually, large, complex programs that we wish to experiment with and modify frequently are best written as a number of self-contained, closed subroutines, with the main program being an executive routine that merely guides the program through the subroutines in the proper sequence. This approach makes such a program simpler to write, to "debug" (eliminate the errors from), and to modify.

SUMMARY

In this chapter we have been concerned with such programming techniques as *looping, instruction modification, table look-up, programmed switches,* and *subroutines.* These are important and powerful techniques for solving difficult problems—so important that special capabilities (such as *indirect addressing, index registers, sense registers,* and the *Branch and Return instruction*) have been incorporated into many computers to simplify the programming of such techniques.

The further we proceed in the programming of computers the more apparent it becomes that our major difficulties lie above the detailed instruction-writing level. The main difficulties arise in devising an overall logic (at the block diagramming level) that will provide a solution to the problem. In the next chapter we will find that techniques have been developed which reduce the work involved in writing the individual machine instructions and in incorporating subroutines into a program. But the overall logical problems will continue to present a major challenge.

EXERCISES

Prepare a block diagram and program for each of the following exercises.

7.1   We have a deck of cards and would like to reproduce a systematic sample of them, consisting of the first card and each thirteenth card thereafter.

7.2   Given an input card containing loan number, loan amount, *yearly* interest rate, and payment amount, we wish to prepare a schedule of the monthly payments on this loan by punching an output card for each such payment showing payment number, payment amount, remaining balance of the loan after the payment, amount of the payment applied to principal, amount of the payment applied to interest, and loan number.

The interest for a payment is computed by multiplying the monthly interest rate by the remaining balance, then this is subtracted from the payment amount to obtain the amount of the payment applied to reduction of the principal. However, on the last payment the regular payment amount may be too much to make the loan come out even, so this payment should be adjusted to repay the loan *exactly*. At the conclusion of one loan, read the next card and repeat the process for the next loan.

The form of the numbers and the wiring of the control panel are described below.

		Input	*Output*
Loan Number	xxxx	word 1	word 1
Loan Amount	xx,xxx.xx	word 2	
Yearly Percent Interest	xx.xx	word 3	
Payment Amount	x,xxx.xx	word 4	word 4
Payment Number	xxxx		word 3
Remaining Balance	xx,xxx.xx		word 2
Amount to Principal	x,xxx.xx		word 5
Amount to Interest	x,xxx.xx		word 6

7.3   Prepare a program that will set memory locations 0100 through 1999 to zero.

7.4   There are 600 numbers of the form xxxxxx.xx stored in memory locations 1000 to 1599. Add these numbers and punch a card with their sum.

7.5   There are 300 job numbers stored as a table in memory locations 1001 to 1300. Associated with each job number is a total of hours worked on that job, and these totals are stored in locations 1501 to 1800. If the job number is stored in location n, then the total for that job is stored in location $n + 500$. Punch a card for each job that will contain the job number and the total hours. The control panel is wired so that Job Number is punched from word 1 and Total Hours is punched from word 2 of the output buffer.

7.6   We wish to read a card containing B and n, and punch the contents of a block of memory into n cards, each containing an address (starting with B) and the contents of that memory location. A block diagram for this problem is given in Figure 7–9.

7.7   A vector **a** is stored sequentially in memory beginning in location A, and a vector **c** is stored in sequential memory locations beginning with location C. Each vector involves n memory locations. Read a card containing A, C, and n (in input words 1, 2, and 3, respectively). Compute the vector product, T, punch T in the output card (from word 1), and stop. You may assume that A, C, and n are of such size that the vectors do not overlap in memory, and so that you may write your program in locations 0000 through 0100. See the section on Vector Multiplication for further discussion of this problem.

In the following four exercises, assume that job rates for jobs number 1 through 500 are stored in memory in locations 501 through 1000, so that the rate (of form x.xx) for job number n is stored in location 500 + n. Your programs for Exercises 7.8 through 7.11 should be written in locations 1600 through 1999.

7.8   We wish to read cards containing man-number, job number, and hours; and for each such card, punch a card to contain man-number, job number, hours, and pay (job rate times hours). The form of the numbers and the control panel wiring are described below.

		Input	Output
Man-Number	xxxxxx	word 1	word 1
Job Number	xxx	word 2	word 2
Hours	xx.x	word 3	word 3
Pay	xxx.xx		word 4

7.9   We wish to read cards containing man-number, job number, hours, and guaranteed rate; and for each such card, punch a card containing man-number, job number, hours, and pay. In this case, pay is computed as hours times job rate or guaranteed rate, whichever is larger. The control panel is wired the same as in Exercise 7.8 except that guaranteed rate (x.xx) is wired into word 4 on input.

7.10   Assume that there are several cards for each man-number in Exercise 7.9 and that they are sorted into man-number sequence. We wish to produce a single card for each man that contains man-number, total hours, and total pay. Pay is computed as in Exercise 7.9, and the control panel is wired as shown below.

		Input	Output
Man-Number	xxxxxx	word 1	word 1
Job Number	xxx	word 2	
Hours	xx.x	word 3	
Guaranteed Rate	x.xx	word 4	
Total Hours	xx.x		word 2
Total Pay	xxx.xx		word 3

7.11   With the same input and output cards, and the computation the same as in Exercise 7.10, we wish to accumulate total job cost for each job number by using the locations 1001 through 1500 for this purpose. Thus the total dollars for job number n would be accumulated in location $n + 1000$. Assume that locations 1001 through 1500 have been cleared to zero before the start of this program.

In the following exercises fill in the effective address of the instruction executed.

Exercise Number	Instruction Written	Contents of Location 0999	I_1	I_2	I_3	Effective Address
7.12	ADA 0999 1000	0004720467+	0142+	0220−	1976+	
7.13	ADA 0999 2000	0004720467+	0142+	0220−	1976+	
7.14	RAA 0999 3000	0004720467+	0142+	0220−	1976+	
7.15	BRU 0999 0100	0004720467+	0142+	0220−	1976+	
7.16	RAA 0999 1100	0004720467+	0142+	0220−	1976+	
7.17	RAA 0999 2100	0004720467+	0142+	0220−	1976+	
7.18	RAA 0999 1100	0004720476−	0142+	0220−	1976+	

Fill in the second line of each of the following exercises.

Exercise Number	Instruction	Contents of Location 0999	A Register
7.19	RAA 0999 0015	0011223344+	5566778899+
7.20	RAA 0999 0070	0011223344−	5566778899+
7.21	RAA 0999 0055	0011223344+	5566778899+
7.22	RAA 0099 0034	0011223344−	5566778899+
7.23	STA 0999 0070	0011223344+	5566778899+
7.24	STA 0999 0003	0011223344+	5566778899−
7.25	STA 0999 0026	0011223344+	5566778899+

7.26 Suppose that in 7.8 the 500 job numbers do not run from 1 to 500 but are of the form xxxxx, and are stored in order (as the arguments in a table) in locations 0001 through 0500 with the corresponding rates in locations 0501 through 1000.

We have a closed Table Look-up subroutine that requires that the following information be located sequentially in the words following the Branch and Return instruction:

    1st word: Search Argument
    2nd word: Location of First Table Argument
    3rd word: Number of Arguments in the Table

This subroutine places the location of the first table argument that is greater than or equal to the search argument in index register 1. The contents of the A and M registers are destroyed. The subroutine is stored in memory in a block starting with location 1900.

Write the program for Exercise 7.8 under the above conditions.

7.27 Write the program for Exercise 7.9 under the conditions stated in Exercise 7.26.

7.28 Write the program for Exercise 7.11 under the conditions stated in Exercise 7.26.

7.29

Consider the square matrix $\quad A = \begin{pmatrix} a_{11}, & a_{12}, & \cdots, & a_{17} \\ a_{21}, & a_{22}, & \cdots, & a_{27} \\ \bullet & \bullet & \bullet & \bullet \\ \bullet & \bullet & \bullet & \bullet \\ \bullet & \bullet & \bullet & \bullet \\ a_{71}, & a_{72}, & \cdots, & a_{77} \end{pmatrix}$

and the column vector $\mathbf{v} = \begin{pmatrix} v_1 \\ v_2 \\ \bullet \\ \bullet \\ \bullet \\ v_7 \end{pmatrix}$.

The product $A \cdot \mathbf{v}$ is a column vector $\mathbf{w} = \begin{pmatrix} w_1 \\ w_2 \\ \bullet \\ \bullet \\ w_7 \end{pmatrix}$

in which each component of this vector is the product of the corresponding row of A times v $(w_i = a_{i1}v_1 + a_{i2}v_2 + \ldots + a_{i7}v_7)$.

The matrix A is stored by rows in memory in 49 locations, starting at location 1000: $a_{11}, a_{12}, \ldots, a_{17}, a_{21}, a_{22}, \ldots, a_{27}, \ldots, a_{71}, a_{72}, \ldots, a_{77}$. The vector v is stored sequentially, starting in location 0900, and we wish to compute w and store it in memory, starting in location 0800. Prepare a block diagram and write a program to perform the above calculation. You may use index registers. The numbers have the following form:

$$a_{ij} = \text{XX.XX}, \ v_j = \text{XX.XX}, \ w_k = \text{XXXXX.XX}.$$

CHAPTER
8 INTRODUCTION TO
AUTOMATIC PROGRAMMING

IN CHAPTERS 6 and 7 we studied the detailed characteristics of the MAC in order to develop an understanding of what computers can do, how they do it, and how the problem must be expressed in terms of machine instructions. After obtaining a thorough understanding of the problem to be solved, the person preparing the program must analyze the problem, devise a step-by-step process which will produce a solution, and express this process as a sequence of instructions which are meaningful to the machine. This overall process, from logical analysis through written machine instructions, is called *programming*. The last step in the overall process of programming, the preparation of the machine instructions from a detailed block diagram, is known as *coding*.

Actually, the procedure for solving the problem can be unambiguously expressed through the block diagram, so the coding can be a relatively straightforward, noncreative task, but one that involves strict attention to detail and a lot of routine effort, such as substituting numeric operation codes for operation abbreviations, writing instruction locations for each instruction, assigning memory locations to data, etc.

Early in the history of the use of computers it became obvious that the computer itself could be used for the routine operations involved in coding. And it was later discovered that the computer could also be used to translate the problem, expressed in a language convenient to the programmer, into detailed machine instructions. This use of the computer to assist in the task of coding is known as *automatic programming* (or automatic coding), and a great deal of effort has been devoted to the development of automatic programming techniques. In fact, automatic programming has become so widely accepted that it is unusual to write a program in pure machine language.

The term automatic programming encompasses a tremendous variety of techniques, ranging from standardized routines which may be used to solve a specific mathematical problem (without any coding at all, or even block diagramming) to translating programs that accept, as input, a problem stated in a language similar to that used in the detailed block diagram and produce, as output, a machine-language program. The computer programs that are available to assist in the coding process (and thus implement automatic programming techniques) are often referred to as the "software" of the equipment. In the remainder of this chapter we will illustrate some important automatic programming techniques and discuss their advantages and limitations.

SYMBOLIC PROGRAMMING

The simplest and one of the most useful automatic programming techniques allows the coder to write the program in a language that closely resembles the machine instructions but expresses them in a more convenient form. In a symbolic system the programmer may use alphameric (alpha-numeric) operation abbreviations instead of operation codes. He need not write memory addresses and keep track of memory, but may use "names" to designate the data or instructions to which the program refers. Furthermore—even if the machine is binary, or has a complex representation of the instruction itself—the programmer may write instructions in a notation (alphabetic or decimal) that is convenient to him.

In a basic symbolic programming system the programmer writes an instruction for each machine-language instruction in the program. He also writes some instructions that describe the form of the data as they enter the computer, the form in which the output is to be presented, and instructions which control the operation of the *assembly program* that translates his instructions into the machine-language instructions.

As shown in Figure 8–1, the symbolic instructions written by the programmer are entered as input into the computer, and the assembly program (or processor) causes the computer to convert these instructions into a machine-language program that is the output of the assembly process. This machine-language program may then be loaded into the memory of the machine just as if it had been written directly by the programmer. The program, as written in symbolic language, is called the *source program.* The machine-language program that will result is called the *object program.* The computer program that translates from the source program to the object program is called the *assembly program,* or the *processor.*

Let us now consider a specific symbolic coding system for the MAC.[1] This is a simplified system which excludes a number of variations that sometimes simplify the coding process but which would only "add to the confusion" at this stage of the learning process.

The form on which the symbolic program is written is shown in Figure 8–2. The top two lines include the name of the problem or program, the name of the coder, the date, and the page number. The heading of the body of the form deserves more detailed discussion. The field headed Line refers to a sequential line number which indicates the order in which the instructions are to be assembled. This is a three-digit number (with a decimal point understood at the

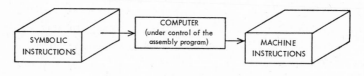

FIG. 8–1

Translating the Symbolic Program

dashed line between the units and tenths position). Thus the first line would be numbered 010, the second line would be numbered 020, and so on. This numbering system makes it possible to insert as many as nine instructions between two lines by writing them on another sheet and numbering them by use of the third digit so that they are between the two line numbers on the original program sheet.

The remaining fields on the form correspond to portions of the MAC instruction as written on a coding sheet. Location indicates the location of the instruction, Operation refers to the alphabetic operation abbreviation, and the Operand field corresponds to the data address of the instruction. There is also a single column field (Index) to indicate the index register tag and another single column field (Indirect) to indicate an indirect address. The field corresponding to columns 25 through 72 may be used for comments, and columns 73

---

[1] This is based upon the IBM 7070 Basic Autocoder description in *7070 Basic Autocoder Reference Manual,* published by International Business Machines Corporation in 1960 (Form No. 28–6078).

Problem

Coder | Date | Page | of

Line		Location		Operation		Operand		Index	Indirect	Comments		Identification	
1	3	4	8	9	11	12		22		25		72 73	80

FIG. 8-2
MAC Symbolic Coding Form

through 80 are used for identification of the program, usually page number and problem number.

You may have noticed that there is no place on this form for partial word indicators in the instruction. Field definition indicators are automatically inserted into instructions by the assembly program. The data fields are defined by means of symbolic operations that provide information necessary for field definition to the assembly program, but which do not correspond to basic machine-language operations.

Symbolic Addressing

In symbolic programming we do not use numeric operation codes but rather the three-character alphameric operation abbreviations, which we have been using in our programming. These abbreviations are written in the operation field.

Both the Location and the Operand fields may correspond to memory addresses, and in order to understand how they are written we must first discuss *symbolic addressing*. A symbolic address consists of from one to five alphameric characters, *the first of which must be alphabetical*. Symbolic addresses are left-adjusted, so that the left-most character is written in column 4 or 12. A symbol stands for a memory location, and whenever the same symbol is encountered within the program the same memory location is substituted for that symbol. For example, if we wish to add an hours field into the A register, we could write ADA HRS rather than using the actual memory location for hours (which might be 0025). When the assembly program first encounters a symbol it assigns a memory address to the symbol and stores both the symbol and its equivalent address in a table. The next time this symbol is encountered it is found by Table Look-up and the same address is substituted for it to make up a machine-language instruction.

In the location field, which corresponds to the location of an instruction, only those instructions which are referred to elsewhere in the program need be assigned symbols. For those instructions that are not referred to (either to be modified or to be branched to), the location field may be left blank and their locations are sequentially assigned by the assembly program.

An actual machine address (also left-justified, but with numeric left-most character) may be used either in the location or the operand field. Note, however, that actual addresses must be used with considerable caution because the assembly program may assign a symbol to that address without recognizing that it has been used for another purpose. The major use of actual addresses in the MAC is for the data address of a Shift instruction, where a conflict cannot arise because this address does not really refer to memory at all.

The operand field corresponds to the data address of a MAC instruction and is usually a symbolic address. However, *literal addresses* may also be used in this field. A literal address is the actual data to be operated on by the instruction—a one to ten digit number *preceded by a + or − sign*. The literal address is used to supply a constant to the program, and the assembly program stores this constant in a memory location and substitutes the location of this constant as the data address of the instruction.

The index field is used to tag an instruction with the number of the desired index register. To tag a data address as an indirect address, a 1 is inserted in the indirect field. If these fields are blank, no index register or indirect address is involved.

Pseudo-operations

When using symbols for addresses it is necessary to establish a correspondence between the symbols and the format of the input and output data. This is one of the functions that is performed by various *pseudo-operations* which are necessary for assembling the program but which are not translated into machine instructions. We will discuss four pseudo-operations: Define Area (DA), Define Constant (DC), Equate (EQU), and Control (CTL).

DA (Define Area). The pseudo-operation DA may be used to reserve and define any portion of memory, such as input, output, or a work area. This operation provides the assembly program with the precise format of the data located in the area being defined. The assembly program then automatically assigns locations and field definition indicators so that the data may be conveniently referred to by symbolic addresses.

A DA operation consists of a header line and one or more succeeding lines with blank operation columns. The DA header line is used to initiate the reservation of a portion of memory and to indicate the number of words in the area. The succeeding entries define the fields within the area and specify the word (or portion of a word) of memory to be reserved for each such field.

In the header lines, the symbol written in the location column specifies the name of the area, DA is recorded under the operation, and the number of words in the area is recorded under the operand. Lines directly below the DA header line contain the names and the starting and ending positions of fields composing the area.

When defining the fields within an area, we must remember that the MAC has the flexibility of operating on a field within a word. When the indicator portion of a machine-language instruction contains field definition digits, these digits specify the portion of the word to be used in the operation. Since a field which bridges two or more consecutive words cannot be operated on with a single instruction, the separate portions of such a field must be given different names. We specify that no single symbolic name can correspond to a field which is included in two or more memory words.

The positions of an area are indicated by word and position within the word. The first word of the area is referred to as word 0, the second word is word 1, the third word is word 2, and so forth. Digits within a word are numbered 0 through 9, from left to right. A *digit position* of an area is defined as a word-number followed immediately by a digit number. For example, the sixth digit (digit 5) of the third word (word 2) corresponds to the digit position 25. Since there may be more than ten words in an area, the word may be designated by a two-digit number. Thus the sixth digit of the thirteenth word would be indicated by 125.

The symbol corresponding to a field is entered under the location column, the operation column is left blank, and the limits of the field are indicated in the operand column. The limits of the field are defined by placing the digit position of the left-most character of the field first in the operand column, followed by a comma and the digit position of the right-most character of the field. In a single-position field the comma and the right-most limit digit indication may be omitted.

For example, suppose we are concerned with an input area in which the control panel of the MAC is wired so that man-number is wired into the low-order five positions of the first input word, rate enters the lower three positions of the second input word, and hours enters the low order three positions of the third word of input storage. We could define the input area as:

Location	Operation	Operand
INPUT	DA	20
MANIN		00,09
RATE		10,19
HRS		20,29

Note in this example that the number of words in the input area has been designated as 20, although only 3 are shown. This is because reading a card destroys the contents of a 20-word block, and we wish to prevent the assembly program from assigning the other 17 words to some other use. We could have many choices for the symbolic designation of man-number and rate. We have chosen to use MANIN for man-number because we wish to punch man-number in our output card, so we must distinguish between the designation of man-number in the input area from that of man-number in the output area.

Why did we designate all ten positions of each word for each field when they only required the lower portion of the word? This was purely arbitrary—we could have accomplished the same thing by designating the limits of MANIN as 05,09 rather than 00,09. However, unless we are using the other part of the word for something else, little is gained by designating a partial word.

On the other hand, suppose we had packed Rate into the upper three positions of the second input word and Hours into the lower three positions:

$$
\begin{array}{lll}
\text{Man-Number} & \text{00000xxxxx} & \text{word 1} \\
 & \text{x.xx0000xx.x} & \text{word 2} \\
 & \text{Rate \quad Hours} &
\end{array}
$$

Then the area definition would have been:

Location	Operation	Operand
INPUT	DA	20
MANIN		00,09
RATE		10,12
HRS		17,19

DC (Define Constant). The pseudo-operation DC may be used to enter numeric or alphameric constants into the program and to assign names to constants for ease of reference. Like the DA operation, the DC operation consists of a heading line and one or more succeeding entries with blank operation columns. The DC header line directs the processor to assign an area in storage to the constants entered directly below. The format of the DC header line is the same as that of the DA header line. It is not necessary to assign a symbol to the constant area unless a symbol is desired for some particular reason. Numerical constants are entered by naming them in the location field and then writing them (preceded by a + or − sign) in the operand column. Leading zeros need not be written.

A five-position alphameric constant[2] may be entered in the same way by specifying its name in the location column and writing an @ symbol, followed by the alphameric constant in the operand column. Any symbol that has been assigned a location by the assembly program may also be specified as a constant by naming it in the location field and then placing the symbol to which it corresponds in the operand field, preceded by a + or − sign. In the illustration below, 0000000015+ would be stored as C1, 0000031416− would be stored as constant C2, the 10-digit numeric equivalent of NET P as C3, the numeric equivalent of AY as C4, and the memory location number assigned to the symbol START would be stored as constant C5.

Location	Operation	Operand
	DC	5
C1		+15
C2		−31416
C3		@ NET P
C4		@ AY
C5		+START

EQU (Equate). The pseudo-operation EQU may be used to equate a symbol to another symbol or an actual address. For example, when two or more people work on the same program two different symbols may be inadvertently assigned to the same item in different parts of the program. The EQU operation may be used to equate one symbol to the other. In using this operation the first symbol is inserted under the Location column, the EQU is placed in the Operation column, and the machine address or the second symbol is placed in the Operand column.

CTL (Control). Two operations are performed by the CTL pseudo-instruction. The first tells the assembly program where in memory to begin the assembly process, and is designated by the

---

[2] Recall that the MAC can store a five-position alphabetic field in a ten-digit word by translating each alphabetic character into a two-digit number.

symbol BEGIN in the Location column. The pseudo-operation CTL is placed in the Operation column, and the memory address at which the program is to begin is placed in the Operand column. Similarly, when the end of the program is reached, the symbol END is placed in the Location column, the CTL pseudo-operation abbreviation is placed in the Operation column, and the memory location of the first instruction in the program is placed under the Operand column. This pseudo-instruction tells the assembly program that this program is complete, and it also causes the assembly program to generate a Branch Unconditionally instruction at the end of the loading process that transfers control to the first instruction in the program and commences its execution.

Assembly of the Program

The source program is punched into cards with one card for each line on the symbolic coding form. The assembly process illustrated in Fig 8–1 actually requires two passes through the machine. On the first pass the machine establishes a symbol table that includes each symbol in the program and the machine address that is assigned to it. As the first symbolic instruction is processed, its location is specified by the BEGIN control operation. As succeeding instructions are read they are assigned sequential locations in memory, and any symbols appearing under the Location column are placed in the symbol table and given the memory address to which they correspond. All symbols corresponding to data and constants (except literals) must be defined by means of the DA and DC pseudo-operations, and these are placed in the symbol table along with their corresponding memory addresses. Finally, the literals are assigned memory locations.

At the conclusion of the first pass, the completed symbol table is in the memory of the machine. This process assigns the instructions in the program to a block of sequential memory locations, the data and constants are assigned to the next portion of memory, and lastly the literals are assigned to the next available memory locations. Thus the entire program is assigned to a continuous sequence of memory addresses.

It should be noted that this memory assignment process has not taken into account the machine addresses that the programmer might have assigned by direct addressing. It is the programmer's responsibility to make sure that any direct addresses that are actually memory locations do not conflict with the memory locations that are assigned by the assembly program. One way he may do this is by using a block of the first part of memory for his machine addresses and assuring, through the BEGIN control operation, that the assembly program begins memory assignment beyond the block that he has used.

For the second pass, the source program cards must be reinserted in the card reader of the computer.[3] As each source instruction is read the operation code is substituted for the operation abbreviation, the instruction is assigned the proper machine location, and the symbol in the Operand column is looked up in the symbol table and assigned its corresponding memory location and any necessary partial word indicators. Likewise, index tags and indirect address tags are inserted to produce a completed machine-language instruction. An output card is punched containing the assembled instruction in single-card loader form in columns 1 to 40. At the same time the assembled program may be listed on the printer, with the symbolic instruction printed alongside the resulting machine-language instruction.

Several possible errors may be detected in the assembly process. For example, any invalid operation abbreviations that occur, as well as symbols that are not properly defined in the program, can be indicated by printing an * beside the erroneous instruction. Thus these errors can be corrected before attempting to run the program on the machine.

Examples

As our first example of a symbolic program, consider the program which we created in Chapter 6 to summarize a deck of transaction cards. To refresh your memory, we have a deck of punched card labor tickets containing man-number, job number, and hours, which we wish to summarize by job number (assuming that the cards are in job number sequence when they enter the machine). The block diagram for this program is presented in Figure 6–24, and the machine-language program is shown in Example 6–32. A symbolic program for this problem is shown in Example 8–1.

First, let us consider the input area definition in lines 20.0 through 22.0. Line 20.0 is the header line in which the DA pseudo-operation is specified for a 20-word input area. The control panel is wired so that the job number is entered in the first word of the input storage and the hours are entered in the second word. On line 21.0 we assign

---

[3] On machines that have magnetic tapes (or other auxiliary file devices) the cards do not have to be sent through the machine a second time since the source information can be read from the file on the second pass.

Example 8–I

Line	Location	Operation	Operand
01:0	BEGIN	CTL	0101
02:0	START	RDC	INPUT
03:0	NEWJB	LDM	JOBIN
04:0		STM	JOBOT
05:0		LDM	HRS
06:0 .		STM	THRS
07:0	OLDJB	BEC	(END)
08:0		RDC	INPUT
09:0		RAA	JOBIN
10:0		SUA	JOBOT
11:0		BZA	(TOTAL)
12:0		PRT	OTPUT
13:0		BRU	(NEWJB)
14:0	TOTAL	RAA	THRS
15:0		ADA	HRS
16:0		STA	THRS
17:0		BRU	(OLDJB)
18:0	END	PRT	OTPUT
19:0		HLT	0001
20:0	INPUT	DA	20
21:0	JOBIN		00,09
22:0	HRS		10,19
23:0	OTPUT	DA	2
24:0	JOBOT		00,09
25:0	THRS		10,19
26:0	END	CTL	START

the symbol JOBIN to the job number as it appears in the input area, and in line 22.0 we assign the symbol HRS to the hours in the input area.

In line 23.0 we set up the header for the two-word output area. Since the punch instruction does not destroy unused portions of the memory block, this output area need only be specified as two words. In line 24.0 we assign the symbol JOBOT for the job number in the output area, and in line 25.0 we assign the symbol THRS to the total hours output.

Note that the six lines described above do not appear on the machine-language programming sheet in Example 6–32. However, to write the machine-language program we had to establish a diagram of the input and output areas (at least mentally) in order to assign addresses to the fields processed by the program.

In the Location column in Example 8–1, the symbol START designates the beginning instruction in the program. The symbols NEWJB, OLDJB, TOTAL, and END are necessary because the corresponding instructions are referred to by means of the data addresses of branch instructions. They indicate the beginning instructions of various blocks in the block diagram.

Since the BEGIN control operation in line 01.0 starts the memory assignment in location 0101, the location column of the assembled program would be identical with that shown in Example 6–32. However, the input area would be words 0119 through 0138, and the output area would be 0139 (for JOBOT) and 0140 (for THRS).

As a second example of symbolic programming consider the problem in Example 7–12 of Chapter 7. In this problem we have a set of labor cost balances for jobs 1 through 500, stored in memory locations 0001 through 0500. We wish to punch 500 cards, each containing a job number and the balance for that job. Figure 7–13 showed a block diagram for this problem; Example 8–2 shows us a symbolic program.

This symbolic program is rather straightforward. Considering the output first, we wish to punch the location (job number) from word 1 and the contents of that location from word 2 of the output buffer, as indicated by the definition of the output area in lines 12.0 through 14.0. The major interest in this example lies in the use of literals in lines 02.0, 07.0, and 09.0. An absolute address is used in line 03.0 as the data address of the LDM instruction. Of course, this address is modified before execution by adding the contents of index register 1 (as indicated in the Index column). An absolute address is also used on line 11.0 to specify the arbitrary data address of the Halt instruction.

After assembly, this program would strongly resemble the program in Example 7–12, except that the output area would be words 1010 and 1011 and that the constants 1, 500, and 501 would be stored in 1012–1014 respectively.

Example 8–2

Line	Location	Operation	Operand	Index
01:0	BEGIN	CTL	1000	
02:0	START	RA1	+1	
03:0	LOOP	LDM	(0000)	1
04:0		STM	CONTS	
05:0		ST1	LOC	
06:0		PCD	OTPUT	
07:0		SU1	+500	
08:0		BZ1	HALT	
09:0		AD1	+501	
10:0		BRU	LOOP	
11:0	HALT	HLT	0001	
12:0	OTPUT	DA	2	
13:0	LOC		00,09	
14:0	CONTS		10,19	
15:0	END	CTL	START	

Macroinstructions

In our discussion of subroutines in Chapter 7 we noted the problem of relocating them so that they fit into the proper memory locations for the program in which they are employed. Now that we are familiar with symbolic programming we recognize that subroutines can be written in symbolic language so that they can be incorporated into the main program in the process of symbolic assembly. Actually the symbolic programming system can be easily extended to do much more than merely make the relocation of subroutines easier, for symbolic macroinstructions can make the process of incorporating subroutines extremely simple.

A *macro-instruction* (frequently called a *macro*) is a pseudo-instruction in the symbolic language that causes the assembly program to insert an open subroutine and tailors that subroutine to suit the locations of the data which it uses. Thus a macro is an extension of the machine language, for it provides the programmer with an instruction which is basically the same to him as a machine-language instruction insofar as what he must do in order to use it. For example, the macro SQR might instruct the machine (through an open subroutine) to take the square root of the quantity indicated by the symbol under the Operand column. As with any machine instruction or subroutine, the programmer must be aware of the details of what the macro does. For example, he must know that the resulting square root appears in the A register, and that the previous contents of the M register are destroyed.

If the open subroutine corresponding to the macro requires several parameters as input information, they may be written on successive lines (in a specified order) in the Operand column. Note that certain macros of general value may be supplied as a part of the symbolic programming system. However, additional macros can be written by the programmer himself and incorporated into the assembly system for his individual use or for other programmers in his installation.

As we mentioned, macroinstructions represent open subroutines, so the subroutine is incorporated into the program every time the macro is specified on the program sheet. Using the macro several times in the same program may lead to a considerable waste of memory, as opposed to using a closed subroutine. Of course it is possible to establish a library of closed subroutines that can be incorporated into the program by the assembly program. If care is taken to write these subroutines so that they are called in the same way, a call macro (CAL) can be established that links the closed subroutine into the main program by specifying the name of the subroutine in the Operand column and listing the symbolic names of the parameters to which the subroutine refers (in the specified order) on succeeding lines of the coding form.

A library of subroutines corresponding to the macroinstructions must be incorporated as a part of the assembly program. As we mentioned, such a library is open-ended; the programmer may create his own macroinstructions and insert them in the subroutine library, thus extending the assembly language to suit his own needs or the needs of a particular installation.

Note that when we introduce macroinstructions we eliminate the one-to-one translation that previously characterized symbolic programming. Macros make it possible for the programmer to create many machine instructions by writing a single line on the symbolic programming sheet.

Advantages

Symbolic programming provides several important advantages over machine-language programming. In the first place, the computer handles the clerical work of assigning memory and of translating symbols to operation codes, thus simplifying the task of programming. Moreover, since the assembly program handles the memory assignment, it is more convenient for several people to work on a program simultaneously, for they do not have to be concerned about interfering with each other in the machine's memory. They do, however, have to agree precisely upon the symbols to be used, although the EQU pseudo-operation is helpful when two programmers inadvertently use different symbols for the same information.

A second advantage of symbolic programming lies in the area of documentation. It is much easier for the programmer to read and understand his program when it is written in symbolic form than when it is written in pure machine language. Moreover, it is much easier for someone who is not intimately familiar with the program to read and understand it in symbolic form. It is extremely important in an installation that any competent programmer be able to figure out what is going on in any program, for programs may outlast the people who prepare them. For this reason alone it is worthwhile to program in symbolic language rather than machine language.

Perhaps the most important advantage of symbolic programming is the ease of making changes. When in a machine-language program it is necessary to add or delete an instruction, all of the instruction locations beyond that point in the program must be changed, and any data addresses referring to these instructions must also be changed. With symbolic programming, however, memory locations are not assigned until after the program has been completed, so an instruction can be deleted by simply crossing it out and one can be inserted by merely writing it with a line number that places it in the proper position. This ability to easily modify the program is of great importance during the writing of the program, during the process of detecting and eliminating errors in the program, and when the program must be changed in order to improve or bring it up to date.

Another advantage of symbolic programming is the ease with which subroutines may be incorporated into the program. In fact, where they can be used macroinstructions make it possible to greatly reduce programming effort by producing many machine instructions from a single line of coding.

Symbolic programming also has some limitations. In contrast to some of the automatic programming techniques which we will discuss later, the programmer still must think in terms of individual machine instructions[4] and (except for the use of macros) he must write at least as many instructions as he would write in pure machine language. Also, machine time is required to assemble the program into a machine-language program, and this machine time may represent a significant cost. When changes are made in the program, it is usually reassembled, and in the process of testing and correction many assemblies may be necessary.

There is no question, however, but that the advantages of symbolic programming outweigh its disadvantages when compared to machine-language programming. In fact, it is safe to say that symbolic programming has essentially replaced machine-language programming except for machines for which no adequate assembly program has been written.

PROCEDURE-ORIENTED LANGUAGES

With the exception of macroinstructions, each symbolic instruction produces but one machine-language instruction. Another characteristic of symbolic systems is the fact that although the symbolic system eliminates the detail of working directly with machine memory addresses, the programmer still must express the problem in terms of the specific instructions which the machine can execute. Thus symbolic programming systems can be referred to as machine-oriented programming languages.

It is possible to conceive of programming languages in which the structure of the language is designed for ease in expressing a class of procedures, rather than simply reducing the effort involved in writing each computer instruction. Many such procedure-oriented programming languages have been devised. For example, COBOL is de-

---

[4] As we will see later, this close correspondence with the basic machine language may have advantages as well as disadvantages.

signed to express data processing procedures in a language strongly resembles ordinary English. ALGOL and FORTRAN designed to express mathematical problems in languages closely sembling mathematics. DYNAMO is designed for expressing industrial dynamics problems, and the various versions of IPL (Information Processing Language) are designed for expressing complex logical decisions involved in the simulation of heuristic processes.[5]

Each procedure-oriented programming system is composed of two elements. First, there must be the language: the set of rules describing how the problem can be expressed so precisely that it can be unambiguously translated into a machine-language program. Second, there must be a processor (frequently referred to as a compiler) : a computer program that accepts the source language as input and translates it into a machine-language program as output (as shown in Figure 8–3). As before, the program expressed in the procedure-oriented language is called the *source* program, and the resulting machine-language program is called the *object* program.

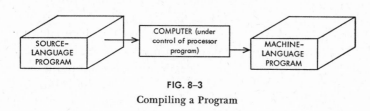

FIG. 8–3

Compiling a Program

FORTRAN

In order to better understand the characteristics of procedure-oriented languages, and to analyze their advantages and limitations, let us consider the FORTRAN language. FORTRAN makes an excellent illustration because it is widely used and because FORTRAN compilers are available for a large number of different types of computers. In the following discussion we make no attempt to present FORTRAN in its entirety, only to illustrate some of its major characteristics.[6] For those who wish to learn to use FORTRAN, several excellent detailed descriptions of this language are noted in the Supplemental Readings at the end of this chapter.

In the FORTRAN language the problem is expressed in terms of statements (as shown in Example 8–3) rather than in terms of ma-

---

[5] For more detailed descriptions of these languages see Supplemental Readings at the end of this chapter.

[6] This discussion is adapted from *FORTRAN General Information Manual*, published by International Business Machines Corporation (Form No. F28–8074–1) , 1961.

chine instructions. Each FORTRAN statement is identified by a number, and is composed of numbers, variables, words, punctuation, and operation symbols. Although considerable flexibility of content is allowed, each type of statement must be written to conform *precisely* to a set of rigid rules governing its form, punctuation, and use.

Numbers that do not change in the program (called *constants*) can be written directly in a FORTRAN statement. Numbers that vary (called *variables*) may be designated by symbols similar to those used for symbolic addresses in symbolic programming systems. For example, 24 and 3.1416 are constants, while JOBNO and HOURS represent variables. In FORTRAN there are two types of numbers: those which involve decimals (called *floating decimal numbers*) and whole numbers (called *integers*). Constants which are integers are written without the decimal point (for example, 2, 4, −35, or 5243) while floating point numbers are written with a decimal point (for example, 243.05 or 143. or −.00325).

Variables that represent integers must begin with one of the following letters: I, J, K, L, M, or N. Variables beginning with any other letter are interpreted to represent floating decimal numbers. The distinction between the type of number or variables is important, for the FORTRAN system handles the decimal points properly with floating point numbers, but when calculating with integers only whole numbers are produced and all fractional parts of the results are simply dropped. Thus, for integers, $5 \div 2 = 2$ and $1 \div 3 = 0$.

A sequence of constants, variables, and operations symbols which indicates a quantity or a series of calculations is called an *expression*. For example, REGPA + OTPAY − DEDS is an expression. Plus (+) and minus (−) symbols exist in punched card code and are handled by most computers, but signs for multiplication and division are not usually available on such machines. Furthermore, it is impossible to represent exponents or subscripts in the usual way, for all symbols must appear on the same line when punched into a card or stored in a computer's memory. Therefore in FORTRAN we substitute operation symbols as follows: * indicates multiplication, / indicates division, and ** indicates exponentiation.

Ordinary Notation	FORTRAN Notation
$A \cdot B$	A*B
$A \div B$	A/B
A^2	A**2
A^N	A**N

Quantities connected by operation symbols must represent the same type of number, either floating point or integer, except that floating point quantities may have integral exponents. Note also that no operation symbols are assumed to be present, so 2B would not be interpreted to mean 2 times B (this would have to be written 2*B).

Parentheses may be used in the usual way to specify the order of operations. For example, A * B + C indicates that we add C to the product A times B, while A * (B + C) indicates that we add B and C and multiply the result by A. Where parentheses are omitted the order is taken to be from left to right within the following priorities: First, any exponentiation is evaluated, then multiplication and division are performed, and, finally, addition and subtraction are performed. For example, in the expression

$$A**B + C*B/E*F**2 - G$$

the A**B would be evaluated first and then the F**2 would be computed. Then C*B would be calculated; this would be divided by E, and this result would be multiplied by F**2. Finally, A**B would be added to C*B/E*F**2, and G would be subtracted to evaluate the expression as:

$$A^B + \left(\frac{C \cdot B}{E}\right)F^2 - G$$

There are three basic types of statements in the FORTRAN language: arithmetic, control, and input-output. Arithmetic statements cause calculations to take place; control statements perform the logical functions in the program (such as branching, looping, and instruction modification); and input-output statements cause cards to be read and punched (or other input-output media to be processed).

Arithmetic statements are always of the form:

$$\text{Variable} = \text{Expression}$$

For example:

$$X = A**B + C*D/E*F**2 - G$$

is an arithmetic statement, and means *substitute* the value obtained by evaluating the expression on the right for the value of the variable on the left-hand side. Note that this substitution meaning for the = sign is different from the ordinary meaning of equality, but it is consistent with our previous notation in block diagrams. As you may recall from Figure 7–2, $i = i + 1$ is nonsense in the usual meaning of equality, but makes good sense when it is interpreted to mean substitute the value $i + 1$ for i.

Example

As a simple example of FORTRAN language, let us consider the problem of summarizing the same deck of cards we used to illustrate symbolic programming. As you recall, we had a deck of punched-card labor tickets containing job number and hours which were sorted in job number sequence. We would like to process these cards and punch a card for each job containing job number and total hours. A block diagram for this problem is shown in Figure 8–4, the same block diagram that we used before except that it is expressed in symbolic notation and ignores end-of-file considerations.[7] The FORTRAN program is shown in Example 8–3.

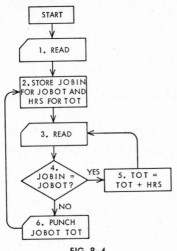

FIG. 8–4
FORTRAN Block Diagram for Group Control

First note that the statements in this program are numbered in the left-hand column. This numbering is purely arbitrary—the numbers need not be sequential or even in ascending sequence, as indicated by the fact that statement 1 is last. Referring to the block diagram, we see that the first block is handled by the combination of statements 100 and statement 1. In statement 100, the 1 after the word READ indicates that the form in which the information appears in the input area is indicated by statement 1. The names of the variables entered from the card (from left to right in the input area) are indicated by the symbols JOBIN and HRS to the right of the READ statement.

Just like the Define Area pseudo-operations in symbolic programming, FORMAT statements indicate the form of the input and

---

[7] End-of-file could be handled by adding an extra "dummy" card to the end of the data deck so that the last meaningful card would be processed properly. Because it is designed primarily for mathematical problems, elementary FORTRAN does not handle data processing end-of-file procedures as well as we would wish.

output data. In this illustration it is assumed that the job number is read into the low-order four positions of the first word of the input storage, and that hours (expressed in the form xx.x) are entered into the low-order positions of the second input word. This information is provided inside the parentheses in the FORMAT statement (statement number 1). The I in I10 indicates that the job number is an integer, and the 10 indicates that it can be considered to occupy all 10 positions of the first word. The F in F10.1 indicates that "hours" is a floating decimal number. The 10 indicates that it occupies the entire second word, and the .1 indicates that the number is understood to have one digit to the right of the decimal point.

If the control panel were wired so that the job number entered the

Example 8–3

Statement
No.

100	READ 1, JOBIN, HRS
101	JOBOT = JOBIN
102	TOT = HRS
103	READ 1, JOBIN, HRS
104	IF(JOBIN − JOBOT)105, 105, 107
105	TOT = TOT + HRS
106	GO TO 103
107	PUNCH 1, JOBOT, TOT
108	GO TO 101
1	FORMAT (I10, F10.1)

upper four positions of the first word, and the hours entered the low-order three positions of the input word, the format statement would be written:

FORMAT (I4, 3X, F3.1)

In this representation I4 indicates that JOBIN is a four-digit integer in the high-order four positions of the word; 3X specifies that the next three digits are to be skipped; and F3.1 indicates that HRS is of the form xx.x located in the low-order three positions of the word.

Statements 101 and 102 correspond to the second block of the block diagram. Statement 101 indicates that the job number just read from the card (JOBIN) is to be substituted for the job number in the output area (JOBOT). Statement 102 substitutes the hours just read from the card (HRS) for the total hours accumulated (TOT).

Statement 103 corresponds to block 3 in the block diagram, and its description is identical with that of statement 100. Statement 104 is a control statement corresponding to the decision block (block 4) in the block diagram. This statement instructs the machine to subtract JOBOT from JOBIN. If this result is negative, go to statement 105; if it is zero, go to statement 105; if it is positive, go to statement 107. Note that a negative number means the old job number is larger than the new job number, so the cards are out of sequence. If we wish to handle this out-of-sequence condition as an error, we could substitute some other statement number for the first 105 and use this new statement to take care of the error condition.

Statement 105 is an arithmetic statement, corresponding to block 5 in the block diagram. It adds hours to the previous total of hours. Statement 106 is another control statement, corresponding to a Branch Unconditionally to statement 103. Statement 107 is another input-output statement that is interpreted in the same manner as READ statement 100. A card is punched with the job number and total hours in the format indicated by statement 1; job number is punched as an integer from word 1, and total hours is punched as a floating decimal number (with one digit to the right of the decimal point) from output word 2.

Notice in this illustration that the programmer is almost entirely divorced from the consideration of the particular machine being used. Only in the construction of the FORMAT statement (statement number 1) need the programmer give any consideration to the characteristics of the machine, and here he must only know the word size and understand that the information from the card is entered through the control panel into certain positions of the input storage.

Inventory Cost Example

The FORTRAN language is specifically designed to be convenient in expressing mathematical problems, especially problems involving the manipulation of arrays of numbers, such as vectors or matrices. Let us consider the inventory cost problem that we used as an illustration in Chapter 7. We have the amounts (denoted by A_i) and the unit costs (denoted C_i) for 500 inventory items stored in memory, and we wish to compute the total cost (T) of this inventory:

$$T = A_1 \cdot C_1 + A_2 \cdot C_2 + A_3 \cdot C_3 + \cdots + A_{499} \cdot C_{499} + A_{500} \cdot C_{500}$$

With FORTRAN we need give no consideration to the specific memory locations in which these numbers are stored. FORTRAN, however, has a means of denoting such arrays through a modified form of subscript notation. Since we cannot indicate subscripts in FORTRAN by moving them down below the line we enclose them in parentheses after the variable. For example, A_1 is denoted A (1), A_2 becomes A (2), . . . , and A_{500} would be denoted A (500).

A block diagram for a machine-language program (using index registers) for this problem is shown in Figure 7–14. A FORTRAN program for this problem is shown in Example 8–4.

Example 8–4

```
 1  DIMENSION A(500), C(500)
 5  FORMAT (F10.2)
 9  S = 0.
10  DO 12 I = 1, 500
11  T = A(I)*C(I)
12  S = S + T
15  PUNCH 5, S
99  STOP
```

Statement 1 establishes the size of the amount and unit cost arrays. The A (500) indicates that the amount array contains at most 500 numbers, and the C (500) indicates that the cost array contains at most 500 numbers. Every subscripted variable in a FORTRAN program must appear in a DIMENSION statement so that the FORTRAN compiler will know how much memory to allot to the array. Note in our illustration that the arrays themselves must be assumed to have been created by an earlier portion of the FORTRAN program.

Statement 5 is an output FORMAT statement indicating that the result is a ten-position field with two places after the decimal point. Statement 9, setting up zeros in the location in which the sum will be accumulated, corresponds to block 1 in Figure 7–14.

Statement 10 is an illustration of a very powerful type of FORTRAN control statement called a *DO loop*. Statement 10 translates to: Execute the following statements, up to and including statement 12, starting with I = 1, then with I = 2, . . . and finally with I = 500.

This statement corresponds to the logic accomplished in blocks 2, 5, and 6 of Figure 7–14. Statement 11 is an arithmetic statement that multiplies $A_i \times C_i$ (in block 3), and statement 12 adds this product to the previous sum (as in block 4). Therefore, the first time around the loop statement 11 multiplies A_1 by C_1, the second time around it multiplies A_2 by C_2, and so on, until it has multiplied A_{500} by C_{500} and the sum has been accumulated as S.[8]

Finally, after the DO loop has been completed, statement 15 causes the result (S) to be punched into a card, as specified in FORMAT statement 5. Statement 99 then causes the computer to stop. The above problem could be easily generalized to handle arrays of any size (but less than or equal to 500) by changing statement 10 slightly so as to read:

$$10 \ DO \ 12 \ I = 1, \ N$$

and by specifying a value of N (either computed or read from a card) somewhere in the program before statement 10.

Functions

Subroutines may be easily incorporated into FORTRAN programs by defining them as *functions*, giving them names (which always end in "F"), and using the names in the FORTRAN statements. For example, the statement:

$$DIST = SQRTF(X**2 + Y**2)$$

would compute the square root of the floating decimal quantity $x^2 + y^2$ and substitute its value for the variable DIST. Again, the programmer must understand *exactly* what the subroutine does, and he must follow all the details of specifying the parameter, or parameters, in the parentheses.

Evaluation

Our discussion of FORTRAN has been elementary and incomplete, but any inference that FORTRAN provides many advantages for preparing mathematical problems for computer solution is more than justified. The other procedure-oriented languages are similarly helpful in solving the types of problems for which they are designed. Such languages, however, also have limitations and disadvantages which, along with their general advantages, we will presently examine. We must also recognize that we are entering a complex and controversial[9] area when we attempt to evaluate the impact of procedure-oriented languages.

Learning a procedure-oriented language is much easier than learn-

---

[8] It should also be noted that statements 11 and 12 could be replaced by the single statement 12 $S = S + A(I) * C(I)$.

[9] To obtain some idea of the depth of disagreement among experts in this area, read "The RAND Symposium: 1962," reported in *Datamation,* October, 1962, pp. 25–32.

ing the details of a specific machine. For example, it is claimed that the mathematically trained person can learn enough about FOR-TRAN in 8 to 12 hours' study to begin to express moderately complicated problems in this language. Thus the cost and time involved in learning enough to use a computer to solve problems is greatly reduced. This is particularly important for those who have no direct interest in computers themselves—who only wish to be able to use them to solve problems that arise in their major field of interest.

Since procedure-oriented languages eliminate most of the details associated with the use of computers, and also generate many instructions from a single line of information, these languages make the task of programming much easier, and reduce the cost and the time required for programming. For example, after the problem has been analyzed and block-diagrammed, a program that would require a week to write in symbolic language might be done in a day with FORTRAN. Moreover, since FORTRAN is easier to understand and involves fewer details, there are likely to be fewer mistakes in the resulting program, so less time and effort is required to eliminate errors. Also, many of the most common errors are detected in the compiling process and are therefore eliminated *before* the program is run on the machine.

Another important advantage of procedure-oriented programming systems, also shared with symbolic systems, is the ease with which programs can be modified. Statements can be added, changed, or eliminated; but the changes incorporated by such recompilation might have been very difficult to make in a machine-language program.

Since such languages are easily read with a minimum of training, they also provide built-in documentation as compared with machine language or even symbolic programs. This can be very important, for it often is necessary to communicate the content of a program to management or to other systems analysts or programmers involved in maintaining or modifying the program. This ease of communication should not be dismissed lightly, for these communication difficulties present some of the most vexing problems confronting the management of data processing organizations.

Finally, one of the most important advantages of procedure-oriented languages is that they are essentially machine independent. A problem programmed in the FORTRAN language can be run (with minor changes, primarily in the format statements) on most IBM computers and on many machines produced by other manufacturers. Similarly, COBOL compilers exist for a number of different machines[10] so that problems expressed in COBOL can be run on many different machines of several different manufacturers.

Machine independence of source-language programs is important in several ways. First, if programs are written in a machine-independent language it is possible to avoid much of the reprogramming cost associated with replacing an obsolete or outgrown machine with a newer and/or larger piece of equipment, for these programs can easily be recompiled for a new machine. Since reprogramming costs can otherwise run into hundreds of thousands of dollars, this is not an insignificant advantage. Secondly, the usefulness of programs of general interest (such as scientific programs) is greatly extended, for they are no longer restricted to a single type of machine. Thirdly, in a large organization that has many plants, it is possible to share data processing programs without requiring each plant to have the same type of computer.

Despite the impressive advantages of procedure-oriented programming systems, they also have some limitations and disadvantages. For example, a minor disadvantage is the cost of the machine time involved in compiling. One study indicates that the cost of compiling COBOL statements ranges from approximately 19¢ per 100 cards to more than $16 per 100 cards, depending upon the machine (and compiler) involved.[11] By the time the errors in a program are eliminated, it has usually been recompiled many times, so these compiling costs can and do add up.

Another minor but irritating problem is that such languages are frequently *almost* (but not quite) machine independent. This is a rather subtle problem, for most compilers will produce the results specified in the manuals that describe the language. However, there are peculiarities of each compiler that involve situations and circumstances that are not specified in the manual. The good programmer learns about these peculiarities of the specific compiler with which he is working, and takes advantage of them upon occasion. Then, when these programs are compiled for a different machine, different outcomes are obtained. This is true even for the various FORTRAN compilers produced for different IBM computers.

The major problem associated with problem-oriented languages,

---

[10] At one time it was specified that only computers for which a COBOL compiler was available would be considered for installation in the Department of Defense. Needless to say, this regulation stimulated the development of COBOL compilers for many different computers.

[11] Reported in *Honeywell EDP Newsletter*, February 1, 1964.

however, is that of object program efficiency. How efficient is the program produced through use of a procedure-oriented language as compared with a program for the same problem coded in a machine-oriented language? This is an illustration of an extremely simple question that has no simple answer, for there are many different considerations that interact to determine the answer in a specific set of circumstances. Hence this question may provoke a heated argument whenever several computer experts get together.

It can be argued that compilers are produced by the most expert programmers, men who should be able to incorporate their advanced techniques and most sophisticated approaches into the programs produced by the translating process, and thus the resulting program should be at least as efficient as one produced by the average run-of-the-mill programmer. On the other hand, one can also see that the process of translating from the procedure-oriented language to *any* machine language program involves a tremendous amount of ingenuity, so the task of writing a compiler that always produces the most efficient program may be almost impossible. Furthermore, much of the expert programmer's extra efficiency may be obtained by looking at the entire program as a unit and taking advantage of this "global" approach to increase efficiency. This is very difficult to do in a compiling process which looks at the program one statement at a time and analyzes it character by character. Thus, although it is possible that the resulting object program from a problem-oriented language could be as efficient as the program produced by an average programmer, it is more likely that such a program will be less efficient. The major question is: *How much* less efficient?

Actually, the answer to this question depends upon the sophistication of the user of the procedure-oriented language as well as upon the inherent efficiency of code produced by the compiler. For example, if the programmer knows absolutely nothing about computers, and consequently has no knowledge of the characteristics of the object program that will be produced, he has no criterion for choosing—on the basis of efficiency—between alternative approaches to expressing the problem. Under these circumstances one can obviously expect inefficient programs to result. On the other hand, if the programmer understands the characteristics of the machine that he is using, and if he has a good knowledge of the results that are produced by the compiler in the translating process, he can obviously make choices in writing the source program that will minimize the inefficiency of the object program.

Perhaps an even more subtle consideration is associated with the very fact of machine independence. As we have seen, the block diagram itself is related to the problems and opportunities that arise in the process of writing the program in machine language. Similarly, machine characteristics may dictate the most efficient overall approach to a problem. Thus when one eliminates the consideration of the peculiarities of a particular machine from the process of design of a program, he also eliminates many possibilities for increased efficiency. When one is not always considering the problem of writing an efficient program in terms of machine instructions, his block diagram is likely to produce a program of reduced efficiency. And when one takes a program that was designed to take advantage of the characteristics of a specific piece of equipment, and recompiles it for running on another machine with different characteristics, it is highly unlikely that the resulting program will be efficient—even if the compiler does an outstandingly efficient job of translating from the source language into the object program.

As an example of the importance of considering machine characteristics when writing a program, a simple problem was written in COBOL in two versions, both of which accomplished exactly the same end result.[12] One version was designed that took into account some elementary facts about the machine involved, while the other ignored the machine characteristics. The first version operated at *ten times the speed* of the inefficient version.

The total cost of solving a problem on the computer is composed of two separate costs: the cost of analyzing the problem and writing the program, and the cost of running the program on the machine. In general, the use of procedure-oriented languages will reduce the first of these costs, but it may increase the second.

From this type of analysis it is obvious that there are a number of problems that should be programmed through the use or procedure-oriented languages. For example, problems that are "one of a kind" (one-time reports and many engineering problems) obviously should be programmed in procedure-oriented languages because the costs of programming are quite large in comparison with the costs of running. On the other hand, the situation may be reversed for a complex data processing problem that is run day in and day out, month after month. In this case total costs may be reduced by investing time and money in producing as efficient a program as possible with a machine-oriented programming language.

12 Daniel D. McCracken, "Object Program Efficiency Revisited," *Datamation*, June, 1962, p. 32.

Thus one may conclude that most installations are likely to utilize more than one programming system. Although there are a few installations that utilize a single procedure-oriented language exclusively, most installations use several programming systems, including a symbolic system and one or more procedure-oriented languages. Each problem is analyzed and a decision is made as to which programming system should be used for that problem. In fact, it is even possible to use more than one programming system on a single problem by writing the major structure of the program in a procedure-oriented language and coding the subloops that are crucial for running efficiency in symbolic language.

To conclude this discussion we should note some important trends. (1) The unit costs of data processing are being steadily reduced by engineering developments that improve the machines, while at the same time the salaries of programmers are increasing. (2) This same improvement makes the machines more complicated and thus more difficult to program in machine-oriented languages. (3) We are making steady progress in designing languages and devising compilers that together produce more efficient object programs and require less time to compile. Consequently, in our attempts to minimize the total costs of preparing the program and running the problem, it appears inevitable that the general tendency must be in the direction of greater and greater use of procedure-oriented languages.

OTHER TYPES OF SOFTWARE

In addition to machine-oriented and procedure-oriented languages there are many other types of software that are of considerable importance. An important category includes the various types of generalized program packages that may be used to solve problems that recur frequently. For example, general programs are available for solving linear programming problems which will accept the data for a problem involving any number of variables (up to a specified limit), and any reasonable number of restrictions, and then calculate a solution to the problem. Other examples of such mathematical programs include matrix inversion routines, correlation and regression analysis programs, and a program that uses quadratic programming to perform investment portfolio analysis.

Another important class of software includes true problem-oriented program generators which accept the specifications of a specific problem and generate a program to solve that problem. An example of this type of system are the "report generators" that are designed to make the preparation of one-time reports easy and convenient on machines such as the MAC.[13] The input to a report generator includes information concerning:

1. The characteristics and formats of the cards used as input for the report.
2. The manipulation and calculation required to produce the information printed on the report.
3. The format of the report, including both the headings required and the specific location in which the results are to be printed.

Given the above information, the report generator produces a program that can be used to cause the computer to read the data cards and prepare the specified report as output.

Similarly, as we will see when we study magnetic tape-oriented machines, generalized sorting routines are available that will accept a description of the tape records and the location of the sorting fields within the records as input, and generate a program that will sort that tape and produce as output a magnetic tape arranged in the specified sequence.

When we study magnetic tape-oriented systems, we will encounter supervisory programs (or operating systems) which actually take over the operation of the computer and allow one to intermix assemblies, compilations, and running of programs, and at the same time will gather statistics concerning the time consumed in running each job. Some operating systems even determine the sequence in which the jobs are run on the machine according to the priorities assigned to each job and the time the job is due. Also, in magnetic tape-oriented systems we encounter input-output control systems that greatly simplify the complex programming problems involved in efficiently utilizing sophisticated input-output equipment.

Finally, there are a large number of utility programs that support the day-to-day operations of a data processing center. These include loading routines, memory dumps, diagnostic programs that assist in eliminating errors from programs, card-to-tape conversion routines, tape-printer routines, file loading and dumping routines, and snappy demonstration programs to impress visitors, such as routines for playing NIM and three dimensional Tic-Tac-Toe, or calculating the

---

[13] For example, see *Report Generator for IBM 1401 Card Systems: Preliminary Specifications*, Form J 29–0215, International Business Machines Corporation, White Plains, N.Y., 1960.

day of the week for any date, or playing music through an amplifier hooked into the computer, etc.

RESPONSIBILITY FOR SOFTWARE

As one can see from the above discussion, the software available for a given machine may be equally as important as the hardware characteristics of the equipment in determining how efficiently it can be used. Thus the machine manufacturer bears the responsibility for providing the automatic programming systems that are necessary to utilize the equipment efficiently. Today most[14] manufacturers accept this responsibility and accordingly schedule production of a new machine and preparation of the software so that *working* software is available when the first machines are delivered.

Many users' organizations exist (particularly in the engineering and scientific computer area) that put pressure upon the machine manufacturer to produce software with certain characteristics, and also cooperate to produce and share programs that have widespread usefulness. Organizations such as SHARE (formed by the users of large IBM scientific computers) and USE (formed by the users of Sperry-Rand computers) have exerted an important influence upon the development of software techniques and upon hardware design as well.

However, the final responsibility for software and its use rests with the individual data processing installation. It is usually necessary to select the software to be used in a specific installation, to establish policies governing its use, and even to modify systems to conform with the specific needs of the installation. Thus many installations have a small group of experts who are primarily concerned with evaluation, development, and modification of software and with educating the installation personnel concerning its use.

SUMMARY

The use of the computer itself to assist in writing programs —called automatic programming—is of extreme importance in the efficient use of computers. Automatic programming is so important, in fact, that very few programs are written in pure machine language. Symbolic programming systems are machine-oriented in that the programmer must think in terms of the machine

---

[14] On second thought, at least *some* manufacturers do this some of the time.

instructions and must write one instruction in the program for each machine-language instruction that is created by the translating process.

Macroinstructions, which translate into more than one machine-language instruction, may be incorporated into symbolic programming systems. Procedure-oriented languages allow the problem to be expressed in a form radically different from the machine language, and make it possible to prepare problems for computer solution with only a slight knowledge of the machine itself and with a minimum of training.

The total cost of using a computer to solve problems may involve costs associated with the following factors: training, writing a program, translating from the source program into the object program, running the program, modifying the program to improve it or adjust it to changes in the organization, documentation of the program, and changing from one type of computer equipment to another. All of these factors may be influenced by the automatic programming systems employed.

EXERCISES

8.1 Define each of the following terms:

a) source program
b) assembly program
c) object program
d) compiler
e) macro-instruction
f) closed subroutine

g) open subroutine
h) literal address
i) report generator
j) FORMAT statement
k) DO loop

8.2 Discuss the advantages of symbolic programming systems.

8.3 Discuss the advantages of procedure-oriented programming systems.

8.4 Discuss the disadvantages of procedure-oriented programming systems.

8.5 Write a program for problem 7–2 in the symbolic programming system described in this chapter.

8.6 Write a FORTRAN program for problem 7–2.

8.7 Assuming that a 200-entry table has already been stored, write a FORTRAN program for Table Look-up. The argument of the table is the variable JOB (I), the table value is RATE (I), the search argument is JOBIN, and we wish to set R equal to the proper rate from the table.

SUPPLEMENTAL READINGS

BAUMANN, R.; FELICIANO, M.; BAUER, F. L., AND SAMELSON, K. *Intro-duction to ALGOL*. Englewood Cliffs, N.J.: Prentice-Hall, Inc., 1964.
A basic introduction to the ALGOL language.

COBOL General Information Manual (Form F28–8053). International Business Machines Corporation, White Plains, N.Y., 1960.
This includes a basic COBOL primer together with a detailed description of the COBOL language.

COLEMAN HARRY L., AND SMALLWOOD, C. *Computer Language: An Autoinstructional Introduction to FORTRAN*. New York: McGraw-Hill Book Co., Inc., 1962.
Presents FORTRAN to the beginner by using a flow-chart-like diagrammatic format of the material.

FISHER, E.P., AND SWINDLE, G. F. *Computer Programming Systems*. New York: Holt, Rinehart & Winston, Inc., 1964.
This book is entirely devoted to the various types of computer software. For each type of system that we have discussed in this chapter, this book goes into detail in describing the language and how the processor accomplishes the translation from source program to object program.

FORTRAN General Information Manual (Form F28–8074). International Business Machines Corporation, White Plains, N.Y. (1961).
A general introduction to FORTRAN that indicates the major variations in this language as it has been implemented for various machines.

FORTRAN, Programmed Instruction Course. International Business Machines Corporation, White Plains, N.Y. (1963).
This course, consisting of five booklets (four chapters and a problem booklet), presents FORTRAN in terms of small "frames" of information, each requiring a response from the participant. These materials are apparently very effective in allowing one to learn to use FORTRAN on his own.

GORDON, G. "A General-Purpose Systems Simulator," *IBM Systems Journal*, September, 1962 (reprinted by IBM as Form 320–1714).
Describes a general-purpose simulation program designed to ease the problems of programming complex simulations by allowing the problem to be described by a simple block diagram language.

McCRACKEN, D. D. *A Guide to COBOL Programming*. New York: John Wiley & Sons, Inc., 1963.
A well-written introduction to COBOL.

———. *A Guide to FORTRAN Programming*. New York: John Wiley & Sons, Inc., 1961.
A well-written introduction to FORTRAN.

NEWELL, ALLEN (ed.). *Information Processing Language—V Manual.* Englewood Cliffs, N.J.: Prentice-Hall, Inc., 1961.

A collection of writings providing information on IPL-V.

PUGH, A. L., III. *DYNAMO User's Manual.* Cambridge, Mass.: The M.I.T. Press, 1961.

This describes the DYNAMO language designed for describing and running Industrial Dynamics Simulations. The system is not very understandable or useful without an understanding of *Industrial Dynamics* by Jay W. Forrester, published by the M.I.T. Press, 1961.

SAXON, J. A. *COBOL—A Self-Instructional Manual.* Englewood Cliffs, N.J.: Prentice-Hall, Inc., 1963.

An introduction to COBOL designed to assist a person to learn to use this language without other help.

9 DEVELOPMENT OF A COMPUTER PROCESSING SYSTEM

IN THE PREVIOUS discussion we have concentrated our attention upon the stored program and how it may be used to control the electronic data processing machine. It is necessary to understand the stored program concept to comprehend the capabilities and the limitations of electronic data processing machines. Moreover, a knowledge of the stored program also enables us to comprehend why electronic computers are so dependent upon people. But there is much more to the use of computers than writing programs, and we are now in a position to consider the entire process involved in converting a data processing area from manual or punched card methods to electronic data processing.

Although the machine program in a sense represents the culmination of the overall process, producing the machine instructions is only one of several steps, and it is one that can be partially mechanized through automatic programming. Even if coding is done through symbolic machine instructions, it usually requires only 20 to 30 percent of the total time involved. It should be emphasized that if the entire process is not properly carried out the proposed electronic data processing application will not be successful. Like the weakest link in the chain, each step is potentially of great importance, for failure of any of these steps can lead to an unsatisfactory result.

DEFINE THE PROBLEM

The first step in this process is defining the data processing problem itself. It is necessary to determine what information is required from the system in the form of reports; what is required from this portion of the system to integrate it into the overall data processing system; where the input information arises; what exceptions can arise and under what circumstances; how many transactions and exceptions of each type are involved; how each transaction and exception should be handled; what files are involved and what information is involved in them; whether results are required on schedule or on demand; and so forth *ad infinitum*. Even if we are merely converting an area as is, the answers to these questions may be far from obvious, for a data processing system is so complex that it usually must be defined by observing it in operation to determine what is being done. Only in the most extraordinary circumstances is it possible to find some individual in the organization who can define in sufficient detail an existing data processing area.

Furthermore, when converting an area to electronic data processing it is not uncommon to attempt to improve upon the results obtained from the old system. Often this improvement is one of the major motivations for the use of a computer, so the problem of defining the data processing area frequently becomes entwined with the fundamental question: What information should be processed and what results should be obtained? Thus, defining the data processing area may not only involve finding out what is being done at the present, but may also include answering the difficult question: What *should* be done? (This subject will be discussed in greater detail in Chapter 14, Systems Analysis and Design.)

It is obvious then that the data processing area must be properly defined; that it may be a time-consuming process; and that it is of crucial importance. It is not so obvious, but it is equally true, that we cannot determine what results we should produce without answering the question: What results *can* we produce, and what are the *costs* involved? In other words, the desirability of data processing results depends heavily upon the cost of obtaining them. This is a complex situation in which we should attempt to minimize the total of two costs: (1) the cost of data processing and (2) the cost of poor performance of the organizational system attributable to inadequate data processing.

The second of these two costs may be difficult to estimate, but there is little justification for any data processing unless it contributes to the performance of the business system. However, the first of these costs—the cost of data processing—is our concern at this time. To determine the most desirable end products we must be aware of the costs of the possible alternatives. Thus, we must move into the succeeding steps of development of a computer processing system, for costs cannot be reliably estimated until some further steps beyond the definition of the problem have been completed.

DEVISE PROCEDURE

The second step in the process is devising a procedure for converting the input information into the results that are required. A procedure usually is expressed in the form of a procedural flow chart showing where the information enters the system, any manual steps that are involved, the files that are maintained, the various machine runs required, and the output reports that are produced. We have encountered procedural flow charts before in our work with punched card machines.

Procedural flow charts superficially resemble block diagrams in that they are both composed of various shaped boxes connected by arrows. What, then, are the differences between procedural flow charts and block diagrams? In the first place, the procedural flow chart is concerned with the *flows* of data from source document to final result while the block diagram is concerned with *how* the processing steps are done.

More specifically, procedural flow charts are concerned with the flows of data *between* machines (only implying what goes on inside the machines) while block diagrams represent in detail what must be done *inside* the machine to accomplish the desired result. Thus, each machine block in a procedure represents an entire machine program, and the procedure integrates these programs together with auxiliary machine and manual data processing steps to produce the required results.

It may be somewhat surprising to discover that, despite the speed of the computer and the power of the stored program, it is usually necessary to break a data processing problem down into several machine runs. Not only does the size of the machine memory restrict the size of the program that can be accommodated, but the fact that files may be maintained in different sequences and that a variety of different outputs are required may also combine to make it necessary to split the processing into a number of different machine runs.

Example

In order to illustrate certain aspects of the overall process involved in converting to electronic data processing, let us consider the rather simple payroll example that we used to illustrate punched-card data processing in Chapter 4. In this example we wished to produce checks and earnings statements, and a payroll register as shown in Figures 4–1 and 4–2. In addition, we wished to produce a labor cost report.

In the example in Chapter 4 we assumed a straight hourly payroll. Let us complicate this somewhat by computing pay on the basis of the larger of the man's guaranteed rate and a rate for the operation he performs (similar to the problems in Exercises 7–9 through 7–11). Let us also change the labor cost report to be a summarization by work order within job within department, as shown in Figure 9–1. In punched card terms this would be minor control on Work Order

Dept.	Job	Work Number	Current Week		Total	
			Hours	Amount	Hours	Amount
13	3	1142	38	79 40	148	327 60
		1253	105	324 66	791	2418 84
		1425	72	175 00	844	1946 18
		1793	16	35 75	16	35 75
		2542	150	342 16	567	1031 82
		2553	93	215 50	270	650 60
			474	1172 47	2636	6410 79
	42	1107	59	142 50	602	1503 46
		1262	127	309 95	1003	2485 00
		1586	88	198 00	115	278 16
		1781	104	236 03	104	236 03

FIG. 9–1

Labor Cost Report

Number, intermediate control on Job Number, and major control on Department Number.

In addition to the results produced in Chapter 4, we wish to prepare summaries by department of regular hours, overtime hours, gross pay, withholding tax deductions, F.I.C.A. deductions, each voluntary deduction, and net pay. And we wish to handle bond deductions so that a bond is purchased whenever sufficient deductions have been accumulated to buy a bond of the designated denomination. On the other hand, there are a number of reports that might be desired from a payroll system that we are not considering, such as deduction registers, employee earnings registers, W-2 forms, and social security and income tax reports to the federal government.

Note that since we are considering a problem that is almost

identical to the one for which we have prepared a punched card procedure, we already have a reasonably well defined problem. Thus, we can concentrate upon the problems involved in developing procedures for using the computer to solve this problem. Our basic sources of input data will be a time card (like the one shown in Figure 4–4) and a labor ticket (as shown in Figure 4–5). However, we may wish to modify these inputs to suit the format of the additional file information—and even the form of the results produced to conform to (or to take advantage of) the capabilities of the equipment we will be using.

As we have frequently remarked before, looking at a finished procedure (or block diagram) seldom gives any indication of the thought processes required in its development. You should therefore pause at this point and ask yourself: What sort of procedure could I devise for preparing this payroll? Or better still: How would I go about devising a procedure for this problem?

Another question we should ask is: What do we really have to do? We must balance attendance hours with job time for each man, calculate the pay of each man (first gross, then net); we must summarize labor costs; and we must prepare the payroll register, checks and earnings statements, and the departmental summaries. How can we group these tasks together to form machine runs?

Initial Procedure

First we might consider modifying the punched card procedure, substituting the computer for punched card equipment where it appears desirable. Since we have changed the method of calculating the payroll, we need to get the rate for each operation into the procedure some way, so we might write it on (and punch it in) the job card. Furthermore, the job cards must stay with the time cards down through the calculation of gross pay since the pay calculation involves both the guaranteed rate for the man and the rate for the operation.

Thus, one approach would be to keep the punched card procedure (Figure 4–7) down through the time audit report. Then we could combine steps 3, 4, and 8 in one calculating run to produce job cards (with labor cost computed and punched for the labor distribution) and a current earnings card for each man. Then, after merging the year-to-date cards, master cards, and deduction cards with the current earnings cards, we could combine the gross-to-net calculation with the printing of the payroll register. At the same time we could punch cards for writing the check and earnings statements with the accounting machine.

Actually, we might even consider performing these two runs together, feeding into the computer the time cards, job cards, year-to-date cards, payroll master cards, and deduction cards, and producing as output the printed payroll register, job cards including job costs, new year-to-date cards, and cards for printing the checks. By

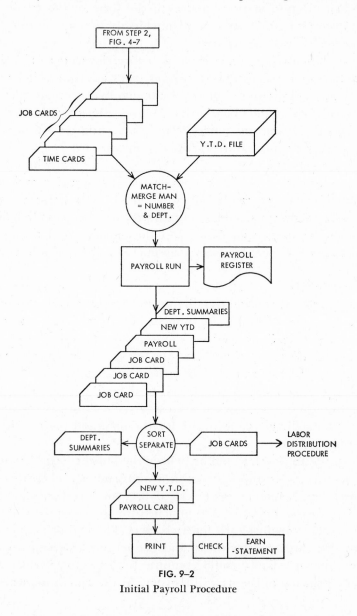

FIG. 9–2

Initial Payroll Procedure

spreading deductions in the year-to-date card and prepunching social security number and exemption code in the time card, we could eliminate the payroll master and deduction files and thereby substantially reduce card volume. Thus we might obtain the procedure shown in Figure 9–2. (Note that this starts after step 2 of the procedure in Figure 4–7.)

As indicated by this procedure, the input to the computer (in man-number and department number order) is a time card, a year-to-date and deduction card, and several job cards for each man. Output is a payroll card and a new year-to-date card (from which the checks and earnings statements can be printed) and several "costed" job cards for each man. After each department is processed, the machine also produces several departmental summary cards. The jobs cards go into a procedure where they are sorted by work order number, job number, and department number to produce the labor cost report shown in Figure 9–1 (and perhaps re-sorted for other reports).

Revised Procedure

This looks like a pretty good procedure, but actually it might be improved by making better use of computer memory. For example, rather than key-punch the operation rate into each job card, we could establish a table of operation rates in memory and obtain these rates by means of Table Look-up.

The procedure in Figure 9–2 punches a lot of cards, and punching is the slowest of the input-output operations. Thus we might establish a table within memory of the active job number and work order combinations and accumulate summaries of labor costs that would be punched at the end of each department and used to print the labor cost report directly.

Now, to proceed with our discussion, we require some volume figures. Let us assume this is a 10,000-man payroll (rather than a 1,500-man payroll as in Chapter 4), so there would be 60,000 job cards, 10,000 time cards, and 10,000 year-to-date cards. Assume also that we have 15 departments, each working on a maximum of 80 jobs per week, with 10 active work orders in each job in each department.

The labor cost table for a department would thus have $80 \times 10 = 800$ entries, and would require two words per entry (one for job number and work order number and the other for accumulating hours and cost), so this table takes up 1,600 words of memory. Also, we might have 100 operation rates to be stored (with operation number and rate in the same word), leaving only 300 words of memory for input-output areas and the program—which probably is not enough memory for so complicated a program.

How could we split this into two runs in order to reduce the memory requirements? One approach is shown in Figure 9–3, which begins after step 1 in the procedure in Figure 4–7. This procedure combines the time audit, gross pay calculation, and labor cost summarization into a first computer run. The gross-to-net calculation, department summarization, and printing of the payroll register are accomplished in a second computer run.

As indicated in Figure 9–3, the input to the first run is composed of the merged time and job cards for each department, preceded by a deck of department labor cost master cards (including a card for every active job and work order combination in that department) that establishes the memory table to accumulate labor costs. The output would be a printed time audit report indicating men for whom the attendance time and job time do not balance, together with job cards that do not correspond to valid job and work order combinations for that department. The punched output would consist of a payroll card for each man containing the information from his time card plus his gross pay. At the end of a department, department labor cost summary cards would be punched from the memory table (while the labor cost master cards are being read for the next department).

The payroll deck is merged with the old year-to-date and deduction cards to provide input to the gross-to-net payroll run, which produces the payroll register, department summary cards, and two cards for each man that can be used to print his check and earnings statement.

The detailed contents of the cards in this procedure would be as follows. First, as input to the first run, the time card would be the same as Figure 4–4 except that it would also include social security number and exemption code. The job card would be the same as Figure 4–5, except that the rate field would not be used. The department labor cost master card would contain department number, job number, and work order number.

The output cards from the first run would be a payroll card that would include all of the information from the time card plus gross earnings, and department labor cost summary cards that would include the information from the department labor cost master card plus total hours and total cost.

In addition to the payroll deck, the input to the second run would include old year-to-date cards containing man-number and department number, year-to-date totals of gross pay, withholding tax, last week's date and net pay, and the following deduction information: bond balance, bond purchase price, community chest, credit union, bonds, hospitalization, union dues, and miscellaneous.

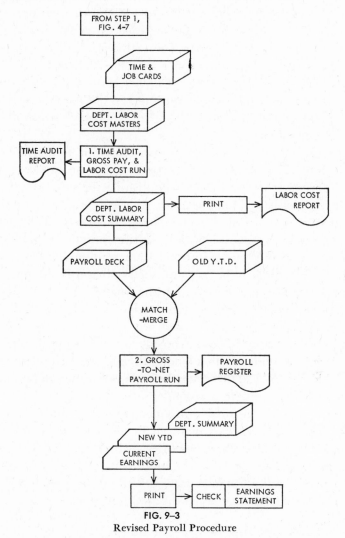

FIG. 9–3

Revised Payroll Procedure

Output from run 2 would be new year-to-date cards with the same fields, but updated information, and current earnings cards containing the information from the payroll card plus current withholding tax and current F.I.C.A. There would be a department summary card for each summary total containing department number, identifying account code, and the total cost.

Evaluation

Is this better than our first procedure? The first procedure punches 10,000 payroll cards, 10,000 new year-to-date cards and 60,000 job cards, for a total of 80,000 cards. Let us calculate the number of cards punched in the first run of this new procedure. First, we would punch 10,000 gross pay cards. Then for each department we would punch 800 cards (one for each entry in the labor cost table). Since there are 15 departments, this is 12,000 cards. On the second run we punch two cards per man, or 20,000 cards. Thus we punch $10,000 + 12,000 + 20,000 = 42,000$ cards in the second procedure as opposed to 80,000 in the first. In addition, we eliminate the time audit tabulation and the sorting and summarization of the labor cost procedure.

As a result of the above discussion we should note that the design of procedures is a rather complex process, for we can conceive of many different procedures for accomplishing the same result. But a procedure consists of breaking down the work to be accomplished into subtasks, each of which can be accomplished on a single machine run. Thus we must consider the resulting programs and estimate their memory requirements in order to determine whether or not a proposed procedure can be accomplished. Obviously the procedures that can be employed depend upon the capabilities of the available equipment as well as upon the characteristics of the job to be done. For example, if the MAC had 4,000 words of memory available we would be able to combine both runs of our procedure into one run.

Also, we have observed that among the many different procedures that could be employed there may be wide variations in the efficiency obtained. For example, our second procedure (Figure 9–3) would require roughly half the machine time of the first one (Figure 9–2). One of the major problems involved in utilizing the computer for data processing is therefore that of devising the most efficient procedure utilizing the available machine. If a good procedure can be found, the mechanization may prove to be very effective, but if a poor procedure is used, it is likely that the application will be economically unsound.

BLOCK DIAGRAMS

The procedure breaks our problem down into machine runs and defines each machine run in terms of its input and output and the processing that is to be accomplished. As we have seen in all our experience with programming, a block diagram must be constructed for the machine program before we can begin to prepare the instructions. Heretofore all our examples and exercises have been rather simple—so much so that our block diagrams have easily fit onto one page. However, when the problems begin to become more realistic, the task of preparing the block diagram becomes much more complex, so much so that it must be approached in stages.

Overall Block Diagram

The first stage might be termed an overall block diagram whose purpose is to express the major logic of the program. Most of the

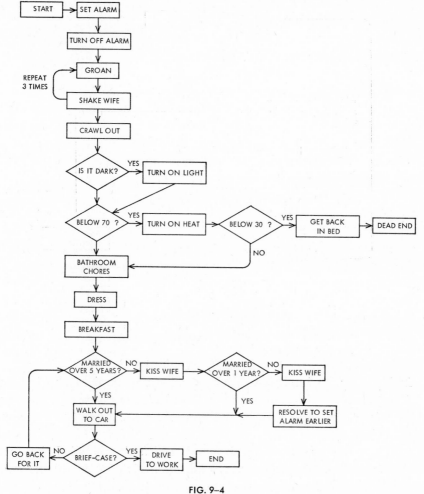

FIG. 9–4

How to Get to Work in the Morning

block diagrams that we have constructed so far have been overall block diagrams, but, since our problems have been simple, it has been possible to include sufficient detail in the overall block diagram to write the program directly from it. However, as we will see in our payroll example, in practical problems this may not be the case.

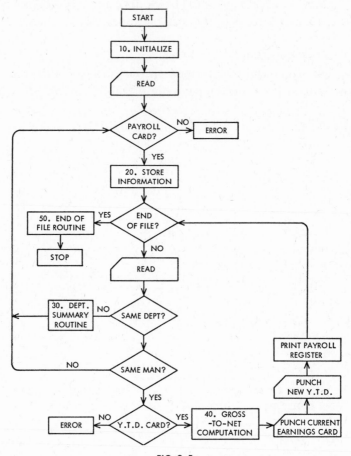

FIG. 9–5
Overall Block Diagram (Run 2)

Incidentally, an interesting illustration of a general block diagram that has been going the rounds among computer programmers for years is presented in Figure 9–4. You might see if you can improve upon its logic.

Although the amount of detail which is included in this type of block diagram will vary from one individual to another and from one situation to another, the overall block diagram should be simple enough to be expressed on a piece of paper of reasonable size, and yet it should adequately exhibit the relationships between the various types of input and output and the major processing steps involved in the machine run. Not only is the overall block diagram valuable in communicating to others the general ideas involved in the machine run, it also forces the person who constructs it to rigorously formalize the basic logic of the program before becoming involved in the myriad details which may conceal important logical errors.

An overall block diagram for the gross-to-net payroll (run 2) program is presented in Figure 9–5. Note that its primary concern is with the type of card read, detecting errors of sequence of input or missing cards for a man, and detecting the end of a department. It does not go into detail about the actual payroll computation, the departmental summarization, the end-of-file processing, or the initialization.

Subsidiary Block Diagrams

Since a block in the overall block diagram may represent several hundred machine instructions, a further breakdown and a more detailed block diagram may be prepared for each of these blocks. In this illustration we have used multiples of 10 to identify these blocks in the overall block diagram so that in the next breakdown we may use the units digit to identify the individual blocks. A more detailed breakdown of block 40 of the overall block diagram is shown in Figure 9–6, in which the blocks are identified by the numbers 41, 42, 43, and so forth.

The resulting diagram may include sufficient detail to enable a program to be written. On the other hand, a further breakdown may be desirable for certain blocks in the semidetailed block diagram, as illustrated in Figure 9–7 for block 41. The notational

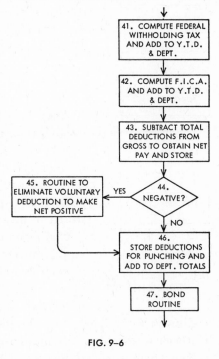

FIG. 9–6

Semi-Detail Block Diagram (Block 40)

system may be expanded by inserting an additional digit beyond the decimal point, and this may be further extended if additional detail is necessary. Thus the blocks in Figure 9–7 are numbered 41.1, 41.2, 41.3, and so on.

It should be obvious that the process of *construction* of block diagrams and the *presentation* of the final results in block diagram form are two separate and distinct entities. The process that one goes through to arrive at a completed block diagram is a complex trial-and-error procedure that is extremely difficult to formalize. Some individuals prefer to follow a logical step-by-step process involving several progressive stages, each in more detail than the previous one. Others, on the other hand, prefer to go directly from the overall block diagram to a quite detailed result. However, no matter which approach is attempted, there are likely to be many revisions before a completed product is achieved, for even after the diagram is logically complete there remains the problem of revising the geometrical presentation so that the eye can easily follow the flow.

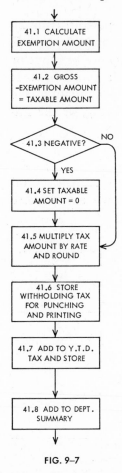

FIG. 9–7

Detail Block Diagram
(Block 41)

CODING

As we have previously noted, the overall process of preparing a machine program is called *programming*. This includes the preparation of the block diagrams and writing the program. The process of converting a detailed block diagram into the machine instructions, which are stored in memory, is called *coding*.

Coding can be done in several ways. For example, machine-language instructions can be written as we wrote them in Chapters 6 and 7. On the other hand, some automatic programming technique is usually used to assist in the coding process. Symbolic programming, in which the coder thinks in terms of machine instructions—but need not be concerned with specific memory locations—may be employed. Or procedure-oriented languages, such as COBOL or FORTRAN, may be used. Using these programming systems the coder need not explicitly consider the detailed machine instructions, for the computer is used to translate from the source language in which he writes to the machine-language instructions.

Once the detailed block diagram has been written and the input and output format specified, it should be a relatively straightforward process to use one of these coding techniques to prepare a program for the machine. This is not intended to imply that the coding process requires no creativity or that its proper completion is a trivial matter, but if the preceding steps have been properly completed, the coding process should require a relatively small percentage of the total time involved.

It is important to recognize that the processes of coding and block diagramming are intimately related, for the detailed block diagram must represent a program that can be efficiently expressed in the language employed, and one which will produce an efficient machine-language program. Thus the process of preparing an efficient, detailed block diagram involves a certain amount of mental program coding.

PROGRAM TESTING

When the program has been written, the fun has just begun, for now it must be run on the machine. And we might as well face facts: If the program is at all complicated, it is highly unlikely that it will run properly and produce the desired results! Theoretically, one should be able to write the program correctly the first time, and certainly one should strive mightily to do so. But, unfortunately, to err is all too human, and programmers tend to incorporate their "fair share" of errors in their programs.[1]

These errors must be detected and corrected before the machine procedure can be used on a routine basis. Program testing, or "debugging," is the process of ascertaining that the program accomplishes the results for which it was intended. It is important to recognize that the process of debugging must begin when the program is originally planned and must be continued as the program is written, for a program that is well planned and carefully written will contain few errors of commission or omission compared with one that is poorly planned and sloppily written. Therefore it is necessary

---

[1] It seems that the average experienced programmer makes about one error for every 30 or 40 lines of coding.

to start with as few errors as possible, for even then it is difficult enough to debug a program; and it may be almost impossible to cope with the task of debugging a complex program with a large number of mistakes.

Two major types of errors cause difficulty in a program. The first type is the *logical* error, where the original planning of the program does not adequately represent the data-processing situation involved. A simple example of this type of error will occur in planning a payroll application if the planner ignores the fact that the total of a man's deductions and taxes may well exceed his gross pay in certain circumstances, thus producing a negative net pay amount. The second type of error is the *clerical* error: the assignment of two different symbols for the same data, the use of a wrong operation symbol, or the omission of one or more instructions.

While the detection and elimination of clerical errors is by no means a trivial problem, techniques have been developed that enable us to cope fairly well with this type of error. The logical errors, however, present an entirely different problem, for they usually represent a fundamental lack of understanding of the data processing situation and are usually detected only after a more comprehensive understanding of the situation has been attained. Thus the debugging process can turn out to be a long, drawn-out affair, with no absolute certainty that it has ever been completed.

As the size and complexity of the program increase, the problem of debugging increases geometrically: it may be very simple to check out a program containing only 30 instructions, but a program involving several thousand instructions may require weeks of work. Thus debugging may account for a significant part of the total cost of producing a complex program.

Program testing is like solving a murder mystery: you obtain certain clues, after which you ask the proper questions to obtain further clues, and so on, until you are able to deduce the identity of the murderer. In our deductive debugging process the programmer must interact with the machine in order to obtain his clues, but his processes of logic and deduction are rather slow, and he must be careful not to have an expensive machine sit idle while he is engrossed in thought. He must also guard against the possibility that under the pressures of time and enthusiasm he will make ill-considered changes in the program that create *more* errors rather than correcting mistakes. Thus it is important that efficient techniques for debugging be developed and that these techniques be *used*. The following discussion will outline some of the techniques that have been developed for debugging.

First, it is worth mentioning again that the best debugging technique is not to make errors in the first place. The programmer must adopt a skeptical attitude both when he is originally writing the program and when he is program-testing. One is tempted to assume that the program is correct until it is proved otherwise, but it is much better to assume the opposite: that the program is wrong until it is proved to be correct. Furthermore, it is helpful if the programmer always keeps two things in mind in writing the program: (1) that the program *must* be debugged; (2) that the program will probably be modified. Both considerations motivate one to use thorough, clear, and accurate documentation and to devise the simplest possible logical structure for handling the problem. The motto "KISS"[2] is most applicable to the programmer's work.

Perhaps it is really too much to ask that one always program correctly, but it is not unreasonable to demand that one at least write his program legibly. Simple misreading at the key-punching stage can introduce numerous errors. Especially troublesome are confusions between O and zero, i and 1, and z and 2. After the symbolic program is key-punched it should be printed from the cards and carefully checked for such simple errors.

Preliminary Checking

Before the program is run on the computer the programmer should carefully check it for both logical and clerical errors. Every program of any complexity should also be carefully checked by another competent programmer. First, he should examine the logic expressed in the block diagrams and test it as best he can to see if it will accomplish the desired results. Then he should go over the actual program to detect clerical errors and deviations from the block diagram. It is amazing how difficult it is for the original programmer to detect the simplest mistakes in logic, but how they stand out like sore thumbs when someone else attempts to read and understand the program.

As was mentioned in the previous chapter, the processors that translate from the symbolic or procedure-oriented language to the object program also do quite a bit of checking for simple clerical errors or omissions. For example, they may indicate invalid operation symbols, symbols that have not been defined (which in turn may disclose cases where simple errors have been made in writing a symbol),

[2] KISS *also* stands for "Keep It Simple, Stupid "

and labels that have not been referred to in the program (which may or may not indicate errors).

Test Data

The ultimate test of a program, of course, is in producing the correct results when it is run on the machine. It is therefore necessary to have input data that can be used to test the program. Usually these input data are of a hypothetical nature, designed to test the various branches of the program with as little machine time as possible. The correct answers for these input data must be available at the time of testing. In addition it is quite helpful if at least one case can be carried completely through on the programming chart itself, showing the intermediate results in the machine registers. Not only must suitable input data and pre-calculated results be available, the input data must be in the input form so that they can actually be read into the machine and processed by the program.

The construction of adequate test data is a challenging task and probably should be begun when the program is being written. Perhaps the main problem in debugging is having so many errors that they interfere with each other and produce such confusing results that the programmer cannot deduce what happened. Accordingly, the first input data should be designed to test the simple logic of the program in handling the normal transactions. Then when these bugs have been eliminated, test data must be available to test the most common exceptions, and, finally, data should be available to force the program through the most devious and unusual exceptional conditions.

Segmentation

An important approach to the testing of complex programs is to break them down into pieces and debug each piece separately. For example, if there are closed subroutines in the program, each can be debugged by itself, since subroutines are self-contained units and do not interfere with the other parts of the program. Even if a program does not use subroutines, major segments of a complex program can still be tested separately by entering correct intermediate results into the machine and starting at the beginning of the segment to be tested. For example, in our gross-to-net payroll program we can first concentrate upon the overall logic in the block diagram in Figure 9–5. Then we might concentrate on block 40 (shown in further detail in Figure 9–6), or on blocks 10, 20, 30, or 50.

Machine Aids to Debugging

Now that we have explored the overall strategy of debugging, the question arises: What do we do when we find that the machine is producing a wrong answer, or no answer at all? First, if an answer is available, we use it to deduce the cause of this result. If the machine stops with an error condition, we attempt to deduce how it could have gotten into such a fix. Of course, the overall strategy is to narrow down the suspect area of the program to a single instruction. At this point it is easy to see why multiple errors make debugging so much more difficult.

As we narrow our search we find it necessary to examine in detail what is going on inside the machine registers and the memory. Although most machines are designed so that a person can sit at the console and examine any register within the machine, and can execute a test program one step at a time, this is an extremely slow and expensive process and should be avoided. Therefore many techniques have been developed that use the machine to produce special output information that the programmer can examine to determine what is going on inside.

A simple but important technique is a program that dumps memory. After the program being debugged has stopped (either with an error or at a designated instruction), the *memory dump* routine can be employed to print out the contents of any selected portion of memory and the contents of the various registers of the machine. This provides the programmer with a snapshot of the contents of memory at a certain time; and he can examine the input and output data, instructions, and intermediate results to see what has happened.

Another debugging aid is a *trace* routine which takes over control of the machine. After each instruction of the program being debugged is executed, the instruction and the contents of the various registers are printed to produce a "dynamic picture" of what is going on. The trace may then be compared with the program listing itself (which represents what the programmer expected), and errors may be isolated and analyzed away from the machine.

A word of caution is in order here, for although the tracing routine is apparently simple its actual use can be extremely time-consuming. The MAC operates at approximately 4,000 operations per second, but it can *print* only 600 lines per minute. Thus to trace a program requiring one second to execute would require about 7 minutes, and would produce about 100 printed pages. To trace a program that would require one minute to run would require 7 hours and produce 6,000 pages of output! For obvious reasons then, *selective traces,* which trace only selected instructions and allow the rest of the program to operate at high speed, have been developed, replacing the simple trace.

Many well-designed symbolic programming systems include macros that make it easy for the programmer to specify that certain instructions be traced and certain blocks of memory be dumped during the debugging process. Such macros make it easy to trace selected instructions, but not the whole program. This is as it should be, for full tracing is expensive and usually unnecessary. Obviously, these macros do not influence the actual operation of the program and so can be removed when the program has been debugged. Writing these debugging macros while writing the program provides an excellent example of the desirability of considering debugging when writing the program.

Procedure-oriented Languages

So far our discussion of debugging has concentrated upon symbolic programming and has ignored the process of debugging programs written in the more complex procedure-oriented languages. As we mentioned in Chapter 8, there should be fewer errors in a program written in a procedure-oriented language than in one written in the detail required by a machine-oriented language. But errors still occur, and they are more difficult to detect and eliminate. The problem is that our debugging techniques are oriented to the detail of what is going on in the machine, but this detail is exactly what the programmer has avoided by using the procedure-oriented language. Unless he understands the machine language and knows in general what his compiler is going to produce from his source language statements, he may be in trouble when it is time to debug.

To overcome this difficulty some languages include provisions that make it convenient during debugging to dump input and output areas and to print values of specified symbols at any stage in the execution of the program. Again, the problems of debugging must be considered when the program is being written.

Effectiveness of Debugging Procedures

The process of checking a long and complicated program usually involves several brief periods of testing on the machine itself, interspersed with long periods of thought (away from the machine) during which mistakes are diagnosed and corrections made and—most importantly—incorporated in the documentation. Most well-run installations have debugging rules and procedures which are designed to discourage programmers from sitting at the console and tying up the expensive computer while searching for errors.

After all the expense and complexity of the debugging process, it is still impossible to prove (with certainty) that a complex data processing program is free from error. In the first place, debugging procedures are relatively ineffective in eliminating logical errors, for it is not likely that synthetic test data, devised to determine whether the program operates as the programmer thinks it should, will include situations that will reveal the subtle misunderstandings that are embodied in logical errors. For example, it is not likely that the programmer will include an exception in the test data—the very existence of which he is unaware. Indeed, a complex program has so many branches that it is almost impossible to design test data that will insure that each instruction in the program will be executed in the process of debugging so as to detect clerical errors.

Even if adequate test data are actually used, it requires substantial additional effort to actually *prove* that this is the case. Thus we can conclude that debugging eliminates *most* of the errors in a program, and *reduces* the likelihood that there are others; but it does not eliminate the possibility that some program errors still remain.

CONVERSION

After the programs are thought to be free of error, another step in the development of a computer processing system is that of converting the application to the use of the electronic computer. This step is far from trivial, for it frequently involves significant changes in the way information (both input and output) is handled by people outside the data processing portion of the organization. The mechanized system must always be integrated into an organization composed of people, and not only is it difficult to foresee all of the consequences involved in the changes that are necessary, it is also imperative to understand that the success of the computer's use may depend upon human factors outside the mechanized procedures.

To gain confidence in the machine program and procedures, as well as to allow the people of the organization to adjust to the changes, it is customary to convert an application to computer processing before abandoning the previous processing method. Thus there is a period of *parallel operation* during which "bugs" in the mechanized procedures, and in adapting people to these new procedures, can be eliminated. Parallel operation usually requires at least two or three processing cycles, and may extend over a period of several weeks or months if major difficulties arise.

Illustration

As an illustration of the problems that can arise in parallel operation and debugging, consider the following selections abstracted from a diary prepared by Fred Gruenberger of the General Electric Company at Hanford, Washington.[3] The application was a file maintenance problem in which a magnetic tape file of some 11,000 300-character master records was updated daily by some 2,000 to 4,000 transactions. This application was converted from a manual processing system and went into parallel operation on December 10.

The conversion job shown here was fairly clean and straight-forward. The problem was well-defined, and the customers were cooperative and able to learn rapidly. Even so, it took six weeks of daily processing to uncover all the troubles and subtle bugs (assuming they are all out now).

Near the end of December a log book was begun which recorded events of each day's run. The following are excerpts from this log. Man-number 88888 is fictitious and was included for debugging purposes. Some of the difficulties related below are more understandable if you realize that records on magnetic tape are invisible, and it is therefore impossible to see what is recorded in the file.

December 29: . . . An overflow condition stopped the machine on man-number 88888. . . . Corrected at console by subtracting a large amount from bucket in question and noting action. Two output tapes disappeared without being printed.

January 6: Job went on at 3:00 A.M. and promptly collapsed. Main parameter card had invalid identification. Error discovered when F. wandered in at 1:00 P.M.

Rerun started at 8:00 P.M. Collapsed again due to some data cards with batch numbers not represented in batch parameter cards. The chief customer was notified and started for his office to get missing data.

Rerun again at 11:00 P.M. with complete data. New trouble: 83 tape read errors. Here F. pulled a boner. Changed typewriter address to address of an on-line printer without noting transfer-back address. . . .

January 7: On machine at 9:00 P.M. All went well till the first of

---

[3] Reproduced, by permission, from *Computing News*, Vol. 5, No. 8, April 5, 1957.

five input cards with an invalid month code. . . . F. batched a console patching. Reloaded and restarted. 20 minutes shot. . . . One report out of balance today.

It seems last three correction cards for 88888 were not processed. No non-metaphysical explanation leaps to mind.

January 9: On at 8:30 P.M. for a special pass—edit the master tape. Pass collapsed immediately due to our cleverness in writing instructions at same place in memory as the tape input area. Correction made and pass proceeded. However, for some 12,000 master records it produced about 20,000 error messages. This program was debugged?

January 17: . . . Regular daily business was processed today by operators, with no intervention on the part of the analysts.

January 21: Utter chaos today. January 21 report shows figures which are impossible. Something is seriously wrong in the master records.

January 22: Glorious recovery. GG found two errors in the program transferring payroll information to our tape. . . . The organization code was at the far end of the master record, not where it belonged. This accounts for a great deal of the trouble of recent dates.

January 28: Another demonstration given today. Smooth as silk. The regular daily run was moved up to 2:00 P.M. for this purpose. Fifth consecutive daily processing handled by operators only. We are tempted to conclude that the job is now successful.

People Problems

The duplication of activities involved in parallel processing may cause serious personnel difficulties, for someone must process the information in the old way, someone must process it in the new way, and it is frequently necessary for others to reconcile the differences in the results. Thus, just when the total work force is about to be reduced because of the mechanization, it must be increased because of the conversion process. This duplication of effort may also occur outside the data processing organization, for those associated with preparing the input information may be forced to follow two different procedures, one which is new and the other which will soon be discarded.

The process of conversion is frequently very trying, for this is the place where we garner the harvest of all mistakes and misunderstandings. Also, a substantial resentment is frequently engendered by the process of change, and the problems that almost inevitably arise during the conversion process are often seized upon by the disgruntled (who may be many and powerful) in an attempt to discredit the whole process of change and those who are associated with it. But these problems will be more fully discussed in Chapter 16.

DOCUMENTATION

Documentation is not a step in the same sense as are those which have been described previously, for it is a *part* of all these steps. It is of such great importance, however, and so frequently slighted, that it must be highlighted here. Perhaps you have heard the couplet:

> Old bankers never die—
> They just lose interest.

This thought applies to programmers with respect to documentation, except—unfortunately—most programmers never *had* any interest in documentation. This is understandable; clear, complete descriptions of complex programs are a chore to prepare, and such documentations must compete for the programmer's attention with the much more glamorous tasks of devising and debugging the programs. Yet without a clear and complete description of the procedures and programs, the entire process comes to naught; for in the long run it is impossible to use programs that you do not thoroughly understand, and it is almost impossible to obtain an understanding of a program without excellent documentation.

As we have mentioned before, it is axiomatic that even the best of systems will eventually be modified. Human memory has a low reliability, and, even if it were accurate, those involved in the original development may no longer be available. Also, it is an extremely complex task to modify a well-documented machine program, and it is almost impossible to modify a poorly documented program. In fact, it may be easier to go back and re-do the entire job rather than attempt to modify a program that lacks adequate documentation.

By clear and complete documentation we mean legible procedural flow charts supported by adequate descriptions and detailed formats of the various records and documents involved; legible and understandable block diagrams at all levels; legible listings of the programs; and test data that can be used to determine if the program is properly performing its intended functions.

Most importantly, this documentation must be *maintained up-to-date through all changes* that occur—through all steps in our process and through future months and years—so that the documentation actually represents the program as it is rather than as it started out in the programmer's mind. One can see that the preparation of detailed documentation not only provides reference material for future use, it also induces those preparing the system to perform their task with thoroughness and precision.

RELATIONSHIPS BETWEEN THE STEPS

As has been described above, the overall process of converting a data processing area from a previous method to the use of an electronic computer involves the following steps: *defining the problem, devising the procedure, preparing overall and detailed block diagrams, coding, debugging, converting,* and *documentation.* Unfortunately, however, these steps are not really sequential and cannot be performed independently of one another. For example, we have noted that to devise an adequate procedure it is necessary to determine how much work can be accomplished on a given machine run. This may involve a rough block diagram of the run and estimates of the amount of memory required for the tables, program steps, and input and output storage.

It is frequently necessary to return from a step near the end of the process to an early step and to re-do previous work. For example, in preparing a detailed block diagram it may become obvious that the program would operate more efficiently if the overall block diagram were modified. At the coding stage we may find that the procedure which breaks the processing down into machine runs is not adequate, for the program may require more memory capacity than the machine has available, making it necessary to return to the problem of devising an adequate procedure. Logical errors, discovered during the debugging or conversion process, can force a return clear back to the problem definition step and consequent reworking of all intervening steps in the process.

It may be observed that the objective of this whole process is to attain an adequate understanding of the data processing problem and to express this understanding in the form of workable procedures and machine programs. Since the problems of data processing are quite complex, it is not likely that a complete understanding of the data processing problem will be obtained at the first attempt. It is usually necessary to begin with a less than adequate understanding and to improve upon this knowledge as we continue through the process, making corrections and repeating steps whenever necessary.

We have concentrated our attention upon the details of each of the steps in this process, and this was justified, for each is of great importance. But even more important to the manager is an awareness of the consequence of the interrelationships between them.

Organization and Personnel

The close interrelationships between the steps in the process of placing an application on the computer has implications as to how the overall process should be carried out. For example, it has been suggested that the problem definition and procedures preparation should be performed by one group of people, the overall and detailed block diagramming by another group, and the coding by a third group. However, in view of the interrelationships between these steps, someone should be assigned responsibility for the entire process, so a team approach is usually taken in which procedures analysts, programmers, and coders work together on a given application from the beginning to the end of the process. Thus, at each step the viewpoints of the procedures analyst, the programmer, and the coder can be taken into consideration.

It is also apparent that in a complex process such as this, in which each step is dependent upon the previous step, a thorough and painstaking job must be done from start to finish. There is no place for sloppy work or inattention to detail. The persons who are involved must be thorough, painstaking, and well organized, and some speed may be sacrificed in the interest of accuracy and precision. A rather broad background is required of the person who aspires to work as a procedures analyst, for he must thoroughly understand the possibilities of the machine so that he can devise procedures for which efficient programs can be prepared. (The organization and staffing of a data processing center are discussed in more detail in Chapter 15.)

Cost Estimation

Furthermore, an understanding of the interrelationships between these steps provides an explanation for the difficulties that have been encountered in estimating the savings or costs associated with acquiring a computer or placing an application on a machine that is already available. Estimates of machine running time must be made on the basis of original definitions of the problem area, and on the basis of the first approximation to a procedure, block diagram, and machine program. Frequently, these estimates are excellent, but it is not uncommon for them to be misleading, for as a more adequate understanding of the problem area is developed, the machine time involved may expand by several hundred percent. This is not to imply that accurate estimates can never be made, or that it is undesirable to attempt to make estimates; it is simply a recognition that at an early stage in the process it is possible for estimates of machine time to be significantly in error, usually on the low side.

If one views the process of converting to computer processing as a straightforward, seven-step process, then it is inconceivable that it could take so long and cost so much as it actually does. This cost and time can only be explained by the fact that these steps are inter-related, and the process involves a great deal of looking forward, taking a stab, and looping backwards.

Furthermore, because of these interrelationships it is difficult to control these costs, for exerting pressure to assure that the individual steps are completed expeditiously may only postpone the recognition and correction of basic difficulties until the latter stages of the process, at which time more work must be repeated. Such work is difficult to administer, for it is not easy to determine how much time pressure should be exerted or even to estimate the amount of time and effort that should be required to complete the overall process.

CONTROL OF ACCURACY

A major problem in the design of mechanized data processing systems is control of accuracy. As compared with humans, machines are exceptionally accurate. However, this does not imply that machine errors do not occur, for errors are made by the best machines. Moreover, any errors that exist in the input information will cause erroneous results.

People appear to have a built-in armor of skepticism with which they view the results of manual processing, so manual data processing is repeatedly scrutinized at each step in the process, and the results are accepted with caution. But the results produced by a machine are accepted with blind faith by some people—although others, resenting the intrusion of the machine into their domain, are eager to use machine mistakes to discredit the entire operation. For these reasons, and also because the intermediate results are not subject to careful scrutiny by humans, special care must be given to the design of procedures by which errors may be detected and corrected.

Three aspects of control of accuracy must be considered in the design of procedures. In the first place, checks must be included which reduce the probability of an undetected error producing erroneous results. Second, once an error has been detected the cost of its correction is influenced by the design of the system. The previous two points are concerned with accidental errors. There is also the possibility of purposeful errors introduced to perpetrate fraud, so the system should be designed to discourage fraud by increasing the probability that it will be detected.

The objective in control of accuracy is not necessarily to eliminate all errors. Rather, we should attempt to minimize the total costs associated with the detection and correction of errors plus the costs caused by the uncorrected errors that are produced.

Considerations associated with the control of accuracy are involved in each step of the overall process of converting to mechanized data processing. At the problem definition stage, for example, the accuracy required of the system must be determined. Procedures must include provision for insuring the accuracy of input information and for the establishment of controls by means of which the accuracy of processing can be checked. Block diagrams and programs must not only produce the desired results but must also include provisions for the detection of errors.[4] The design of procedures and programs may also be influenced by the desirability of developing restart procedures by means of which correct processing can be resumed after errors are detected. Debugging is an important consideration in the control of accuracy, for the objective of debugging is to eliminate errors in the program itself, and erroneous programs produce inaccurate results.

Auditors are also concerned with the accuracy of data processing results and therefore should take an active part in the overall process of design and installation of a mechanized data processing system. The auditor has a viewpoint and training that makes him valuable in establishing accuracy controls and in designing adequate test data for use in debugging.

It is important that the procedures be designed so as to include provisions for an adequate audit trail. On the other hand, the auditor must understand the capabilities and limitations of computers so that he can adapt his requirements to the new equipment without necessarily requiring that traditional audit trails be produced in exactly the same form, for this may be both inefficient and unnecessary when computers are used.

---

[4] Those who are interested in specific techniques that may be incorporated in programs and procedures for control of accuracy should refer to Felix Kaufman's *Electronic Data Processing and Auditing* or the IBM booklet, *The Auditor Encounters Electronic Data Processing,* which are cited in Supplemental Readings at the end of this chapter.

SUMMARY

To convert an area from manual processing to electronic data processing it is necessary to obtain an understanding of the data processing problem and to express this understanding in the form of procedures and machine programs. There are several steps involved in this process: defining the problem, devising procedures and block diagrams, writing and debugging the programs, parallel operation and conversion, and documentation. Each of these steps presents its own peculiar problems, but the major difficulty is associated with the fact that the overall process is not straightforward but loops back upon itself as misunderstandings come to light.

In the first step of this process, problem definition, it is necessary to decide upon the results to be obtained. But it is illogical to specify the results to be produced by a data processing system without regard to the cost of obtaining them; and costs are related to the procedures used, the equipment available, the form in which the results are presented, and the type and amount of information obtained. Thus it is important that management, who in the final analysis must specify the results required, be aware of the necessity for adapting results to the requirements of technology and that management encourage efforts to design effective systems, taking into account both the cost and the value of information. It is equally important that management realistically plan for the time and costs involved in the preparation necessary to produce programs and to convert to electronic data processing.

EXERCISES

9.1 *a*) Describe each step involved in converting a data processing area from manual processing to electronic data processing.

b) How are these steps interrelated?

9.2 *a*) What is the difference between logical and clerical errors that may exist in a program?

b) Why is it difficult to devise adequate test data for debugging a program?

c) Describe some useful machine debugging techniques.

d) How can you prove that a complex program is free of errors?

9.3 Why does the most efficient procedure for a particular application depend upon the characteristics of the machine to be used? What influence does this have on the possibility of using a compiler language to make it easy to change from one machine to another?

SUPPLEMENTAL READINGS

The Auditor Encounters Electronic Data Processing (Form F20–8057). Prepared by Price Waterhouse and Co. and published by International Business Machines Corporation, White Plains, N.Y.

An excellent presentation of the effect of the use of electronic data processing equipment upon the auditor and of techniques that can be used in the control of accuracy.

CHAPIN, NED. *An Introduction to Automatic Computers.* Princeton, N.J.: D. Van Nostrand Co., Inc., 1957.

Pages 106 to 128 discuss approaches to the process of defining the data processing problem.

Document and Accounting Controls (Form C20–8060). International Business Machines Corporation, White Plains, N.Y.

Discusses techniques for control of accuracy in mechanized data processing systems.

Flow-charting Techniques (Form 320–8152). International Business Machines Corporation, White Plains, N.Y.

Describes in detail different types of block diagrams and flow charts; and discusses the symbols on the standard IBM flow-charting template and describes their use.

KAUFMAN, FELIX. *Electronic Data Processing and Auditing.* New York: The Ronald Press Co., 1961.

This book discusses control of accuracy and the relationships between the auditor and electronic data processing.

LEEDS, H. D., AND WEINBERG, G. M. *Computer Programming Fundamentals.* New York: McGraw-Hill Book Co., Inc., 1961.

Chapter 10 presents an excellent discussion of debugging.

MCCRACKEN, D. D.; WEISS, H.; AND LEE, T. *Programming Business Computers.* New York: John Wiley & Sons, Inc., 1959.

Chapter 3 discusses flow charting and various types of block diagrams and their uses.

MEYERS, W. E., AND SCHMIDT, R. N. *Electronic Business Data Processing.* New York: Holt, Rinehart & Winston, 1963.

Chapters 15 through 17 present a slightly different approach than ours to procedural flow charts and the various types of block diagrams.

OAKFORD, ROBERT V. *Introduction to Electronic Data Processing Equipment.* New York: McGraw-Hill Book Co., Inc., 1962.

Chapter 5 includes a comprehensive discussion of debugging programs for intermediate computers.

10 APPLICATIONS OF INTERMEDIATE COMPUTERS

INTERMEDIATE electronic data processing machines, such as the basic MAC, may be integrated into a punched-card data processing system, providing it with the capabilities of the stored program and the processing advantages of a memory of several thousand digits. Such machines have achieved a remarkable popularity, and thousands of them are in use in the United States.

As one would expect, a general-purpose computer is usually used in many different data processing procedures. Because almost every organization has a payroll, this is probably the most frequent application area for intermediate computers. Payroll is not necessarily the most important application for most such machines, but when a computer is obtained for several uses, payroll is likely to be one of them.

Other areas in which intermediate computers are frequently used are inventory accounting, cost accounting, sales analysis, materials control, and engineering calculations. In reference to the latter, it is not uncommon for firms that obtain a computer primarily for data processing to allocate a portion of its time to the engineering department, and this frequently results in a significant improvement in the effectiveness of the engineering effort.

The above discussion has been concerned with the use of intermediate computers in general manufacturing organizations. However, a surprising percentage of the intermediate computers have been used in such special industries as fire and casualty insurance, public utilities, wholesaling, life insurance, federal and state governments, railroads, and petroleum. For example, of the first 400 IBM 650 computers ordered, about 60 percent were in special industries. In such industries, the use of an intermediate computer may be justified on the basis of one or two special jobs that have sufficient volume or importance to support the cost of the computer.

It should be emphasized that a tremendous amount of ingenuity goes into most data processing applications. Frequently, applications that are called by the same name are completely dissimilar when examined closely. Each use of a data processing machine must be expressly tailored to the situation in which the machine is being used—so far, it has not been found possible merely to transplant applications from one industry to another (or even from one company to another within the same industry) without extensive revision.

Therefore the illustrations included in this chapter have not been chosen primarily to illustrate how an electronic computer should be used in typical situations. The primary purpose of each illustration is to present interesting ways in which the capabilities of the computer can be applied to data processing. In particular, several of these examples provide illustrations of how an ingenious use of memory can simplify data processing procedures.

PARTS REQUIREMENTS PLANNING

Manufacturing organizations frequently produce a variety of end products. However, although the same factory may be producing hundreds of different items, for purposes of efficiency these items usually are constructed from a relatively small number of standard parts or components. For example, in the automotive and home appliance industries it is customary to produce a basic stripped model, a standard model, and a deluxe model of each product that are identical in 90 per cent of their parts. And even in industries that produce to customers' specifications, most products are mostly composed of standard assemblies and parts.

The above discussion is not intended to prove that a small number of parts is involved in production of our modern complex mechanisms, but it does indicate that the number of parts involved is much less than if each end item were entirely different from every other end item. This interchangeability of parts, although allowing production efficiencies, also provides some difficulty in planning for production. To break a production schedule down into the quantities of required individual parts, it is necessary to consider (for each individual part) all the end items in which it appears and then to add up all these separate requirements to obtain a total requirement for the part.

This process of "exploding" the production schedule to the individual parts involved is necessary to procure those parts that are purchased and to plan production for those parts that are made within the organization. Unfortunately, however, a production schedule is usually dynamic rather than static: it is subject to frequent changes as the result of variations in the demands of the market, labor conditions, raw material prices, inventory policies, and moods of management.

When a schedule changes it is necessary to reflect the effect of the changes upon the required parts, and if several thousand parts and several hundred items are involved it is apparent that a lot of data processing is required. Furthermore, *time* is an extremely important consideration, for the ability to meet the new schedule depends upon acquiring the required parts in the proper amounts at the right time. Any delay in exploding the schedule to parts is too much to suit those who are charged with the responsibility for obtaining, canceling, or scheduling the parts involved and controlling the inventories of these parts.

Punched Card Procedures

Parts requirement explosion has therefore been one of the popular applications of standard punch card equipment, and the following approach has frequently been used. Two basic types of information are necessary to explode a schedule to basic parts: the schedule itself and a bill of materials for each end item.

For planning purposes, most schedules involve several periods of time (days, weeks, or months). In this case, the first period is a firm schedule, the next period is less definite, and succeeding periods are usually forecasts for planning purposes only. Such a schedule is presented in Figure 10–1.

Model	Periods					
Number	1	2	3	4	5	6
12A	50	50	75	70	60	40
12B	25	30	30	30	30	35
127C	0	0	20	30	40	50
203X	100	100	100	100	100	100
204	30	20	10	0	0	0
607	0	0	25	0	0	25

FIG. 10–1

Assembly Schedule

The schedule is punched into cards, with one card for each line on the schedule, as shown in Figure 10–2.

For each end item (hereafter referred to as a *model*) a bill of materials is required. A *bill of materials* is a list of the parts and

Model Number	1	2	3	4	5	6	
0012B	00025	00030	00030	00030	00030	00035	

FIG. 10–2
Schedule Card

materials required to build the model, along with the required quantity of each part or material (see Figure 10–3).

A card is also required for each line on each bill of materials. In fact, the bill of materials is frequently maintained in punched card form and printed (when required) by means of a punched-card

BILL OF MATERIALS	
	Model 12B
Part #	Usage Quantity
123	4
2322	1
2323	1
4460	5
4723	1
4725	8

FIG. 10–3
Bill of Materials

accounting machine. Thus, we have a permanent file of cards, such as the one shown in Figure 10–4.

The usual punched card procedure (see Figure 10–5) involves key-punching the schedule cards, sorting them to model-number sequence, and hand pulling or selecting by use of a collator the bill of

Model Number	Part Number	Usage	
0012B	00123	004	

FIG. 10–4
Bill of Materials Card

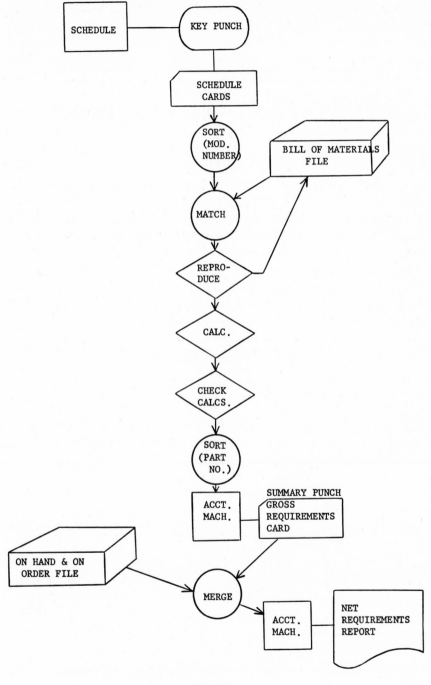

FIG. 10–5
Punched Card Procedure for Requirements Determination

materials decks for each of the models appearing in the schedule. These bills of materials decks are reproduced to obtain working decks, and the proper schedule card is filed ahead of each active bill of materials deck. A punched card calculator can then be used to pick up the scheduled quantities for each period for a given model, multiply these quantities by the usage of each part, and to punch the resulting requirement for each period of the schedule into the part card itself.

Then the resulting cards may be sorted to part-number sequence to get all of the cards for each part number together so that they may be summarized on the accounting machine, where a total require-ments card for each part may be summary punched. These cards may then be merged with a file of inventory balance cards to produce a net requirements report showing the on-hand balance, the on-order bal-ance, the requirements for each of the coming periods, and the net shortage or overage resulting.

The above procedure is relatively simple in principle and suffers from only two major defects. The first of these is the time it takes to complete the procedure. For example, if there are a total of 15,000 active parts and 500 end items there may be 180,000 cards in the bill of materials file, 100,000 of which may be active for any given schedule. Even with considerable overlapping and duplication of machines it would require about a week of processing (on a two-shift basis) before the requirements reports would begin to be printed. Although a week is not particularly long for this amount of work, *any* time required to do this processing is usually just that much too long.

The second problem cannot be disposed of easily and it is one which we may tend to overlook: the problem of maintenance of the bill of materials file—the continual process of adding new models and keeping up with the changes made by the production and engineering departments on the current models. If this file is to be useful for forecasting purposes it must accurately reflect the current shop practice, and it is surprising how many changes must be made each week to keep this file current. Usually a second file (called a *where-used* file) is maintained to make it easier to keep the bill of materials file current. A where-used file has exactly the same cards in it as the bill of materials file, but it is maintained in part-number sequence. Thus, when the engineering department substitutes one part for another, the cards which are to be replaced may be found together in the where-used file and replaced as a group. These cards can then be used to locate the individual bills of materials in which cards must be changed.

Computer Procedure

Of course, several approaches may be considered when using a computer for the determination of parts requirements. One procedure that has been widely used is presented in Figure 10–6. The

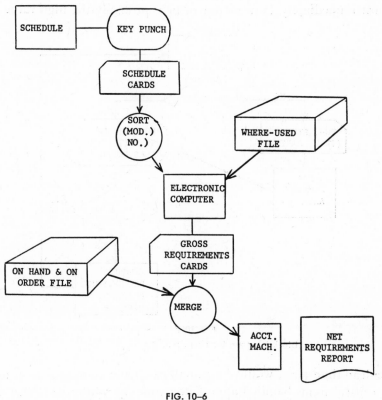

FIG. 10–6

Computer Procedure for Requirements Determination

schedule for all models is stored as a table in the memory. Instead of using the bill of materials file (as in the normal punched card approach), the where-used file is used. It is passed through the computer (in part-number sequence) and, as each card for a given part number is read, a Table Look-up on model number is used to find the forecast for the model, and the contribution of that model to the requirements for the part is computed. Thus, after all of the cards for a given part number have been read, the total requirement for that part is summarized for punching into an output card. A general block diagram for this computer run is shown in Figure 10–7.

For the volumes discussed above, the computer procedure would require only about one day's work on a two-shift basis, which is an important time improvement. However, this time is misleading because it refers to the total time to complete the entire job. But in this procedure the first results would become available after only a few hour's time, and the planners could begin to work with them almost immediately. As a matter of fact, probably the high-value or

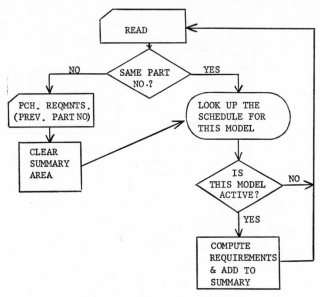

FIG. 10–7

Block Diagram for Requirements Calculation

long-lead-time parts would be put through the computer first, and the critical items handled almost immediately, while the "nuts and bolts" could be processed later.

It should be noted that this approach has several limitations, which must be considered in light of the individual circumstances. The first of these is the size of the memory. If the schedule involves a large number of models or extends over a considerable number of periods, the memory of the computer may not be sufficient to store the entire schedule. Furthermore, it is frequently desirable (in order to reduce the size of the bill of materials file) to first break the model schedule down into requirements in terms of subassemblies, and then repeat the process to find the individual parts requirements. This is known as a two-stage explosion. Frequently, the situation will call for a multistage explosion. Where the explosion involves more than one stage, the output of the first stage becomes the schedule for the second, and thus the memory required to store the schedule for succeeding stages may get quite large. In these cases, however, it may be possible to divide the end items into small groups (which have little or no interchangeability of parts between them) for processing separately, thus reducing the overall problem to several smaller problems that can fit into memory.

It is also readily apparent that the above computer procedure is rather inefficient when only a small percentage of the models is active in a given production schedule, for in this case only a relatively small proportion of the cards read by the computer would actually be involved in the requirements calculation. In such situations it may be possible to increase speed by spreading several usages in each where-used card or to separate the models into active and inactive categories. Then the active models may be processed by the above approach, while bills of materials for active models from the inactive file may be processed by the punched card approach.

AUTOMOBILE INSURANCE RATE CHECKING AND CODING

When an automobile insurance policy is sold, a copy of the completed application is usually forwarded to the home office of the insurance company. Here it is checked for accuracy of the premiums, and statistical and management codes (required by the various rating organizations) are assigned. These codes enable the rating organizations to make studies of insurance in force and of losses in the various categories with which they are concerned. Until recently it was impossible to mechanize the functions of rate checking and coding because they were performed by clerks who referred to rating books and coding tables to assign the proper codes and rates to the individual coverages afforded by the policy.

With the advent of the memory capacity of the intermediate electronic computer it became possible to mechanize this process and to perform both of these operations at the same time. Seven types of coverages (bodily injury and property damage, medical, collision, comprehensive, wind, combined additional, and towing and labor) may be involved in any automobile insurance policy, and the premium for each depends upon from one to six different factors (such as state, private passenger classification, age of driver, type of car, and limits desired). In addition, at least ten different codes must be assigned to each policy to facilitate later statistical analysis.

To enable its salesmen to determine the premium on a given policy, most companies publish a rating manual that contains as many as 100 pages of instructions and tables. For a computer to be able to check the rating it would appear that the entire book would have to be stored in the computer's memory. This seems impossible, for if we calculate the amount of memory required to store all of the tables in the book it will usually add up to many times the available memory capacity. Herein lies the interest in this application, for by examining the tables involved, and combining the knowledge of how the tables were originally derived with the logical and computing capabilities of the machine, it is possible to reduce the memory requirements to the amount available in most intermediate computers.

The rating manuals were prepared with the capabilities and limitations of people as the primary consideration. Thus, whenever possible, tables were substituted for computations. Of course, the numbers in these tables do not occur by happenstance: they are based upon underlying relationships that enable the table to be constructed from basic information. Furthermore, the rating manuals use many techniques to minimize the possibility of human errors and confusion, such as printing the same table in several places when it is to be used under a number of different circumstances.

Thus there are a number of ways in which the memory requirement can be reduced. In the first place, consideration can be restricted to the tables involved in rating policies for one state at a time because the policies for one state can be easily processed as a group before we proceed to the next state. In addition, an examination of the tables which apply to a given state reveals that they contain a tremendous amount of duplication. For example, there may be 35 territories within a state, and a large table for each of these territories, but there may be only five *different* tables in this group.

As an illustration of how calculation may be substituted for memory, consider the determination of the premium for bodily injury or property damage. To find the premium for bodily injury coverage, a table in the rating manual is used which provides the premium for limits 5/10 (meaning $5,000 per person and $10,000 per accident) on the basis of territorial schedule and private passenger class, as shown in Figure 10–8. If the limits are other than 5/10, we must also refer to the table in Figure 10–9 to find the

Type and Class	Terr. 5		Terr. 6		Terr. 7		Terr. 8	
	B.I.	P.D.	B.I.	P.D.	B.I.	P.D.	B.I.	P.D.
Private Pass.								
Class 1A	$19	$19	$25	$19	$18	$14	$14	$17
Class 1B	21	20	29	22	21	17	16	20
Class 1C	27	27	35	26	26	20	20.	24
Class 2A	35	35	45	34	33	26	25	31
Class 2B	40	40	51	39	38	30	29	35
Class 2C	48	48	62	47	45	36	35	42
Class 3	32	32	41	31	30	24	23	28

FIG. 10–8

Table for Bodily Injury Coverage

premium. Thus to find the premium for bodily injury for class 1B in territory 7 with limits of 15/30, we would consult the table in Figure 10–8 and find $21.00. Then, under 15/30 in Figure 10–9, we would find the premium of $26.88. With a computer, we can replace the table in Figure 10–9 by noting that there are certain percentage relationships between the 5/10 rate and all of the other rates, as shown below:

10/20 . . . . 120%		50/100 . . . . 145%
15/30 128		100/100 147
20/40 133		100/300 154
25/25 130		200/200 155
25/50 136		250/250 158
50/50 139		

MASTER INCREASED LIMITS (Even Dollar Rates)											
Rate	10/20	15/30	20/40	25/25	25/50	50/50	50/100	100/100	100/300	200/200	250/250
$10	$12.00	$12.80	$13.30	$13.00	$13.60	$13.90	$14.50	$14.70	$15.40	$15.50	$15.80
11	13.20	14.08	14.63	14.30	14.96	15.29	15.95	16.17	16.94	17.05	17.38
12	14.40	15.36	15.96	15.60	16.32	16.68	17.40	17.64	18.48	18.60	18.96
13	15.60	16.64	17.29	16.90	17.68	18.07	18.85	19.11	20.02	20.15	20.54
14	16.80	17.92	18.62	18.20	19.04	19.46	20.30	20.58	21.56	21.70	22.12
15	18.00	19.20	19.95	19.50	20.40	20.85	21.75	22.05	23.10	23.25	23.70
16	19.20	20.48	21.28	20.80	21.76	22.24	23.20	23.52	24.64	24.80	25.28
17	20.40	21.76	22.61	22.10	23.12	23.63	24.65	24.99	26.18	26.35	26.86
18	21.60	23.04	23.94	23.40	24.48	25.02	26.10	26.46	27.72	27.90	28.44
19	22.80	24.32	25.27	23.70	25.84	26.41	27.55	27.93	29.26	29.45	30.02
20	24.00	25.60	26.60	26.00	27.20	27.80	29.00	29.40	30.80	31.00	31.60
21	25.20	26.88	27.93	27.30	28.56	29.19	30.45	30.87	32.34	32.55	33.18
22	26.40	28.16	29.26	28.60	29.92	30.58	31.90	32.34	33.88	34.10	34.76
23	27.60	29.44	30.59	29.90	31.28	31.97	33.35	33.81	35.42	35.65	36.34
24	28.80	30.72	31.92	31.20	32.64	33.36	34.80	35.28	36.96	37.20	37.92

FIG. 10–9

Increased Limits Table

PRIVATE PASSENGER AUTOMOBILE SECTION Territory 4													
$50 Ded. (72) Class			$100 Ded. (74) Class			$150 Ded. (75) Class			$250 Ded. (76) Class			Age Groups	Symbols
1	2	3	1	2	3	①	2	3	1	2	3		
$22	$31	$27	$10	$14	$12	$ 8	$12	$10	$ 6	$ 8	$ 7	1	
21	29	26	10	13	11	8	11	10	6	8	7	2	A
20	28	24	9	13	11	7	11	9	5	7	6	3	
19	26	23	9	12	10	7	10	9	5	7	6	4	
26	37	32	12	17	15	10	14	12	7	10	9	1	
25	35	30	11	16	14	10	13	11	7	10	9	2	B
23	33	29	11	15	14	9	13	11	6	9	8	3	
22	31	27	10	14	13	9	12	10	6	9	8	4	
30	43	37	14	21	18	11	16	14	9	13	11	1	
29	41	35	13	20	17	10	15	13	9	12	10	2	ⓒ
27	39	33	13	19	16	⑩	14	13	8	12	10	③	
26	37	31	12	18	15	9	14	12	8	11	9	4	
34	49	43	16	23	20	13	18	16	10	14	12	1	
32	47	41	15	22	19	12	17	15	10	13	11	2	D
31	44	39	14	21	18	12	16	14	9	13	11	3	
29	42	37	14	20	17	11	15	14	9	12	9	4	

FIG. 10–10
Collision Insurance Table

Thus, with territory 7, class 1B, and increased limits of 15/30, we would find the basic rate of $21.00 and multiply it by 128 percent to obtain the $26.88 premium.

The table in the rating manual is quite complex for collision insurance, with the premium being determined by territory, symbol (for type and model of automobile), deductible amount, class, and age group, as shown in Figure 10–10. For example, to find the $150 deductible collision premium in territory 4 for a car corresponding to symbol C, class 1, and age group 3, we would find $10 corresponding to the circled identifications in Figure 10–10. However, it is necessary to store only the premiums for two deductible amounts ($50 and $100) since all of the others may be expressed in terms of these. For example, the $150 deductible premium is 80 percent of the $100 deductible premium. The premiums for the various age groups can likewise be expressed as a percentage of the premium for age group 1, and the class premium can be expressed as a percentage of class 3. Thus Figure 10–10 can be reduced to the small table in Figure 10–11, combined with a certain amount of logical analysis and computation. Note that the table in Figure 10–11 (for 17 different symbols) involves only 17 words of storage—if the information is tightly packed.

Territory 4		
$50 Ded.	$100 Ded.	Symbol
$27	$12	A
32	15	B
37	⑱	ⓒ
43	20	D
47	23	E

FIG. 10–11
Condensed Collision Insurance Table

For the example circled in Figure 10–10, looking up the $100 deductible and symbol C in Figure 10–11 we find $18.00. To convert to $150 deductible, we multiply by .8 and get $14.40, and to convert to age group 3 we multiply this by .9, obtaining $12.96. The amount for class 1 is 80 percent of this; so, rounding to the nearest dollar, we obtain the $10.00 premium found in Figure 10–10.

Such techniques make it possible to store all information necessary for checking rates and assigning codes to policies written in a typical state in less than 1,000 words of memory. It should be mentioned that mathematicians also frequently store tables in condensed form to save memory. When necessary, they use high-order interpolation techniques to reconstruct the detailed results.

In this application, input to the computer would be a card (punched from the policy application) containing the type of automobile, the age of the driver, location, types of coverage, the premium assigned, etc. The output would be a statistics card which could be used for statistical analysis, and if the agent made a mistake in assigning the premium the machine would punch out a corrected rating card.

One of the casualty companies that uses an electronic computer for this application operates on a decentralized basis, with about ten regional offices which handle the billing for the policies. At these regional offices the cards are punched from the policies and sent over telephone wires to the home office, where they are checked and coded by the computer. For renewal policies, billing cards are sent to the regional offices to write bills in advance of renewal. Their volume of approximately 10,000 policies per day is handled in about 2 hours' computer time, reducing the number of clerks required under the previous manual procedure by about 40. The computer is available for the rest of the working day for such applications as payroll, life insurance calculations, and statistical applications.

PUBLIC UTILITY BILLING

The calculation of gas, water, and electric bills by public utilities has been a popular punched card application. Basically, it is quite simple: given a card in which the current meter reading and previous readings are punched, it is only necessary to apply a rather simple rate and calculate the amount of the bill. If it were *actually* this simple, however, there would be no need for a computer. The need for an electronic computer is apparent only after an investigation of the by-products required and the great variety of exceptions which can occur.

The exceptions involved include checking the "reasonableness" of the consumption in order to detect meter reading errors, estimating consumption for meters that were not read, prorating bills that are for less than the normal billing period, and handling the various types of meters that may be used in a single city.

In the computer approach to utility billing, all of the exceptional situations can be handled in a single run. In the standard punched card approach, each situation requires a special procedure (or manual handling or review). Furthermore, no sorting is involved in the computer procedure: the meter cards are processed in the same sequence in which they are read and need never be removed from this sequence.

Bill Calculation

When the card is read into the machine, the previous reading is subtracted from the present reading to determine the consumption. Reading dates are subtracted to determine whether the account to be billed is for a full month or for a prorated period, and the accounts are processed accordingly.

The computed consumption is compared with previous months, and an audit is performed to determine the accuracy of the reading. If this month's use compares reasonably with the preceding months', the normal calculation routine is followed. However, if the use is higher or lower, a *subroutine* is followed, and the account is given further programmed scrutiny to check for the "obvious" meter errors which can be corrected by suitable programming. If the type of error cannot be determined, the bill may be calculated as is and an indication punched so that the card may be selected for clerical review or discussion with the customer.

In cases of missed readings, an estimated consumption is calculated by utilizing an average of the previous months' usage. Such factors as season can be taken into account, duplicating the process an estimating clerk would follow. Where the preceding month was also estimated, the computer can find the last actual meter reading and from it recalculate successive preceding usages to project an estimated current reading and consumption. Usually, company policy limits the number of times that a bill can be estimated without actually reading the meter, and the computer can check to see whether the preceding month's estimation was the last one allowed. If this is the case, it can prepare a special card to indicate that the meter must be read.

In a given city there may be several rate structures, depending upon the type of customer and the type of service he receives. Each of these different rate structures is divided into several *consumption steps,* and a different rate is charged for consumption within each step (the rate usually decreases as the consumption increases). For example, the typical rate structure may have a flat charge of $1.00 for the first 15 kilowatt-hours (*kwh*) or less, the next 35 *kwh* cost $.05 apiece, the next 50 *kwh* cost $.04 apiece, the next 100 *kwh* cost $.03 apiece, and everything over 200 *kwh* costs $.02 per *kwh*.

This rate structure may be expressed in the computer by means of the table shown in Figure 10–12. In this table the correction factor for each rate step is obtained by subtracting from the total bill at the maximum consumption of the previous step the product of the rate under consideration times the same consumption. The $1.00 correction factor in the illustration is a flat charge. To obtain the second correction factor we subtract from the $1.00 the product 15 times $.05 (or $.75) to obtain the $.25 correction factor. The total bill for 50 *kwh* would be 50 times $.05 plus $.25, or $2.75.[1] Subtracting 50 times $.04 (or $2.00) from $2.75, we obtain the third correction factor of $.75, and so forth. Then, to compute the bill for 250 *kwh*, we would multiply 250 times $.02 and add the correction factor of $3.75 to obtain $8.75, which agrees with the long calculation based upon the original statement of the rate structure.

Step (*kwh*)	Multiplier	Correction Factor
15	.00	1.00
50	.05	.25
100	.04	.75
200	.03	1.75
9999	.02	3.75

FIG. 10–12
Rate Table

The rate structure is stored in the computer memory, with each step requiring one location. Thus, if a company has 30 rates, each of which has 5 steps, only 150 storage locations are required. The computer calculates the bill by locating the appropriate rate and step by means of Table Look-up, multiplying the consumption by the rate, and adding the correction factor to the product. Prorated bills are computed by projecting the consumption to a one-month base, performing the bill calculation at that base, and adjusting the

---

[1] Fortunately, this is the same total as we get by the regular way of calculating this bill, which would be to charge $1.00 for the first 15 *kwh* and $.05 each for the remaining 35 *kwh* to obtain $1.00 + .05 (35) = 1.00 + 1.75 = $2.75.

calculated amount by the prorate percentage previously figured. The ability to store all of the applicable rates within the machine ensures that bills for all the various types of customers can be calculated without any prior review or sorting operation.

Desired By-Products

Among the most interesting aspects of this application are the statistical summaries which are desired. The rate departments of many companies find it necessary to have complete statistics on the number and size of bills rendered customers for each of the company's rates. For example, they may wish to construct a graph for each rate in which the horizontal axis represents the number of kilowatt-hours for each bill, and the vertical axis tabulates the number of bills at each consumption (as illustrated in Figure 10–13).

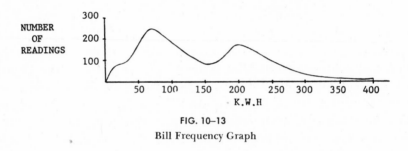

FIG. 10–13

Bill Frequency Graph

We would prefer to accumulate all these statistics in summary form in memory (as a by-product of computing the bills), but since there may be 30 rates and up to 99,999 consumption steps in a rate, it is easy to see that it is not possible to store these summarized statistics for the entire rate structure. However, analysis shows that most customers are billed on relatively few rates and that most customer consumption falls within definite limits. If storage is reserved for the most frequently occurring rates and bill sizes, over 90 percent of all bill statistics can be stored, with the remaining 10 percent punched into detail bill frequency cards during the bill calculation. These detail cards, together with summary frequency cards punched from the memory, can be used to easily obtain a complete summarization of all bill statistics.

Frequently a summarization by dollar amounts of the bills within each rate structure is desired. As in the above case, the summaries may be developed during the bill calculation by accumulating totals in memory for the most frequently occurring classifications and punching special cards for classifications which occur infrequently. Also, a total of customers, meters, consumption, and gross and net billing amounts is accumulated during bill calculation and is punched in a control card when the last account of each control unit is completed. This card is later used for automatic control of the accounts receivable cycle-balancing operation.

The above discussion is a greatly simplified description of the program involved in public utility bill calculation. It may be deduced, therefore, that the computer program itself is very complex. The ability of the stored-program machine to handle all of these complexities in a single run makes it possible to replace an extremely cumbersome combination of punched card and manual procedures with a relatively straightforward and highly automated process.

OVERHEAD COST DISTRIBUTION

The distribution of costs between the various operating and service departments in a business can be a complex problem, for the total costs for any one department are not known until the costs from other departments are distributed to it, while the total costs of the other departments may also be dependent upon the total cost of the first department. Although many approximate solutions to this problem have been developed, it can be solved with mathematical precision through the solution of a set of simultaneous linear equations. Since the advent of the electronic computer it is not only practical to use this mathematical solution but actually less expensive than obtaining an approximate solution manually.

Iterative Technique

The technique used is an iterative procedure in which approximate solutions are improved by repeated calculation until the desired accuracy is reached. To illustrate the method we will consider a case in which only four departments are involved (denoted by A, B, C, and D). The first column of the table in Figure 10–14 indicates that 15 percent of the total costs of department A is charged to department B, and 15 percent of the total expense of department A is charged to department D. The initial direct costs (totaling $36,000) are given by the last column. Our objective is to redistribute this $36,000 total, taking into account the transfers indicated in the body of the table.

In order to calculate the total cost associated with each deparment,

Dept. from Dept. to	A	B	C	D	Direct Costs
A	--	10%	15%	15%	$ 8,000
B	15%	--	20	10	7,000
C	--	10	--	30	9,000
D	15	15	10	--	12,000
TOTAL	30%	35%	45%	55%	$36,000

FIG. 10–14

Cost Transfer Table

the information in Figure 10–14 may be expressed in equation form as follows:

$$(1) \quad A_T = .10B_T + .15C_T + .15D_T + 8,000$$
$$(2) \quad B_T = .15A_T + .20C_T + .10D_T + 7,000$$
$$(3) \quad C_T = .10B_T + .30D_T + 9,000$$
$$(4) \quad D_T = .15A_T + .15B_T + .10C_T + 12,000$$

Using the initial direct costs for each department as our first approximation for the total costs for the departments ($A_T = 8,000$, $B_T = 7,000$, $C_T = 9,000$, $D_T = 12,000$), then substituting these values into the right-hand side of equation 1, we obtain a better approximation for A_T:

$$A_T = .10(7,000) + .15(9,000) + .15(12,000) + 8,000$$
$$= 700 + 1,350 + 1,800 + 8,000$$
$$= 11,850$$

Then, using this new value for A_T, along with the old estimates for B_T, C_T, and D_T, and by substituting in equation 2, we obtain:

$$B_T = .15(11,850) + .20(9,000) + .10(12,000) + 7,000$$
$$= 11,777.50$$

Likewise, using $A_T = 11,850$, $B_T = 11,777.50$, $C_T = 9,000$, and $D_T = 12,000$, and substituting in equation 3, we obtain:

$$C_T = .10(11,777.50) + .30(12,000) + 9,000$$
$$= 13,777.75$$

Now, using $A_T = 11,850$, $B_T = 11,777.50$, $C_T = 13,777.75$, and substituting in equation 4, we find:

$$D_T = .15(11,850) + .15(11,777.50) + .10(13,777.75) + 12,000$$
$$= 16,921.90$$

This completes the first iteration. For the second iteration we repeat the above process, always substituting the latest available approximations for A_T, B_T, C_T, and D_T:

$$A_T = .10(11,777.50) + .15(13,777.75) + .15(16,921.90) + 8,000$$
$$= 13,782.70$$
$$B_T = .15(13,782.70) + .20(13,777.75) + .10(16,921.91) + 7,000$$
$$= 13,515.15$$
$$C_T = .10(13,515.15) + .30(16,921.91) + 9,000$$
$$= 15,428.09$$
$$D_T = .15(13,782.70) + .15(13,515.15) + .10(15,428.09) + 12,000$$
$$= 17,637.49$$

The results of succeeding iterations are summarized in Figure 10–15 where we may observe the process of convergence toward the correct solution. Notice that the improvement in accuracy of the totals between iterations 6 and 7 is less than $4.00, while the last two iterations agree to the nearest dollar for each department. Although even better accuracy could be obtained by a few more iterations,

Iteration / Dept.	3	4	5	6	7	8
A_T	$14,311.35	$14,411.56	$14,446.78	$14,453.65	$14,455.07	$14,455.37
B_T	13,996.07	14,071.30	14,101.81	14,106.80	14,108.01	14,108.26
C_T	15,642.77	15,750.19	15,764.42	15,768.30	15,769.07	15,769.24
D_T	17,810.21	17,847.45	17,858.73	17,860.90	17,861.37	17,861.47
Total	$61,760.40	$62,080.50	$62,171.74	$62,189.65	$62,193.52	$62,194.34

FIG. 10–15

Results of Succeeding Iterations

because of the usual inaccuracies in the assignment of the original percentages, this accuracy is probably ample. But to determine a formal stopping point we may compare the total of all of the departments (last line in the table in Figure 10–15) for a given iteration with the same total for the previous iteration and agree to terminate the procedure when this difference is less than a specified amount (in this case $1.00).

Having obtained the total cost, it is easy to use the column totals of the table in Figure 10–14 to determine the percentage of the total costs remaining and to calculate the net costs for each department, as below:

$$
\begin{aligned}
A_N = A_T - .30A_T &= .70A_T = \$10,\!118.76 \\
B_N = B_T - .35B_T &= .65B_T = 9,\!170.37 \\
C_N = C_T - .45C_T &= .55C_T = 8,\!673.08 \\
D_N = D_T - .55D_T &= .45D_T = 8,\!037.66 \\
&\ \ \text{Total} = \$35,\!999.87
\end{aligned}
$$

Since the total direct charges were \$36,000, this procedure produced excellent accuracy in the above illustration. It should be noted that this method is quite different from the usual elimination method that you may be familiar with, and it may not converge for all sets of simultaneous linear equations. However, this iterative method always converges for the type of equations that arise in overhead cost allocation.

Computer Program

It is not difficult to program the above procedure for a computer. This has been done for a firm which has 90 departments and about 625 interdepartmental transfers. In this case the percentages in the equations to be solved were stored in memory in the following form:

Percent	Dept. to	Dept. from
xx.xx	xx0	0xx

These percentages are stored in sequential locations, with a zero word between equations. Words 0000 through 0090 may be used to record the approximate solutions as they are developed. Assuming that the percentages are stored properly in memory, and that the direct cost for the departments are stored (in location 0000 through 0090) as the first approximation, the block diagram in Figure 10–16 may be used to calculate the total costs for each of the 90 departments.

The entire program for reading all the information into the memory of the computer, computing the total costs for each of the departments, computing the net costs for each department, and punching the results into cards requires less than 300 program steps. Adding 100 locations for accumulating the department totals and

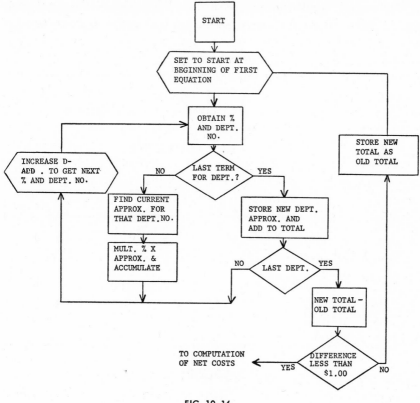

FIG. 10–16
Overhead Cost Calculation

100 locations for the initial direct costs, 1,300 locations remain for departmental distribution percentages.

For the problem in the firm just cited, the solution—using the MAC—requires about ten iterations at two seconds per iteration. The total problem, including loading the program, loading the percentages and initial direct costs, and printing the results, requires less than four minutes. This is equivalent to some 300 hours of desk-calculator labor (required for an *approximate* solution), and provides a good illustration of "computer power."

SUMMARY

Each of the above illustrations provides an example of the ingenuity required in the design of computer applications. In the material-requirements explosion an entirely different file sequence was necessary to take advantage of the capabilities of the computer. In the automobile insurance rating and coding procedure it was necessary to analyze how large tables (developed for use by the insurance salesman) had been constructed so that they could be condensed to fit into the computer's memory. In this illustration the proper entry in the full table is recomputed each time it is needed, and a similar approach is often taken to the determination of the surrender value of life insurance policies.

The public utility billing illustration shows how the branching capability of the electronic computer makes it possible to handle numerous and rather complicated exceptions in a computer program. It also demonstrates how memory may be conserved in accumulating summary information by allocating memory only to the high-volume categories and handling the low-volume categories in another way.

The use of mathematical techniques in an accounting problem is shown in the overhead cost allocation example. When a computer is available, powerful mathematical techniques may become practical, not only simplifying the data processing problem but also providing a better solution.

EXERCISES

10.1 Describe the difference between a bill of materials file and a where-used file. Using each of these files, outline a data processing procedure for determining parts requirements.

10.2 If carried to its logical conclusion, what are the outputs of a materials control system? Does the procedure discussed in this chapter provide these outputs? What is needed before such outputs can be produced?

10.3 Describe some techniques for conserving memory in storing tables. Why don't we use these techniques when the tables are to be used by people?

10.4 Suppose we have utility bills representing consumptions ranging from 1 to 10,000 kwh. If we wish to tally the number of bills of each size between 40 and 140 kwh, how could we exclude the other bills? (Answer with a block diagram.)

10.5   *a*) What is an iterative procedure?
      b) What is meant by convergence of an iterative procedure?
      c) What is a set of simultaneous linear equations?
      d) Are there other ways to solve simultaneous linear equations? How?
      e) How can overhead cost allocation be expressed in terms of simultaneous linear equations?

SUPPLEMENTAL READINGS

Application Development 19—Type 650 for Public Utility Customer Accounting (Form 32–6153). International Business Machines Corporation, 590 Madison Avenue, N.Y.

A description of the use of a 650 computer for utility billing (as discussed in this Chapter).

Application Report 75—Overhead Cost Allocation (Form 32–9360). International Business Machines Corporation, 590 Madison Avenue, N.Y.

This presents the example of overhead cost allocation included in this Chapter and briefly discusses the solution of the equations using punched card calculators.

JEWETT, GRANDJEAN G. "Distribution of Overhead with Electronic Calculators," *The Journal of Accountancy* (June, 1954), pp. 698–701.

Discusses distribution of overhead and the use of electronic computers to solve the resulting equations.

Type 650 for Fire and Casualty Insurance Applications (Form 32–6160). International Business Machines Corporation, 590 Madison Avenue, N.Y.

A discussion of rate checking and coding of automobile insurance policies, using the 650 computer.

11 MAGNETIC TAPE FILES

SO FAR, our discussion of electronic computers has been confined to machines that are similar to the basic MAC. Such machines have all the major characteristics of computers, but they are limited to punched cards for machine-processable input and output. Such machines, of course, are of substantial importance, and we have concentrated our attention upon them because of our concern with the major concept associated with the computer; namely, the stored program. However, we are now in a position to go on to the added power and complexity of machines with machine-processable files.

The adding of machine-processable files and more powerful input-output facilities to the computer contributes greatly to its potential for data processing. First, such devices release the computer from dependence upon the punched card as an input and processing medium. Secondly, these devices provide a tremendous increase in speed of data flow that makes it practical to utilize internal speeds many times faster than the 4,000 operations per second illustrated by the basic MAC.

There are two general types of machine-processable files. *Random access* (or *direct access*) files are devices which make it feasible to skip around within the file, processing transactions without regard to the order in which they occur. In *sequential access* files, on the other hand, transactions must be sorted into the proper sequence before the file can be used. Chapter 11 will be concerned with sequential access files, provided by means of magnetic tapes, and random access files will be discussed in Chapter 12.

CHARACTERISTICS OF MAGNETIC TAPES

Magnetic tapes provide a concise, accurate, speedy, and relatively inexpensive method of recording information in a form in which it can be processed by machine. In addition to being used for input and output, magnetic tapes are also used for storage of file information. The magnetic tape used for electronic data processing is similar to the plastic tape used for ordinary tape recorders, except that it is usually wider and is manufactured to more rigid quality specifications. Although some machines have used tape up to 3 inches wide, most are between ½ and 1 inch wide, and a single reel will contain 1,500 to 3,000 feet.

Information is read from, and recorded on, magnetic tapes by read-write heads, which are electromagnets with an extremely small gap between the poles (see Figure 11–1). As the tape passes over the gap in the read-write heads, pulses of electricity flowing through the coil of the heads causes the coating of the plastic tape to be magnetized in a pattern that indicates the bits to be recorded. When the tape is again passed over the read-write head, this pattern of magnetized spots on the tape induces pulses of current in the coil of wire (similar to the pulses that recorded the information in the first place) so that the tape-recorded information can be read. These pulses may be written (or read) at very high rates of speed (up to hundreds of thousands of bits per second), and the magnetized spots on the tape are very densely packed together (up to hundreds or even more than a thousand bits per inch).

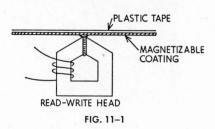

FIG. 11–1

Information Representation

The magnetic tape is wide enough so that several read-write heads can be placed side-by-side within the width of the tape. Thus the four bits for a single binary-coded-decimal digit can be recorded widthwise by using four read-write heads to provide four channels on the tape.

Magnetic tapes provide not only high speed and high density recording, they also provide excellent reliability and accuracy; in fact their error rate compares favorably with punched card reading and punching. However, the tremendous speeds attainable mean that a tremendous amount of data can be written and read—so a very low error rate can still give rise to frequent errors. Thus it is only prudent to provide some method for detecting (and perhaps correcting) errors, especially if this can be done with little additional cost. Fortunately, the addition of a *check* bit (also called a *redundancy* bit)

MAGNETIC TAPE

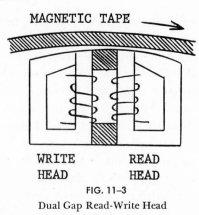

Digit Recorded			
3	4	5	0

Check Bit	1	0	1	1
8	0	0	0	0
4	0	1	1	0
2	1	0	0	0
1	1	0	1	0

WRITE   READ
HEAD   HEAD

FIG. 11–2

Binary-Coded Decimal with
Odd Redundancy Check

FIG. 11–3

Dual Gap Read-Write Head

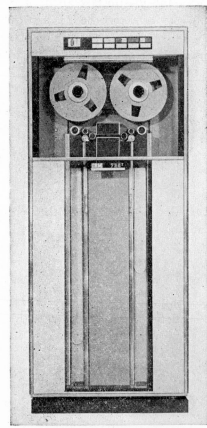

Courtesy of International Business Machines Corp.

FIG. 11–4

IBM Magnetic Tape Unit

to the four-bit binary-coded-decimal code provides a self-checking capability at little added cost. This check bit is generated automatically by the tape unit, as the digit is written, so as to produce an odd number of one-bits in the resulting five-bit character (see Figure 11–2). Then, as the tape is read, the tape unit checks to see that there is an odd number of one-bits in each digit, and the unit indicates an error if there is not.

Errors in reading tape may be corrected by backspacing the tape and reading it again. If the information is properly recorded, it should be read properly on the second attempt. But what if the mistake was made when the tape was written? Here we are in real difficulty, for now we do not have the original information from which the record was written, so such errors are difficult (if not impossible) to correct when the tape is read. For this reason many tape units use a dual-gap read-write head (shown in Figure 11–3). The information is written by the left-hand side of the mechanism, and when each digit passes over the gap on the right-hand side it is read and checked for validity. Thus, if a writing error is made, it is known at the time of writing, and the tape can be backspaced and rewritten (or a bad spot on the tape can be skipped) to provide readable information.

A magnetic tape unit is constructed so that a reel may be easily mounted for processing and easily removed after processing is com-

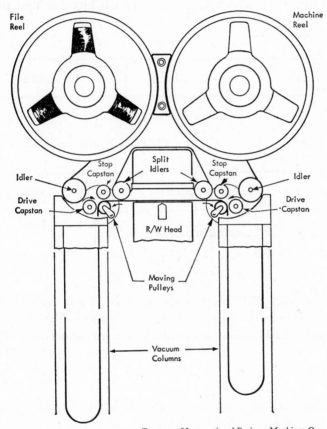

Courtesy of International Business Machines Corp.

FIG. 11–5
Tape Feed Mechanism

pleted. The tape unit is designed to transport the tape over the read-write heads between two reels. To make it possible to start the tape in a few milliseconds, the movement of the tape itself is isolated from the motion of the reels by providing some slack tape between the tape reels and the mechanism which pulls the tape over the read-write heads. As shown in Figures 11–4 and 11–5, one method of controlling this slack is by running the tape into vacuum columns. Vacuum switches in these columns are used to control the rotation of the reels so that adequate slack is maintained both before and behind the read-write head.

Tape Records

On an ordinary tape recorder, sound is recorded continuously from one end of the tape to the other, and the tape is in continuous motion. In contrast to this, information on the computer tape is recorded in blocks, with a gap between each block so that the tape

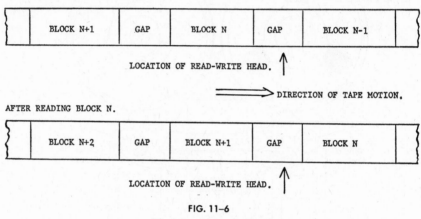

FIG. 11–6

Blocks on Magnetic Tape

can come to a stop and start again between blocks, as shown in Figure 11–6. The time required to start the tape and to get it up to the proper speed for reading each block has an important influence upon the effective speed of reading or writing the tape. For the various machines, this start time ranges between 3 and 40 milliseconds.

Thus, magnetic tapes are similar to punched cards in the sense that a single Read instruction reads an entire block of information into memory. However, there is no control panel associated with the magnetic tape units, so there can be no rearrangement when a block is transferred between memory and the tape.

In most machines a tape block has no address while on tape, but each Read instruction enters the next block character-by-character into a specified group of words within the memory of the machine. However, magnetic tape blocks are usually much larger than 80 characters. (Also, because the writing of new information erases the old, magnetic tape may be reused.)

The number of words in a tape block is specified by the program when the tape is written. To minimize the unused portion of the tape (the inter-record gaps) and to maximize speed, it is desirable to make the blocks on the tape as long as possible. Since a file record may be relatively short (a numeric punched card would be eight words), it is often desirable to group several file records into one tape block (as shown in Figure 11–7 where each tape block con-

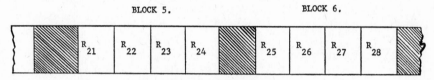

FIG. 11–7
Four Records in a Block

tains four file records). Thus it becomes necessary to distinguish between a *tape* record (or *block*) and a *logical* record, which is a record in the file. It is convenient to *think* in terms of logical records, but the program must be written to handle the tape blocks and separate them into logical records for processing.

Speed

The raw speed (or character rate) at which information may be read from or written upon magnetic tapes is a function of the number of bits per inch per tape channel, the number of channels, and the speed at which the tape moves. As we have noted, the effective speed of reading or writing also depends upon the starting and stopping time between blocks, and upon the length of the block itself.

For a machine such as the MAC it is possible to have several different models of tape unit available for use, with different levels of performance and cost. For example, we might have five-channel tapes with densities of 220, 550, or 1,100 bits per inch, and tape speeds of 50, 100, or 150 inches per second. Thus we would have the character rates shown in Figure 11–8. Each character rate is obtained by multiplying the characters per inch by the speed in inches per second to obtain the rate in characters per second.

By providing 9 rather than 5 channels across the tape, we could read (or write) two digits at once and double the character rate for each of the above combinations of density and tape speed. Thus we would have 18 different combinations of bit density, number of channels, and tape speeds, providing character rates from 11,000 to 330,000 digits per second. Note that the word in the MAC is 10 digits plus sign, so to obtain the number of words per second we would have to divide the number of digits per second by 11 to obtain speeds from 1,000 to 30,000 words per second.

Density in Digits per Inch

		220	550	1,100
	50	11,000	27,500	55,000
SPEED IN INCHES PER SECOND	100	22,000	55,000	110,000
	150	33,000	82,500	165,000

FIG. 11–8

Character Rate in Digits per Second

The start-stop time of the tape unit depends upon the speed at which the tape moves. The time required to read a word is obtained by dividing the number of words per second into one. This information is summarized in Figure 11–9. The rental price of such tape units may vary from $350 per month for the slowest tape to around $2,000 per month for the fastest.

Time per Word (Microseconds)

	Tape Speed (Inches/second)	Start-Stop Time (Microseconds)	220 (Digits/inch)	550 (Digits/inch)	1,100 (Digits/inch)
Five-	50	15,000	1,000	400	200
channel	100	10,000	500	200	100
	150	7,500	333	133	67
Nine-	50	15,000	500	200	100
channel	100	10,000	250	100	50
	150	7,500	167	67	33

FIG. 11–9

Start-Stop Time and Time per Word
(in Microseconds)

To indicate the importance of the block length in determining the effective speed of a tape unit, let us consider the five-channel, 550-bit per inch, 100-inch per second tape unit that has a nominal speed of 5,000 words per second. If we read (or write) 10-word blocks our effective speed is 833 words per second; 100-word blocks give an effective speed of 3,333 words per second; and 200-word blocks give an effective speed of 4,000 words per second. As indicated by Figure 11–10, the effective speed seems to be gradually approaching 5,000

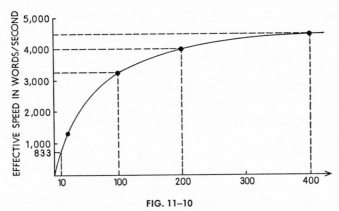

FIG. 11–10

Effective Speed as a Function of Block Length
(5,000 Word/second Nominal Speed)

words per second, but the spectacular speed improvements have been obtained by the time we reach 200-word blocks.

Magnetic Tape Instructions

Several interesting programming considerations are involved in the use of magnetic tapes for input and output. The machine must be informed which of the possible tape units to read from or to write on. Some method must be devised for determining when the end of a reel of tape has been reached, and provision must be made for rewinding tapes so that they can be removed from the machine. There is the possibility of backspacing to reread a record, so certain tape errors may be corrected through programming instead of by stopping the machine. Also, on some machines, it is possible to read a tape backwards as well as forwards, which is sometimes advantageous.

Since we may have many tape units attached to a single computer, and each unit may require as many as seven operation codes, we could easily run out of available combinations in our two-digit operation code. Fortunately, none of the tape operations involve any possibility of field definition, so we may use the field definition digits (positions 8 and 9 of the instruction) to designate the tape unit.

Thus we need provide only seven different operation codes to control the magnetic tapes.

73 RMT (*Read Magnetic Tape*). This operation causes the magnetic tape unit, designated by positions 8 and 9 of the instruction, to read the next tape block into the computer memory starting in the location specified by the data address. If the block on tape is so long that it runs over the top of memory, the information that cannot be placed in memory is lost, but the tape continues to move and stops in the next inter-record gap.

For example, RMT 1700xx03 reads the next block from tape unit 03 into memory, starting with location 1700. If the tape block contains 200 words they would be placed in locations 1700 through 1899, replacing the previous contents of this block. On the other hand, if the tape block contains 400 words the first 300 would be read into locations 1700 through 1999 and the remaining 100 words would be lost. Note that the programmer may not know how many words are in the next block, but he must provide a memory area large enough to accommodate the largest block that could be on the tape or risk destroying important information (instructions or data) in memory or losing part of the data from the tape.

When writing tape we must tell the machine which tape unit to use, where in memory to start, and how long a block to write. To indicate the end of the block we use a word containing a special symbol called a *record mark* (1111 in binary-coded-decimal). A record mark can be entered into memory from load cards, just like any other constant in the program, and must be stored after the last word of the block to be written.

74 WMT (*Write Magnetic Tape*). This operation code causes a record to be written on the designated tape unit. This record begins with the memory location specified by the data address, and ends with the word preceding the first word containing a record mark. If no record mark is encountered, the tape record is terminated when the contents of the highest word in memory have been written.

If there is a record mark in word 1800, the instruction WMT 1600xx05 will write a 200-word block on magnetic tape unit number 5. If there is no record mark in memory this instruction will write a 400-word block containing the contents of words 1600 through 1999.

75 TBS (*Tape Backspace*). This instruction causes the indicated tape to be backspaced one record. The record is not read, but after the instruction has been executed the record can be read by a Read

Tape instruction. Of course, the Backspace instruction can be repeated several times if it is desired to go back several records.

End-of-File Procedures

One consideration in the use of magnetic tape is that of rewinding it when its end has been reached. Unfortunately, this problem cannot be solved by simply allowing the tape to run completely out, as we do with a motion picture projector. A method must be devised for detecting the end of the tape and rewinding it through machine programming. This is further complicated by the necessity to detect and correct (when possible) tape reading and writing errors.

Actually, the meaning of *end-of-file* depends upon whether the tape is being written on or read from. If we are writing on a tape it is necessary to detect the physical end of the tape so that we do not attempt to write beyond the end. On the other hand, in reading the tape we wish to know when we have read all the information that was written on it even if the physical end of the tape has not been reached.

Both conditions can be handled by means of an end-of-file indicator for each tape unit. When writing, this indicator is turned on by a reflective spot affixed a few feet from the physical end of the tape. When reading, this indicator is turned on through a special character on the tape written by the following instruction.

76 WET (Write End-of-File Tape). This instruction writes a one-character block on tape that sets the end-of-file indicator when it is read. This indicator may be interrogated by Branch instructions.

50 BET (Branch End-of-File Tape). This instruction examines the end-of-file indicator of the designated tape unit. If the indicator is on it is turned off and the next instruction is taken from the location designated by the data address. If the indicator is off, the next instruction is taken from the next sequential memory location.

77 RWT (Rewind Tape). This instruction causes the selected tape unit to be rewound, a high-speed operation that takes about one minute. Then the tape may be dismounted by the operator or read again by the computer.

These last three instructions are used in the following way: When writing, a Branch End-of-File Tape instruction is given after each Write instruction. When a Branch occurs, a Write End-of-File Tape instruction must be given before rewinding so that the end-of-file indicator will be turned on when the tape is read.

When reading the tape, a Branch End-of-File instruction is given after each Read Tape instruction. The end-of-file routine then rewinds the tape and takes any other action desired to terminate the processing of that tape.

Error Detection

As we have previously indicated, magnetic tape units are mechanical devices which must operate within very close tolerances. When information is recorded at a density of several hundred bits per inch on a flexible tape, even a small particle of dust can interfere with the reading or writing of information. This is not to imply that magnetic tape units do not perform satisfactorily, but it indicates that built-in checks should be incorporated in their design whenever possible, and that they must be properly maintained and carefully used.

To aid in the detection of errors, the redundancy bit is carried in an extra channel on tape and each *byte*[1] of information may be checked to see that the proper number of 1 bits are present when reading and writing. (Such checking when writing depends upon the use of dual-gap read-write heads.) By automatically writing suitable extra redundancy characters at the end of each tape block it is possible to add further strength to the automatic detection scheme, and even to provide methods of reconstructing certain types of erroneous data.

Whether reading or writing, the detection of an error in a block sets an error indicator that may be interrogated by the following instruction.

39 BST (*Branch on Signal Tape*). This instruction interrogates both the end-of-file and the error indicators. If either (or both) of these indicators is on a Branch occurs and the *error* indicator is turned off. The purpose of this rather strange instruction is to make it possible to reduce the number of instructions in the main loop by handling both end-of-file and errors (which should occur relatively infrequently) with a single instruction. If a branch occurs it is necessary to give a Branch End-of-File Tape instruction to determine whether the branch was caused by an error or an end-of-file condition.

When a single file requires several reels of tape it is usually desirable to use two tape units for input and two for output for the file. When the first reel of the file is completed it can be rewound and replaced by a new reel while the machine processes the next reel

---

[1] The configuration of bits written simultaneously across the tape is sometimes called a *byte*. In our five-channel tape a byte represents one digit; on the nine-channel tape a byte represents two digits.

(which is mounted on the other tape unit) thus overlapping several minutes of tape-handling time for each reel involved. This tape unit switching is accomplished by instruction modification that changes the tape designation digits in the instruction.

A typical end-of-file routine for an input tape is illustrated in the block diagram in Figure 11–11. When a read error occurs, ten

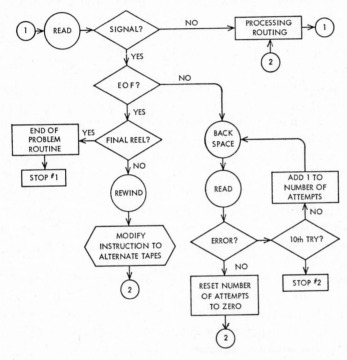

FIG. 11–11
End-of-File and Error Routines

attempts are made to read the record correctly before the machine is stopped. Input tape units are alternated by the end-of-file procedure. Similar routines are required for each of the Read or Write instructions in the program.

The necessity for many such routines in a program makes special input and output macros in the symbolic programming systems very appealing. In such a macro it would be necessary to provide symbols for the location of the end-of-run routine and to designate the primary and alternate tape units.

Tape Handling and Control

As was mentioned previously, the high density of recording and the rapid motion of the magnetic tapes combine to make them rather sensitive. The performance of tape units does not depend entirely upon the equipment itself, but tape reliability may be significantly influenced by how the tapes are handled and stored by the machine operators. For optimum performance, magnetic tapes should be handled very carefully and always protected from dirt—whether in storage or in use.

Particles of dust on the surface of the tape can cause reading or writing errors by increasing the distance between the tape and the read-write heads. Dropping or squeezing a reel of tape can crimp or nick its edges and affect the alignment of the channels with respect to the read-write heads. In short, *extreme* care against damage and dust must be taken in mounting, transporting, and storing magnetic tape reels, and this involves intensive training and constant supervision of personnel, spotless housekeeping, and humidity and dust control in the machine room and tape storage areas.

A human cannot read the information on a piece of magnetic tape: a machine must be used to read it. To machine operators, however, one reel of tape looks very much like another, and a typical installation may require several thousand reels of tape in its various processing runs. It is therefore necessary to establish identification procedures to insure that the proper tape reels are used at the proper times. This problem is further complicated by the fact that magnetic tape can be used over and over, so that a reel of tape that cannot be used today (because the information recorded upon it is still needed) may become available for use next week. If the wrong reel of tape is placed on the machine for input, the processing will be in error. Usually this situation is easily detected and corrected. However, if the wrong reel of tape is mounted on the machine for output, the information on that reel is destroyed when the new information is written. For this reason many tape units are constructed so that a special plastic *file protect ring* must be affixed to a tape reel before the tape unit can write on the tape (see Figure 11–12). Needless to say, it is desirable that operators be instructed *never* to put a file protect ring on a tape reel—this should be the function of *one* person who is in charge of all the tapes.

A visible label must be placed on each tape as it is written, showing the job on which the tape is used, the tape unit on which it must be mounted, the date when it was written, the date after which it may be reused for other purposes, and so forth. Most well-run, large installations employ a tape librarian whose full-time job is to maintain control over the magnetic tapes and file protect rings and to see that the proper reels are used at all times.

In addition to written labels for human use it is usually desirable to write a magnetic label on each tape so that the machine program can check to see that the proper tapes are mounted on the correct tape units. This is accomplished by using the first record written on the tape as an identification record, this record containing such information as the tape serial number, the date when the tape was placed in service, the number of times it has been passed through the machine, the date on which the present information was written, the

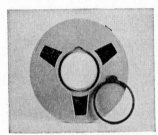

Courtesy of International Business Machines Corp.

FIG. 11–12

File Protect Ring

date it may be used for other purposes, and program identification information such as the run number, tape unit address, and reel number.

Instructions can then be incorporated in the starting routines and the end-of-file procedures which will check to see that all of the input tapes are properly mounted and that the output tapes may safely be written upon, as well as place a current label on the output tapes. These tape labels may also be used for gathering usage statistics which can be analyzed to determine when the tapes are worn to the point that they should be retired from service.

Needless to say, these extra routines complicate the programming and (more importantly) require a considerable amount of memory. In this connection, it should be noted that an extra tape unit may be used to store parts of the program that are executed infrequently. For example, we may store the end-of-file and error-correction routines on such a tape unit and read these routines into the main memory of the machine only when they are needed. If several such routines are written on one reel of tape, bringing the proper one into the memory may involve searching through several records on the tape to find the desired routine. This searching process may seriously delay the program, so this technique is most useful for storing portions of the program which are seldom used (such as those discussed above).

BUFFERING

Let us consider the timing considerations involved in the use of magnetic tapes on the MAC. Suppose we are processing cards against a tape file and printing the result. The information from a 20-word block on tape is combined with the information from a card to produce printed results. We will consider a moderately slow tape-unit that reads 2,500 words per second with a 15 millisecond start-stop time. The time (in milliseconds) to read a 20-word block is $15 + .4 (20) = 23$ milliseconds.

The card reading and the printing are buffered, and require 100 milliseconds. Thus, if processing requires 77 milliseconds or less, the MAC will operate at its full card and printer speed, as shown in Figure 11–13. Even if the total of tape time and process time exceeds

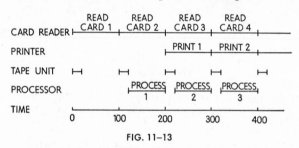

FIG. 11–13

Timing Diagram of Tape Operation on Basic MAC

100 milliseconds, the added time from tape reading is relatively insignificant as a percent of the total time (a maximum of 23 percent) and, with a faster tape unit, this delay would be reduced.

Expressed another way, the MAC performs around 4,000 instructions per second, so it requires 250 microseconds per instruction. Each word read from tape takes 400 microseconds, which is less than two instructions per word (of course, the 15 millisecond start-stop time is the eqivalent of 60 instructions). Thus even with rather slow tapes there is little to be gained by buffering the tapes to allow overlapping of reading, writing, and computing. And if we use faster tapes there is even less need for buffering.

Faster Machines

As we have stated before, the basic MAC is a building-block machine, for we can add magnetic tapes, additional memory capacity, and even more card readers and printers to the basic configuration.

But this building-block concept can be carried even farther, for we might also build a version of the MAC that has a faster memory and executes instructions faster than the basic MAC but has the same logic in that it operates with the same instruction set. Thus a program written for the basic MAC would operate on the faster version, and vice versa.[2]

Thus we could have a version of the MAC that would execute 20,000 instructions per second, another than would execute 100,000 instructions per second, and another that would execute 500,000 instructions per second. Of course, we could also have memory sizes ranging up to 10,000 words or (by using the sign position of the instruction as a part of the address) up to 20,000 words.

Now consider the version of the MAC that performs 100,000 instructions per second. This is 10 microseconds per instruction, and this machine can execute 10,000 instructions while reading one card or printing one line. Consequently, since much data processing work involves only a few hundred instructions per transaction, if the transactions are read from cards, the main frame (processor) and memory of the machine might be idle more than 95 percent of the time, waiting for the next card to be read. Therefore such machines are usually operated exclusively with magnetic tape input and output.

Of course, if the major data processing machine operates exclusively with magnetic tape input and output, there must be some way to get transaction information onto magnetic tape and to print the results that are produced on magnetic tape. This can be accomplished by having one or more small, slow computers which are used to convert cards to tape and to print and/or punch results from tape. The basic MAC, for example, could be simultaneously converting information from punched cards to blocked-tape records and printing results from blocked-output records on tape. Thus card-to-tape and tape printing are off-line operations that are performed independently of the tape-oriented major data processing machines.

Now let us consider the desirability of tape buffering with our 100,000 instruction per second machine. Here the 23 milliseconds required to read a 20-word record on a 2,500 word per second tape

---

[2] Of course, if we were building a faster machine we might choose to design an entirely different set of instructions to take advantage of features we could engineer into the advanced model. But the point is that logic and speed can be independent, and there may be many advantages in producing machines with various speeds and capacities but with the same logic (as in the IBM 360 series).

unit would represent 2,300 instructions at 10 microseconds per instruction. Even with the faster tape units, 750 instructions can be executed during the start-stop time for a block. As with punched cards on the slower version of the MAC, it is very desirable on the faster machines to be able to overlap tape reading and writing with computing.

Data Channels

Recall that the card input buffer on the basic MAC is a 20-word block of nonaddressable additional memory that assembles the information from the card as it is read one row at a time. When the card is completely read, a Read Card instruction transfers the contents of the buffer into memory and begins to feed the next card. This transfer from buffer to memory requires about 5 milliseconds, so 95 milliseconds of computing remain before the cycle can be repeated.

For magnetic tapes this type of buffering would be awkward for several reasons. First, a card is of a fixed length while a tape block may contain only a few words, or several hundred. Since the buffer would have to be large enough to contain the largest record, either the amount of extra memory required would be large or the block length would have to be restricted—or perhaps both. Secondly, the card is read row-wise, so information from all columns must be accepted as it appears. However, the tape is read digit-by-digit, so the buffer would be filled one byte at a time. Thus the entire buffer memory need not be available to the tape all at once, but only one byte at a time.

Therefore a different approach is taken to provide buffering of magnetic tapes. A *data channel* is a device that accepts information one byte at a time from tape, assembles this information into words, and interrupts processing for one memory cycle while this assembled word is transferred into memory. Thus the data channel uses the memory of the machine itself to assemble the record being read, with two single-word buffers and a special address register being used to coordinate the tape units with the memory (as shown in Figure 11–14). In this system the tape is connected to the single-word buffer A, which is filled a byte at a time. When this buffer is full, it transfers its contents to buffer B so that buffer A can be refilled from the tape.

Then the machine processing it interrupted for one memory cycle while the contents of buffer B are stored in the location given by the special address register, 1 is added to the contents of the register, and the machine continues processing while the next word is read from tape. The flow of information is reversed on output, with the data channel taking a word of memory into buffer B, transferring it to A, and feeding it to the tape a byte at a time as required.

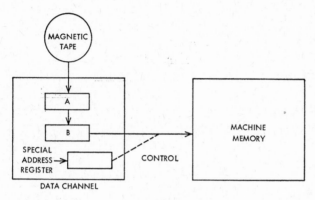

FIG. 11–14
Input Data Channel

Now let us consider timing, using a moderately fast nine-channel tape unit with a start-stop time of 10 milliseconds and reading at a nominal rate of 10,000 words per second (100 microseconds per word). To read a 200-word block would require $10 + 200(.1) = 30$ milliseconds. If the memory cycle of the machine is 5 microseconds, the 200 interruptions would require $200 \times (.005) = 1$ millisecond, so processing would be interrupted only 1 millisecond for each tape block, and 29 milliseconds would be available for processing. In this time the machine could execute 2900 instructions. In other words, the interruptions involved in tape reading require only about $3\frac{1}{3}$ percent of the main frame time.

Note, however, that the main memory itself is used for buffering. Therefore we must provide two input areas for each input tape, one to assemble the record and one from which to process it. If we have several input and output tapes with long records, a good deal of memory may be required for input and output areas, so a large memory may be desirable on a tape-oriented machine.

Like tape units, modules of memory, card readers, etc., data channels are also building blocks that may be added to the machine configuration as required. Let us consider an example to illustrate the effect on processing time of different numbers of data channels. In our example we will read records from two tapes (A and B), then process them and write the results on tapes C and D. This is a fairly typical operation on tape-oriented machines.

First, consider the case where there is no buffering (and no data channels). As shown in Figure 11–15, no overlapping is possible, so one cycle requires the time to read tapes plus the time to process plus the time to write tapes.

```
TAPE A          READ A
TAPE B                   READ B
PROCESS                         PROCESS
TAPE C                                  WRITE C
TAPE D                                         WRITE D
          ←─────────────────────────────────────→
                        ONE CYCLE
```

FIG. 11–15

Tape Processing without Data Channels

If two data channels are available, one can be used for the input tapes and one for the output tapes. Thus input, output, and processing can be overlapped as shown in Figure 11–16. Here we are reading one pair of records, processing the previous pair of records, and writing out the results of the records whose processing has just been completed. Thus if the processing time is less than the time required to read both input records, the time for one cycle is reduced to the time required for reading the tapes.

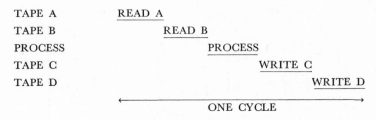

FIG. 11–16

Tape Processing with Two Data Channels

In the previous illustration we are "input-output–bound," for the main frame is idle part of the time waiting for reading and writing to be completed. In such cases we might reduce the cycle time even more by adding two more data channels. As shown in Figure 11–17, reading from both tapes, writing from both tapes, and processing can now be overlapped to reduce the cycle time to the time required for processing. Note that we are now process-bound, so further speeding up of input and output will not increase the speed.

Of course we must recognize that in most applications the processing time will vary from transaction to transaction, so sometimes it may exceed input-output time and sometimes not. Also, we usually must decide upon a machine configuration for a mix of different applications with varying mixtures of input, output, and processing times. However, the objective is to put together a configuration from

TAPE A	READ A_N	READ A_{N+1}	READ A_{N+2}
TAPE B	READ B_N	READ B_{N+1}	READ B_{N+2}
PROCESS	PROCESS$_{(N-1)}$	PROCESS$_{(N)}$	PROCESS$_{N+1}$
TAPE C	WRITE C_{N-2}	WRITE C_{N-1}	WRITE C_N
TAPE D	WRITE D_{N-2}	WRITE D_{N-2}	WRITE D_N

$$\xleftarrow{\hspace{3cm}}\text{ONE CYCLE}\xrightarrow{\hspace{3cm}}$$

FIG. 11–17

Tape Processing with Four Data Channels

available building blocks that will be as efficient as possible (in terms of results per dollar) for the mixture of applications which we wish to process.

Instructions

In our discussion of unbuffered tapes on the MAC we designated which tape unit is to be operated by the two digits in positions 8 and 9 of the instruction (that are used also as partial word indicators). If we add data channels we may assign each tape unit to one of the data channels, with a maximum of ten tapes on each channel. Thus we may use the first digit (position 8) to designate the data channel and the second digit to indicate the tape unit. For example, if we have four data channels and three tapes on each channel, we would designate them as shown in Figure 11–18.

Tape Numbers

		0	1	2
Data Channel Number	0	00	01	02
	1	10	11	12
	2	20	21	22
	3	30	31	32

FIG. 11–18

Tape Designation

If we are reading from tape 2 on data channel 1 (designated by 12), and give a second Read instruction before the first block has been completely read, an interlock causes the central processor to be delayed until the channel has completed the operation under way. To use this time for other purposes we might wish to be able to inquire whether the channel is busy—before giving another Read instruction.

51 BCB (Branch if Data Channel Is Busy). This instruction queries the data channel designated by position 8 of the instruction. If this channel is busy a branch occurs. If the channel is available, the next instruction is taken from the next memory location. The use of this instruction will be discussed later under the topic of Multiprogramming.

With large blocks of input which may need to be transferred to an output or a processing area, it is desirable to have instructions that will move blocks of information from one part of memory to another quickly and easily. In order to move a block from one place to another it is necessary to designate the beginning location of the block, the memory location where the block is to be stored, and the number of words to be moved. This requires two instructions.

67 RCV (Receive). The data address of this instruction indicates the location of the first word to which the block is to be moved. Positions 8 and 9 of this instruction give the high-order two digits of the number of words that are to be moved. This instruction has no effect unless it is immediately followed by the following instruction.

68 TSM (Transmit). This instruction causes a block of data to be moved from memory locations that begin with the location specified by the data address of this instruction to memory locations that have been indicated by the preceding Receive instruction. The two low-order digits of the number of words moved are designated by positions 8 and 9 of this instruction, while the two high-order positions are designated by the same positions of the Receive instruction.

The data is moved one word at a time, starting with the first word of the block. Each word transferred requires two memory cycles, so the time to move a block is the number of words times two times the memory cycle time.

For example, the following sequence would move a 200-word block from memory locations 4100–4299 into locations 4600–4799:

> RCV 4600 xx02
> TSM 4100 xx00

The following sequence would move a 1234-word block from memory locations 7000–8233 into memory locations 6000–7233:

> RCV 6000 xx12
> TSM 7000 xx34

Note that the above blocks overlap, but the words in 7000–7233 are transmitted before they are replaced by new information. It is not possible to reverse this and move the information from 6000–7233 into 7000–8233 because the information in 7000–7233 would be replaced before being moved.

PROCESSING MAGNETIC TAPE FILES

Magnetic tapes are used for input of transactions, output of results, and for maintaining file information. Since on most machines the tape records are not addressable, a record must be read into the machine memory before it can be identified. To obtain a single record from a magnetic tape file it is usually necessary to start at the beginning of the tape and examine each record until the machine reaches the record for which it is searching. Therefore it is not efficient to search a tape file for just one record, for on the average it would be necessary to examine half of the file to find it. Although magnetic tapes operate rapidly, it still takes several minutes to read a reel of tape, and a minute (or even a few million microseconds) for each file reference is too time consuming.

Therefore, magnetic tape files are utilized in much the same way as the punched card collator (described in Chapter 3). The master file is maintained in sequence upon tape, and it corresponds to the file in the primary feed of the collator. The transaction tape, sorted into the same sequence as the file, corresponds to the cards in the secondary feed of the collator. Thus the active items from the file may be selected by using the branching ability of the computer to accomplish the functions of the collator. Moreover, through the use of the computer the active items can be processed and returned to the file concurrently with this process of collation. Thus, instead of merely selecting active items for further processing in other machines (as the collator does), the computer with magnetic tapes combines the processing function with file reference and updating.

To use magnetic tape files efficiently, therefore, the same basic approach is adopted that is used with punched card equipment. We collect a batch of transactions, sort them into the same sequence as the master file, and proceed through the master file in sequence to process the entire batch. Since magnetic tapes are processed in a sequential manner, they may be called *sequential access* files, as opposed to *direct access* files in which it is feasible to go directly to any item and process it individually. (Direct access files will be discussed in Chapter 12.)

For technical reasons, it is impossible in most machines to read a record from a magnetic tape, alter it, and write it back on the same magnetic tape in replacement of the old record. Even if it were possible to perform this operation, it might not be desirable because the original file information would be destroyed in this process, making it difficult to go back and reconstruct a correct record when errors are made.

When the transactions affect the contents of the file, the master file is usually read and rewritten on a new tape; those records that must be altered are changed, and the inactive records are merely copied. Then the updated master file is used as input during the next proc-

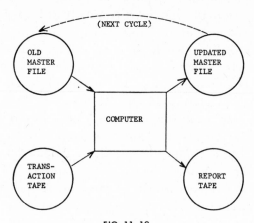

FIG. 11–19

Magnetic Tape File Processing

essing cycle. This basic approach is illustrated in Figure 11–19.

It should be noted that the approach of rewriting the entire file each time it is processed makes accuracy of tape writing an important consideration, for there is the possibility of creating errors in inactive records. Also, if the machine is buffered, or if it can read and write tapes simultaneously, it takes no extra time to rewrite the file. But if the machine cannot overlap operations, rewriting the entire file may be so uneconomical that more complex techniques must be devised for efficient processing with unbuffered machines.

Let us consider a general block diagram for a typical magnetic tape file processing run in which we wish to process transactions against the master file, produce an output record for each transaction, and update the master record. We may have no transactions on some master records, in which case we merely rewrite the record. On other master records we may have one or more transactions. In Figure 11–20, M designates the identification field of the master record being considered and T designates the identification field of the transaction record that has been read.[3] Note that this block diagram treats the problem in terms of logical records and ignores the programming problems involved in buffering, blocking, and end-of-file and error routines.

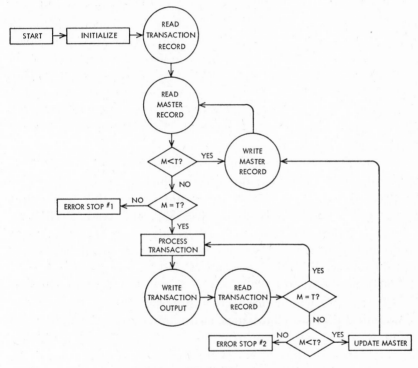

FIG. 11–20

General Block Diagram of a Typical File Processing Run

Let us go through this block diagram with some synthetic data to see what would happen under certain conditions. M (2431) means the number 2431 is the identification of a master record, and T (2576) means that the number 2576 is the identification of a transaction record. Consider the following data, and note that there is no master record for T (2617) and that T (2615) is out of sequence:

---

[3] $M < T?$ is read: Is M less than T?

Transaction Records	Master Records
T(2576)	M(2554)
T(2583)	M(2576)
T(2583)	M(2577)
T(2617)	M(2583)
T(2629)	M(2604)
T(2615)	M(2629)
	M(2631)

Following the block diagram in Figure 11–20, we would read T (2576) and M (2554). Since M (2554) is less than T (2576), we would write M (2554) and read M (2576). Now M (2576) equals T (2576), so we would process this transaction, write a record for T (2576), and read T (2583). M (2576) is not equal to T (2583), but T (2583) is greater than M (2576), so we would update the master record, write M (2576), and read M (2577). This master record is less than T (2583), so we would write M (2577) and read M (2583), which equals T (2583).

We would process this transaction, write a record for T (2583) and read the next transaction record, which is another T (2583). M (2583) equals T (2583), so we would process this transaction, write another output record for T (2583), and read T (2617).

Now T (2617) is not equal to but *greater* than M (2583), so we would update the master record, write out a record for M (2583), and read M (2604). This is less than T (2617), so we would write M (2604) and read M (2629), which is not less than or equal to T (2617); so we would reach error stop No. 1.

Assuming that we could start again by reading the next transaction, T (2629), and comparing it with M (2629), we could find equality, process this transaction, write an output record for T (2629), and read T (2615). Now T (2615) is not equal to M (2629) and T (2615) is not greater than M (2629); and so in this case we would reach error stop No. 2.

SORTING MAGNETIC TAPES

As has been discussed previously, magnetic tape machines usually process transactions against a file that is in sequence, and the transactions must be placed in that same sequence before processing. Thus it is necessary to be able to sort information on magnetic tapes. However, because a magnetic tape is a continuous ribbon, the individual records cannot be physically shuffled as can punched cards. Fortunately, it is possible to use the computer itself to re-arrange the information on magnetic tapes and thereby accomplish the same result obtained with a punched card sorter.

The most common method of sorting magnetic tape records involves a process of merging the small sequences on the original tape to form longer sequences, repeating the merging process with these sequences to form longer sequences, and so on, until a single sequence is built up. A minimum of four tape units are used for this process—two for input and two for output.

Sorting Illustration

Suppose we have a magnetic tape containing records identified by the three-digit numbers shown in Figure 11–21. It should be emphasized that we are concerned not only with these numbers but also with the records which they identify. We wish to sort the records so that they are in sequence according to these identifying numbers (as the sorting key).

In Figure 11–21 the first four numbers are already in sequence and the next five form a sequence—as do the next three and the last three numbers. The end of a sequence is indicated by a step-down condition—a number followed by a smaller one.

To merge these sequences and form longer sequences, we first separate this original tape into two tapes. If we place the original tape on unit A, on the first pass we will produce tapes C and D, as shown in Figure 11–22. In this procedure we write records on tape C until the end of the first sequence is reached; then we write on tape D until the end of the next sequence;

021
142
343
565
007
380
786
960
965
253
275
613
849
376
477
814

FIG. 11–21

Sorting Example: Input

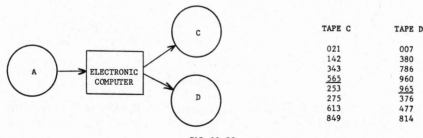

FIG. 11–22

Sorting Example: First Pass

TAPE C	TAPE D
021	007
142	380
343	786
<u>565</u>	960
253	<u>965</u>
275	376
613	477
849	814

on C till the end of the next sequence; on D till the end of the next, and so on, switching output tapes at the end of each sequence.

At the conclusion of this pass we may remove the input tape from tape unit A and replace it with another reel of tape, thus preserving

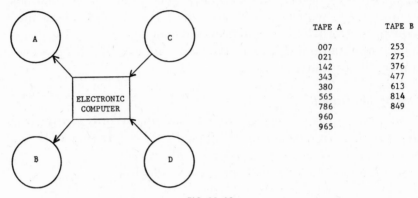

TAPE A	TAPE B
007	253
021	275
142	376
343	477
380	613
565	814
786	849
960	
965	

FIG. 11–23
Sorting Example: Second Pass

the information in its original sequence. The next pass requires a fourth tape unit. In this pass tapes C and D become the input and tapes A and B are the output, as shown in Figure 11–23. As we merge tapes C and D, we write on tape A until the end of the first output

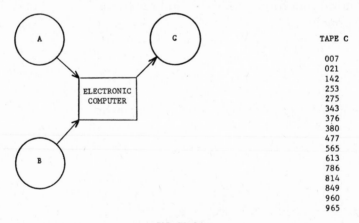

TAPE C
007
021
142
253
275
343
376
380
477
565
613
786
814
849
960
965

FIG. 11–24
Sorting Example—Final Pass

sequence; then we write the next sequence on B, then switch back to A, and so on.

On the next pass tape units A and B become the input and C and D the output. However, as shown in Figure 11–24, only one sequence is produced, so we never switch to tape D, and the sorting process is completed.

The foregoing process is accomplished by a series of comparisons among the sorting keys in the record just read from the first input tape, the record read from the second input tape, and the last record which has been written. Records are thus written in ascending se-

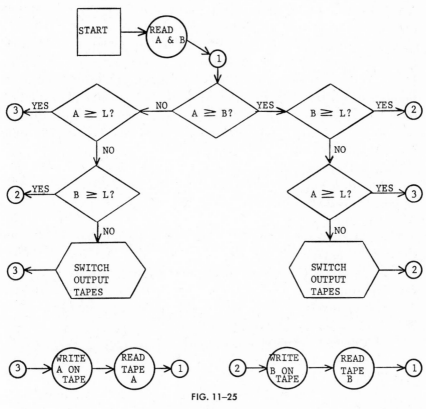

FIG. 11–25

Basic Logic of a Sort Pass

quence on one output tape until both input records are smaller than the last record that was written, when a new sequence is started on the other output tape. The block diagram in Figure 11–25 illustrates the basic logic of a single sorting pass. In this diagram, A represents the sorting key of the last record read from tape A, B represents the key of the last record read from tape B, and L represents the key of the last output record.[4] Again, in this block diagram we are dealing

---

[4] $A \geq B$? is read: Is A greater than or equal to B?

with logical records and are ignoring considerations involved in blocking records. End-of-file and error detection are also ignored.

Although it applies directly only to those passes in which there are two input tapes, with a small change in interpretation the block diagram of Figure 11–25 will serve for the first pass also. If we substitute "Read from tape A into Input Area A" for "Read tape A," and "Read from tape A into Input Area B" for "Read tape B," then A represents the identification of the record from Area A, and B represents the identification of the record from Area B.

Let us follow through to the block diagram of Figure 11–25 with the example of Figure 11–21 and try to obtain the result of Figure 11–22. At the start, we read 021 into Area A and 142 into Area B. The number 021 is less than 142, so we ask if 021 is greater than the last record written. Since we have written no previous records, the answer is yes, and we go to ③ and write 021 on tape C, read 343 into Area A and go to ①.

Now 343 is greater than 142, so we ask if 142 is greater than the last record written. Since 142 is greater than 021 we go to ② and write 142 on tape C, read 565 into Area B, and go to ①. At this point A = 343, B = 565, and L = 142.

Thus, A ≧ B? is answered no; but 343 is greater than 142, so we write 343 on tape C and read 007 into Area A. Now A = 007, B = 565, and L = 343, so again we take the left path on the block diagram. But A is not greater than L, so we ask if B is greater than L. The answer is yes; so we go to ② and write 565 on tape C, read 380 into Area B, and return to ①.

At this stage A = 007, B = 380, and L = 565. Thus A is not greater than B, A is not greater than L, and B is not greater than L; so we switch from tape C to tape D and go to ③. Then we write 007 on tape D, read 786 into Area A, and return to ①. This may be continued with the remainder of the input records.

By a similar process, it is easy to verify that the block diagram of Figure 11–25 produces the results shown in Figure 11–23 from those shown in Figure 11–22—assuming that we always call the input tapes A and B and call the output tapes C and D. We can also verify the results of Figure 11–23 by this process.

Number of Passes Required

In the above procedure the total number of sequences on the output tapes is cut in half on each pass after the first. Working backwards from the last pass (which has only one sequence), we see in Figure 11–26 that the preceding pass had two sequences, the one before that had four, the one before that had eight, the one before that had sixteen sequences, and so on. Thus, at the start of a process requiring N passes (after the first), there were a maximum of 2^N sequences.[5] Conversely, if there were 2^N sequences (or less) evenly divided on two tapes, the sort could be completed in N passes at the most.

Suppose we wish to know how many passes (after the first) will be required to complete the sorting of a tape. If we know the number of sequences on the two tapes at the end of the first pass (denoted by K),[6] then we can determine the number of additional passes (de-

	Number of Sequences	N = Number of Passes to Complete the Sort	2^N
At the end of the last pass	1		
At the beginning of the last pass	2	1	2
At the beginning of the next-to-last pass	4	2	4
At the beginning of the 3rd-from-last pass	8	3	8
At the beginning of the 4th-from-last pass	16	4	16
At the beginning of the 5th-from-last pass	32	5	32
At the beginning of the 6th-from-last pass	64	6	64

FIG. 11–26

Sequences and Number of Passes to Complete the Sort

noted by N) that will be required to complete the sort by choosing N as the smallest whole number that will satisfy the relationship $2^N \geqq K$.

For example, if there are 1,500 sequences after the first pass, 11 more passes will be required because $2^{11} = 2,048$ (which is greater than 1,500), while $2^{10} = 1,024$ (which is less than 1,500). The difficulty in estimating the number of passes required to sort a tape is that we usually do not know the number of sequences on a tape at the

[5] 2^N is read: 2 to the Nth power, or the product of N 2's; $2^1 = 2$, $2^2 = 4$, $2^3 = 8$, $2^4 = 16$, etc.

[6] As will be seen in Exercise 11.4 at the end of this chapter, in addition to splitting the original tape into two, the first pass may reduce the total number of sequences on the tapes. Thus K may not be the number of sequences on the original tape.

start but only know the number of records. Thus we are forced to estimate the number of sequences, using whatever information we have. If the file is already in order, there is only one sequence; and if the file is originally in reverse sequence, it is easily verified that the first pass produces sequences of length two.

Actually, however, the accuracy of the estimate of the number of sequences is usually not as crucial as one might suppose. For example, in the foregoing illustration any estimate between 1,025 and 2,048 would still indicate 11 passes after the first. Furthermore, the machine will take the necessary number of passes, no matter what we estimate.

The writing process described above is called a two-way merge. It is possible to use three input tapes and three output tapes and obtain a three-way merge; and corresponding higher-order merges may be devised. If we let T represent the number of *input* tapes used, the corresponding formula obtained is:

$$T^N \geq K$$

Costs and Time for Sorting

In illustration of the time required for sorting, and to obtain an indication of the costs involved, let us consider a faster version of the MAC. This faster machine has a 5,000-word memory and executes an average of 50,000 instructions per second (20 microseconds per instruction). It has two data channels and ten medium-speed magnetic tape units that read at 7,500 words per second (133 microseconds per word) with a 7.5 millisecond start-stop time and a recording density of 550 digits per inch. Rewind time is one minute.

If machine rents for $25,000 per month on a one-shift basis, or for $37,500 per month on a two-shift basis, this corresponds to a direct hourly cost of $142 per hour on a one-shift basis and $107 per hour on a two-shift basis. However, adding the costs of operators, supplies, space, power, etc., we obtain figures in the neighborhood of $175 and $140 per hour, respectively. In our cost calculations we will assume two-shift operation and will use the $140 per hour figure.

Suppose we wish to sort a file containing 50,000 ten-word records, blocked so that there are 50 logical records per tape block (500 word blocks). We will assume that there are 15,000 sequences after the first pass.

To estimate the total time for a given sort we need to know both the number of passes required and the amount of time for each pass.

For the low-order merges we can assume that the processing time is overlapped by the tape time (for reasonable record sizes) so that the total time per pass is determined by the number of blocks in the file.

Each block requires $7.5 + 500\,(.133) = 73.5$ milliseconds. Since there are 1,000 blocks on the tape, one pass of the tape takes 73.5 seconds plus 60 seconds for rewinding,[7] a total of 133.5 seconds per pass.

First, consider a two-way merge. If we have 15,000 sequences after the first pass, then 14 additional passes will be required since:

$$2^{14} = 16,384 > 15,000 > 8,192 = 2^{13}$$

Therefore 15 passes are required, and we have a total time of $15\,(133.5) = 2,002.5$ seconds. Thus at $140 an hour it would cost about $78 to sort this file using a two-way merge.

It should be noted that the two-way merge is probably the least efficient method of sorting on magnetic tape. For example, a three-way merge would reduce the number of passes after the first to nine since:

$$3^9 = 19,683 > 15,000 > 6,561 = 3^8$$

Therefore the total number of passes would be reduced from 15 to 10 and the cost would be reduced to around $52.

This looks like a good thing, and we have plenty of tape units, so perhaps we should consider a four- or a five-way merge. However, let's look at memory requirements. For buffering we need two input areas for each input tape and two output areas. With a three-way merge this is eight 500-word blocks, or a total of 4,000 words. A four-way merge would require ten 500-word blocks—which uses up all the memory and leaves no room for the program! Therefore we might wish to increase the memory size of our machine to allow higher-order merges when sorting.

Another approach that may reduce sorting time is that of sorting several records into sequence in the memory of the machine during the first pass. Thus we might internally sort each tape block into sequence, so that at the end of the first pass we would have only 1,000 sequences. In this case, seven passes after the first would be required since:

$$3^7 = 2,187 > 1,000 > 729 = 3^6$$

---

[7] All tapes rewind simultaneously.

The internal sort of the block of 50 records could be programmed as a two-way merge, using memory areas instead of tapes. However, this internal merge might not be completed within the time available when reading or writing a block (approximately 70 milliseconds). Assuming that this would require 100 milliseconds, we would be compute-bound on the first pass, and it would require 100 seconds plus rewind time, or 160 seconds. The total time for this sort would be $160 + 7 (133.5) = 1094.5$ seconds, and the cost would be approximately $43.

As will be discussed later, some machines are able to perform simultaneous functions (sorting and other work, for example), and the sorting only delays the other work by the amount of internal processing time involved in the sort. Since internal processing time may be substantially less than the tape time involved, the cost of the sorting may be further reduced.

It should be obvious at this point that many variations in method can be used to sort magnetic tapes. Likewise, there are a number of techniques for internal sorting. The best method for any given situation will depend upon the characteristics of both the equipment and the file that is to be sorted.

In the above discussion we have neglected the time necessary to mount and dismount tapes to get on and off the machine. This setup time might well amount to several minutes, and each minute costs close to $2.50 on this machine. For small jobs that run only a few minutes, the setup time may be the most important component of cost, so the best way to increase efficiency would be to reduce setup time. By providing extra tape units and utilizing automatic executive routines to load and start a new program (using other tape units) immediately when the old one is completed, it is possible to use the machine almost continuously while the reels are being mounted and removed. And many data processing organizations utilize such techniques to improve efficiency.

Cards versus Tape

If this same file were represented by 50,000 cards, and we were sorting on a six-digit numeric key, 6 passes would be required. Using a 1,000-card-per-minute sorter, and assuming an operating efficiency of 60 percent, it would require 300,000 card passes, or about 500 minutes to sort the file. However, the punched card sorter rents for less than $1.00 per hour, and an operator can be obtained for about $3.00 per hour, so the total cost of sorting the punched card file would be about $33.

Since the time for comparisons is small compared to the tape time, even if the sorting key is so long that we must compare on several words, the sorting program is still input-output bound. Thus the time required for sorting magnetic tapes is essentially independent of the length of the sorting key. But the time necessary to sort punched cards depends upon the number of card passes required, which depends upon the number of columns involved in the sorting key, and whether the key is alphabetic or numeric. If the sorting key were eight digits or four alphabetic characters, the costs of tape sorting and card sorting would be about the same, and tape sorting would be less expensive than card sorting for larger fields.

However, it should be emphasized that the total cost of all the applications must be considered—not just the costs of sorting—when comparing the economics of a punched card system with that of a magnetic tape electronic data processing system. Furthermore it is frequently possible (when desirable) to sort transaction cards on a punched card sorter before converting the resulting sorted file to magnetic tape for processing through the computer. It should be noted that it is also frequently possible to utilize the memory of the computer to eliminate or reduce the necessity for sorting, and thus to reduce the cost and complexity of the procedures involved.

Several people have noted that a special-purpose machine (requiring only limited capabilities as compared with a computer) could be designed to take over the tape sorting burden from the expensive computer main frame, as well as to perform the functions of extraction from a file and subsequent merging. Or a basic MAC, with slow tape units and renting for around $7,000 per month,[8] might be employed for these functions.

Unfortunately, both the special-purpose and the small general-purpose machines are restricted to low-order merges with small tape blocks, and therefore cannot employ the powerful techniques of the large computers; so they show no spectacular economic advantage over the large machines for sorting.

Generalized Sort Routines

To sort one magnetic tape requires a slightly different sorting program than to sort another tape. This is caused by differences in the record size, the number of records per block, and the location of the sorting key (or keys) within the record. However, it is not neces-

---

[8] Such a machine would normally be available in a tape-oriented data processing installation for converting cards to tape and for printing tapes.

sary to write a new sorting program for each different tape that is to be sorted: "generalized sort routines" are usually available from the machine manufacturer as a part of the machine software. Each generalized sort routine utilizes a particular sorting technique and is capable of modifying itself to fit various formats of files.

The record size, the number of records per block, and the location within each record of the sorting key (or keys) may be entered into the machine by means of a punched card or the first record on the tape. The first phase of the generalized sort program then utilizes this information to modify the sorting routine itself to produce (for example) a three-way merge which will apply to the particular tape under consideration. This process requires but a few seconds to be completed, and then the machine proceeds to use the generated program to sort the file.

INVENTORY CONTROL, ACCOUNTS RECEIVABLE, AND BILLING ILLUSTRATION

To illustrate how a tape data processing machine may be used, let us consider an illustration that combines the elements of invoicing, billing, accounts receivable, and inventory control into one procedure. Let us assume that we carry about 50,000 different items in inventory at five different warehouses; that we receive an average of 2,000 orders each day with an average of six items on each order; that we have an average of 2,000 receipts and adjustments per day; and that these 14,000 line items each day involve a considerable amount of duplication, only 8,000 items being active on the average day.

As each order arrives we would like to check it against the inventory record to see if we can ship the items requested, and, if not, to backorder them for later shipment. Then we write a priced and extended invoice which shows warehouse location so that the stock can be conveniently "pulled" by referring to a copy of the invoice. Before writing the invoice, however, we update the accounts receivable record and check to see that the customer's credit limitations have not been exceeded. Periodically, the accounts receivable file can be analyzed for collection follow-up.

Although the processing described above requires a considerable amount of record keeping and clerical effort, it is the area of inventory control that provides the major motivation for the use of an electronic computer in such a situation. By maintaining accurate and adequate usage information, along with on-hand and on-order balances, it is possible to reflect the effect of each transaction upon the inventory status and to immediately signal when it is desirable to procure, expedite, or dispose of surplus.

Furthermore, when some action should be taken, adequate information concerning the status of the item, the various vendors, and the probable usage can be automatically provided to the person in charge of controlling the inventory for that particular item. This allows the *people* involved to concentrate on the problems associated with managing the inventory rather than spend their time looking up records and checking balances to determine which items need their attention. By reducing outages and preventing the accumulation of excessive quantities of obsolete items, this "management by exception" technique should provide significant increases in the return on the money invested in inventory.

It should be apparent, however, that the effectiveness of inventory control will depend upon the decision rules that are devised for setting reorder levels, expediting levels, and deciding when to dispose of surplus. If we do not know enough about our inventory problems to devise effective rules, we cannot expect the computer to do a satisfactory job of inventory control, for the computer is utterly dependent upon the rules we devise and the program we write. At least one organization that tried this approach has found to its dismay that they did not know enough about their inventory control problems to make this approach successful. (An inventory simulation that is useful for testing various approaches to inventory management will be discussed in Chapter 17.)

Procedure

As the customer orders are received, a card (containing the customer number, item number, and quantity ordered) is punched for each item on each order. These cards are combined with similar cards for those items that are received into the warehouse and for those items that are being ordered from the vendors. The resulting 14,000 cards are sorted into item-number sequence and converted to magnetic tape for processing in Run 1 against the master inventory file (which is also in item-number sequence), as shown in Figure 11–27.

The master inventory file contains such information as item number, description, unit price, unit cost; total orders and backorders for each of the past six months; on-hand balance, on-order balance, backorder balance, reorder level, expedite level, disposal level, and warehouse locations at each warehouse; a maximum of three vendors, an indication of the person in charge of inventory control for this item, and codes indicating the inventory control rules to be applied to this item. We will assume that each master inventory

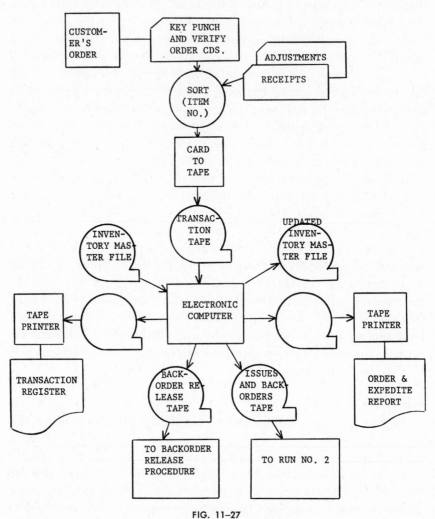

FIG. 11–27

Run 1: Inventory Processing

record requires 50 words, and that these are grouped six records to each tape block.

As discussed previously, this machine cannot selectively alter records within a tape file, so it is necessary to read and rewrite the entire master inventory file to change the 8,000 active records among the total 50,000 inventory records in the file. Since the machine can read and write at the same time, no additional time is required; and an important safeguard against machine malfunctioning is obtained because the input information is not destroyed. If the output is found to be in error (or unreadable), it can be reconstructed by reprocessing the old input tape.

To have something to refer to when questions arise, and to provide an audit trail, a transaction register is produced that lists each inventory activity, showing the warehouse number, item number, type of transaction, old balance, transaction amount, and resulting new balance, as well as the date of the last transaction so that the activities on an item may be traced by hand if there is any question about it.

Each active item is examined to determine whether it should be ordered, expedited, or disposed of. If any of these actions are indicated, a report is prepared that contains most of the information in the master inventory record, so that the proper person has the information necessary to take the indicated action.

The receipt of some items may allow backorders to be released, and a tape indicating the items and quantities involved is provided to go into a backorder release procedure.

The issues and backorders tape is actually an invoice tape; it contains (for each item ordered) all the information needed to write a line on the invoice. However, this tape is in item-number sequence, so that the items for a given invoice are scattered more or less at random. This tape then becomes the input to Run 2, which sorts it to customer-number sequence so that the body information may be combined with heading information to write the invoice.

Run 3 combines this tape with a customer master tape, maintained in customer-number sequence, which contains name and address, standard shipping instructions, and accounts receivable information. The output from Run 3, shown in Figure 11–28, includes a tape from which invoices may be printed, an updated customer master tape, a transaction register tape, and an exception tape which notes such situations as missing customer records or the exceeding of allowable credit.

Let us now consider Run 1 in greater detail. The general block diagram of Figure 11–29 represents an acceptable overall logic for this run—assuming we understand that the symbols referring to tape reading really mean "Read another block if we have exhausted all of the records from the previous block." If the block is not exhausted, a read-tape symbol simply means to process the next record of the tape block. The write-tape blocks should be similarly interpreted. In Figure 11–29 the symbol T represents the item number of the record being processed from the transaction tape, and the symbol M represents the item number of the record being processed from the inventory master tape. This block diagram resembles the general block diagram shown in Figure 11–20, except that in Figure 11–29 the transaction processing is broken down into three separate routines.

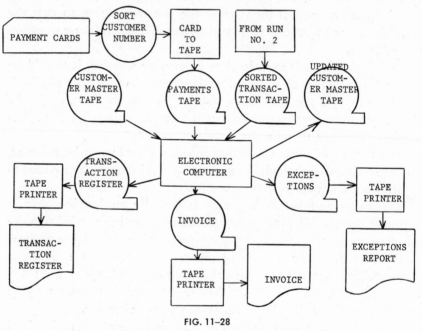

FIG. 11–28

Run 3: Invoice and Accounts Receivable

Time Estimation

One of the most interesting aspects of planning for an electronic computer installation is the problem of estimating the time required for each processing run. This is an extremely important problem in deciding whether or not to install such a machine, or deciding whether or not to place a given application on the electronic computer.

Historically speaking, there are numerous instances when the time estimates upon which the decision to procure a machine was based

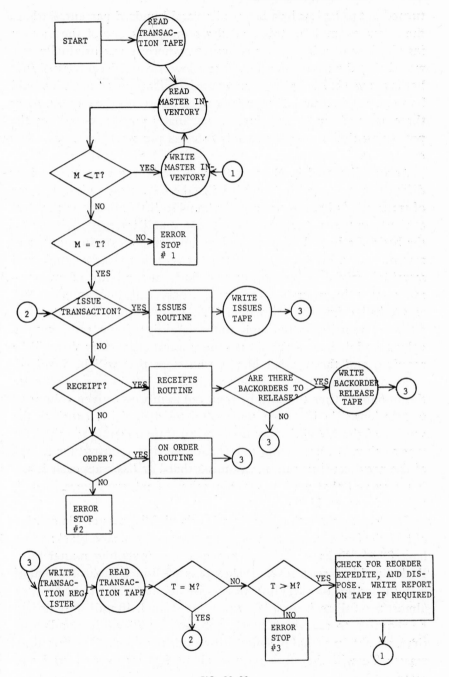

FIG. 11–29
Overall Block Diagram for Inventory Run

turned out to be low by a factor of several hundred percent. Perhaps the classic example of this difficulty occurred at one of the pioneer installations of a large-scale computer, where it was originally estimated that the payroll for 12,000 employees could be processed in 2 hours per week. As the problem was originally programmed, it would have required around 20 hours per week to process the payroll. After three *years* of reprogramming, it was finally possible to reduce the processing time to approximately 8 hours per week for some 7,000 employees.

As was discussed in Chapter 9, when designing a procedure it is difficult to estimate how long it will take to process a given volume of transactions because we usually know so little about the problem at the time that we require the estimates, and we must estimate on the basis of a hypothetical procedure involving a certain number of machine runs. Frequently we begin by ignoring a large number of seemingly trivial exceptions, only to find—at the point of programming—that the program actually requires several times as many steps as we had originally estimated. The point is that accurate time estimates require a thorough understanding of the problems involved, and unerring estimates of the amount of memory that will be required and the number of program steps that will be involved.

Even *after* the program is written it is not always easy to estimate the amount of time that will be required to process a given volume of transactions. To illustrate some of these difficulties, consider the version of the MAC that we used to illustrate the time required for tape sorting. Let us attempt to estimate the time required for Run 1 of the previous illustration, assuming that our basic appoach is satisfactory and that we know the number of program steps in each block of Figure 11–29.

First we consider the tape time involved. The master file consists of 50,000 50-word records, grouped six records per tape block; so we have 8,334 blocks of 300 words each in our inventory master tape. Each tape block requires six inches, plus a 3/4-inch gap, for a total of 6.75 inches per block. Thus we require about 4,688 feet of tape, or almost two full reels. At 7,500 words per second, 40 milliseconds will be required to read each block, and, adding 7.5 milliseconds start time, we obtain a total of 47.5 milliseconds per block. Our inventory master file will therefore require about 396 seconds to read and rewrite.

When converting cards to tape we can produce a 10-word record for each card, blocked 10 records per block. The 14,000 cards produce 1,400 tape blocks of 100 words each, and we will assume that the issues and backorders tape is of a similar form but contains only 1,200 blocks. Our output to be printed will be written out with a 12-word record for each line, which will be grouped 10 records per tape block. The transaction register tape will be composed of 1,400 blocks of 120 words each, and its writing can overlap the reading of the transaction tape. Thus we require 25 seconds to write the issues and backorders tape and 33 seconds to write the transaction register tape. The amount of time for the backorder release tape and the order and expedite report tape is quite difficult to estimate because we do not know how many backorders will occur a day or how many order and expedite reports will be written per day, for these volumes depend upon the effectiveness of our inventory control methods. If we estimate 1,000 four-line order and expedite reports per day, and 500 backorders to release per day, then about 11 seconds will suffice for these tape outputs. Total tape time will therefore be estimated as $396 + 25 + 33 + 11 = 465$ seconds excluding rewind time.

Referring to Figure 11–29, let us assume that the issues routine averages 300 executed instructions, that the receipts routine averages 200 executed instructions, the on-order routine averages 100 executed instructions, and the routine that checks for reorder level averages 500 executed instructions. Also assume that each master record requires 20 instructions to move it into the processing area and to determine whether or not it is active. Thus a tape block that has a single issue activity requires $6 \times 20 + 300 + 500 = 920$ executed instructions, which require about 18.4 milliseconds at 50,000 operations per second. Of the 47.5 milliseconds required to read a block from the master tape, about 45 are available for computation, so it is evident that we are tape-bound if there is only one transaction per block.

Two issues activities on a single record in a tape block would require $6(20) + 2(300) + 500 = 1220$ instructions, or 24.4 milliseconds. Similarly, issues on two records within the same block would involve $6(20) + 2(300 + 500) = 1720$ instructions, or 34.4 milliseconds—and we are still tape-bound. However, issues on three records within the same block would require $6(20) + 3(300 + 500) = 2520$ instructions, or 50.4 milliseconds, 5.4 milliseconds of which would not be overlapped by the master tape time.

Thus, we must face such questions as: *How frequently will we have three or more records active in one tape block?* And such questions can be rather difficult to answer. In our present illustration it is likely that such occurrences will be rare enough to be insignificant, so our total time will be approximately the tape time plus the rewind time plus the setup time.

However, we must recognize that, if the tapes were faster or the records shorter, or if the machine were slower or the executed routines longer, to produce good time estimates we would have to determine how frequently we might have various types of multiple transactions within a tape block. In such cases it is rather difficult to estimate the time, and this time will vary from one run to another because of the chance variations in such co-occurrences.

LIFE INSURANCE FILE PROCESSING

A life insurance company does not produce a product in the ordinary sense of the word: the main "product" of the life insurance "factory" (home office) is paper work. Thousands of clerks may be employed in the process of maintaining the necessary information and records associated with the hundreds of thousands (or even millions) of life insurance policies in force with the company.

Acutely aware that their major home office costs are associated with paper work, life insurance companies were among the first nongovernmental organizations to investigate the use of electronic data processing equipment. Metropolitan, Prudential, John Hancock, Pacific Mutual, and Franklin Life all installed large-scale electronic data processing systems before 1957, and all but the smallest companies use computers today. In fact, some of the smaller companies have cooperated to form data processing centers for joint use.

Most of the processing involved in home office operations is concerned with the maintenance and processing of files of information concerning the various aspects of individual policies. Before the introduction of the computer it was necessary to maintain 10 or 20 separate files of policy information for punched-card and manual processing.[9] Punched card files might include the name and address file, the billing file, the policy loan file, the dividend file, the valuation file, and the commission file. Manually processed files might include the application file, the alphabetic index file, the

---

[9] Much of this information about insurance files was obtained from notes on a talk by R. M. Roehm, "Application of the Type 650 with Tapes to Ordinary Life Insurance," at Endicott, New York, July 15, 1955.

policy register file, the premium history file, the dividend file, and the loan history file. In short, information concerning any given policy was spread out in many files.

This multiplicity of files was necessary because of the limited size of the punched card and because of the physical difficulties associated with referral by large numbers of people to a single file. For the information to be conveniently available to the people using it, a separate file was provided for each different use to which the information could be put. The existence of these many files (containing overlapping information) required a considerable amount of duplication of effort and led to confusion when it was necessary to make changes or to answer inquiries pertaining to a given policy. Perhaps the major advantage of using electronic data processing equipment is the consolidating of these files for processing and reference.

The ability of the computer to handle long and complex programs that involve many decisions, combined with the virtually unlimited length of the magnetic tape record, made it possible to consolidate these many files into one master file that contains such information as policy number, amount of insurance, date of issue, age at issue, premium anniversary date, dividend option, rating, basic dividend rate, gross premium, net single premium, name of insured, address of insured, loan principal, loan interest, rate of loan interest, commission, commission-split percent and agent number for two or more agents, office, and so forth. The length of this record ranges from around 240 to 500 characters, depending upon the company. From the machine standpoint, three basically different types of operations are involved.

The first is file maintenance: keeping the master record up to date with respect to changes that can occur affecting the policy (such as changes in name or address of the insured, changes in the method of premium payment, instituting a loan on the policy, cancellation of the policy, changing a beneficiary, or starting a new policy). Almost all magnetic tape data processing involves a surprisingly large amount of file maintenance—the hidden, nonproductive aspect of data processing which may turn out to be more time-consuming than the productive processing.

The second type of processing arises primarily as a function of time or payment associated with the policy. Bills must be sent, commissions and dividends must be calculated, payments must be accounted for, loan payments must be billed and accounted for, and accounting and statistical information must be gathered.

The third basic type of operation is the process of answering inquiries about the status of the various policies. Although the volume of inquiries is not significant compared with the other two types of operations, the basic procedural approach is usually determined by the company policy with respect to handling inquiries. Most of the file maintenance and processing operations could be accomplished on the basis of a monthly cycle, but when it is realized that hundreds of thousands—or even millions—of records may be involved in the master file, it can be seen that it is desirable to pass this file through the machine as seldom as possible. However, inquiries concerning status must be handled with reasonable promptness, and several basic approaches have been taken which represent compromises between the problem of file reference and the economics of processing.[10] A few of these are outlined below:

1. Back up the magnetic tape file with visible records in the home office which may be used for answering inquiries. In this case, the processing cycle can be weekly or monthly.
2. Decentralize the handling of inquiries to the field (usually a district office). In this situation, the home office furnishes machine-prepared status records to the field for visual reference when answering inquiries. This decentralization usually provides excellent service to the policyholder.
3. Process the master file daily for 24-hour service on inquiries.
4. Process the file and handle references on a weekly basis.
5. Process, on a daily basis, an abbreviated premium status tape containing the information needed to answer the usual questions, along with the date of the last transaction (so that other questions can be answered by reference to the transaction register). The complete master file can be processed on a weekly or monthly cycle basis.
6. Maintain the records in some type of random access file (see Chapter 12).

Ideally, it would be highly desirable to process all of the different types of transactions and file references against the master file in one machine run, as shown in Figure 11–30.[11]

However, because of the variety of transactions, the amount of processing to be accomplished, and the many different types of insurance that are in force in a given company, an extremely large

---

[10] See *Electronic Data Processing System—Ordinary Life Insurance* (Form 32–6804), International Business Machines Corporation, 590 Madison Avenue, New York.

[11] Figures 11–11 and 11–12 are adapted from similar illustrations in *IBM 705—III: Consolidated Functions; Ordinary Life Insurance* (Form 32–7924), International Business Machines Corporation, 590 Madison Avenue, New York.

and complex program would be required. Because of the size of the program and the many input-output areas involved in the approach illustrated in Figure 11–30, it is unlikely that the 5,000 words of memory of our illustrated machine would be enough, so we would probably be forced to split this into two or more machine runs (as illustrated in Figure 11–31).

The first run (and the *only* run involving the entire master file) is used to select from the master file those records that are actually active for processing on one or more subsequent runs. As can be seen

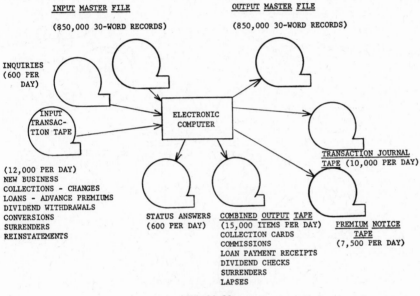

FIG. 11–30

Combined Processing Run

from the diagram, the output of these subsequent runs is merged back into the file the next time the master file is processed.

The approach described above is known as the *consolidated functions* approach, in which all of the processing associated with the insurance policy is accomplished through the use of the machine. For a small- or medium-sized company, such an approach is necessary to justify the cost of a machine. However, some of the largest insurance companies have been able to economically justify the use of the equipment for only one or two of these processing functions. For example, the first Univac acquired by the Metropolitan Life Insurance Company was fully occupied with the actuarial and reserve calculations on its 37,000,000 policies, and Metropolitan has installed

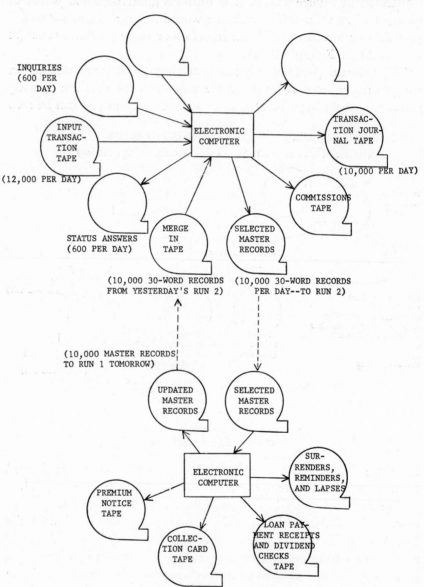

INPUT MASTER FILE

(850,000 30-WORD RECORDS)

OUTPUT MASTER FILE

(850,000 30-WORD RECORDS)

INQUIRIES
(600 PER
DAY)

INPUT
TRANSAC-
TION
TAPE

(12,000 PER DAY)

ELECTRONIC
COMPUTER

TRANSAC-
TION JOUR-
NAL TAPE

(10,000 PER DAY)

COMMISSIONS
TAPE

STATUS ANSWERS
(600 PER DAY)

MERGE
IN
TAPE

SELECTED
MASTER
RECORDS

(10,000 30-WORD RECORDS
FROM YESTERDAY'S RUN 2)

(10,000 30-WORD RECORDS
PER DAY--TO RUN 2)

(10,000 MASTER RECORDS
TO RUN 1 TOMORROW)

UPDATED
MASTER
RECORDS

SELECTED
MASTER
RECORDS

ELECTRONIC
COMPUTER

SUR-
RENDERS,
REMINDERS,
AND LAPSES

PREMIUM
NOTICE
TAPE

COLLEC-
TION CARD
TAPE

LOAN PAY-
MENT RECEIPTS
AND DIVIDEND
CHECKS
TAPE

FIG. 11-31

Processing Split into Two Runs

additional large-scale computers to convert other areas of processing to the computer systems.

The Franklin Life Insurance Company installed a Univac in March of 1955.[12] Its master file consists of 240-digit records maintained in policy number within due-date sequence. Some 80 different programs (including sorting, collating, editing, and processing runs) are involved in their consolidated functions approach. One of the most difficult problems associated with installing a computer is converting manual files to magnetic tape; and Franklin Life required more than a year to convert these files to magnetic tape.

EFFICIENCY CONSIDERATIONS

In the life insurance processing that is presented in Figures 11–30 and 11–31, we are reading and rewriting a master file of 850,000 30-word records in order to process 10,000: only one out of every 85 records that we read and rewrite is active.

Activity Ratio

The ratio of active records to records read is called the *activity ratio*. In the previous example the activity ratio is 1/85, which is relatively low. The total time required for a low-activity ratio processing run is primarily determined by the total time required to read (and write) the file, for on inactive records the machine is badly tape-bound. For example, to read and rewrite the 850,000 30-word records on our illustrative version of the MAC would require a little over one hour. If there are 30 milliseconds of un-overlapped processing on each active item (which is a rather generous estimate), 10,000 items would require five minutes of additional processing, so the total time would be about one hour and five minutes.

Suppose we doubled the activity ratio by processing 20,000 active records. The un-overlapped time would now be ten minutes, and the total time would be one hour and ten minutes rather than one hour and five minutes; we would process an additional 10,000 transactions in only five more minutes. By doubling the processing volume we increase the time (and cost) by less than 8 percent. Thus there is always pressure to increase the activity ratio in order to increase efficiency and reduce the cost per transaction processed.

---

[12] A. C. Vanselow, "Franklin Life Installs a Computer," *Pioneering in Electronic Data Processing* (Proceedings of the Second Annual American Management Association Electronics Conference, February 27–29, 1956).

Delay Time

Why do we encounter low activity ratio file processing? If transactions occur uniformly over time, then to process a batch of transactions we must wait for enough transactions to accumulate for a suitable batch. If we wait long enough, a large number of transactions will accumulate and the activity ratio will be relatively high. But if we are under time pressure to process each transaction quickly and get the results, we cannot wait for a large batch to accumulate, and we must process with a low activity ratio.

In the insurance illustration, for example, if we accumulate our transactions for a month we might have close to 250,000 activities on our file, and we would have a respectable activity ratio of 5/17, or almost 1/3.

Let us consider the average delay, D, between the time that a transaction occurs and the time when the results of that transaction are available. Suppose T is the time in hours between the beginning of two successive processing runs, and P is the time in hours required for processing. Consider the diagram in Figure 11–32.

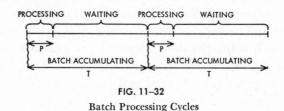

FIG. 11–32

Batch Processing Cycles

If a transaction occurs after the first processing run starts, it misses that batch and must wait until the next run starts. Thus the next batch accumulates over time period T, and the average transaction waits for $T/2$ hours for the next processing run to begin. But the results are not available until the processing run is over, so the average delay time is $D = T/2 + P$.

In many batch processing applications we have the following conflict. To decrease the average delay, we would like to decrease the time T between processing cycles. But this decreases the batch size, decreases the activity ratio, and reduces the efficiency of processing. Expressed another way, if we wish to reduce costs by increasing the batch size, we must do it by increasing T, which increases the average delay.

In situations where delay time is not crucial in determining the value of data processing results, we can accumulate batches large enough for efficient processing, and batch processing is efficient and effective. But where the delay time is crucial and cannot be large enough to accumulate efficient batches, batch processing (and thus magnetic tape and punched card processing) are not very satisfactory. Batch processing frequently produces considerable tension between those whose concern is cost and those for whom timeliness is essential.

Multiprogramming

There are other ways to improve the efficiency of low activity files. Consider the timing chart in Figure 11–33 that shows the activity of the main frame and the tapes on a low activity file. File block 3 is active, and its processing requires more time than reading block 4, so

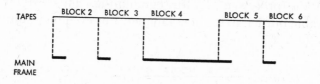

FIG. 11–33
Timing Chart of Low Activity File

reading block 5 is delayed. On the other hand, it requires little main frame time to determine that inactive records are inactive, and the main frame must wait until the next tape block has been completely read.

In our previous block diagrams of such programs we would, after reading a record, execute a few program steps to determine if the record is active, and if not, give instructions to write the old record and read the new one. But since the new record has not been read, the machine delays execution of this Read instruction and waits till the data channel is free.

Instead of giving these Read and Write instructions, suppose we gave a Branch if Data Channel Busy instruction, and transferred to some other program to use the main frame time until the data channel is free again? We might obtain the timing chart shown in Figure 11–34.

Of course, in the alternate program, we would have to check every once in a while to see if the data channel is free, and when it is, transfer back to the file program. This approach is called *multiprogramming* or *parallel processing*.

If four or more data channels are available, it is possible to process two low-activity files simultaneously, or to perform card-to-tape or tape printer operations as a by-product of other processing, therefore eliminating the need for this expensive auxiliary equipment. It should be noted that multiprogramming requires that two or more programs be stored in memory at once, so its effective use depends upon having a large capacity memory. It should also be emphasized that, as far as processing is concerned, only one program is operating at a time—only the input-output functions are being overlapped. But this approach allows the most expensive and powerful component of the machine—the processing unit—to be in continuous use.

Note, however, that there must be some rather complicated co-ordination between the programs that are being juggled back and forth in the process of multiprogramming. This may provide a considerable burden to the programmer. But even more burdensome

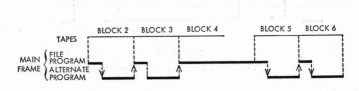

FIG. 11–34

Timing Chart for Multiprogramming

is the fact that it may not be known, when a program is written, what programs it might be multiprogrammed with. We should be able to operate any two programs together (having suitable characteristics, of course) so that we can make best use of machine time. Obviously, it is desirable that our automatic programming systems be designed for multiprogramming purposes so that the assembly program can be used to integrate programs. This will be discussed further in the following section.

Supervisory Systems

We have mentioned the fact that the manual tasks of mounting tapes, loading programs, starting new jobs, etc., can require a good deal of time. When we use a faster machine, it completes an individual job quicker, so it can process more jobs. Therefore there are more setups, so setup time consumes a greater proportion of the total time available. Combined with the fact that faster machines are also more expensive, this leads to the conclusion that we must give serious thought to the question of how we can operate a large, fast machine efficiently.

This problem has been attacked by means of *supervisory systems,* or *monitors,* which are programs that take over many of the tasks normally performed by a console operator. The various programs to be run are placed on a reel of magnetic tape, and the monitor loads the program and runs the problem. While the first problem is running, the monitor may print out instructions to the operators to mount tapes for the next job on spare tape drives, so when the first job is done, the second can be begun immediately, and so on. Thus jobs can be intermixed: a sort, a short debugging run, an assembly, a production job, a scientific calculation, etc.

The monitor can stack programs in the file (if random access files are available), decide (on the basis of established priorities and decision rules) upon the order in which they are to be executed, and print out suitable instructions to the operators. If the operators do not get all the tapes mounted on time for one job, the monitor can sneak in another job that does not require special input/output tapes and use the time that would otherwise be wasted. Also, the monitor would have the responsibility for selecting programs to be multi-programmed and would perform the necessary adjustments to run them together.

It therefore becomes apparent that the monitor itself can become a rather large and complex program. It is part of the software, but is also the mechanism which integrates all the other software. It may also require that all programmers design their programs so that they can be run in compliance with the restrictions imposed by the monitor. In short, a monitor is a *necessary evil* if a large, fast, tape-oriented electronic computer is to be used efficiently for a variety of jobs.

SUMMARY

Magnetic tapes provide both high-speed input and output and machine processable files for computers. Magnetic tape files must be processed sequentially, for the delays involved in skipping back and forth in such a file are so large as to be intolerable. The faster the internal speed of the computer, the more desirable rapid input and output becomes, so magnetic tapes—buffered by data channels—are usually the major input and output for large, fast computers.

Such tape oriented machines require off-line, card-to-tape, tape printers and tape-to-card facilities, which may be provided by one or more smaller and slower machines (such as the basic MAC with tapes).

Information is recorded on magnetic tape in blocks, each of which is read or written by a single instruction (as are the cards in the basic MAC). A tape block, however, may be composed of one or several data records. Compared with punched cards, magnetic tapes are much faster and more concise; they provide much greater flexibility in record length; they are reusable; and they provide more processing flexibility because they can be rewound and/or backspaced without human intervention. On the other hand, the information on tape is invisible, so humans cannot refer to the information recorded on them without the aid of a machine.

The processing of magnetic tape files is generally similar to the basic approach used in punched card processing. Batches of transactions are accumulated, sorted into the same sequence as the file, and processed as a group while reading (and usually updating) the entire file.

Thus it is necessary to be able to sort records on magnetic tape. Although a number of techniques may be used, the basic method of tape sorting involves the merging of sequences, to obtain longer sequences, until a single sequence is finally produced. Unlike the punched card operation, the time required is essentially independent of the number of characters in the sorting key.

The activity ratio of a file-processing run is the number of active file records divided by the total number of records in the file. If the activity ratio is low, the central processor is idle much of the time. Thus there is motivation to increase the activity ratio by increasing the size of the batch, thereby increasing the average delay between the time a transaction occurs and when results are obtained. Faster magnetic tape units and the ability to multiprogram are machine developments that make low-activity file processing more efficient. Although magnetic tape files are quite efficient and provide very desirable data processing systems when it is feasible to accumulate batches of transactions for processing, they are not very satisfactory in situations where it is necessary to process each transaction (or inquiry) immediately.

More sophisticated software is necessary for efficient programming and operation of large, fast, tape-oriented electronic data processing machines. Fortunately, the characteristics of the tapes themselves, combined with the larger memories available on such machines, make it possible to provide more sophisticated software and to employ monitoring systems to increase operating efficiency.

EXERCISES

11.1 Consider our illustrative machine, with tapes recorded at 550 digits per inch and a ¾ inch inter-record gap. These tapes read and write 7,500 words per second (.133 milliseconds per word), with a start-stop time of 7.5 milliseconds. We have 30,000 12-word records to record on such tape.

a) If these records are recorded in 12-word blocks, how many feet of tape are used and how much time would be required to read the tape.

b) If these records are recorded in 240-word blocks, how many feet of tape are used and how much time would be required to read the tape?

11.2 At 1,000 lines per minute, how long would it take to print 30,000 lines on an on-line printer? How much main frame time could be saved by writing this information on magnetic tape (as in part a of Problem 11.1) and by using an off-line printer? (Assume that the run would be input-output bound and that there is no multiprogramming with the printer.)

11.3 Since magnetic tape can be read so fast, is buffering of tapes as important as was buffering of cards? Why?

11.4 Consider the sequence of records identified by the numbers 25, 03, 17, 80, 46, 15, 77, 17, 03, 01, 25, 98, 62, 02, 33, 17.

a) How many sequences are represented in the above list?

b) Follow through the block diagram in Figure 11–26 with the above list. How many sequences are on the output tapes?

c) How many passes (after the first) will be required to sort the above list using a two-way merge?

11.5 Consider a file containing 15,000 100-word records grouped into into blocks of 500 words. This file is estimated to contain 3,700 sequences. The sorting key is a 20-character alphabetic field.

a) How many passes (including the first) would be required to sort this tape using a two-way merge?

b) How many passes (including the first) would be required to sort this file using a three-way merge?

c) Using the machine described in Exercise 11.1, how much time would be required to sort this file using a two-way merge?

d) How much time would be required to sort this file using a three-way merge?

e) Suppose that on the first pass we internally sort the file into sequences of 20 records. How many more passes would be required to sort this file with a two-way merge?

11.6   *a*) Upon what file characteristics does the time to sort a magnetic tape file depend?

       b) Upon what file characteristics does the time to sort a punched card file depend?

       c) Upon what machine characteristics does the time to sort a magnetic tape file depend?

11.7   *a*) What are the advantages of magnetic tape over punched cards as a processing medium?

       b) What are the advantages of punched cards over magnetic tape as a processing medium?

11.8 Describe the general approach used to process magnetic tape files.

11.9 Some computers can read a tape record, backspace, and write an updated record on the same area of the tape. For low-activity file processing, should such a machine be buffered? If 10 percent of the records are active, and backspacing requires the same time as reading a record, how much more tape time would such a machine require to process a file than a buffered machine that reads and rewrites on a separate tape?

11.10 Prepare a semi-detailed block diagram for the Read Master Record tape symbol in Figure 11–20 to show how the reading of the master file could be handled with six records in each tape block.

11.11 How does the problem of handling inquiries affect the procedures that are used for processing files?

11.12 What is multiprogramming? Why is it important?

11.13 What are the characteristics of batch processing? What are its advantages? What are its disadvantages?

11.14 What is a monitor system? Under what circumstances are such systems important?

11.15 The block diagram in Figure 11–11 does not detect errors in the last block of a file. Modify this block diagram to detect such errors.

SUPPLEMENTAL READINGS

GREGORY, R. H., AND VAN HORN, R. L. *Automatic Data-Processing Systems*. San Francisco, Calif.: Wadsworth Publishing Co., Inc., 1960.

    Chapter 9 discusses file processing and describes various sorting techniques.

IBM Magnetic Tape Units (Form A22–6589). International Business Machines Corporation, White Plains, N.Y.

    This manual describes the operation of IBM magnetic tape units and the process by which information is recorded and organized on tapes. It also mentions tape labeling and recovery of data from damaged tapes.

LEEDS, H. D., AND WEINBERG, G. M. *Computer Programming Fundamentals*. New York: McGraw-Hill Book Co., Inc., 1961.

    Chapter 5 discusses the tape input-output on the IBM 7090. Chapter 11 considers in detail, he problem of efficient producion, discussing supervisory programs and multiprogramming.

McCracken, D. D.; Weiss, H., and Lee, T. *Programming Business Computers.* New York: John Wiley & Sons, Inc., 1959.

Chapter 10 describes input and output devices and the use of buffers. Chapter 15 discusses various methods of sorting, both internally and with magnetic tapes.

Slater, R. E. "Electronic Data-Processing in an Insurance Company," *Pioneering in Electronic Data-Processing.* (From proceedings of the second annual AMA Electronics Conference, February 27–29, 1956, and published as Special Report No. 9, by the American Management Association, New York.)

A discussion of the early use of a Univac at John Hancock Mutual Life Insurance Company.

Sorting Methods for IBM Data Processing Systems (Form F28–8001). International Business Machines Corporation, White Plains, N.Y.

Describes various tape sorting techniques and discusses the selection of the best approach for a given situation.

12 RANDOM ACCESS FILES

AT THE CONCLUSION of Chapter 11 it was observed that both magnetic tape and punched-card data processing involve the accumulation of a suitable batch of transactions that are processed as a group. Thus the delay involved in processing a transaction includes not only the processing time itself but also the time necessary to accumulate the number of transactions needed to form a batch. In certain situations the delays involved in batching cannot be tolerated, or the time required to pass the entire file through the machine to process just a few records is excessive. Hence magnetic tapes are not always suitable for storing file information.

Fortunately, however, devices have been developed that provide storage for large files of information in such a manner that a single record can be extracted for processing without scanning the other records in the file. Such devices are called *direct access* or *random access* files. Since the time necessary to locate the next active record in most such files depends upon the position in the file of the previous record processed, such files are not truly random access. In one machine, for example, this time may vary from 100 to 300 milliseconds, depending upon how far it is necessary to go from one record to another. But in random access files it is feasible to go directly from one record to another. Thus the term *direct* access is probably preferable to *random* access, although the latter term is more commonly used.

RANDOM ACCESS DEVICES

There are several different means by which random access storage can be provided. Like magnetic tapes, most random access devices record information in the form of minute magnetized areas on a media that is in motion past the read-write heads.[1] Also, information in random access files is brought into the main memory of the machine in blocks that are similar to the blocks of information on magnetic tapes, and the information in the file is not accessible to the program until it has been brought into the main memory where each word of the record is addressable.

However, there is an important difference in how these records are obtained. With magnetic tape, the *next* block on that tape is entered into the memory of the machine when a Read Tape instruction is given. With random access files, each file block is identified by a number that is called the file address, and it is therefore possible to designate any block in the file and bring it into the main memory.

Since some form of physical motion is required, there is usually a delay between the instant when the desired record is specified and when it can be transferred into memory. The extent of this delay is a characteristic of the type of device employed, but it can range from a few milliseconds up to a second or more, depending upon the distance that must be transversed in moving from the current location in the file to the new position. This delay is made up of two parts: (1) the time required to position the record in relation to the read-write head (or vice versa), and (2) the time required to actually read the record. The first delay corresponds to the time required to move from one active record to another in a magnetic tape file, and the second delay corresponds to the time required to read the tape block. The magnitude of these delays is obviously an important characteristic of a random access file.

Magnetic Drums

A magnetic drum is a cylinder rotating on its axis (see Figure 12–1). Read-write heads are spaced around the surface of the drum, and each can read or write upon the "track" that passes under that read-write head. Formerly used as the main memory of many smaller computers, magnetic drums have been largely replaced by magnetic cores for this purpose, but they are still employed for random access file storage.

Read-write heads can be grouped together—as they are on magnetic tape—so that all of the bits for a digit are recorded at the same time (called *parallel by bit*), or a single read-write head can write

---

[1] An exception is the use of minute dots on photographic film for some large files that can only be read, not written, by machines.

the bits for a digit one after another, and then the bits for the next digit, and so on (called *serial by bit*). Most magnetic drums are serial by digit and by word: the digits in a word are recorded one after another, and the words are written one after another (as on magnetic tape). However, it is possible to have drums in which information is recorded with a separate read-write head for each bit in a word so that an entire word is written or read at the same time. Of course the more information that is recorded in parallel, the faster it can be written or read.

A typical magnetic drum file might record 500 words written serially (by bit and by digit) in each track, and might have 400

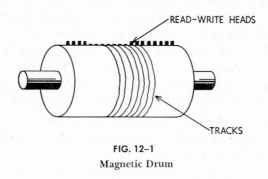

FIG. 12–1

Magnetic Drum

tracks—for a total storage capacity of 200,000 words (2,000,000 digits plus 200,000 signs). Such a drum might rotate at 2,000 revolutions per minute (30 milliseconds per revolution). If the file were organized into 100-word addressable records it would hold 2000 records. If there were no more than five such files on a machine, all the records could be addressed with a four-digit number, with the numbers 0000–1999 referring to the records in the first unit, 2000–3999 referring to the records in the second unit, and so on.

The delay time in reaching a record would be the time required for the drum to rotate into the position where the desired record is about to pass under the read-write head. On the average this will require half a revolution, or 15 milliseconds. Since there are five records on each track, the time to read or write a record would be the time required for 1/5 a revolution, or 6 milliseconds. Thus the total average delay for obtaining any record would be about 21 milliseconds.

Since much of the cost associated with such a file is made up of the cost of the read-write heads and the electronic circuits that switch to the proper head, it is possible to reduce costs by providing a single read-write head mounted on a mechanism that moves it from track to track (see Figure 12–2).

A typical file of this type might store 1,000,000 words on 2,000 tracks, with 500 words per track. In addition to the rotational delay discussed above, an average delay of 333 milliseconds is involved in positioning the read-write head on the proper track. Of course this positioning delay varies with the distance moved between tracks, and ranges from about 40 milliseconds (when going to an adjacent track) to 540 milliseconds (when jumping from one end of the drum to another).

READ-WRITE HEAD

FIG. 12–2

Movable Read-Write Head

By placing 40 read-write heads on a movable mechanism we could reduce the positioning delay to around 60 milliseconds, for the mechanism would then have to move a maximum of only 50 tracks. We would also have another advantage, for all of the information on 40 tracks (20,000 words) would be available for processing without moving the access mechanism. As we will see, we may be able to take advantage of this characteristic when organizing the file.

In general, when we go from fixed to movable read-write heads we increase the delay—and also increase the capacity—while keeping the cost about the same. Thus we may trade off delay for capacity, or either of these for cost.

Magnetic Disks

A magnetic disk file is composed of several flat, circular, magnetically coated disks that are mounted together on a single shaft and that rotate like a magnetic drum. Data may be recorded on the surfaces of the disks by small read-write heads inserted between the disks. Thus each disk surface provides a number of concentric tracks, as shown in Figure 12–3.

Like magnetic drums, magnetic disks may have either fixed or movable read-write heads. With fixed read-write heads, the magnetic disk file operates just like a magnetic drum, for the only delay involved in obtaining a record is rotational delay. However, because of the greater surface area of the disks, more information can be recorded in the same volume than can be recorded on a magnetic drum. A typical fixed-head disk file might store 5,000,000 words and have an average rotational delay of 20 milliseconds.

A widely used type of disk file has movable read-write heads attached to a comb-shaped mechanism that moves in and out between the disks, as shown in Figure 12–4. In such a mechanism there is a read-write head for each disk surface, and when the mechanism is set in one position a track on every disk can be read or written with

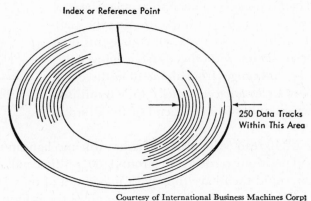

Index or Reference Point

250 Data Tracks
Within This Area

Courtesy of International Business Machines Corp!

FIG. 12–3

Magnetically Coated Disk

only rotational delays. More than one such access mechanism can be placed on a single disk file, so two machines—each with its own access mechanism—can share a single file.

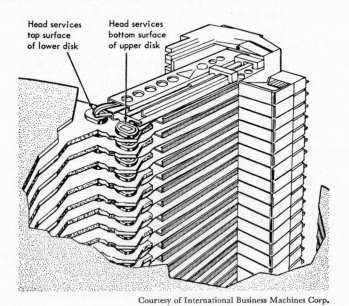

Head services
top surface
of lower disk

Head services
bottom surface
of upper disk

Courtesy of International Business Machines Corp.

FIG. 12–4

Read-Write Head Arrangement

A typical unit of this type (see Figure 12–5) might consist of 50 disks (100 disk surfaces) with 400 data tracks per disk and 500 words per track—for a total capacity of 20,000,000 words. The average delay time for positioning the heads is 200 milliseconds, and 50,000 words are accessible within a cylinder that is composed of the tracks specified by a single position of the access mechanism. The disks

Courtesy of International Business Machines Corp.

FIG. 12–5

Magnetic Disk File

rotate at 2,000 revolutions per minute, so a complete revolution takes 30 milliseconds.

Another type of disk file has only one pair of read-write heads mounted on an access arm that is shaped like a turning fork. As shown in Figure 12–6, this access arm moves from one track of a disk to a position outside the stack, then up or down to another disk, and then in to the desired track of that disk. This process requires a maximum of 8/10 second to go from the innermost track of the top disk to the innermost track of the bottom disk, and an average of

6/10 second is required to move from one file record to another.

One characteristic of all the random access files discussed so far is that their information is always available to the machine, whether it is needed or not. This is in contrast to magnetic tape units, where a reel can be removed and stored when it is not being processed,

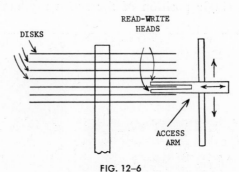

FIG. 12–6

Dual-motion Access Arm

and the tape unit can be used to process other reels of tape. By changing reels, a tape unit provides access to an unlimited amount of information, but the random access files described above cannot be changed because the access mechanisms are permanently attached to the drums or disks upon which the data is written.

There are, however, magnetic disk files whose disks can be conveniently removed from the disk unit and stored like magnetic tapes.

Courtesy of International Business Machines Corp.

FIG. 12–7

Magnetic Disk Pack

One such file is composed of six disks, mounted in a protective cover, as shown in Figures 12–7 and 12–8. Weighing less than 10 pounds, these "disk packs" can be removed from the drive unit and replaced by another pack in about one minute. The drive unit uses a comb-like access mechanism that provides an average delay of 150 milliseconds in positioning the head. The capacity of such a file is about 1,400,000 words.

Courtesy of International Business Machines Corp.

FIG. 12–8

Magnetic Disk Pack Drive Unit

Magnetic Cards

Another method of storing records so that they are directly accessible is on flexible plastic cards (or strips) with a magnetizable coating. These cards can be arranged in packs of several hundreds. To obtain a record, the proper card is selected from the pack and wrapped around a rotating drum where information may be read or written by read-write heads, as on a magnetic drum.

A typical file unit might include eight packs of 256 cards apiece, with 20,000 words on each 16- by four-inch card, for a total storage of 40,960,000 words per file. The time to select a card and wrap it around the drum is around 350 milliseconds, and there is an average rotational delay of 30 milliseconds before reading a record. Once the card is positioned, the entire 20,000 words can be read in about 4 seconds.

This type of file has several appealing features: (1) The card packs may be removed and replaced with others, just as reels of magnetic tape or disk packs, so a unit gives unlimited file storage and more than 40,000,000 words on line in a single unit; (2) Like the disk units that have a comb-like access mechanism, once the card is positioned a large number of records becomes available after only rotational delay; (3) The cost per digit is very low for such a file.

RANDOM ACCESS FILES ON THE MAC

As an example of how random access files might be controlled by a computer, let us consider the large magnetic disk file (with storage for 20,000,000 words) that we have described above. This file is composed of 50 disks with 400 tracks per surface and 500 words per track. It has a comb-like access mechanism that provides an average delay time of 200 milliseconds for positioning the read-write heads.

This file may be organized into 200,000 100-word records that are numbered in the following manner. We start with the outermost track on the top surface of the top disk, and number the five records on that track 000000 through 000004. Then the five records on the same track of the bottom surface of the top disk would be numbered 000005 through 000009. Working down the outermost cylinder, the top five records of the bottom disk would be numbered 000490 through 000494, and the five records on the bottom of the bottom disk would be 000495 through 000499. Then we would begin again at the top of the next cylinder with records 000500 through 000504, and so on.

Thus we number the records in the file from 000000 through 199999.[2] If we divide the identification number of a record by 500, the quotient gives the number of the cylinder (numbering from the outside in) and the remainder indicates the position within the cylinder. Dividing this remainder by 5, we obtain the disk surface

---

[2] We could add four more file units to the system by using the addresses 200000 to 399999 for the next unit, and so on.

number as the quotient and the position of the record on the track as the remainder.

For example, consider record 097645. Dividing this by 500 we obtain a quotient of 195 and a remainder of 145. Thus the record is in cylinder 195. Dividing 145 by 5 we obtain a quotient of 29 and a remainder of 0, so the record is the first record on disk surface number 29 (the bottom surface of the fifteenth disk from the top).

To obtain a record from the file we first load its address into the M register. The low-order six positions of the M register specify the file location of the record, and the high-order position of the M register determines the size of the record to be read or written. If this position is a zero, the record is the 100-word record specified by the address. If this position is other than zero, the record consists of the entire 500-word track on which the record specified by the address is located. For example, suppose the contents of the M register are 0000127431. Then this specifies the 100-word record that is designated by the number 127431. But if the M register contained 1000127431, this would specify the entire 500-word track of records 127430, 127431, 127432, 127433, and 127434.

78 SEK (Seek). This instruction transmits the address of the record from the M register to the disk file and starts the access arm in motion. Then the regular programming of the computer may continue while the access arm moves into position to read the record specified by the address.

79 RDD (Read Disk). If the access arm is in motion, the machine program is delayed until it comes to rest. Then the machine checks to see that it is positioned so that the record whose address is in the M register can be read. If not, the Disk Error indicator is turned on and the program proceeds to the next instruction. If everything checks out, the record (either 100 or 500 words) whose address is specified by the number in the M register is read into the block of memory starting with the location given by the data address.

Information is recorded in the disk in the same five-bit redundancy-checked code that is used on magnetic tapes. If a redundancy error is detected while reading, the Disk Error indicator is turned on at the conclusion of the Read operation.

80 WRD (Write Disk). Just as with the Read Disk instruction, the machine will wait until the access mechanism is positioned, if this is necessary, and then verify that the access mechanism is positioned on the track designated by the address in the M register. If it is not, the Disk Error indicator is turned on and the program proceeds (without writing anything) to the next instruction. When the mechanism is properly positioned, the 100- or 500-word record— whose first word is designated by the data address—is written in the proper record position in the file.

81 WCK (Write Check). This instruction *reads* the record specified by the contents of the M register and compares it digit by digit with the corresponding record in core memory whose location is given by the data address. If the two are not exactly the same, the Disk Error indicator is set.

52 BDE (Branch on Disk Error). If the Disk Error indicator is on, this instruction branches and turns it off. If the Disk Error

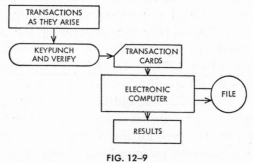

FIG. 12–9

Typical Random Access File Procedure

indicator is off, this instruction is treated as a No Operation instruction.

Timing

The above operations make it possible to do three desirable things when processing random access files. First, we can overlap Seek time with any processing that can be done at that time. Secondly, we can always check to make sure that the transfers of information to and from the file are performed accurately. This is particularly important (as we will see later) when writing in the file, for this operation destroys the previous contents of the file and there is nothing to go back to if an error occurs. Thirdly, we have flexibility to fit the size of the file record to the characteristics of the data file.

In many random access file operations we read transaction information into the machine in the sequence in which the transactions arose (without sorting). The file record corresponding to the current transaction is obtained, the transaction information is combined with the file information for processing to produce some output information and to update the file record, and the file record is rewritten in the file so as to be available the next time it is required. Thus we have the conceptually simple procedure shown in Figure 12–9.

The typical sequence of these operations is indicated in the block diagram in Figure 12–10. Now consider the timing of these operations. Block 2 should require only a few milliseconds. If the Seek operation is random, it will require an average of 200 milliseconds, and block 3 should be overlapped with this. Block 4 requires, on the average, half a revolution (15 milliseconds) to arrive at the beginning of the record and 6 milliseconds to read it (if it is 100 words), for a total of 21 milliseconds. The processing time in block 6 depends upon what we are doing, but the time between the beginning of the Read instruction and the beginning of the next Write instruction must be some multiple of 30 milliseconds (at least one revolution). Likewise, the Write and the Write Check instruction require one revolution (30 milliseconds) plus 6 milliseconds, for a total of 36 milliseconds.

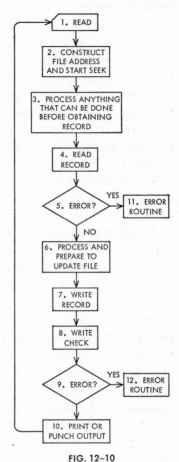

FIG. 12–10

Typical Random Access Processing

Combining the above figures we find that blocks 2 through 9 will require $200 + 5 + n(30) + 36$ milliseconds, where n is the number of disk revolutions during processing. If n is 1, this is a total of 281 milliseconds, which slows down card input to around 220 cards per minute.

Of course if the file is small enough to be placed in fewer than 400 cylinders, the average access time can be reduced, and perhaps considerably. For example, if the file requires only 50,000 records, they can be placed in 100 cylinders, and the average access time can be reduced to around 120 milliseconds per seek, reducing the total time from 281 to 206 milliseconds (corresponding to almost 300 cards per minute).

Data Channels

Now let us consider the faster version of the MAC that we discussed in Chapter 11 in connection with magnetic tape files. This machine can perform around 50,000 calculations per second and is usually operated with magnetic tape input and output in order to take advantage of this processing speed. But the use of this faster machine does not change the time analysis presented above because all of this time is associated with the file operations. Thus the fast machine would operate at the same throughput speed (in transactions processed per minute) as the basic MAC. It is obvious that although random access files are fairly well balanced to the speed of the basic MAC, there is a serious mismatch with the faster machines, where 200 milliseconds represents 10,000 instruction executions.

About the only way to overcome this speed discrepancy is to operate these files in a sequential manner, or to multiprogram or operate several files simultaneously so seek time and read-write time can be overlapped with processing. In order to overlap read-write time, the files are attached to the larger machines through data channels (as are magnetic tapes). To overlap seek time effectively we need an instruction that allows us to test to see whether the access mechanism has completed its movement.

53 BDR (Branch if Disk is Ready). This instruction checks to see if the access mechanism of the file specified by the two-digit number in positions 8 and 9 of the instruction is positioned for reading or writing. If the access mechanism is stationary, a branch occurs. If the access mechanism is in motion, the instruction is treated as a No Operation.

The BDR instruction allows the machine to switch to other processing during the seek time, checking back every few milliseconds to see if the seek has been completed. The machine may also set access arms in motion on several files and then use the BDR instruction to poll them one by one to process the information as it becomes available.

ORGANIZATION OF FILES

An interesting question associated with the use of random access files is: Given a transaction, how do we find the file record associated with that transaction? This may seem to be a trivial question, for we have the identification information from the transaction (for example, the item number) and all we want is the file record that has the same identification. To avoid difficulty with words, let us clarify our terminology. The data processing file is a group of records and each group has an identification number, which we will call the *control* number for that record. The physical file is a random access device that stores blocks of information that are designated by file addresses. As with magnetic tapes, the logical record may or may not be the same size as the block in the file, so the file block associated with an address may contain one or more logical records.

Now let's restate our question: Given the control number of a logical record, how do we find the address of the file block in which the record is stored? If we could store the records in the file so that the control number and the file addresses were the same, we would have no problem. But the control numbers may have more digits than the file addresses, or they may be alphabetic, or there may be many large gaps in the control numbers that would represent wasted file space.

Control numbers are identifying numbers that may have other purposes in the data processing system than that of designating the location of a record in a random access file. For example, the item numbers that identify items in inventory are frequently assigned according to coding systems which may be used to classify these items for analysis purposes or to indicate the particular characteristics of the items themselves. It is seldom convenient to assign item numbers consecutively because new items are always entering the system and obsolete items are being removed. A typical item-numbering system for 10,000 to 15,000 items (which could theoretically be handled through the use of a five-digit code) might involve eight-digit item numbers, where the right-most two digits are a material code, the left-hand two digits are an item-use classification, and the remaining four digits are arbitrarily assigned.

You may have recognized that this problem is quite similar to the Table Look-up problem discussed in Chapter 7. In Table Look-up the "argument" corresponds to the control number and the function corresponds to the file record. The basic difference between the present problem and Table Look-up is not so much in the task to be accomplished as in the location of the desired information. Because of the rapid access to core memory, it is feasible to examine a large number of arguments in the process of Table Look-up. But with the files located in relatively slow random access files, it is impractical to examine a similar number of individual file records to find the one desired. Therefore other approaches that involve relatively few accesses to the file must be devised to find the file block that contains the record for a given control number.

Arrangement of records in a file so that the file address can be quickly found from the control number is called the file *organization*. There are two basic approaches to file organization: *sequential* organization, in which the master records are located sequentially within the file (as they are on magnetic tape), and *random* organization, in which the records are scattered about without apparent rhyme or reason. Note, however, that sequential and random here refer to *how the file is organized, not how it is processed,* for transactions can be processed in random sequence with either method.

Sequential Organization

In files in which a large number of logical records may be made available with a single motion of the access mechanism, a sequential file organization may be effective. As you recall, both the disk files (that have comb-like access mechanisms) and the magnetic card files have this property, for once the access mechanism has been positioned —or the card has been wrapped around the drum—many records can be read.

Although the file is organized sequentially (like magnetic tape files), we wish to avoid going through them sequentially. Therefore, in the main memory of the machine we store a table of control numbers that indicate what cylinder or card the record is on, and we use Table Look-up to develop the file address for the seek operation. Then on the first track of the cylinder (or the first record of the card) we would have another table indicating the address within the cylinder (or card) at which the records are stored.

Let us consider how this would work for the magnetic disk file on the MAC. Suppose we have the inventory file described in the illustration in Chapter 11. Here we have 50,000 master records requiring 50 words per record. Thus we would need 25,000 100-word file blocks for this master file, which we could store in 53 cylinders, as follows.

Use the first track of each cylinder to store the index to that cylinder, which would consist of the 480 control numbers of the higher of the two file records in each block. The last 15 blocks in the cylinder would be used to store records that might be added to the file. Then, in the memory of the MAC, we would store a 53-word table consisting of the control numbers of the last record in each cylinder. We will start the table in location 1000 and use the first 53 cylinders (numbered 000 through 052).

Now, given an item number of a transaction, we perform a Table Look-up to find the cylinder. If 1023 is the location of the first control number that is greater than or equal to the search argument, the cylinder is number 23, and the address of the first record in that cylinder is 011500 (23 × 500). This would be combined with a 1000000000 (indicating that we want to read the entire track) to obtain 1000011500, which would be placed in the M register for a seek operation. Then the Read Disk would place the second table in memory and we would perform another Table Look-up to get the block address. Since the access mechanism is already located on that cylinder there would be no further seek time to obtain this block. The control number of the first file record in the block would be compared with that of the transaction, and if they are not the same the control number of the second record in the block would be examined. If this is not the record sought, the three overflow tracks (at the bottom of the cylinder) would be examined record by record until the file record is found or it is determined that the record is not in the file.

Thus the file record would be obtained with two Table Look-ups and one Seek, plus at least two file reading operations (more if the record is in an overflow area). The file is packed rather densely, using 53 × 500 = 26,500 addresses for 25,000 records to give a 94 percent utilization of the file. Most of the slack is due to the provision for overflow records, which is very important in accommodating file growth and turnover. Were there no overflow areas, the records in the file would have to be moved down to add a new item. Even with relatively little change in the file, this could be rather awkward.

Random Organization

Another approach to assigning file locations to records is to devise a formula that converts the control number into a file address. Usually we wish to convert a block of numbers with many gaps into a smaller block with few gaps. But there are two problems here. The first is that of gaps—addresses that do not have any control numbers which are converted to them. Secondly, there may be duplications—several control numbers may be converted into the same address. If there is room for several (M) file records in each block, duplication is desirable, but *too many* duplicates (more than M) becomes a problem.

Both of these problems may be reduced to manageable proportions by conversion techniques that produce results that are essentially random, for such techniques tend to smooth the resulting number patterns and to reduce both the number of gaps and the number of addresses corresponding to too many control numbers. A *chaining* technique may be employed to use the gaps to store the overflows caused by excessive duplication.

A popular method of converting from control numbers to addresses is *prime number division*. To use this method, a prime[3] number is chosen that will limit the range of the resulting addresses. To find the address for a given control number we divide the control number by the prime, throw away the quotient, and use the *remainder* to determine the file address. Note that the same prime number is used as the divisor for all control numbers in a given file, so the resulting file addresses are less than this prime divisor.

For example, in the above illustration we have 50,000 50-word records, which would go into 5,000 disk tracks. To reduce the overflows we should provide some slack, so let us take the prime 5501 (which provides about 10 percent slack). When we load the file we read the first record, divide its control number by 5501, and obtain the remainder. Since we want a track address (which is a multiple of 5) rather than a record address, we multiply the remainder by five to calculate the address of a disk track, and place this record as the first one on that track. The record for the next control number that converts to that track is stored as the second record on the track, and so on, until we fill up the track with ten records (or run out of records).

What happens when an eleventh record comes along whose control number converts to the same track? We would merely have the machine save it until after all the remaining records had been completely loaded. At that point there should be some tracks that are not completely used, and we should have collected a number of records that have been similarly rejected because there was no room for them on the calculated track.

These records are overflow records and would now be read back into the machine. The machine again goes to the proper track. Finding it full, the machine is programmed to examine the other tracks in that cylinder until it finds an unused space. When an unused space is found, its address is stored on the original track as the

---

[3] A prime number is a number that cannot be factored into the product of smaller numbers. Thus, 2, 3, 5, 7, 11, 13, 17, 19, 23, 29, 31, and 37 are primes. Tables of prime numbers are available.

overflow address, and the overflow record is stored in that address. If we have another overflow record for the track, it would be stored on the same track as the first overflow record. If there is no room there, then the machine would search out another empty spot and insert another overflow address in the previous overflow track. This process is continued until all of the master records are stored in the file.

Now, to process a transaction, this process would be repeated. The address of the track would be calculated by dividing the item number by 5501, multiplying by 5 (to get the first record of a track), and adding 1000000000 to indicate that an entire track is desired. The ten records on that track would be brought into the computer and their control numbers examined one by one. If the record is found, it is processed. If it is not found, the overflow address is used to bring in another track, which is examined record by record. This "chaining" process continues until the record is found or the end of the chain is reached (in which case the record sought is not in the file).

Summarizing this process we can say that we calculate a file address, move the access mechanism to the proper cylinder, read a track, and examine the records on that track sequentially till we find the record sought or until we come to the end of that track. If necessary, we read another track on that cylinder and repeat this process. Obviously, this process can be used to locate any record in the file, but it is desirable that there be relatively few long chains of overflow records.

The less slack we leave when packing the records into the file, the more overflows we are likely to have. Experience has shown that if 10 to 15 percent slack is allowed, overflows do not usually present a problem, and if they do, it may be profitable to use a slightly different prime as the divisor because this redistributes the records into addresses in a different manner. An analysis of the distribution of addresses resulting from any conversion scheme can be obtained by using the computer to convert the control numbers (without loading the file) and to summarize the results.

To add records to a file organized in this manner presents no problem, for the machine merely follows the chain to the end and adds a link (if necessary) to insert the new record. Records can be removed simply by erasing them. After a good deal of this changing, of course, it may be better to dump the file and reload it. Also, if some master records are known to be more active than others, they can be loaded into the file first and thus be assured of being in the front of the chain rather than at the end.

Best Organization

Of course, the decision upon sequential or random file organization depends upon the type of processing that one is doing, the characteristics of the equipment used, and the relative value of speed and file space.

In general, the sequential file organization provides better utilization of file space, but random file organization is faster for processing transactions in random sequence, for it requires no Table Lookups and usually only one Read File operation. Adding and deleting records is more convenient with the random organization.

It is possible, and sometimes desirable, to sort transactions and then process them sequentially against a random access file. Both methods of file organization can process sequential transactions, but sequentially organized files require less seek time. Note, however, that prime-number division maintains a semblance of sequence, since if two control numbers are in sequence and close together, the resulting remainders are also likely to be close together.

If we wish to prepare periodic reports in control-number sequence from the file records, sequential organization is preferable. Random organization, by contrast, requires skipping around, and also requires the input of a sequential list of all the control numbers in the file so that the records can be processed in that sequence.

SYSTEMS ADVANTAGES

Figure 12–9 indicates that the basic approach in using random access files is deceptively simple. The transactions are entered into the machine as they occur and are processed against the file, updating it and producing the required output.

Simplified Procedures

One of the major advantages of random access files is their ability to simplify procedures by eliminating the typical cycles of sorting and processing against this file, resorting and processing against that file, etc. With random access files the transaction may be entered into the machine, processed against one file, processed against another, etc., until it has updated all the pertinent files.

Not only can random access files store master files, they can also store programs (or portions of programs) as well. Therefore, when complex processing is required special subroutines can be quickly called into memory from the files, so it may not be necessary to break the procedure down into as many machine runs because of restricted memory space.

Reduced Delay

Another major advantage of random access files is that of reduced delay time. Since there is no necessity for batching and sorting, it is possible to process transactions as they arise and to produce results without extensive delay. As we have seen, the handling of inquiries is a major problem in batch processing systems. But in random access systems the files are always up to date and regular processing can easily be interrupted momentarily to extract the information required to handle an inquiry.

Real-Time Processing

As was mentioned in the previous chapter, the delays involved in batch processing are often natural delays and little advantage can be obtained by reducing them. But elimination of the *necessity* for such delays opens new and relatively unexplored possibilities for changing the entire nature of the data processing system—from a passive recorder of history (which, of course, is valuable for making many important decisions) to an active participant in the minute-to-minute operations of the organization. It becomes possible to process data in *real-time*—so that the output may be fed back immediately to control current operations. Thus the computer can interact with people on a dynamic basis, obtaining and providing information, recording the decisions of humans, or even making some of these decisions.

In order for machines to interact with people in real-time data processing, it may be necessary for data to be gathered *on-line,* rather than through documents that are collected, key-punched, verified, and read into the machine at a central location. This requires devices by which information can be entered directly into the computer from remote locations and results can be transmitted directly back. Such devices, along with communications networks, will be discussed in Chapter 13.

Large Machines

Although there is a troublesome mismatch between the speed of most random access files and the processing speed of a large, fast computer, there are some significant systems advantages that may be obtained by using random access files to improve the throughput of such machines.

We have noted the desirability of monitor supervising systems that perform many duties of the console operator in order to reduce the setup delays that are involved in going from job to job. On a tape-oriented computer the various utility programs, assembly and compiling systems, and the programs to be executed are all stored on tape (along with parts of the supervisory program). When it is time to change from one job to another the spinning of a good deal of tape may be required to obtain the program to be run, call in the proper compiler or assembler, assemble the program, obtain the necessary subroutines, etc. This is particularly time-consuming for small problems whose preparation time may exceed the actual running time. With random access files the systems can all be in the file, and everything can be obtained without tape-searching delays.

Furthermore, in order to reduce setups, it is desirable to batch together those jobs that require the same tape unit and printer setups. A random access file can be used to allow the machine to perform this batching and to schedule its own input and output. The computer accepts jobs as they are provided and places them in the file, then it decides (on the basis of scheduling and priority rules) in what sequence to run the jobs. As new jobs are submitted they are fitted into the sequence to provide dynamic scheduling. Output can also be collected in the files and batched for efficient printing.

SYSTEMS PROBLEMS

Along with their impressive systems advantages—and perhaps *because* of some of them—random access files also introduce some systems problems that must at least be mentioned.

Control of Accuracy

Several characteristics or techniques of random-access data processing make control of accuracy more difficult than in batch processing. In the first place, transactions may be introduced into the system as they occur, with different types of transactions intermixed and without any reference to the sequence of these transactions. Therefore, it is much more difficult to establish control totals, which are conveniently accumulated in batch processing and provide much of the basic information for subsequent control of processing accuracy.

As we have seen, in altering a file record the original record **is** destroyed when the updated record is returned to the file. Although current information is always present within the file memory, historical information required to reconstruct the current information is not. Therefore, if the current record is not readable, or if it contains some mistake because of machine malfunctioning or errors in the input information, there may be no convenient way of reconstructing the correct information.

When random access files are utilized in real-time processing, direct manual entry of certain information may be provided through the use of keyboard entry stations. For example, warehouse receipts may be entered into the records by means of a typewriter located in the warehouse. Needless to say, such a method of entering information is rather prone to error compared with our usual procedure of key-punching and verifying. Furthermore, it may also be more difficult to control, for anyone who has physical access to a remote entry station can modify the records within the machine. And as operating people become involved in data entry they are apt to be more concerned with their major tasks rather than with the sideline of data entry. They do not see themselves as "professional" data processing specialists, and it is difficult to instill in them a proper respect for the importance of accuracy.

It is also more difficult to provide an adequate audit trail with random access files. Since random access processing usually requires no sorting of input information, and no intermediate summarizing of transactions, the usual listings, which are prepared as a by-product of these batch-type operations, are no longer conveniently produced and therefore are not available to provide an audit trail.

We have said that control of accuracy may be a difficult problem in using random access files, but the difficulties are not insolvable; the systems designer, however, must be aware of them and provide solutions when the system is designed.[4] For example, he may incorporate in the programs many more checks of reasonableness and consistency of the input information than would ordinarily be necessary. He may design the system so that a remote entry station cannot be operated without a special key or coded combination, and in this way control the ability to change crucial file information. And he may produce a transaction register, with a line for each transaction, that shows the balances before the transaction, the transaction itself, and the resulting balances, along with a reference to the date

---

[4] Extended discussions of control of accuracy techniques which are applicable to random access files are listed in the Supplemental Readings at the end of this chapter.

and page number of the previous transaction. It then becomes possible to trace transactions that have affected a given record by finding the last activity, then referring to the previous activity, which refers to the previous one, and so on.

To provide a point to which we can return if anything goes wrong, it may be necessary to dump the master file periodically by writing it on magnetic tape or punching it into cards. This can consume much time. For example, to punch the contents of a 20,000,000-word disk file into cards would require 167 hours at 200 cards per minute (assuming the file could be punched into 2,000,000 cards). Even dumping this file on high-speed magnetic tape would require at least 40 minutes. (This, incidentally, is a pretty good argument for having magnetic tape units on machines with random access files.)

What If the Machine Breaks Down?

In designing any system it is necessary to consider the question: What if the machine breaks down? But especially in a real-time system, in which the machine is an integral component in minute-by-minute operations, this may become an extremely important question. Operations may have to stop or some method of bypassing the machine must be devised. Sometimes this is easy, for it may not be difficult to switch to manual processing of the essential information. However, in cases where the processing is crucial to important operations, it may be desirable to go so far as to have duplicate equipment on a stand-by basis to take over processing in case of machine failure.[5]

EXAMPLES OF RANDOM ACCESS FILE PROCESSING

In this section we will consider two examples of the use of random access files for data processing. The first is an inventory control, billing, and accounts receivable operation in which quick service to the customer is of great importance. The second is an illustration of improved management control in a business organization.

Wholesale Grocery Application

As an illustration of the use of a random access file, consider the combination of warehouse inventory control, billing, and accounts receivable for a large wholesale grocery. Since markups are relatively

---

[5] Both the SAGE and the SABRE systems have duplications for this purpose.

low in the grocery business, wholesalers compete actively with one another on the basis of service. Thus the ability to provide the desired items as quickly as possible is of great importance. An up-to-the-minute knowledge of inventory position, along with the ability to process an order as a unit without waiting for a batch to be accumulated, provides significant advantages for random access processing.

The wholesaler we will discuss carries about 3,000 items in stock, which he sells to approximately 300 customers in his area. These customers order from a preprinted order form, furnished by the wholesaler, on which they simply indicate the desired number of each item printed on the form. The average order includes about 300 items, and the total volume involves around 35,000 line-items per day. An average of 300 different items is received into the warehouse each day, and a "slot" system, in which receipts are placed in any slot that is available when they arrive, is used in the warehouse.

Within the file memory of the machine we require two types of records, one for items in inventory and the other for customer information. On the basis of cards key-punched from the order, we wish to prepare an invoice, to maintain accurate inventory records, to notify management of shortages which are developing, to maintain accounts receivable information concerning each customer, and to provide information concerning the warehouse location (slot number) so that the order may be easily assembled for shipment.

The record for each inventory item should contain such information as the item number (which, in this case, can correspond to the file address), description, pack and size, unit price, unit cost, unit weight, class of merchandise, minimum stock balance, total on hand, and three or four combinations of slot number and quantity stored in that location. The item record must therefore be about ten words long.

The customer record should include customer number, both the "sold to" and the "ship to" name and address, the routing, and a history of orders for which payment has not yet been received. Thus each customer record might involve up to 50 words of information.

For this application we might consider a stripped-down version of the MAC, with a card reader and punch (as in the basic MAC), a 300-line per minute printer, and a single disk pack unit similar to that in Figures 12–7 and 12–8. Such a machine configuration might rent for less than $3,000 per month.

The overall procedure used is shown in Figure 12–11. Input order cards, punched from the preprinted order form, would include store number and eight items (stock number and quantity) spread across

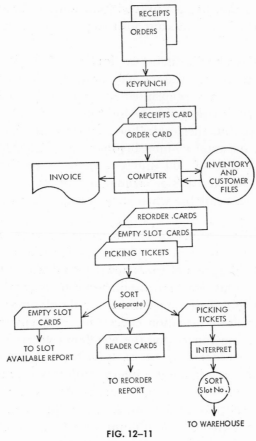

FIG. 12–11
Inventory and Invoicing Procedure

the card to reduce the number of cards involved. Receipts would be entered into the computer from cards in which item number, quantity, and slot number would be recorded.

Output from the machine would include the invoice, picking tickets (which would be interpreted and sorted to picking sequence before being sent to the warehouse), empty slot cards, and reorder cards. Periodically, analyses of inventory position, turnover, etc., could be produced from the master inventory file.

In addition to the heading information, the invoice would include (for each item) the item number, slot number, description, pack and size, unit price, and the dollar amount (quantity times price). Out of stock items not shipped would also be indicated. For the entire invoice there would be printed a dollar total, discount (if any), net amount, and the total weight of the order.

This program should operate at around 200 lines (and cards) per minute output, so the total processing time should be between three and four hours for the 35,000 line-items, plus heading lines, plus miscellaneous output. Key-punching the input cards would involve around 40 hours per day, so six key punches and operators would be required. The computer required for this job would rent for less than $3,000 per month; and key punches, sorter and interpreter would add a few hundred dollars to the total monthly machine rental. It is likely that the same job could be accomplished for about the same money through the use of standard punched card equipment, but the procedure described above provides important advantages in terms of inventory control information, speed of processing the individual orders, and ability to promptly answer questions concerning the availability of individual items.

Consolidated Manufacturing Control Operations

When utilizing random access files, it may be possible to return to the old manual bookkeeping approach of reflecting the influence of each transaction on various records as the transaction occurs, thus keeping all records up to date at all times. In a job-shop situation, the labor ticket prepared for payroll purposes contains information which can also be used to keep track of the progress of each order in the shop and to analyze machine efficiencies.

By maintaining within memory three types of files, we can use the information on the labor ticket to maintain an employee's pay record, to maintain a current status of each job within the shop (including where it stands with respect to the schedule and to standard cost), and to accumulate statistics concerning the performance of each machine in the shop.

Since the record for each active job includes the schedule for that job and standard cost data for each operation—both of which could be compared with actual performance—management can be provided with exception reports that highlight those jobs which are behind schedule or on which excessive costs are occurring. Since the status of each job is up to date at all times, inquiry stations may be used to interrogate the file whenever desirable to answer questions about the status of any order in the shop.

Furthermore, raw material and in-process inventory balances can be maintained, and raw material requirements can be forecast on the basis of the projected production schedules. But the really spectacular potential achievements lie in the relatively unexplored area of shop scheduling. A modest approach to this problem may be taken by working backwards from the due date of the order through each operation, thus providing a scheduled starting date for each operation that will allow the order to be completed on time. Then, given these starting dates for each operation on all orders within the shop, it is possible to prepare a rough forecast of machine load and manpower requirements that may be used to forecast bottlenecks which will arise when attempting to meet the schedule.

A considerable amount of research effort is currently being expended in attempts to devise techniques which can be used to efficiently handle the minute-by-minute decisions concerning which job should be done next when an operation is completed and a machine in the shop becomes available. (A simulation technique for studying this problem is discussed in Chapter 17.) As such dispatching procedures are developed, it becomes possible to design real-time control systems in which direct data entry from the shop is combined with information in random access files to evaluate progress and make current shop operating decisions so as to achieve optimal overall performance of the shop.

SUMMARY

There are many different devices, ranging from large magnetic drums through magnetic disks to magnetic card files, that provide large amounts of file storage that may be processed without regard to sequence. Such devices, however, differ in size, in average delay for obtaining a record, and in cost per digit stored.

Although many variations in the use of random access files are possible, the basic approach is to enter each transaction in the sequence in which it occurs, obtain the necessary file records, process the transaction, update the file records, and produce the desired output. This may be contrasted with the batching approach where a batch of transactions is accumulated, sorted into the sequence of the file, and processed against the file to produce results and to update the file.

The major systems advantages of random access files are the procedural simplicity (for example, lack of sorting) that is possible, the drastic reduction in the delay between the time when the transaction arises and the time at which the results are available, and the consequent possibility of real-time data processing where the data processing system actively participates in current operations.

One interesting problem in using random access files is that of file organization. There are two basic approaches: sequential organization, in which the file records are stored in sequence and Table Look-up is used to locate the file record for each transaction; and random organization, in which prime number division is used to compute the file location from the control number, and chaining is used to handle overflow. Other systems problems that may arise in the use of random access files are control of accuracy, re-creation of information that might be destroyed, and provision of alternate procedures for use when the equipment is not available.

Random access files are not well matched with the processing speeds of the larger and faster machines. However, they may be quite useful on such machines for program storage and input-output queuing in connection with automatic monitoring systems.

Random access files offer important alternatives to the systems designer, and they may be combined with magnetic tape files on the same machine to make combination sequential-random processing possible. In general, if batching delay is not a problem, and efficient procedures for batch processing can be developed, sequential processing with magnetic tapes will cost less than random access processing. However, if delays are crucial, and begin to force uneconomically sized batches—or to make batch processing impractical—then random access files are an attractive alternative. Furthermore, random access files combine with on-line input-output devices to open up the possibility of real-time data processing (that is impossible with batching techniques).

EXERCISES

12.1 How does the basic approach to processing with random access files differ from the approach used with punched cards or magnetic tape files?

12.2 Discuss the advantages obtained through the use of random access files?

12.3 Discuss the systems problems associated with the use of random access files?

12.4 Describe the sequential method of file organization. How is the record for a transaction found in such a file?

12.5   Describe the random method of file organization. How is the record for a transaction found in such a file?

12.6   Why do random access files present problems in the area of control of accuracy?

12.7   Suppose we have a random access file in which are stored inventory records identified by item number. How could we make a list of the items that are out of stock?

12.8   What is involved in inserting a new record in a random access file? In deleting a record? How would these problems be handled in magnetic tape files?

12.9   Suppose we have a random access file in which are stored inventory records identified by item number. We attempt to find a record for an item that is not in the file. What would happen? If we were processing a similar magnetic tape file, what would happen if we attempted to find an item that was not in the file?

SUPPLEMENTAL READINGS

BUCHHOLZ, WERNER. "File Organization and Addressing," *IBM Systems Journal,* June, 1963, pp. 86–111.

   This is a comprehensive description and discussion of various methods of organizing and addressing random access files.

Disk Storage Concepts (General Information Manual, Form F20–8161). International Business Machines Corporation, White Plains, N.Y.

   An excellent general discussion of random access processing with magnetic disk files. Includes discussions of the systems advantages of random access files, file organization, techniques of control of accuracy, and bypass and restart procedures.

HILLEGASS, J. R., AND STATLAND, N. "Random Access Storage Devices," *Datamation,* December, 1963, pp. 34–45.

   A survey description of many different types of random access files, with a discussion of the advantages and limitations of each. It includes a discussion of costs for both random and sequential processing, and presents a chart showing the characteristics of the random access files available at that time. There are other articles on random access files in this issue of *Datamation.*

In-Line Electronic Accounting, Internal Control and Audit Trail (Form F20–2019). International Business Machines Corporation, White Plains, N.Y.

   A discussion (prepared by Price Waterhouse and Co.) of the problems of control of accuracy and provision of an audit trail when using random access files. Outlines techniques for solving these problems.

13 OVERVIEW OF
ELECTRONIC COMPUTERS

OUR STUDY of punched card equipment, the basic MAC computer, magnetic tape, and random access files has shown that a wide variety of mechanized data processing equipment exists. The previous presentation has been designed to emphasize the most important characteristics of the equipment and the major ideas involved in its use for data processing.

The characteristics of the MAC were chosen to be as representative as possible of the characteristics of computers, while at the same time avoiding (when possible) confusing complexity. It should be noted that the designer of any computer has quite a number of choices to make, and these choices result in variations in certain characteristics of machines. In this chapter we will discuss some of these basic variations.

Although we have mentioned the possibility of real-time data processing, we have considered few of the equipment or communications factors involved. Furthermore, the building-block approach makes it possible to have a tremendous variety of possible machine configurations, and we should be aware of the general nature of these possibilities. In this chapter we will also discuss communication between machines, additional input-output devices, building-block concepts, and ways of combining these building-blocks into more sophisticated machine systems.

VARIATIONS AMONG MACHINES

As was pointed out in Chapter 6, various coding schemes can be used to represent information in the computer. The MAC uses binary-coded-decimal representation that requires 4 bits per digit. For alphabetic information, the MAC uses an 8-bit (2-digit) code, while many machines use a 6-bit code that will represent both alphabetic and numeric characters.

Pure binary[1] representation, in which combinations of the digits 0 and 1 are used to represent any number in much the same way as the individual digits are represented in binary-coded-decimal notation, is the most efficient means of storing and computing with numeric information. Thus machines intended primarily for computation (rather than data processing) frequently use pure binary notation.

In the modern building-block concept the same basic machine can be used for either data processing or for scientific computation, or for a mixture of both. To enable a processor to be an effective block in either a scientific computer or a data processing machine, it is not uncommon to have a dual method of representing information, with a word being considered as composed of 36 binary digits or six alphanumeric characters (bytes) of 6 bits each.[2] In such machines two sets of arithmetic instructions exist, so that a Binary Add can be used to add binary information and a Decimal Add can be used for decimal information. In such machines the instruction is usually considered to be a binary word. Thus addresses are binary numbers, which explains why the memory size of so many computers in some power of 2 (2048, 4096, 8192, 32768).

In long computational problems involving thousands of additions, subtractions, multiplications, and divisions, the intermediate results may be numbers about which we have very little intuitive feeling concerning size; hence the problem of keeping track of the decimal point when writing the program is quite difficult. So that the machine itself can keep track of the decimal point, many computers include instructions which operate directly upon numbers expressed in floating decimal notation (which is described in Appendix C). Of course, a binary machine uses an automatic floating *binary* point rather than a floating decimal point. Thus we may have a third way in which information may be represented in the memory of a machine, for in floating point notation one portion of the word represents the digits of the number and the other portion of the word is an exponent that indicates the location of the decimal point.

---

[1] For a more complete description of binary notation see Appendix B.

[2] Some machines use a 48-bit word that can also accommodate eight 6-bit characters. Others use a 32-bit word that accommodates four 8-bit bytes, or 64-bit "double words" that hold 8 such bytes.

Variable Word Length

The memory of the MAC has been organized into words of ten digits and sign, each of which is designated by an address. Several computers that are designed primarily for data processing employ another approach to the organization of memory. Instead of recording information in memory in words of a specific length, these machines are able to handle each field (whether a single character or many characters) as an individual unit of information.

Rather than being composed of words of a fixed length, the memory of such machines is organized so that each character has its own address. A field is addressed by its right-most (or in some machines, its left-most) position in memory, so the other limit of the field must be designated in some way. This may be done by indicating the length of the field in the instruction; or the other end of the field may be indicated by a special character, by a special bit position in the character code, or by sensing the sign of the field.

For example, one such machine addresses the right-most position of the field and denotes the left-most limit by adding an extra bit to the 6-bit alphanumeric character code. In this machine we might allocate memory *positions* 20 through 29 to name, 30 through 34 to man-number, 35 through 37 to hourly rate, 38 through 40 to overtime hours, and 41 through 43 to regular hours. If we denote the field definition bit by a circumflex ($\wedge$) over the character, the record for Mr. T. C. Mits might appear in an input area as below:

$\wedge$							$\wedge$			$+$	$\wedge$	$+$	$\wedge$	$+$	$\wedge$	$+$
M	I	T	S			T	C	1	2	3	4	5	2	5	0	0	8	3	4	0	0

20 21 22 23 24 25 26 27 28 29 30 31 32 33 34 35 36 37 38 39 40 41 42 43 44 45 46

Thus, to obtain his name, we would address 00029; to obtain his man-number (12345), we would address 00034; to obtain his regular hours worked (40.0), we would address 00043; and to obtain his overtime hours (08.3), we would address 00040.

Notice that the allocation of memory in such a machine is quite similar to the allocation of columns in a punched card: the maximum number of positions that a field can require must be allotted to that field (as shown in the field for overtime hours). Since we must locate the fields by means of the address of the units position, the number of characters devoted to each field must remain fixed so that these addresses will be the same from record to record.

Machines in which memory is organized in the manner described above are said to have *variable field* (or *word*) *length*. However, the length of a particular field is not really variable; it must be fixed, just as the size of a field on punched cards must be fixed. But the ability to allocate the required number of positions (and *only* the required number of positions) of memory (or of magnetic tape) to each field allows us to make the maximum use of the available memory. On the other hand, an additional digit is required in the data address on a machine in which each memory position is addressable. Also, since characters must be obtained from memory one at a time, such machines inherently operate in a serial fashion: they operate on one character at a time, so that the time to perform an operation is proportional to the size of the field. Note that the use of the partial word indicators in the MAC accomplishes essentially the same thing for a fixed word-length machine as does variable word-length memory organization.

Elimination of Control Panels

The control panels on the MAC computer simplify input and output, for information can be easily rearranged and edited by the control panel wiring. However, control panels have their disadvantages too, for they must be changed between jobs, which adds to setup time, and their flexibility is restricted by the number of selectors they have. Thus many machines do not employ control panels but instead use special instructions to make input-output editing easier.

If a machine is alphabetic and has variable word length, there is little need for rearranging information on input, for each field is directly addressable and minus signs are usually read in as zone bits in the units position of the field. Likewise for punched output: the information can easily be set up in memory to correspond with the card format.

Printing, however, requires some additional editing, for we frequently wish to insert decimal points, dollar symbols, and minus signs. And since nonsignificant zeros are unsightly, we may wish to eliminate them by replacing them by blanks. For example, we might wish to print the field 0024736 as $248.37 CR. To handle such a situation we might store a "skeleton" $- - - - -.- - CR in memory and use a Store for Printing instruction to insert the digits in the proper positions and eliminate the leading zeros.

To eliminate the control panel in a fixed word-length machine like the MAC we would need a way to condense numeric information from the alphabetic (two-digit) mode into regular numeric for processing. For example, cards might always be read column-by-column in alphabetic mode into a 16-word block. Then we could have a Condense instruction that would take 10 positions of two-digit coded information, eliminate the left-hand digit of each pair, and enter the right-hand digits into the A register.[3] The sign would be determined by the left-hand (zone) digit of the units position. Thus:

$$9\ 5\ 9\ 1\ 9\ 7\ 9\ 3\ \underline{9}\ 9$$

would enter to the A register as:

$$5\ 1\ 7\ 3\ 9\ +$$

while:

$$9\ 5\ 9\ 1\ 9\ 7\ 9\ 3\ \underline{7}\ 9$$

would be entered as:

$$5\ 1\ 7\ 3\ 9\ -$$

Of course, the exact number of digits obtained from a given word of memory would be determined by the partial-word indicator positions of the instruction. We would also need a Store and Expand instruction to reverse this process, and some Store, Expand, and Edit instructions for printing.

Order Structure

Because its instruction includes only one data address, the MAC is called a *single-address* machine. Other machines use a *two-address* instruction with an operation code and two data addresses:

Op.	A	B
xx	xxxx	xxxx

Such an order structure allows the computer to add two numbers together with a single instruction. For example, the instruction Add to Memory (ADM) might cause the contents of the location specified

[3] Recall that in alphabetic mode each column translates into a two-digit number. The left digit indicates the zone punch, while the right digit is the numeric punch. A no-zone translates to a 9 (so numeric columns all have 9 as their left digit), a y-zone translates to an 8, an x-zone translates to a 7, and a zero-zone translates to a 6.

by the B address to be added to the contents of the location specified by the A address, with the result replacing the previous contents of the location specified by the A address. Two-address logic also permits a three-way Branch instruction where one path would be taken on minus, another path on zero, and a third path on plus.

There are also *three-address* machines, in which an instruction has an operation code and three data addresses, A, B, and C:

Op.	A	B	C
xx	xxxx	xxxx	xxxx

Such a machine requires no arithmetic registers, for A denotes the location of one factor, B denotes the location of the other factor, and C denotes the location at which the result of the operation is to be stored. It should be observed that the word size must be large here unless the memory is small, or unless alphabetic addressing is used, so that each address requires but three positions.

There are variable field-length machines for which the instructions have a variable number of addresses (ranging from zero to 3), depending upon the operation code. For example, the stop code requires no data address; an instruction to add field A to field B and to store the result in location B requires two addresses, and so forth. Thus each instruction uses a minimum of memory space.

COMMUNICATIONS

We have mentioned the fact that communications facilities exist by which it is possible to transmit data in machine-processable form from one location to another. This transmission can be off-line, where data are read from some input medium (punched cards, for example), transmitted to another location, and written in some machine-processable form (magnetic tape, for example). Or the transmission can be on-line: from some reading device directly into a computer, or from a computer to some remote output device, or even from one computer directly to another.

Types of Lines

Communications lines of several different qualities (or band widths) are available. The quality of the line determines the number of characters per second that can be transmitted over the line. For example, the lowest-quality lines transmit around 8 to 12 characters per second, the usual voice-quality telephone line will transmit around 400 digits per second, and lines are available that will transmit close to 100,000 characters per second.

Lines connecting equipment within a plant are frequently owned by the company, but communications facilities for longer distances are usually furnished and maintained by public communication companies such as the telephone and telegraph companies. This type of business is of growing importance to the communications companies, and there have been predictions that within the next 10 or 15 years as much as half of their revenue will be derived from data transmission.

Courtesy of International Business Machines Corp.

FIG. 13–1

Remote Card Reader, Printer, and Entry Unit

When there is sufficient volume of communications between two or more locations it is feasible to obtain leased lines connecting the locations. Such lines may be leased for any period of the day (8 A.M. to 5 P.M., or for 24 hours) and may be used for any mixture of voice communication, written communication, and data transmission.

If the volume of transmission between any two points is too small to justify leased lines, it is possible to use "dial-up" facilities in which data are transmitted over the normal telephone switching network, and the connection is dialed and paid for as is a long-distance call.

In data communications systems, in addition to the lines, the communications company furnishes standard terminal equipment to convert signals produced by digital input equipment to signals suitable for transmission on the line, and to reconvert back to signals suitable for data processing equipment at the receiving unit. Data processing manufacturers produce a great variety of input, output, and data gathering equipment designed to be attached to these terminal facilities. This equipment includes paper-tape readers and punches, serial card readers and punches, parallel card readers and punches, magnetic tape units, and a variety of small remote input stations that combine information from punched cards, punched plastic badges, and from keyboards or dials (see Figure 13–1).

Most such communications devices utilize self-checking codes (redundancy bits) and transmit special checking characters with each block of data in order to detect errors in transmission. As we know from watching television, communications facilities occasionally are interrupted, and errors may also occur, so the reliability of

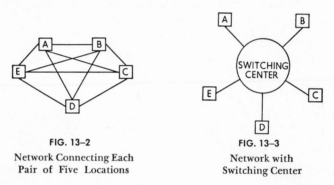

FIG. 13–2
Network Connecting Each
Pair of Five Locations

FIG. 13–3
Network with
Switching Center

the communications system and provision for error detection and correction are important concerns of the data processing systems designer.

Communications Networks

If a company has n different locations, each of which must communicate with all the others, the number of lines required to directly connect each pair of locations is $n(n-1)/2$. This number increases rapidly as n increases, and the resulting network becomes complex and expensive (see Figure 13–2). The cost of the network can usually be drastically reduced by introducing a switching center which is connected to each location and which routes messages between the proper pairs of locations (see Figure 13–3).

In the past, such switching centers have involved output of the messages (into punched paper tape, for example) and human action to retransmit the message to the proper destination. Now, however, special-purpose computers are being used to perform this function automatically, with random access memory used to store incoming messages until the proper line is available to send them on to their destination.

Multiplexing

When several low-speed or low-activity devices are to be attached to a single high-speed device, it is desirable to provide some way of allowing access for each of the slow or infrequently used devices to the fast one. This may be accomplished by means of a device called a *multiplexor*.

In its simplest form a multiplexor is simply a switching mechanism (see Figure 13-4) that queries the input lines, in turn, to

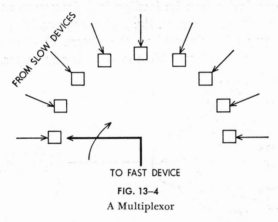

TO FAST DEVICE

FIG. 13-4

A Multiplexor

determine if any device is ready to transmit. When a device is ready to transmit, the multiplexor connects it to the fast device until it completes its message and then proceeds to examine the other lines in sequence until another activity is encountered. In such a system, if a second device is ready to transmit while the first one is transmitting, the second one must wait until the first has finished its message. If several activities occur simultaneously, the last one in line could be forced to wait for a substantial period of time, but this type of multiplexing is frequently quite satisfactory for connecting manual entry devices to a computer.

Multiplexors may be very helpful in reducing the cost of a data network, for they allow one moderate-speed line to substitute for many slow-speed lines that might otherwise be poorly utilized (see Figures 13-5 and 13-6).

A more sophisticated type of multiplexor incorporates a small, 2-character buffer for each input line. The switching device connects to each of these buffers and empties them in sequence so rapidly that

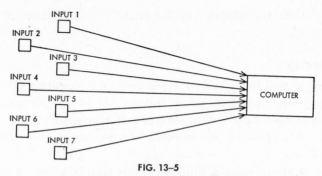

FIG. 13–5

Data Collection without Multiplexing

all the slower devices can be feeding in information at their maximum speeds. Then, of course, the high-speed receiving device must have some way of unscrambling the stream of characters that it receives in order to reassemble the resulting messages.

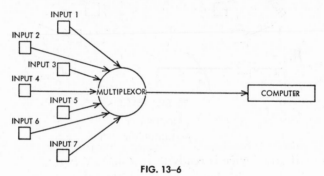

FIG. 13–6

Data Collection with Multiplexing

INPUT-OUTPUT DEVICES

So far in our discussions of input and output we have confined our attention to punched cards, magnetic tape, and line printers. There are a number of other types of input-output devices that are of growing importance.

Magnetic Ink Character Readers

Equipment is available for reading information printed in a special type font (E13B) with ink that is magnetizable (see the bottom of the check in Figure 13–8). Each digit is scanned horizontally by several read heads, and the resulting pattern of pulses is interpreted to determine the character read. If the character is unrecognizable, an error may be indicated.

Magnetic ink character readers may be used to enter printed information directly into a computer at speeds comparable to the speed of punched cards. Also, a magnetic ink character reader may be combined with a sorter to obtain a machine that will sort paper documents according to the information printed in magnetic ink on the documents (see Figure 13–7).

The major applications of magnetic ink character readers are in banking. In terms of total volume, one of the largest single data processing problems is that of handling the billions of checks that are processed in the United States each year. From the time that it is

Courtesy of International Business Machines Corp.

FIG. 13–7
Magnetic Ink Reader-Sorter

issued until it is posted to the proper depositor's account, a check is cleared through an average of 2.3 banks and is sorted and totaled about six times.[4]

Most data processing is concerned with the manipulation of information. However, check processing is more complicated than this, for the check has importance as a document, and the document itself must be processed along with the information.

Since a single check may be processed by many different banks, a common machine-processable language is required to make mechanization practical. The American Bankers Association has established specifications for information content, format, and character design

---

[4] See E. L. Van Deusen, "The Coming Victory over Paper," *Fortune*, October, 1955.

for a magnetic ink recording system that is readable both by people and by machines. A sample check, encoded along the bottom with these magnetic ink symbols, is shown in Figure 13–8.

Much of this information, such as the routing symbol, transit number, and account number, may be preprinted on the check before it is issued. Equipment is available from several manufacturers for encoding the variable information, including the amount, on the check during the proof operation.

As we have mentioned, equipment is available that can sort checks encoded with magnetic ink symbols and can enter the encoded information into a computer. Thus checks can be sorted whenever necessary, at the bank where they are cashed and at other points in

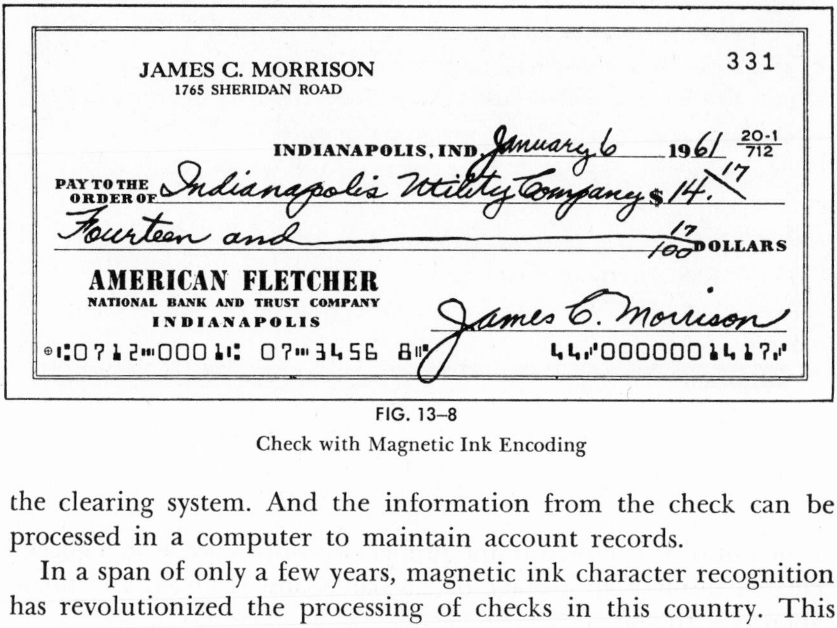

FIG. 13–8

Check with Magnetic Ink Encoding

the clearing system. And the information from the check can be processed in a computer to maintain account records.

In a span of only a few years, magnetic ink character recognition has revolutionized the processing of checks in this country. This revolution is an interesting one, for it required concerted action by an entire industry and by most of its customers. Because each bank processes a high volume of checks drawn on other banks, a single bank using magnetically encoded checks could not efficiently employ such equipment unless other banks also encoded their checks. And in order for a bank to encode its checks the people who write them have to use checks that are designed for this technique and preprinted with certain magnetic ink characters. Even banks too small to use the equipment themselves had to preprint checks with symbols so that they could be processed by other banks.

Optical Character Readers

Devices exist that will read uppercase alphabetical and numerical symbols printed on documents. At present, such devices require that the information to be read be printed in a specific type font (or a few similar fonts at most), but developments indicate that such restrictions will gradually be relaxed.

Optical character readers scan each character with a beam of light, and the reflection provides a pattern of black and white that is translated by a photoelectric cell into a pattern of impulses that will be decoded if the machine recognizes the character. Again, if the character is unrecognizable, an error may be indicated.

Optical character readers have their major applications in areas (such as public utility and insurance billing) where many notices are sent out and returned with a payment. The notice contains all the information required to enter the payment transaction into the data processing system when it is read by the optical character reader. Of course someone must still open the mail and verify that the payment is for the proper amount, but the expensive key-punching and verifying steps are eliminated.

As optical character readers become more versatile and reliable, and as their price is reduced, it seems logical to expect that they will take over many of the input tasks now being accomplished by key-punch and verifier operators.

Voice Output

Several devices are available that allow computers to talk directly to people. In these devices spoken words are recorded on a magnetic drum or disk, as in a voice recorder. Each word is assigned a code, and the computer then assembles a message by specifying the proper sequence of codes that select the words to produce the desired spoken message.

Such a device is in use for stock market quotations. Any subscriber to the service can dial the code number of the desired stock over the phone and instantaneously receive a voice report giving Bid and Ask prices, price of last trade, the volume of trading up to the present, the opening price, and the highest and lowest prices for the day.

Graphical Displays

A number of devices can display information from computers on the face of cathode-ray tubes, similar to a TV screen (see Figure

13–9). Such devices have been extensively used in scientific computing installations—where the results must often be placed in graphical form anyway—thus eliminating both the voluminous printing of numbers and the subsequent tedious plotting of the graphs.

There are also military systems (such as SAGE) in which such devices present tactical information to the decision-maker in pictorial form. And such devices can be used to achieve a very high printing speed by displaying an entire page of printed information,

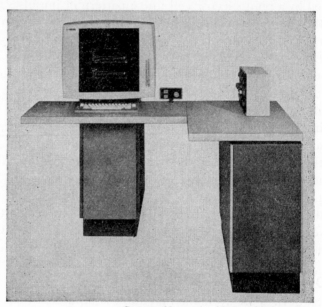

Courtesy of International Business Machines Corp.

FIG. 13–9

Graphical Display Unit

photographing it, and then displaying another page. The photographic image can then be printed by means of xerography.

Cathode-ray displays show substantial promise as components in computer-controlled teaching machines, for they can communicate both written information and diagrams to the student. By means of an *electronic marker,* small amounts of information can be written on the surface of the display tube and entered into the memory of the machine, so the student's response can be indicated in this manner. It seems likely that such display devices will become more and more important as we learn how to employ computers to interact with people in learning and problem-solving situations.

Desk Sets

Any number of devices are available that communicate via keyboard entry with computers and that print computer output by means of slow printers. For example, there are window posting machines, designed for use in savings banks, that accept keyed information concerning the customer number and the type and amount of the transaction. This information is used to update the account record in random access files in the computer and to print out a record of the transaction in the customer's passbook (which is inserted into the machine).

Similar devices are available for almost any type of interrogation activity. One such device, about the size of a small adding machine, is used by several airlines to handle reservations. To determine seat availability on a certain flight, the agent selects a metal plate on which the schedule for flights to the desired destination are printed. When this plate is inserted into a slot in the desk set, notches in the edge of the plate furnish the central machine with the address of the record associated with these flights. By pressing buttons on the face of the machine, the agent may inquire about a specific flight on a certain date, and lights on the machine will indicate the status of that and other flights to the destination. If one or more seats are to be sold (or canceled), the proper buttons are depressed, and the information is recorded in the memory of the machine, which thus maintains the current status of each flight.[5]

BUILDING-BLOCK CONCEPTS

Although we have mentioned that the MAC is an illustration of a "building-block machine," we have not really discussed what is involved in such a concept. The design of machine modules, that can be assembled in different combinations to provide various machine capabilities, is of great importance, not only from the standpoint of flexibility but also from the standpoint of cost. Since computers are very complex mechanisms to design, there are tremendous fixed costs involved in designing and setting up production for such a machine. By means of modular design the same basic machine is suitable for a much wider range of uses, and many more machines can be sold.

---

[5] The SABRE System, which will be described later in this chapter, does much more than merely maintain a seat inventory, and thus requires a more flexible desk set than the one described here.

Thus the fixed costs can be spread over a larger number of machines, which reduces the average cost of each machine and produces lower prices.

Another obvious advantage of building-block machines is that it is possible to tailor a machine to the specific requirements of the jobs to be done, while also maintaining the flexibility to easily expand these capabilities as the volume or complexity of the jobs increases. This is especially important because both data processing and scientific computing tend to expand in volume as we learn how to exploit the characteristics of the computer to accomplish things we would never dream of attempting when we first considered the use of a computer.

There are two aspects of modularity. First, the logical structure of the machine must allow for expansion (perhaps even beyond anything that is feasible at the time when the basic logic must be determined). For example, in order to expand the number of input-output units there must be some way that sufficient instructions can be incorporated in the order structure to handle the additional number of types of units. If the memory may be expanded there must be sufficient digits in the data address portion of the instruction to address the additional memory. In this regard, it would be awkward to expand the MAC memory to more than 20,000 words (and even this would require the use of the sign of the instruction).

The second aspect of modularity is engineering. Input-output units and data channels must be designed with standard *interfaces* so that, no matter what happens inside the devices, they all produce and/or accept the same electrical signals. Thus these modules can be connected with each other in a variety of combinations. In particular, a machine may employ several data channels, and any data channel can control a mixture of input-output units.

As we have pointed out in connection with the MAC, there need be no direct relationship between the logic of the machine and the means by which the results are obtained. For example, with exactly the same order structure we might have one slow machine, which performs arithmetic in serial, digit-by-digit fashion, and a fast machine which performs arithmetic simultaneously on all digits of the word in parallel. Thus, with the same basic logic it is possible to have a number of different pieces of hardware that cover a wide range of cost and capability.

By means of modular construction we can choose from among

several basic arithmetic speeds, memory sizes, numbers of data channels, and numbers and types of input-output devices so as to provide an extremely large number of possible combinations. Not only can we connect input-output units to machines, we can also interconnect two or more computers to provide multicomputer systems for certain purposes. A growing tendency in the computer industry is to standardize the interfaces among components so that it becomes possible to combine components (or machines) from several manufacturers to assemble the desired system.

RANGE OF EQUIPMENT

As pointed out above, the building-block concept makes it very difficult to categorize computers in any hard and fast manner, for the different configurations of a single basic machine may fall into several different categories. Nevertheless, in order to provide a feeling for the wide variety of different capabilities that are available in computers, we will present some general types of computers under the following classifications.

Key-operated Input

A number of small computers are designed to expand the capabilities of key-operated posting or billing machines. These machines typically use ledger cards, selected by the operator, for file information. But, in addition to the printed information on the card, there may be provision for magnetic recording so that account information (account number and current balances) can be automatically entered into the machine from the ledger card. Then the transaction information is entered on the keyboard, the transaction is processed by the computer, and the results are printed and recorded magnetically on the ledger card. Other output devices, such as paper-tape punches and additional printers, may be added to these computers to provide additional records or reports.

Desk Computers

The machines in this category are primarily used as personal tools by engineers and scientists in solving small- to moderate-sized computational problems. Such machines, selling for between $30,000 and $100,000, or renting for between $1,000 and $3,000 per month, usually require no special installation facilities, and many of them can be plugged into any 110-volt outlet. They usually have relatively slow, punched paper-tape input and typewriter output, and many are binary machines.

Such machines are frequently operated on an "open shop basis"; that is, the engineers program and run their own problems rather than use an organization of computer specialists for numeric analysis, programming, coding, and running.

Small Data Processing Machines

These machines, exemplified by the basic MAC, are relatively modest in cost, and rent for between $1,000 and $5,000 per month, but they differ from the previous category in that they are usually not binary and, although they do not process magnetic tape, they have more extensive input-output facilities than the desk computers. This category includes a wide variety of equipment, which is based upon line printers and high-speed paper tape or buffered punched card input and output.

Many of these machines are designed to fit into punched card data processing systems by replacing enough sorters, collators, accounting machines, and calculators to justify their cost. Some of the most successful of these machines combine the principles of punched card machines and computers by using a combination of wired and stored programming for control, thus reducing the memory required for storing the program.

Random Access File Processors

Renting for between $1,500 and $4,000 per month, these machines are designed to process transactions against a random access file. Most of them are rather slow in computing ability and are designed for on-line processing of transactions at speeds of 10 to 100 transactions per minute.

Small Card and Tape Combinations

These machines, renting for between $3,000 and $10,000 per month, employ magnetic tape files, but also use punched card input and direct printer output for much of their processing. They are characterized by the fact that their internal speed is not great enough to make it desirable that they be strictly tape-oriented, yet it is feasible for them to use magnetic tapes for file processing with direct entry of transactions from punched cards.

The basic MAC, with magnetic tapes added, is an illustration of this type of machine. Such machines may be quite efficient for simple processing of large-volume but low-activity ratio files, or they may be used for off-line input-output in large-scale computer installations. Some of them are the equivalent of the early large-scale machines in processing ability.

High-Speed Computers

Renting for from $12,000 up to hundreds of thousands of dollars per month, these machines are capable of executing from 50,000 to millions of instructions per second. They are, typically, building-block machines, and their cost is heavily influenced by the size of the memory, the number of data channels, and the type and amount of input-output and file equipment included in the configuration.

Most such machines are entirely tape-oriented; or they have a relatively large number of input-output devices with provision for multiprogramming so as to keep many of them operating at once.

MULTIMACHINE CONFIGURATIONS

Let us now investigate some of the machine configurations that may be obtained by connecting two or more computers.

In an installation in which the main processor is tape-oriented there are usually one or more small machines to convert from cards to tape so as to print tape results. As shown in Figure 13–10, they may

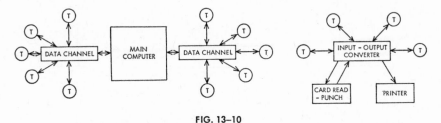

FIG. 13–10

Tape Computer with Input-Output Computer

not be connected in any way. After building a tape from cards on the small machine, it is then necessary to dismount the tape from the small machine and remount it on the large one. For printing output, the tape must be removed from the main computer and mounted on the peripheral machine.

To avoid the bother and the time delays involved in mounting and removing tapes, it is possible to allow the two machines to communicate with each other through shared magnetic tape units, as shown in Figure 13–11. The switching that determines which machine is connected to which tape unit may be manually controlled by the operator; or it may be controlled by one of the machine programs, with an indication of the switch setting being transmitted to the other machine.

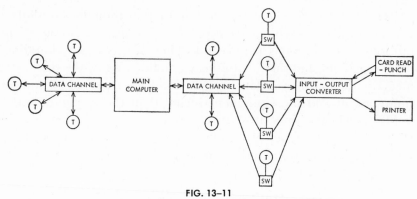

FIG. 13–11

Computers with Shared Tape Units

Another approach to communications between computers is to allow them to share a random access file (as shown in Figure 13–12) rather than a tape unit. This allows more flexibility because the file can have two access mechanisms, and thus the two machines can be connected to it at the same time. In addition to transmitting input

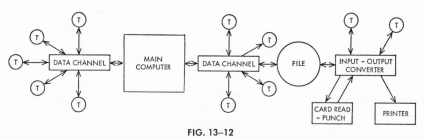

FIG. 13–12

Shared File System

and output information back and forth, they can now communicate with each other by leaving messages in designated file records, with each machine examining its "message box" every so often to see if the other wants anything.

Another possibility is to have two machines communicate with each other by transferring information back and forth, from one memory to another, through a data channel. One such configuration is shown in Figure 13–13, in which there is one computer that handles all input-output tasks (including scheduling) and transmits problems to its large, fast "slave" for solution.

Such a configuration makes a lot of sense in a scientific computing installation where the turn-around time for some jobs is crucial for the progress of the research. The input-output processor can accept jobs as they are fed in and store them in the file. There it can determine the sequence in which they are processed on the basis of the length of the job, how long it has been waiting, and the priority assigned to the job. Thus the jobs that require quick answers can be handled promptly while those that are not so urgent can be used to keep the slave processor busy when it would otherwise be idle. Thus

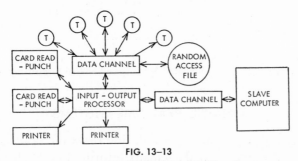

FIG. 13–13
Input-Output Processor with "Slave"

the fast, expensive machine is always kept busy computing, while the input-output processor handles all the input and output devices and the scheduling so that the delay before running a problem is determined by priority rules. Needless to say, such a system requires a rather comprehensive and sophisticated supervisory program.

With such a configuration it is possible to add small "satellite" computers at remote locations and to connect them to the input-output processor. Small jobs might be handled by the satellite computer itself, but jobs that require greater computing power could be transmitted to the input-output processor and handled in the same manner as the jobs it receives from its own card readers. If the satellite jobs are accorded a sufficiently high priority, the computations might be handled by the large computer and returned so quickly that one might not even realize that the satellite itself did not solve the problem.

Another approach to communication between computers is to allow them to share the use of a high-speed memory, as shown in

Figure 13–14. To avoid conflicts in the use of this memory they incorporate instructions that allow one machine to reserve a position of the memory for its exclusive use. Some of the largest, most powerful machines are multimachine configurations of this type, sharing memory between several small machines and an extremely fast computer.

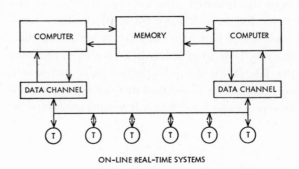

ON–LINE REAL-TIME SYSTEMS

FIG. 13–14

Two Computers with Shared Memory and Shared Input-Output

ON-LINE REAL-TIME SYSTEMS

There is a growing interest in on-line real-time systems, both for process control and for management information. Such large, complex machine systems incorporate suitable input-output devices, multiplexing, communications networks, random access files, and perhaps multimachine concepts.

Process Control

In the process industries there are many on-line real-time systems in which a computer is an integral part of a closed control loop that operates a process. Such a system requires devices that collect data concerning the state of the process, transducers that convert this information to digital form, multiplexors that channel the information to the computer, and devices that actuate controls on the basis of computed results. Such systems require equipment of high reliability, for if the computer will not operate, the process must be shut down or returned to manual control.

The SABRE System

One of the largest civilian on-line real-time data processing systems is the SABRE system, designed to handle reservation and operating information for the entire American Airlines system. As illustrated in Figure 13–15, reservation offices, ticket counters, and flight dispatchers all over the United States are connected through multiplexors and long-distance telephone lines with a large dual-computer system.

When a customer requests a reservation the agent queries the

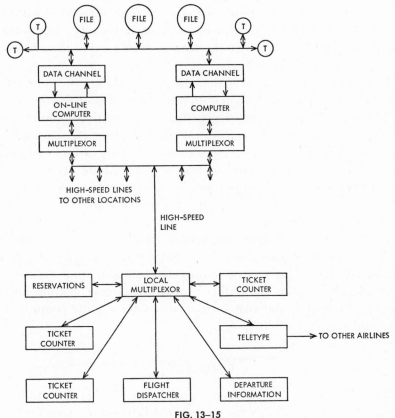

FIG. 13–15
The SABRE System

SABRE computer to determine if the desired space is available. If it is, the reservation is made and the agent enters the following information into the system: name of the customer who made the reservation, telephone number at which he can be reached, who will pick up the tickets and when, and such miscellaneous information as special menu requests, need for a wheelchair, or desire to rent a car. All this information is stored in the random access files, along with the space availability on all flights up to a year ahead, and with much of the 1,000,000-instruction program for the computer.

This system is an active control facility, for it keeps up with changes in the status of the reservation and/or the flight operations. For example, if the customer does not pick up his tickets on time, the computer notifies the agent and instructs him to get in touch with the customer. If the customer cancels, the seats are immediately returned to available status and people on the wait list can be notified. If space on a connecting airline is required, the computer sends a message requesting the space, and follows it up if no reply is received within a specified time. If the flight schedule is changed, the computer notifies the agent to get in touch with the customers affected so that they can adjust their plans accordingly.

In Figure 13–15 we observe that although there are two computers in the system, only one of them is on-line at any time. The other is for backup and is switched on-line when the first requires maintenance. When not operating on-line, the backup computer can be used for normal batch processing of regular data processing or for computing work. Incidentally, in some on-line systems where accuracy and reliability are extremely important, both computers work separately all the time (except if one is down) and compare answers to see that no mistakes have been made.

In the SABRE system the multiplexors are actually special-purpose stored-program computers that collect messages and store them until they can be sent on to the other components of the system. Such special purpose computers provide extremely flexible multiplexing, buffering, and switching facilities for on-line communication and computer networks.

SUMMARY

There are a number of basic variations in the way that numbers and alphabetic characters are represented in memory, ranging from fixed to variable word length, and from pure binary to 6- and 8-bit alphanumeric codes. Many machines employ a mixture of possible representations, such as a combination of pure binary, binary floating point, and a 6-bit byte with a 36-bit basic word.

Many machines do not employ control panels and must provide special instructions for editing and rearranging input and output information. Instruction formats include single-address, two-address, and three-address instructions, or some combination of these.

A wide variety of input-output devices is available for use with computers: magnetic ink and optical character readers, voice output, graphical display units, and a host of key-operated input-output units. Through the use of multiplexors and communications lines, these input-output units can be combined with one or more computers and direct access files to provide a variety of exotic equipment configurations, some of which may be used as on-line real-time systems.

Perhaps the most important concept that makes this wide variety of configurations possible is modular or building-block design. Under this concept the logic of the computer may be divorced from the hardware used to implement it, so that there can be a wide variety of components with standard interfaces that make it possible to interconnect the components as required to meet the needs of the system.

EXERCISES

13.1   What do we mean by variable word length? What are its advantages and disadvantages?

13.2   In a three-address machine we have an instruction that adds one number to another and stores the result.

a)   How many single address instructions would be required to obtain the result of this three-address instruction?

b)   If we wish to compute and store the sum of 10 numbers, how many three-address instructions would be required?

c)   If we wish to compute and store the sum of 10 numbers, how many single-address instructions would be required?

13.3   What is a multiplexor?

13.4   Describe the "building-block concept." Why is this concept of major importance to the producer of computers? Why is it important to the user of computers?

13.5   What is the difference between check processing and most other data processing?

13.6   What problems must be solved in the mechanization of check processing?

13.7   What are the differences between an inventory of airplane seats and an inventory of finished goods?

13.8   Prepare a market forecast for computers for the next ten years. For which types of machines do you forecast the greatest growth?

13.9   Study the computers produced by some computer manufacturer. Does this manufacturer produce machines that compete in each classification discussed in this chapter?

13.10   What is an on-line system? What is a real-time system?

13.11   Why are the following of importance to on-line real-time systems:

a)   Communications networks?

b)   Multiplexors?

c)   Random access files?

13.12 Discuss the advantages and the limitations of magnetic ink and optical character reading equipment.

SUPPLEMENTAL READINGS

BURCK, GILBERT. " 'On-Line' in 'Real-Time,' " *Fortune,* April, 1964.

In addition to describing the SABRE system, this excellent article discusses the management potential of on-line systems and describes progress toward attainment of such systems in industry.

FREDKIN, EDWARD. "The Time Sharing of Computers," *Computers and Automation,* November, 1963, pp. 12–20.

Discusses experiments in the use of computers to interact with people in problem-solving and teaching situations.

IBM TELE-PROCESSING (Systems Summary, Form A24–3090). International Business Machines Corporation, White Plains, N.Y. (1963).

This little booklet includes brief descriptions of various types of communication terminal equipment produced by IBM.

JOHNSON, ROBERT W. "Digital Data Display Systems: An Assessment," *Computers and Automation,* May, 1964, pp. 12–17.

A discussion of the major types of cathode-ray display equipment. This article is followed by a pictorial report on such display units; and there is another article in the same issue on the applications of and market for such displays.

MACDONALD, NEIL D. "The IBM System / 360," *Computers and Automation,* May, 1964, pp. 32–36A.

A description of the IBM System / 360. This system emphasizes modularity concepts, flexible input-output, and provision for handling communications devices; so it provides a good illustration of many of the concepts discussed in this chapter.

REAM, NORMAN J. "On-Line Management Information," *Datamation,* March, 1964, pp. 27–30.

Discusses real-time management information systems, and describes various basic configurations of equipment that may be used for on-line systems. This issue includes several other articles on real-time systems, and Mr. Ream's article is continued in the April, 1964, issue of *Datamation,* in which he discusses installation and implementation problems.

REPACI, C. M. "Considering Data Communications?" *Computers and Automation,* March, 1964, pp. 16–18.

A brief description of the types of data communications facilities available from the Bell Telephone System.

VAN GELDER, HANS. "On-Line Stock Quotation," *Datamation,* March, 1964, pp. 37–40.

A description of the stock quotation system produced by Teleregister Corporation that replies verbally to telephone inquiries.

SYSTEMS ANALYSIS
AND DESIGN

PREVIOUS PORTIONS of this book have been concerned with the mechanization of data processing. To explain how computers may be used for this purpose, a substantial portion of the preceding material has been devoted to the characteristics of various types of equipment. However, illustrations of how the equipment is applied to data processing have been included, and the overall process of converting an area to electronic data processing has been discussed in Chapter 9.

In Chapter 9 the process of development of a computer processing system was described in terms of problem definition, devising procedures, block diagramming, coding, debugging, conversion, and documentation. The basic assumption was made that equipment had already been specified, and it was pointed out that problem definition is an extremely complex area that would be discussed more fully later.

In another framework, the overall process of development of a computer processing system can be divided into three activities: design of the system, implementation of the design, and operation of the system. The first of these is concerned with definition of the problem and the devising of a system that provides an adequate solution. The implementation portion is concerned with the processes of detail block diagramming, coding, debugging, and conversion. Our concern in this chapter is with the definition of the systems problem and the devising of a system that provides a solution that can be implemented.

As discussed in Chapter 2, the entire business organization may be considered as a total system, in which the management information system is a crucial subsystem. Despite the fact that the electronic computer is an extremely powerful data processing tool, the results obtained from the mangement information system are primarily dependent upon the effectiveness with which the system itself was designed rather than upon the specific equipment employed. Thus serious consideration must be given to the techniques involved in the analysis and design of information systems.

There are three major steps in the process of designing an information system. First, it is necessary to obtain an understanding of the total business system and the existing information subsystem. Secondly, the results that *should* be obtained from the information system must be specified. Finally, equipment must be specified and procedures devised that efficiently obtain those results. Obviously, these three steps are interrelated both by the techniques used and by their dependence upon each other.

PRELIMINARY IDEAS

Systems analysis and design is an extremely challenging activity, composed of a mixture of detailed investigation, analysis of relationships, and synthesis. It is usually considered to be a team activity, for it is desirable to have more than one point of view applied to the problems, and two (or more) individuals may stimulate each other to arrive at solutions that would not have been reached separately.

Before examining a structured approach to the task of systems analysis and design, it is important to recognize some of the characteristics of this task and to consider some basic ideas that guide us.

Obtaining Information

Organizational and information systems may be quite complex, and to understand them it is usually necessary to obtain, organize, and assimilate a great deal of information. In general, this information must be obtained either from written sources—publications, files, memos, etc.—or from talking with people. Thus the systems analyst must be familiar with the sources of written information concerning the organization, and he must also understand the organization well enough to know with whom to talk in order to obtain accurate information. Most importantly, he must be adept at the techniques of *obtaining* information from people.

Without the cooperation of those being interviewed, the task of describing a complex system is literally impossible. Even with the whole-hearted cooperation of everyone concerned, this task is still extremely complex. Thus a primary prerequisite for success as a systems analyst is the ability to elicit the cooperation of people. The systems analyst who antagonizes everyone with whom he comes in contact is foredoomed to failure.

How can the systems analyst obtain cooperation? This question cannot be answered in a few words, and this book is not intended as a guide to personality development, but a few comments that are pertinent to the specific human relations problems involved in systems analysis may be of value.

In the first place, the systems analyst must be careful to go through the recognized organizational channels. If the cooperation of his supervisor is not obtained before approaching a worker, justified resentment is likely to result. Courtesy demands that the results of any investigation be reported to the supervisor involved and that gratitude be expressed to him and his subordinates for their cooperation.

The systems analyst should always remember that the mere fact of someone's probing into how people are performing their jobs is likely to make everyone apprehensive, and therefore somewhat resentful. Thus the systems analyst must overcome the temptation to intermix the process of obtaining information with the process of redesigning and improving the system. Nothing causes resentment faster than for the systems analyst to indicate during an interview that the job is not being done properly. Suggestions for improvement not only make it more difficult to obtain information about the system, they also make it harder to implement later changes because those affected can begin to fight the changes that much sooner. Also, until a thorough understanding of the entire system is acquired, it is highly desirable that the systems analyst maintain an open mind concerning what the system should be. Since those being interviewed are likely to be quite sensitive to the reaction of the systems analyst, he must be careful not to indicate disapproval by direct comments, questions, facial expressions, or tones of voice.

On the other hand, the interviewer should be sensitive to the person's attitudes toward the system, for these attitudes may indicate both problems and opportunities. The systems analyst should encourage those he talks with to suggest problems and improvements, and if these suggestions are fruitful he should remember to credit the person responsible. The interviewer must also develop the ability to discriminate between fact and opinion. He should carefully check his information against alternate sources, and he should be sure to interview people on both sides of controversial subjects.

The systems analyst should recognize that he is imposing upon the time of everyone with whom he talks, for they are primarily concerned with getting the job done. Even with the most efficient use of time, the interviewing process is lengthy and tedious and often involves several interviews with each person. It is important that the systems analyst be well prepared for each interview so that the required information can be obtained as quickly as possible. He should record the information in an orderly manner, and be punctual for each appointment.

Before each interview the analyst should carefully study the situation and decide what information he should attempt to obtain. Then he should prepare an outline that can be filled in during the interview to make sure that the desired information is obtained without undue wandering. Of course, excessive efficiency can be most irritating, so the systems analyst must develop a feeling for the attitude of those being interviewed and conduct himself with a suitable mixture of casualness and efficiency.

The interviewer must walk a narrow and difficult line, for without arousing antagonism he must probe deeply into individual conduct and thought processes. Those being interviewed may not understand that a description of the routine part of a job is only the beginning of the task, so they may not comprehend the necessity of isolating and examining each seemingly trivial exception. The systems analyst must continually employ Kipling's "honest servingmen":

> I keep six honest servingmen
> (They taught me all I knew);
> Their names are What and Why and When
> And How and Where and Who.

But care must be taken to minimize the resentment and antagonism that may be aroused by the use of these servingmen.

Creativity

The design of information systems involves a great deal of creativity. There are no foolproof rules or procedures that can be followed to guarantee that an optimal (or even a satisfactory) system will result. And when one observes the process of systems design in various organizations, he is immediately struck with the fact that inspiration seems to play a significant role in the design of superior systems.

We do not completely understand why one person is more creative than another, nor do we know *how* to be creative. However, a number of men[1] have studied creative people and have arrived at some general conclusions about how they approach problems—conclusions that appear to be helpful in stimulating creative thinking in the rest of us.

The first step in the solution of a problem is to define it so that it can be given concentrated attention. Creative ideas do not occur at random; they are usually the result of hard work and study that is specifically directed at a well-defined problem. (This important step in the design of data processing systems will be described in succeeding portions of this chapter.)

Secondly, creativity is based upon knowledge. Thus the systems analyst should concentrate upon extending his knowledge of data processing equipment and its use. He must keep up with new developments in a rapidly changing field, and any new machine manual or procedure write-up may contain an idea that will be invaluable sometime in the future. For example, the applications discussed in Chapter 10 include several approaches to the use of memory that may be of great value in entirely different situations. And, as was emphasized in Chapter 9, it is imperative that the systems designer have a comprehensive knowledge of the equipment for which he is designing procedures, for the efficiency of a procedure often depends upon taking advantage of specific equipment characteristics.

Thirdly, creativity depends upon the development of a multitude of alternative approaches to the solution of the problem. In the long run, the systems designer who quits when he discovers a workable solution to the problem at hand is not likely to be successful, for there may be several other radically different approaches, one of which may be definitely superior to all the rest. The designer should let his imagination roam unfettered. He should collect and record all ideas that occur to him without regard to their practicality; consider all existing ideas and knowledge in all possible combinations and relationships; and use each new idea as a steppingstone to another by attempting to combine it with another approach—modifying it, extending it, adapting it, reversing it, and rearranging it. In the design of systems, as well as in other creative processes, the larger the store of possible alternative solutions that can be created, the more likely the development of a satisfactory solution.

---

[1] For references see the Supplemental Readings by Mee and Polya.

Basic Systems Concepts

As was mentioned in Chapter 2, one of the most important concepts associated with systems is that of a hierarchy of subsystems. Thus it is possible to view the system as a large "black box" whose contents (whether people, transistors, wheels, gears, rocks, electronic computers—or a vacuum) are unknown. We might assume that what must go on in this black box can be determined by what goes into it and what comes out of it, and, in a sense, these inputs and outputs define the system. But, if we were able to peek into this black box, we might find it filled with smaller black boxes, whose contents are again unknown, but which are related to one another by flows of information. Again, the operations that must be performed by each of these black boxes are determined by their inputs and outputs. Conceptually, this process of opening black boxes can be continued until we reach a point where it is possible to directly examine the remaining black boxes and obtain an understanding of how the inputs are converted into the outputs.

Thus in systems analysis we search for meaningful ways to break a system down into subsystems, but this breakdown process is carried only as far as is necessary to get to subsystems of manageable complexity. You may recognize that this approach is a familiar one, for we have employed it in preparing the various levels of block diagrams for machine programs.

It should be noted that the above approach starts with the entire system and breaks it down into simpler and simpler components. Alternatively, another approach might be attempted which would start with the details of the system and combine them to represent the overall system. Working from the top down is by far the more effective approach, for it provides a framework for organizing the effort in a logical way, and it also produces an integrated representation of the system, for we are always concentrating attention upon the interrelationships between the subsystems rather than viewing them from the inside out and running the risk of ignoring these interrelationships.

Another basic concept of systems design that was introduced in Chapter 2 is that of the feedback control loop (or servomechanism). As shown in Figure 14–1, control depends upon two basic factors: (1) the existence of goals to be obtained and (2) the flow of information in the control loop. In the control loop, information about the performance of Operations is collected and organized so that it may be compared with the goals (objectives, expectations, and performance criteria) specified. If the goals are being satisfactorily attained, then the control process goes no farther. But if there are deviations, then it is necessary to decide what to do to produce the desired results, and this decision must be implemented.

This concept has a number of important consequences. First, it points out the importance of the information subsystems for satisfac-

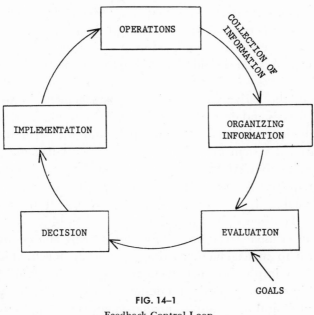

FIG. 14–1
Feedback Control Loop

tory performance of the organizational system, and thus for satisfactory performance by *management*. Secondly, it illustrates the important relationships between the goals or objectives of an organization and the design of the data processing system. Without organizational goals there is no reason to collect and process information. And without a thorough understanding of these goals it is impossible to consider designing an information system. Furthermore, we will use a knowledge of goals to provide criteria for breaking the system down into subsystems.

The concept of the feedback loop also provides criteria for evaluating information systems and subsystems on the basis of performance. It is the performance of the control system that is important, not just its cost, or its "gimmicks," or the equipment that it employs. The measurement criteria must be related to the ability of the control system to detect deviations from the objectives and to institute and implement effective corrective action.

Management Interaction with Systems Design

Management has the responsibility of directing the operations of an organization. Top management defines the goals of the organization and devises the basic strategies and policies by which the organization pursues these objectives. And an important management responsibility is that of structuring the organizational system so that it can compete effectively and can prosper in an ever changing and competitive environment. Thus, the design of the crucial information subsystem should be a primary concern of management at all levels.

Without the active participation of management in the task of systems analysis and design, the entire effort is foredoomed to failure, for the basic goals of the organization and the structure of the organizational system must be determined by management, not by the systems analyst. And the degree of understanding of these matters that is required for systems design makes it mandatory that the systems analyst have frequent opportunity for frank and direct give-and-take discussion of questions concerning objectives, policies, and organizational structure. Thus the systems analyst must have free access to management at the appropriate levels. This is not intended to imply that management must perform all the tasks involved in systems analysis and design; that would be both impossible and undesirable, but unless management is willing to participate in certain aspects of this task, it is extremely unlikely that an effective system can be designed.

Furthermore, even the best-designed system is useless unless it is implemented, and all the work that went into the design of an unimplemented system is wasted. Implementing a new information system usually requires drastic changes throughout the organization, and most people are inherently opposed to such changes, for they pose all sorts of real and imagined threats to the security of the individual. Thus the systems designer must cope with an extremely difficult selling problem. If management has not participated in the design of the new system, then the selling task is difficult (even if the system is worthwhile), but if management has participated throughout the process, most of the selling should have been accomplished as a consequence of this participation, and the system is "bought" by management rather than "sold" by the design group.

For both of the above reasons it is necessary that there be considerable interaction between management and the systems analysis team during the process of systems analysis and design. The Study Organization Plan proposed in the following sections provides for frequent reporting to management and for considerable management interaction and participation.

Consequently, a systems design effort must be mandated by the top management of the organizational component within which it is to be conducted. Since systems design involves a great deal of effort and cost, it must be well planned and its objectives and scope must be carefully specified. The systems design team must be aware of any constraints on the degree of change allowable in inputs, outputs, organizational relationships, or tools to be employed. And a time schedule and budget for the study must be determined and agreed upon. In fact, before a study of any magnitude is begun, the statement of objectives, scope, constraints, and schedule should be expressed in written form to reduce misunderstandings.

A Structured Approach

Systems analysis and design cannot be accomplished by a straightforward step-by-step process, for it involves a complex mixture of information acquisition, analysis, and creative synthesis. However, precisely because it is such a complex task, it is highly desirable to develop a basic methodological approach that provides a framework within which creative solutions can be developed. This framework should guide the systems analyst so that he is encouraged to consider everything pertinent to his task and to employ suitable techniques, but it must also be flexible enough to be applicable under many different circumstances, and it must foster rather than stifle creativity.

As we noted above, systems analysis and design must be a planned rather than a haphazard effort: both time and cost goals must be established, and progress of this work must be monitored against these established goals. Thus the task must be broken down into intermediate stages, effort must be allocated to each stage, and target dates for their completions must be set.

A major problem of systems analysis is obtaining the necessary information, but assimilating and making sense out of the immense amounts of information obtained is an even greater problem. Thus our basic approach should incorporate standard documentation techniques that encourage the acquisition of the most pertinent information, and that present it in a meaningful form.

The Study Organization Plan, developed by IBM, is a basic

methodological approach to systems analysis and design that satisfies the requirements stated above. It is a comprehensive plan for implementing the total systems approach, but it embodies sufficient flexibility to be applicable to many situations, ranging from a complete systems design study of a large organization down to a study whose purpose is to convert a manual area to punched card data processing. The task of systems analysis and design is viewed as a series of three interrelated steps:

1. Understanding the present business;
2. Determining the requirements of the system;
3. Designing the new system.

There is a substantial controversy among systems analysts about how much effort should be invested in studying the existing system before attempting to design an improved system. The traditional approach has been to study the existing data processing system in great detail: to follow pieces of paper around and document each operation performed, recording what is done and how it is accomplished. This viewpoint holds that only after a detailed understanding of the existing system has been obtained should the design of an improved system be attempted.

Other systems analysts believe that detailed study of an existing system is wasteful, and that it tends to reduce creativity by starting the analyst's thinking in the "ruts" of the old system. They prefer to concentrate attention on the results the system should produce, and then set out to devise the most effective system for producing those results without regard to what has been done in the past.

Both viewpoints have merit, but each contains some weaknesses. The first method is expensive and time-consuming and may stifle creativity, and thus lead to only marginal improvements. On the other hand, information systems are so terribly complex that the results they should produce may not be apparent without some examination of the existing system. Furthermore, the realities involved in making changes in organizations dictate that the analyst must understand the present system so that he can obtain the confidence of management and demonstrate the superiority of the new system. Moreover, since changes are disruptive and expensive, the system should not be changed capriciously; only necessary changes should be made.

The Study Organization Plan synthesizes the best of these two approaches. It provides a logical framework within which to gather information about the present system that will be useful in designing and selling an improved system. Yet it does not go into the unnecessary details of *how* operations are performed in the existing system; it concentrates instead on *what* is accomplished.

The following three sections are abstracted from the IBM manuals on the Study Organization Plan (also cited in Supplemental Readings at the end of this chapter). Those who wish a more comprehensive presentation of this subject should consult these publications.

PHASE I: UNDERSTANDING PRESENT BUSINESS

The objective of Phase 1 of the Study Organization Plan is an understanding of the present business and the present information subsystem which provides a sound basis for an analysis of information system requirements and design of a new system. The information obtained is organized into a report called the Present Business Description. First, the business is described in broad, general terms in the General Section. Then it is described in the Structural Section in terms of inputs to the business system, operations performed, outputs produced, and resources employed. Finally, in the Operational Section, the business system is described in greater detail: in terms of subsystems called *activities*.

General Section

This section should contain a clear and concise description of the business in terms of its history, the industry background, the goals and objectives of the organization, its policies and practices, and, finally, any pertinent government regulations affecting the company. The history of the organization should be concise, but it should identify the major milestones that have influenced the present position and course of the business.

Important historical information includes ideas, attitudes, and opinions of key management and research personnel, excerpts from the original charter, reasons for starting the company, mergers and spinoffs, expansion or curtailment of product lines and services, and reasons for changes in name or products. In addition, the growth of the physical plant and numbers of employees over the years is mentioned, along with a very general identification of products and services.[2]

The industry background relates the business to the industry in which it operates. The nature of the industry is summarized in terms

---

[2] *Study Organization Plan: The Method, Phase I* (Form F20–8136). International Business Machines Corporation, White Plains, N.Y. (1963).

of the market it serves, its distribution channels, the major competitors, and growth trends in the industry. Each major competitor should be briefly analyzed in terms of its profit performance, industry position, strengths and weaknesses, and potential market. And the firm being studied should be analyzed and contrasted with its major competitors and with the industry as a whole.

A clear understanding of the goals and objectives of the organization is absolutely necessary for effective systems analysis and design. This may well be a troublesome area, for in most organizations these goals are not stated explicitly, or they are stated in such general terms as to be useless for systems analysis. For example, most businesses would have as a major objective the earning of a profit to provide a fair return on its investment. But such a goal must be supplemented by more specific objectives whose attainment will lead to the attainment of this overall objective. Such specific objectives might be to produce and sell a product or a service; to increase sales by 10 percent per year; to develop new products in a certain area, etc.

It is obvious that the systems analyst is in no position to determine the goals of the organization. Therefore he must somehow stimulate management to formulate these goals in usable form. This is frequently done by the iterative process of the systems analyst proposing a set of objectives, discussing them with management, revising them, discussing them, and continuing this process until agreement on this important topic is reached.

Policies and practices are the general attitudes, ideas, and philosophies that guide the organization in the attainment of its objectives. They include the general ethics of the organization and its attitudes toward employees, suppliers, customers, and the general public. They also include the company attitude toward advertising and promotion, the general philosophy of the company as to how it can best serve its customers, and the practices by which it intends to reach its goals.

Government regulations at the local, state, and national levels may enable the firm to do business, or restrict its activities, or affect the way it must keep its records. But only those government regulations that have an impact on the organization should be discussed in this report.

Structural Section

In this section the business is viewed in terms of the model shown in Figure 14–2. A business functions by receiving *inputs* from suppliers, *operating* upon them to produce *outputs* which are distributed to customers. In this process it employs human, financial, and physical *resources*. Pertinent statistics concerning these major elements of the business can be displayed on an enlarged diagram of the model.

The products of the company should be listed, and the statistics that show their distribution as a percent of sales and a percent of profit should be presented. Historical trends should be exhibited, and future plans and expectations should be projected.

The type of market should be described in terms of its basic characteristics of size, distribution channels, promotional and advertising strategies, and types and intensity of competition. Special attention should be given to seasonal or other cyclical characteristics. The customers should be categorized and analyzed by size, volume, industry, and location. And the location of sales offices, warehouses, and major sales outlets should be indicated on a map. Again, historical trends and future plans should be emphasized, for the systems analyst must acquire a picture of the future market and its characteristics.

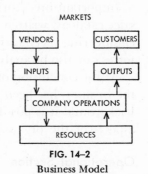

FIG. 14–2
Business Model

The inputs of materials and services, and their sources, are analyzed to reveal important characteristics that inputs may imprint on the business. Input materials should be classified by major type, with breakdowns of annual and unit costs, lead times required, and projections of trends. Major sources of supply should be classified by annual dollar volume. Competitive conditions and practices in the supply market should be summarized and any apparent future changes should be noted.

The facilities, inventories, personnel, and financial resources that are used by the company should be listed and analyzed, and future trends should be noted. The Facilities list should include land, buildings and their use, and significant production facilities. Information on location and area, whether the facilities are leased or owned, and plans for new facilities should also be included. Of special interest in a systems study are data processing equipment and communications facilities.

Financial information concerning the company is usually available from company reports, although detailed breakdowns of these figures (and even overall figures for some companies) may be confidential. Again, past trends and future projections are of particular interest.

The personnel resources of the company should be analyzed by type, skill, and cost. Information on the history of labor relations, local labor markets, turnover statistics, fringe benefits, and management attitudes toward labor should be collected. Again, past trends and future projections are valuable. An up-to-date organizational chart of the company should be obtained or created.

The various physical inventories of an organization serve as buffers that compensate for fluctuations in the production and demand for raw materials, parts, assemblies, and end items. The types of inventories maintained should be ascertained, and each type should be categorized and analyzed by total investment, unit cost, rate of usage, distribution of age, and by various cross-classifications (such as rate of usage by unit cost). The methods of inventory control employed should be noted.

Important inventories of information, such as files of information, sales catalogs, written procedures and policies, computer programs, engineering specifications, etc., should be listed. Information inventories can also be analyzed by size, rate of usage, turnover, and age.

At the conclusion of the General and Structural stages of Phase I, the business has been described in general terms. With this general background it is possible to delve more deeply into the Operational aspects of the organization.

Operational Section

One of the major tasks in Phase I is breaking the total business system down into subsystems called *activities*. An activity is a group of related operations that are *directed toward the fulfillment of one or more goals of the organization*. As a subsystem, an activity should be relatively self-contained and should have a minimum of interrelationships with other subsystems. For example, the following might be considered as activities: Develop new products; Manufacture standard products; Procure raw materials; Produce parts; Create demand and distribute products.

There are two basic approaches to the definition of activities. The *deductive* approach examines the goals defined in the General section and deduces the activities that are required to attain these goals. If the goals are unusually well-defined, or if the systems study is restricted in scope, the deductive approach may be quite satisfactory.

The *inductive* approach goes into the organization department by department and documents the *operations* observed. After all the operations are documented, the analyst attempts to group them into activities that can be related to the basic objectives of the organization. It may require considerable ingenuity (and a good deal of trial and error) to achieve an acceptable activity, which must then be subjected to management scrutiny to verify that the viewpoint developed is meaningful to management.

Whether the deductive or the inductive approach is initially employed, each probably should be checked against the other in

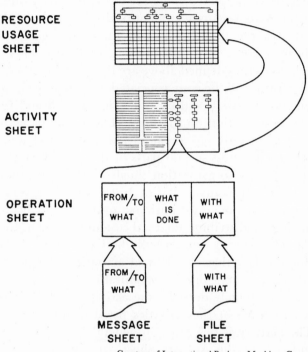

RESOURCE
USAGE
SHEET

ACTIVITY
SHEET

OPERATION
SHEET

FROM/TO WHAT	WHAT IS DONE	WITH WHAT

FROM/TO WHAT	WITH WHAT

MESSAGE
SHEET

FILE
SHEET

Courtesy of International Business Machines Corp.

FIG. 14–3

Documentation Structure of the Operation Section

order to increase the number of alternative groupings that are considered. Thus the operational groupings arrived at by deduction should be checked by studying the operations being performed, and by rearranging them to form other possible groupings. And the activities arrived at by induction should be contrasted with the deductive groupings and all discrepancies should be noted and investigated.

One must recognize that these initial definitions of activity subsystems are only preliminary: they may be repeatedly modified as the study progresses. They do, however, provide the structure for both investigation and documentation.

Documentation becomes important at this point, for it provides a framework for gathering and analyzing the pertinent data, which form a basis for the definition of systems requirements in Phase II and for the design of a new system in Phase III. The five forms employed are named and related to each other in Figure 14–3.

The summary form in the Operation section is the Resource Usage Sheet. The company organization chart (down to a suitable level of detail) is completed along the top of the chart, and a column under each box represents a segment of the organization. In the first horizontal area the total yearly cost for each organizational sub-unit is broken down into categories, as in Figure 14–4.

Then the activities defined above are listed in the other horizontal areas of the form, and the costs associated with each of these activities in each of the organizational units are determined and recorded in the appropriate position on the form. There may be activities that are performed in only one organizational unit, and there may be activities that cut across several parts of the organization, and there may be parts of the organization (such as administrative services) that are involved in many activities. In cases where several activities are performed in one organizational unit, it may be difficult to determine how to distribute the total cost among them. Incidentally, a miscellaneous activity must usually be included in the analysis to correct for the fact that the defined activities may not encompass everything that is done in the organization.

To more completely describe the activities, an Activity Sheet is completed for each of the activities listed on the Resource Usage Sheet. The activity is described in general flow chart form on the right-hand side of the Activity Sheet (rectangular boxes indicate *operations* performed and "flower pot" boxes represent inputs, outputs, and files). These flow charts are intended to be general, and they describe *what* is done rather than *how* it is done.

On the left-hand side of the form is a ruled-off area for recording important information about the operations, inputs, outputs, and files depicted in the flow chart. For each input and output, average and peak volumes are indicated. For each file we record the average and maximum number of references per day, the amount of time it is in use per day, and whether the access is sequential or random. And the time (including waiting time) for the completion of each operation is recorded for both normal and peak loads. Any other pertinent characteristics of the inputs, outputs, files, and operations are also recorded in this area.

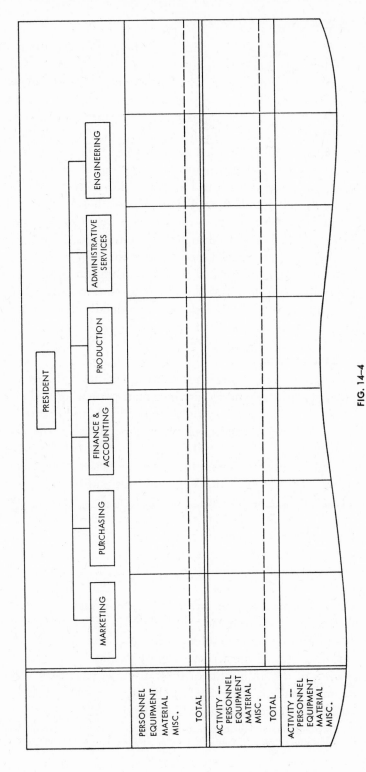

FIG. 14–4

Resource Usage Sheet

Finally, the detailed characteristics of the operations, files, and input-output messages are recorded on supporting Operation Sheets, File Sheets, and Message Sheets.[3] The Operation Sheet is organized to describe each operation in terms of the inputs and events that "trigger" the operation, the processing steps performed, the outputs produced, and the resources employed. Volumes, elapsed time, and frequency data are also recorded on this form.

Note that the above documentation provides substantial flexibility, for the depth of detail can be determined by the analyst. For example, the Activity Sheet flow chart may be rather general and be supported in detail by Operation Sheets, or it may be very detailed and thereby eliminate the need for Operation Sheets. Likewise, the File and Message sheets may be completed for only major inputs, outputs, and files. The purpose of the documentation is to assist the analyst in obtaining and analyzing useful information. Therefore the amount of information gathered and the detail of presentation depend upon the purposes of the analyst.

Report to Management

To make sure that the systems team has an adequate picture of the existing business system, and to convince management of this fact, at the conclusion of Phase I of the study the results should be presented to management in a formal, written report. This report should include the purpose of the study and the results of the general portion of the study, with emphasis on the environment of the company, on its position in this environment, and on its goals and policies. It should also include the structural model, the definition of activities, and the information presented in the Resource Usage Sheet. Supporting documentation below the Activity Sheet level should be relegated to the Appendix.

This report should be concise and readable, and should employ graphic presentation whenever possible. It should emphasize the insights obtained into the performance of the present business system, and it should indicate the areas where it appears that further effort can profitably be expended to improve the system.

The presentation of the written report should be followed by a formal review of the highlights of the report, which in turn should stimulate management's reaction to the framework that has been established for succeeding phases of the study. If this framework is

---

[3] Detailed descriptions of these forms are available in International Business Machines Corporation's *Study Organization Plan: Documentation Techniques* (Form C–20–8075) .

not satisfactory to management, that fact should be ascertained at this time. If the framework appeals to management, then it is advantageous to make sure that everyone is aware of the progress that has been made.

PHASE II: DETERMINING SYSTEMS REQUIREMENTS

The objectives of this phase are to determine what the system is required to do and to specify how the performance of the system can be measured. Up to this time attention has been concentrated upon the present and the past, but from now on the orientation is toward the future.

The output of Phase II is a report called the Systems Requirements Specification, which describes the basic characteristics of the future system, breaks it down into activities, specifies required inputs, outputs, operations, and resources for each activity, and describes the factors to be used to evaluate a subsystem designed to perform the activity.

In the process of determining the systems requirements it is necessary to re-examine the basic goals of the organization—and perhaps to modify them to produce a statement of objectives which is oriented toward the future. Then the activities required to attain these goals must be determined: either by the modification of existing activities or by the creation of new activities. These steps are by no means routine, for they may require a great deal of analysis and synthesis carried out through an iterative process of trial, testing, and checking with management.

Then each activity must be analyzed in terms of its *required* inputs, outputs, operations, and resources. Again, this is a repetitive activity that may loop back into previous steps in the process. As an activity is being characterized in its qualitative aspects, consideration should also be given to the quantitative aspects of the activity: When, how many, how large, and how can its performance be measured? Finally, the results of this analysis and synthesis must be organized into the Systems Requirements Specification.

Goal and Activity Alignment

In Phase I an attempt was made to discover the goals of the organization and to relate the activities being performed to these goals. In Phase II *management* must be encouraged to re-examine these goals and to make them as specific as possible, and especially to make any modifications that will make sure that these goals express the future objectives of the organization—for it is the needs of the future that the new system must satisfy. The long-range plans of the business (if there are any) are a valuable source of information for they may *express* the goals for the future, or reveal that the current expression of goals is inconsistent with these plans.

In Phase I the activities were defined in terms of operations in the existing system directed toward present goals. In Phase II there are two opportunities for significant improvement. First, if the goals have been modified, the activities may also need to be modified to achieve these new goals. However, even with the same goals it is possible (or even probable) that their achievement could be improved by restructuring, replacing, adding to, or modifying the existing activities. It is here that creativity can yield a handsome payoff, so it is well to remember the principles of creative thinking discussed previously—and particularly to note that creativity requires time, hard work, and a conscious effort to produce new combinations and alternatives.

After activities have been modified it is necessary to be rather specific about their definitions, for they may exist only in the minds of the systems study group and must therefore be carefully explained to management. Each activity must be described in terms of its scope and its boundaries. This description tells what is included in the activity and, to avoid confusion, it may also tell what is *not* included. The resulting descriptions should be compared with the Activity Sheets from Phase I to check for consistency and to insure that anything omitted was left out on purpose. Finally, the new activities must be reviewed and evaluated by management so as to keep everyone informed of progress, to make sure that the reformulated activities are reasonable, and to allow management to make known its preferences concerning the sequence in which these activities should be analyzed.

Activity Specifications

The major task of requirements specification is to determine precisely what each activity is required to do in terms of the outputs it must produce, the inputs it must accept, the resources it must use, and the operations it must perform. A good way to approach this problem is first to consider the outputs. After they have been determined, it is possible to infer what inputs are required and to specify the operations that must be performed and the resources that must be employed. Alternatively, it is possible to begin by specifying the inputs and then work in the opposite direction. Actually, it is usually necessary to refine this specification through several iterations, and in this process it may be desirable to use one beginning point at one time and another the next.

The outputs of an activity are usually related to the goals to which the activity contributes or they are required as inputs for some other activity. They may be subject to constraints which aid in specifying their information content or even their form. For example, government regulations, customer acceptance, or industry practice may determine the content of earnings statements, invoices, bank statements, social security and income tax reports, etc.

As we have seen in much of our work with computers, the *logic* framework is usually the most difficult part of an operation to determine and to specify precisely. In analyzing operations it is necessary to determine the cause-and-effect relationships that govern the transformation of inputs into outputs, and to specify the "triggers" that cause operations to take place. The decision logic of an operation is often expressed in terms of a block diagram. In situations involving complex logic, *decision tables*[4] provide both a documentation technique and a method of analysis.

The required operations may be determined by observation of the present system, by deduction of the steps necessary to transform inputs into outputs, or by experimentation with a real system or simulation of the proposed system.[5] Of course, whenever we work with the present system we must be sure to compensate for the fact that the requirements of the future may be different from those of the present. And whenever we experiment with actual or simulated systems we must be sure that we are working with a reasonably valid representation of the system we are studying.

The resources required include people, equipment, facilities, inventories, and information resources (files). In indicating the resources required, we must be careful to specify only those that are actually required and to be as general as possible so that we will not needlessly constrain the process of systems design in Phase III.

However, if there are constraints on the resources that cannot be violated, they should be specified. For example, management may have specified that any equipment employed must rent for less than

---

[4] Decision tables and their use will be described in a section near the end of this chapter.

[5] System simulation and its use is discussed in Chapter 17.

$10,000 per month; or the available amount of office space may be limited; or it may have been specified that the processing be done at the home office rather than be decentralized to the branches.

In addition to a detailed description of each activity, quantitative data concerning the activity must be developed. These data must be associated with the future rather than with the past or the present. Inputs and outputs must be described in terms of peak and average volumes, cycles, and trends. The operations must be analyzed in terms of the number of times per day each logical process (branch of the block diagram) must be performed, how frequently files must be referred to, how many arithmetic operations must be performed, etc. Resources must be expressed in numbers of people of each skill classification required and by the specific equipment to be used (where these are specified at this stage). The general characteristics of files (such as size in characters, access requirements, retention rules, peak and average volume of updating messages, etc.) should also be given.

Inventories present special difficulties, for although it may be obvious that an inventory is required, the *amount* that is necessary may be difficult to estimate. This amount is related to the volume and pattern of the demands which the inventory must serve and to the decision rules employed in the management of the inventory. Of course, some of this quantitative information concerning inventory levels may not be determinable at this point, for inventory performance may depend upon the characteristics of the system that will be designed in Phase III. However, the patterns of demand should be described, and any constraints imposed on the performance of the inventory (such as the average time to serve a demand or the permissible percent of stockouts allowable) should be stated.

At this point each activity should be clearly specified in terms of its inputs, outputs, operations, and required resources; and this specification and the associated quantitative data should be recorded on special forms, as in Phase I. Operations logic should be described by block diagrams or decision tables. Note that the above description is intended to specify exactly *what* the system is required to do, but it should be as free as possible from constraints concerning *how* it is to be accomplished. It is obvious that this is not accomplished by a straightforward step-by-step process but requires much repetition and experimentation to arrive at a specification that blends realism and creativity to obtain requirements that provide the basis for improved systems performance.

Performance Measurement Criteria

In order to provide guidance for systems design in Phase III, it is necessary to establish the criteria of performance which the system must satisfy. This requires that we first select characteristics that are important indications of the performance of the system and specify how they may be measured. Then we must specify minimum and desired values (or ranges) of each of these parameters.

It would be nice if there were an easy way to specify the performance of a system in terms of a single unit of measurement, such as dollars per transaction, or seconds of delay, or the ability to handle a certain number of transactions per day. Unfortunately, however, there is seldom only one such characteristic that is of importance, and there are many difficulties in combining them into a single measure of effectiveness.[6] Therefore, for each activity we will specify the criteria which are important measures of the performance of that activity in contributing to its goals.

The following list includes several major measurement categories, but others may also be important in specific cases:[7]

1. Cost—operating, maintenance, unit.
2. Time—response (input, operations), access, elapsed, cycle, process, turnover.
3. Accuracy—frequency and number of errors, significance of errors.
4. Reliability—stability, durability, life.
5. Security—legal, safety.
6. Quality—appearance, tolerance.
7. Flexibility—variability, sensitivity.
8. Capacity—average load, low load, peak load.
9. Efficiency—performance ratios.
10. Acceptance—customer, employee, managerial, shareholder.

After deciding upon the important measurement factors, a rating scale should be constructed for each factor for each activity. As shown in Figure 14–5, this scale may include indications of the present system's performance (where there is comparability between the present and future system).

The task of specifying acceptable ranges for each measurement

---

[6] This problem is of major concern in Operations Research, and most introductory books on this subject contain an extensive discussion of these difficulties and possible ways to avoid or solve this problem.

[7] This list is quoted from *Study Organization Plan: The Method, Phase II* (Form F20–8137), International Business Machines Corporation.

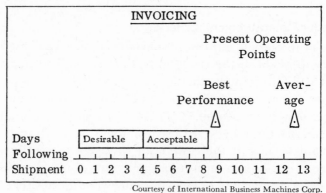

Courtesy of International Business Machines Corp.

FIG. 14–5

Rating Scale for Invoicing

factor may be difficult, for this may be hard to pin down. It is tempting simply to put down a number that is better than the present system, but this decision will be an important determinant of the system designed in Phase III and therefore deserves careful thought. In fact, it is likely that the determination of these ranges cannot be done by the systems analyst alone—management must

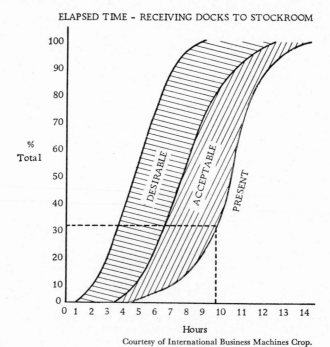

Courtesy of International Business Machines Crop.

FIG. 14–6

Distribution Curves as Performance Criteria

participate in this task. The interplay between the systems analyst and management during the process of determining acceptable values for performance criteria may have important by-products, for the perceptive systems analyst can obtain significant indications of hidden opinions, prejudices, values, and pressures on management, all of which may be invaluable in designing a new system.

After acceptable and desirable values are determined, they should be shown on the rating scale (as in Figure 14–5). Some performance measures cannot be realistically specified in terms of average or of maximum values but must be shown by distribution curves, as in Figure 14–6. The dotted lines on this figure indicate that 30 percent of the total number of items processed is handled in 10 hours or less, but it would be desirable if they were handled in less time (in 3 to 6 hours).

Systems Requirements Specification Report

At the end of Phase II a Systems Requirements Specification Report that incorporates the results of the Phase II analysis must be presented to management. This report should include a packet for each activity, preceded by a summary section which integrates the activities and sets forth the impact of the overall analysis on the performance of the entire business system. Thus the activity subsystems must be related back to the overall systems performance.

In each activity packet there should be a statement of the (perhaps new) goals and objectives, and a precise statement of the scope and boundaries of the activities. Then the activity should be described in terms of its inputs, outputs, operations, and required resources, and this specification should be backed up (perhaps in the Appendix) with documentation such as flow charts, decision tables, specifications of input and output requirements, etc. Finally, the measurement factors and performance criteria for the activity must be presented (preferably graphically).

As at the end of Phase I, this report must be carefully reviewed with management, for unless management really understands it and approves its contents, the study team does not have a firm basis for going on to design the new system.

PHASE III: DESIGNING THE NEW SYSTEM

The objective of Phase III is to create a management information system that best satisfies the requirements of the organization, as set forth in the Systems Requirements Specification produced in Phase II. This system must be described, documented, and evaluated, and a plan for implementing the system must be devised.

Again, the process of systems design is almost impossible to describe because its essence is creativity, and the complex trial-and-error processes that lead to creativity are not well understood. However, we can attempt to apply the general approaches to creativity that were described earlier in this chapter, and we can specify a structural approach to the task of systems design which can serve as a guidepost along the way.

First, it is desirable to analyze each activity separately and to develop several alternative approaches to the performance of each activity. Then we consider the entire system, analyze the interactions among activities, and modify the subsystems to take advantage of these interactions. Then we determine the most effective equipment configuration for each of the various overall systems designs under consideration, evaluate each overall design as implemented, and select the best system. Finally, this system must be evaluated in terms of its impact on the performance of the organization, and it must be documented for presentation to management.

Basic System Design

In order to begin the basic system design it is desirable to start with the "dominant" activity—the activity that involves the most cost, or appears to be most inefficient in the present system, or is most crucial to the performance of the overall system, or is of major concern to management. Then each element of this activity should be analyzed to determine its characteristics and to establish alternate ways in which it could be handled.

Input characteristics are frequently crucial to systems design because much time, effort, and expense may be involved in converting information into machine-processable form. The characteristics of the input data must be scrutinized and exhaustively questioned. Can inputs be batched, or must they be handled on an individual basis? Can this input be created in machine-processable form rather than be converted to this form? What are the accuracy requirements of input—how much verification is necessary? Can inputs be entered directly into the system, or should they be edited, verified, and converted to a machine-processable form on an off-line basis? Can inputs be processed in random sequence, or must they be sequenced before processing? Are there time constraints on the inputs? Are there significant fluctuations in input volume that will affect system performance?

The content and form of output may have significant impacts upon the design of the system, and should be similarly scrutinized. Should output be produced on a routine basis, or only on demand? Should output be printed, or must it be in display or audio form—or should it be in machine-processable form for entry into another subsystem or for re-entry into the same activity? How much summarization of the output is desirable? What are the requirements on format, readability, number of copies desired, and types of forms to be used? Can output be produced off-line? Must output be distributed to remote locations?

As a result of the above analysis it should be possible to begin to eliminate methods of input and output and to specify possible approaches, such as punched card, magnetic tape, off-line printer, remote input-output units, graphic display, character sensing, etc.

Possibilities for processing may also be examined to determine the character and complexity of the operations involved. Should processing be random or sequential? What are the accuracy and audit requirements? Is the operation primarily logic, or arithmetic, or Table Look-up, or file reference? Can exceptions be processed separately, or must all exceptions be included in the main procedures? Can processing be interrupted? How automatic must the system be?

The characteristics of the files are frequently of major importance to systems design. How large is the file? How frequently is the file referenced? How fast does it grow? How frequently must it be updated? Can several files be consolidated? In how many ways is the file referenced, and is there more than one control key?

After examining the characteristics of the various elements of the activity, basic design alternatives should be considered. Design alternatives are built around design concepts which provide the framework for processing. Here is an opportunity to apply a basic approach to creativity: concentration upon the formulation of many possible alternative design concepts. These concepts may be created especially to fit the situation, but they may also be adapted from past experience and from a broad knowledge of approaches that have been useful in other situations.

As examples of design concepts, let us recall the illustrations in Chapter 10 of the use of the basic MAC. Each illustrated an important design concept. The parts requirement example was an illustration of transaction-file reversal. Instead of processing the new schedule as the transactions against the bill of materials file, the bill of materials (in where-used sequence) was processed as the transactions against the schedule stored as a table. The insurance rate-checking and coding illustration was an example of the concept of recalculation as a substitute for reference to large files. The utility billing example incorporated the concept of handling the bulk of the transactions in one run and processing the unusual exceptions in another way. And the overhead cost allocation illustration showed how mathematical techniques might provide design concepts for data processing. Other design concepts that we have discussed include file consolidation, real-time systems, and centralized processing for decentralized operations through communications networks.

After considering as many design concepts as possible, along with various combinations of these concepts, it will be obvious that some are more appealing than others. Those that appear promising should be investigated further and tentatively evaluated, and those that survive this process should be described in a *generic* system description. The generic system description is a general description of an approach to processing, but it is not expressed in terms of detailed machine specifications, nor are the details of a procedure included. This generic description may be expressed in narrative form or in terms of a general flow chart.

After the above process (resulting in one or more generic descriptions) has been completed for each major activity, it is necessary to consider the interactions between subsystems and to combine them into generic descriptions of several basic approaches to the overall management information system. Frequently there will be opportunities for file consolidation among activities, or for the elimination of input-output interfaces between activities.

There may also be incompatibilities among the preferred design alternatives of the various activities. For example, a generic procedure for one activity may be based upon real-time response through a communications network, while another activity may be based on a concept of uninterrupted batch processing. If both these activities are to employ the same equipment, compromises may have to be worked out or another design alternative may have to be adopted for one of the activities. This is frequently accomplished by selecting the most attractive approaches to the one or two dominant activities and then adapting the other activities to the resulting constraints.

At the conclusion of the basic system design stage there should be several alternative generic designs for the overall information system. If this process has been carried out in a thorough and creative manner, the resulting alternatives should provide a number of well-thought-out and attractive alternative systems, all of which have been designed to contribute to the overall objectives of the organization. Which of these alternatives is the best depends upon the costs and systems performance obtained when each is implemented with specific equipment.

System Selection

System selection involves the development of the most efficient equipment configuration for each alternative generic system design, evaluation of the cost and performance of each design alternative as implemented with the selected equipment, and the selection of the best of these systems.

For a given design alternative, the first task is to hypothesize types of equipment that might reasonably be considered. This task is simplified by the fact that cost constraints and performance criteria are usually specified in the Phase II report. For example, if the present cost of the entire system does not exceed $7,000 per month, and no improvements are being considered that radically alter the operations of the business, it is logical to eliminate consideration of large-scale tape-oriented computers. Instead, punched card equipment, card-oriented computers, small computers with random access files, or small computers with tape files might logically be considered. Constraints in the delays involved in producing some reports might eliminate certain types of equipment, leaving only a few basic types. However, there still may be considerable complexity because several manufacturers may produce equipment of each basic type that should be considered.

In this process of considering basic machine alternatives it may become obvious that certain criteria developed in Phase II are particularly expensive to satisfy. For example, the requirement that certain information be available by 4:00 P.M. may require a fast machine that can do the job in one shift, although the information could be produced before 8:00 A.M. the next day by using a slower machine on a two-shift basis. Under such circumstances it would be well to consult with management to see if the time saved is worth the extra cost involved.

After the most promising equipment configurations for each system alternative have been specified, it is necessary to get down to detailed analysis of procedures and machine specifications. Although many combinations of equipment and design alternatives may have to be evaluated, at least we are back to familiar ground, for we have frequently encountered this type of problem in preceding chapters. For each alternative, the procedure must be broken down into machine runs, file organization must be specified, rough block diagrams prepared, and total run time estimated. (Note, however, that we are now able to modify the equipment characteristics in order to improve the efficiency of the system, where before we assumed that the equipment available was fixed.) The number and type of input-output units, channels, and file units, the amount of memory, and the special features (such as floating-point arithmetic) may be modified as the detailed procedures are being formulated. Again, it is desirable to begin this process with the dominant activities and then modify the equipment specifications where necessary to accommodate the other activities.

After this process has been completed for each combination of a design alternative with an equipment configuration, the costs associated with each such combination can be determined. Then it is necessary to choose the most effective combination in terms of the "profit" it produces; i.e., the difference between the cost of the system and its value. In this selection process we use the performance criteria established in Phase II and subject each criterion to the question: What is this type of performance really worth? In answering this question we must also consider some additional factors, such as the cost of converting to the new system, the flexibility of the system for accommodating unforeseen developments in the future, and so on.

In the above discussion we have outlined an approach to a very complex problem, but we have emphasized the iterative nature of the reasoning involved. We wish to design a system that will maximize the profit it produces—that maximizes the difference between the value of the information and its cost. To do this we must specify certain design objectives, design a system to achieve these objectives, specify equipment to achieve this system, and, finally, determine the cost involved.

Unfortunately, these costs may be quite sensitive to the postulated performance criteria, so it may be necessary to ask: What would happen to cost if these criteria were relaxed? It is important that management recognize the sensitive nature of the relationships between performance and cost, and that management be willing to become involved in the value judgments and decisions required to iterate toward the most profitable system.

The New System Plan

The design of the new system has not been completed until a report has been presented that describes the system, presents its advantages and its costs, and describes how it can be implemented. This report is of great importance because it provides much of the information that management must use in deciding whether or not to implement the new system. Besides being carefully prepared, it should also be aimed at the audience that will make this decision.

The information generated in the systems study must be summarized in this report. The summary should include an abstract for top management that succinctly presents the characteristics of the new system, an objective appraisal of its advantages, benefits, and savings, the new system's operating costs (as contrasted with those of the present system), and the time and cost investment involved in implementing the new system.

This report should also include a presentation for operating management that describes the new system in sufficient detail so that its effect upon the day-by-day operations of the business can be evaluated. This presentation should include more detailed charts than are presented in the management abstract. It should also include a presentation of the proposed equipment configuration that includes pictures and descriptions of the individual units, and it should describe the impact of the new system on the organization structure and personnel requirements.

Detailed plans for implementing the new system should be developed and presented in this report in terms of the activities required (such as detailed system design, programming, debugging, installation of the equipment, and conversion), and also in terms of the time, cost, and skills required. These matters will be given further consideration in Chapter 16.

Finally, the cost and value of the new system must be presented and contrasted with the present system. To determine the performance of the new system it may be necessary to simulate all or part of the system and observe the results obtained. Simulation is frequently required in situations with complex interactions and close timing that may involve queues of transactions waiting for processing.

In summary, the new system plan should be a "selling" document that presents the advantages of the new system which have been created by the complex interaction of the systems design team and management. But it must be more than just a sales pitch, for it must include a realistic analysis of the impact of the new system on the performance of the organization and it must contain a plan for implementation. Thus it also serves as a firm foundation for successful implementation and operation of the new system.

DECISION TABLES

In the preceding discussion of systems analysis and design we have frequently referred to a technique of analysis that is sufficiently important to warrant further treatment in this section. Logical networks of branching questions, which we have heretofore presented in block diagram form, can also be expressed by means of *decision tables*. The latter means of presentation has two major advantages. First, by ignoring the order in which the branching questions are asked, the basic logic involved can be expressed in a simpler and more concise form. Second, the decision table form provides a framework for analysis which makes it easier to check to see that all the logical possibilities have been considered.

The upper portion of a decision table is concerned with conditions (or questions) that determine what should be done, and the lower portion is concerned with the actions to be taken. The conditions and actions are written in the left-hand (or stub) portion of the table, where there is one line for each condition or action. The columns of the table correspond to rules, directions, or instructions. Each rule corresponds to a specific set of conditions, and states the actions that are to be taken when those conditions are satisfied.

Example

Suppose we are handling $5.00, $3.00, and $1.00 ticket orders for a play and the application asks whether the customer will accept tickets in a lower-priced section if the seats requested are sold out. A decision table for our analysis is shown in Figure 14–7. Rule 2 states that if seats for $5.00 requests are not available, but $3.00 seats are available—and the customer will accept lower-priced tickets— send him $3.00 tickets and return $2.00 per ticket.

Several important characteristics of a decision table can be observed in this illustration. First, a blank square under a rule number means that the condition is immaterial. If the condition must *not* be satisfied, this is indicated by an N. But *all* the conditions for a rule (both positive and negative) must be satisfied simultaneously if the rule is to be applied. Note also that the rules are mutually exclusive: the conditions for one and only one rule can be satisfied by any ticket request. Therefore, the order in which rules are considered makes no difference, and the order in which the conditions are examined has no influence on the choice of a rule. However (although it is not illustrated in the example), the actions are to be performed in the order in which they are listed.

The entry in the first line of the Figure 14–7 decision table is part of the *condition,* not a Yes or No direction. Similarly, the entries in rows 6 and 7 describe a part of the *action* to be taken. Both of these lines are said to be in "extended entry form," while those containing

Table No. 1 Rule	1	2	3	4	5	6	7	8	9
Request is for	$5	$5	$5	$5	$3	$3	$3	$1	$1
$5 seats available	Y	N	N	N					
$3 seats available		Y	N		Y	N	N		
$1 seats available			Y			Y		Y	N
Will accept lower-priced seats		Y	Y	N		Y	N		
Send tickets costing	$5	$3	$1		$3	$1		$1	
Refund per ticket		$2	$4	$5		$2	$3		$1

FIG. 14–7
Decision Table for Filling Ticket Orders

only Y's, N's, or blanks are said to be in "limited entry form." Either form can be used for a line, but any line must be *either* extended entry *or* limited entry, *not both.* An equivalent table in limited entry form is shown in Figure 14–8.

Note that the limited entry table is usually longer than an equivalent extended entry table, but the columns in the extended entry table are usually wider (because it usually takes more space to write a condition than to write a Y or N). Note also that in limited entry form analysis of the conditions, to determine whether all the necessary rules have been expressed, is relatively straightforward. For example, examining Figure 14–8 we might ask: Could more than one type of seat be requested in a single order? If the answer is yes, the number of rules would have to be expanded, or the table would have to be used more than once for processing orders with requests for more than one type of ticket.

Linking Tables Together

In order to link decision tables together we may specify (as one of the actions) *where to go next in the procedure.* Thus the last action

Table No. 1 Rule	1	2	3	4	5	6	7	8	9
$5 seats requested	Y	Y	Y	Y	N	N	N	N	N
$3 seats requested	N	N	N	N	Y	Y	Y	N	N
$1 seats requested	N	N	N	N	N	N	N	Y	Y
$5 seats available	Y	N	N	N					
$3 seats available		Y	N		Y	N	N		
$1 seats available			Y			Y		Y	N
Will accept lower-priced seats		Y	Y	N		Y	N		
Send $5 tickets	X								
Send $3 tickets		X		X					
Send $1 tickets			X			X		X	
Refund $5 per ticket				X					
Refund $4 per ticket			X						
Refund $3 per ticket							X		
Refund $2 per ticket		X				X			
Refund $1 per ticket									X

FIG. 14–8

Limited Entry Decision Table

line may be an extended entry row with "Go to," and a table name (or number) would be inserted under each rule.

Furthermore, it is possible to specify that a decision table is *closed,* and then it is employed as though it were a closed subroutine. Closed tables are entered by an action row which says "Do table n." After table n is completed it does not itself specify where to go next, but instead the next step in the procedure is specified by the next action line following the "Do table n." Thus, in addition to expressing complex branching logic, decision tables can incorporate closed subroutines.

It is apparent that decision tables are a powerful supplement, or substitute, for block diagrams. The more complex the logic, the more appealing decision tables become. However, to translate a decision table into a machine program it is necessary to decide in what order to ask the questions so as to provide the most efficient program. Among other things, this may depend upon the relative frequency with which the rules will be employed. Given such information, it appears feasible to design procedure-oriented programming languages that convert decision tables directly into machine programs.

SUMMARY

The information system is crucial to the effective performance of an organization. It should be viewed as an integrated system whose design is of major importance to management. Not a very "straightforward" task, systems analysis and design involves a good understanding of the organization, considerable creativity, and the active participation of management.

A structural approach to systems design—based upon IBM's Study Organization Plan—has been outlined to provide guidance in the creative task of designing a new data processing system. This plan involves three phases: Understanding the present business, Determining systems requirements, and then Designing the new system.

Much of the effort in understanding the present system is concerned with the goals, policies, and environment of the organization. Then the present system is described in terms of activities, which are subsystems structured around the goals of the organization. A basic description of these activities—expressed in terms of what is done rather than how it is accomplished—is obtained and documented.

In Phase II, the goals of the organization are re-examined and then modified so as to conform to our projection of the *future*. Activities are then realigned to accord with these goals. Finally, performance measures are devised for these activities and expressed in quantitative terms.

The design of the new system is based upon the understanding and targets produced in the first two phases. A basic principle of creativity is to devise a large number of alternatives from which to choose, and the systems designer accordingly calls upon all his experience and ingenuity to develop a number of attractive alternatives. Each of these alternatives must be implemented with one or more sets of suitable equipment, after which it is possible to compare results and select the most favorable design-equipment combination. Finally, the most favorable alternative must be evaluated to determine its impact on the organization, and implementation plans must be developed.

One important feature of the structure outlined above is its emphasis upon the place of management in the task of systems design. This structural approach not only provides for management participation where required, it also insists upon adequate documentation and *communication* with management at the end of each phase.

This procedure, however, is by no means as straightforward as it may seem: much interaction between phases and many iterations are necessary to produce an effective system. The output results desired and the procedures and equipment used are intimately related because the desirability of a particular set of results is heavily dependent upon their costs, which are determined by the procedures and the equipment employed. Since the basic objective of data processing is to contribute to management control, the systems analyst and the manager must cooperate in the design of a data processing system that will maximize the data processing profit: the difference between the value for management control of the information produced and the cost of producing it.

EXERCISES

14.1 What are the most important abilities required for success in systems analysis and design work?

14.2 If you were beginning a system study, what types of meaningful intermediate targets might you set when planning the overall allocation of time and effort?

14.3 What are the most difficult problems involved in obtaining a representation of an existing data processing system?

14.4 Why and how is management involved in the task of systems analysis and design?

14.5 *a)* Is it reasonable to compare two computers feature by feature (that is, amount of memory, arithmetic speed, tape speed and density, word size, instruction format, etc.) ? Why?

b) What information in addition to the above is required to decide upon the type of equipment that should be employed?

14.6 Analyze problem 6.32 by means of a decision table.

14.7   Analyze the following narrative problem[8] by means of a decision table.

When the quantity ordered for a particular item does not exceed the order limit and the credit approved is "OK," move the quantity-ordered amount to the quantity-shipped field; then go to a table to prepare a shipment release. Of course, there must be a sufficient quantity on hand to fill the order.

When the quantity ordered exceeds the order limit, go to a table named "Order reject." Do the same if the credit approval is not "OK."

Occasionally the quantity ordered does not exceed the order limit, credit approval is "OK," but there is insufficient quantity on hand to fill the order. In this case, go to a table named "Back order."

SUPPLEMENTAL READINGS

Basic System Study Guide. International Business Machines Corporation, White Plains, N.Y. (1963).

This 40-page booklet describes the Study Organization Plan. It is aimed at the man in a small organization who knows something about equipment but has had little experience in systems analysis and design.

Decision Tables—A Systems Analysis and Documentation Technique. International Business Machines Corporation, White Plains, N.Y. (1962).

Describes and illustrates the use of decision tables; also includes some excellent and rather complicated examples.

DIXON, PAUL. "Decision Tables and Their Application," *Computers and Automation,* April, 1964, pp. 14–19.

Presents a description of decision tables and illustrates their use.

IBM Study Organization Plan: *The Approach* (Form F20–8135); *The Method, Phase I* (Form F20–8136); *The Method, Phase II* (Form F20–8137); *The Method, Phase III* (Form F20–8138); and *Documentation Techniques* (Form C20–8075). International Business Machines Corporation, White Plains, N.Y. (1963).

These booklets describe in detail the Study Organization Plan outlined in this chapter, and contain much illustrative material that is of great value in understanding the approach presented.

MC DONOUGH, ADRIAN M. *Information Economics and Management Systems.* New York: McGraw-Hill Book Co., Inc., 1963.

In addition to an interesting discussion of the value of information, this book presents a structure of concepts that are important in systems analysis and design work.

MEE, JOHN F. "The Creative Thinking Process," *Selected Readings in*

---

[8] This problem is taken, by permission, from *Decision Tables—A Systems Analysis and Documentation Technique,* published by International Business Machines Corporation (Form F20–8102) p. 8.

Management, pp. 150–55. Fremont A. Shull, Jr. (ed.) . Homewood, Ill.: Richard D. Irwin, Inc., 1958.

An excellent discussion of the creative thinking process.

OPTNER, STANFORD L. *Systems for Business Management.* Englewood Cliffs, N.J.: Prentice-Hall, Inc., 1960.

This book is devoted to the principles and techniques of systems analysis and design. In addition to an excellent presentation of the importance of planning and scheduling systems work, it also includes a number of checklists that are useful to the systems analyst. Ten short cases are included at the end of this book.

POLYA, G. *How to Solve It.* Princeton, N.J.: Princeton University Press, 1948.

This interesting little book is concerned with the development of a general approach to the solving of problems. Although written for teachers of mathematics, it is easily understandable and is useful for anyone who must solve problems.

15 THE DATA
PROCESSING ORGANIZATION

A COMBINATION of inadequate administration and organizational problems associated with the data processing function has been responsible for many of the difficulties that have arisen in the use of electronic data processing machines. Frequently, data processing is poorly organized and administered without attracting attention, but when a computer enters the picture the resultant centralization of data processing, together with the costs involved, combine to make these inadequacies painfully apparent. In connection with these problems, two closely related questions arise. First, where does the data processing function fit into the overall organizational structure? This important question will be discussed in Chapter 16. Second, how should the data processing function be organized and administered? This question, and others associated with it, will be discussed in the present chapter.

The following discussion will be based on the assumption that our major concern is the establishment of an effective data processing system for management control of the organization. The number of people and type of equipment involved depend upon the size of the organization and its data processing problems, but the basic tasks to be accomplished and the difficulties to be overcome are essentially the same, whether the organization is large or small.

A variety of approaches may be taken in organizing the data processing function. Figure 15–1 shows one possible organization, and while it is by no means the only effective possibility, it includes most of the functions that must be performed and thus can serve as a framework for further discussion. When appropriate, the characteristics desirable in those who fill these jobs will be described.

455

OVERALL MANAGEMENT

The importance of placing the right man in the position of manager of data processing cannot be overemphasized, for the success or failure of the entire mechanization effort is as dependent upon his managerial ability as upon any other single factor. The introduction of a computer or a punched card system entails a myriad of administrative problems, some within the data processing organization itself and others involved with the consequent changes in other parts of the organization.

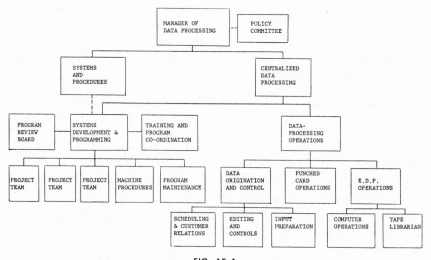

FIG. 15–1

Typical Organization for Data Processing

The function of the manager of data processing is to plan and administer the operation of the data processing system. He has responsibility for the design and implementation of a data processing system that will provide the information required for adequate management control of the organization. Although only the centralized portion of the data processing *work* is under his direct control, he is responsible for the *planning* necessary to achieve an integrated information system.

This position is difficult to fill, for the manager of data processing must possess a variety of capabilities. In the first place, he must operate on a relatively high level within the organization, and, to be effective, he must have the confidence and respect of the entire organization. He must possess a depth of vision capable of comprehending the information requirements of the entire organization, and must have the ability to lead the various components of the organization to accept an integrated data processing system. In addition to having a natural ability to sell ideas, he should be a master of the strategies involved in getting things done, for he must know who must be sold, when to attack—and when and how to retreat. He should be an excellent administrator, for he will be responsible for planning and administering a complex process of change, extending over a period of several years, during which a succession of interrelated steps affecting the entire organization must be scheduled and accomplished. Finally, although not primarily concerned with technical details, he must be capable of assimilating enough of the technology of data processing to be able to interpret its significance for the data processing function and for the entire organization.

Many difficulties that have plagued organizations which have ordered computers arose because the responsibilities of the manager of data processing have been placed upon the shoulders of men who were technically qualified, but had neither the administrative ability nor the reputation within the organization to successfully perform the required functions. The assignment of the proper man to this position can be accomplished only if management is committed to the proposition that data processing is important, for such men are scarce and of great value.

The first question asked, of course, is: Where can we find a man with these qualifications? There is a temptation to search outside the organization for some experienced electronic data processing man to fill this position. However, experience has shown that this man must come from within the organization, for his success or failure will depend upon his knowledge of the organization and managers with whom he will be working, his reputation within the company, and his administrative ability. Such men can be found in most successful organizations. The major problem is that they cannot be spared. Any man that can be spared for this job probably should be automatically disqualified.

If the organization is planning ahead, rather than attempting to institute a crash program, it is possible to bring in a good man from outside and allow him to serve in an advisory capacity for a year or two. Then, if he shapes up well, he can be given line responsibility for the data processing function.

This brings up the question of timing: When should this position be created? A qualified man should be placed in this position *before* the decision is made to acquire a computer, for the most effective way to decide whether or not to get a computer (and if so, which one) is to develop and use portions of the organization shown in Figure 15–1 for this purpose. There is little to be gained from excessive haste in acquiring a computer, and most organizations are far from ready to use one when it arrives. In contrast to a crash program, it is highly desirable to take the time required to find the proper man, acquire and train the people required, thoroughly study the data processing system, and decide upon the data processing tools that should be used.

If, after doing this, it is decided that a computer is not required, it will be because a better way to achieve the data processing objectives of the organization has been devised.

The Data Processing Policy Committee

A common practice has been to establish an electronic data processing policy committee, composed of the heads of the areas which may be affected by the mechanization, to make basic policy decisions concerning the management information system. It should be emphasized that the establishment of such a committee is no substitute for obtaining a manager of data processing with the capabilities outlined above. Also, many of the decisions that have sometimes been made haphazardly by such a committee should be made on the basis of an analysis by a competent systems and procedures group (as outlined in Chapter 14).

However, even with a well qualified manager of data processing and a competent systems and procedures group, a functioning policy committee is still required to establish fundamental objectives. It can also perform a valuable service by assuring the cooperation of the entire organization in the development and installation of an integrated data processing system.

Systems and Procedures

One of the most important groups reporting to the manager of data processing should be the group concerned with systems and procedures planning for the entire organization. The fact that in many organizations the only such group is referred to as *office methods* or *office procedures* and is primarily concerned with the details of paper work and forms design is a reflection of the fact that this important function is frequently neglected.

As was emphasized in Chapters 2 and 14, the basic problem

associated with data processing is determining what information is necessary for proper management control. A second problem is how such information can most efficiently be provided.

These two problems are interrelated, of course, for the desirability of information is at least partially determined by the cost of providing it. The major function of the systems and procedures group should be the solution of such problems. This group should be concerned with designing the overall data processing system and with devising its general procedures. Since they are responsible for the design of an integrated system that may involve manual steps, semi-mechanized steps, punched card processes, and the use of an electronic computer, the members of this group must have an understanding of the capabilities and limitations of all data processing tools. And, since this group is responsible for expressing the overall system objectives, those who compose it must thoroughly understand the objectives and policies of management.

Such an organization is not created instantly; it must be developed over a period of years. The development of such a group should precede the acquiring of a computer, for this decision should be made on the basis of systems requirements that have been specified by the systems and procedures group. If a competent systems and procedures group does not exist in an organization, its development is of infinitely greater importance than the acquisition of a computer or any other data processing tools, for without proper overall objectives and a satisfactorily designed data processing system, tools alone are not likely to provide a solution to data processing problems.

Management of Centralized Data Processing

The manager of centralized data processing is frequently titled "manager of mechanized data processing" or "manager of electronic data processing." He is in charge of both the development and the operation of mechanized systems. During the installation of a mechanized data processing system he has the responsibility of developing a technical staff, programming and installing the computer, and converting the data processing to the mechanized system. Obviously, this also is a key position in the organization.

Besides being a man of proven administrative ability, the manager of centralized data processing must also be something of a salesman, for the attitude of the personnel outside the data processing organization toward mechanization of data processing will be favorably or unfavorably affected by his personality. Although he need not be a professional machine programmer, he will be called upon to make decisions that involve technical questions, and so should have a certain amount of technical ability. Again, it is desirable that this man come from within the organization rather than be hired as an expert from outside.

In many companies the positions of manager of data processing and manager of centralized data processing are combined, and this can be satisfactory. However, the distinction between them is that the top position is primarily concerned with the overall data processing policies and objectives of the organization, while the manager of centralized data processing is more concerned with the means by which these objectives may be attained and with the administration of the internal operation of the centralized processing organization. Neglect of either job gravely jeopardizes the successful utilization of electronic data processing equipment.

Two basic tasks are involved in a data processing center. As will be discussed in Chapter 16, the period between the ordering of a computer and its installation must be devoted to systems development and programming. The computer is gradually put to productive use in routine data processing operations, but the development of new systems and the improvement of old programs continues at a high level for a long, long time. Because routine operation and the development of new systems are dissimilar activities, they are performed by separate portions of the organization.

SYSTEMS DEVELOPMENT AND PROGRAMMING

The detailed design and implementation of mechanized procedures and the writing and debugging of machine programs are the responsibility of the systems development and programming group. As shown by the dotted line in Figure 15–1, there must be close coordination between this group and the systems and procedures group to insure that decisions concerning what data processing areas to mechanize are properly influenced by technical considerations.

Where the two positions of manager of centralized data processing and manager of data processing are combined, these two systems groups are also merged. Again, the two groups represent the particular viewpoints of the two managerial positions, which, if they are combined, requires that adequate consideration be given to the planning of both overall data processing and the mechanized portions of the system. With a single group there is a strong tendency to concentrate exclusively on the mechanized aspects and to ignore the less glamorous manual and semimechanized techniques.

The program review committee, composed of the best systems analysts and programmers in the organization, has the function of reviewing proposed procedures to determine whether they are likely to result in efficient computer programs and of monitoring development of programs to see that an efficient and integrated system is produced. Proper use of such a committee can prevent many of the mistakes which tend to plague new organizations of inexperienced men.

The training and program coordination function associated with systems development and programming is responsible for the development of a uniform philosophy for flow diagramming, block diagramming, and programming, including the selection or development of suitable automatic programming systems for the organization. Such standard procedures and philosophies will substantially reduce the communication difficulties within the organization, as well as the problems involved in debugging and in the future modification of programs and procedures. This group is also charged with keeping the entire organization "educated" on the latest technical developments in programming and equipment; and is responsible for the training of new personnel.

If the electronic data processing group is to function efficiently, the above functions must be effectively performed. Those performing these functions *must* be expert technicians, and, if they do not already exist in the organization, it is acceptable to hire experienced men from outside.

Organization of Systems Development and Programming

The systems development and programming group may be organized in a variety of ways. For example, it may be organized according to the functions of procedures development, block diagramming, and programming, with a separate group performing each function for all applications. As was discussed in Chapter 9, because of the interrelationships between the steps in the overall process of converting to computer processing, it is better to organize this group in teams, each of which is responsible for the systems analysis, block diagramming, programming, debugging, and conversion of an entire application. Usually a team consists of from two to five people, headed by a senior systems analyst.

Personnel for systems analysis and programming usually come from within the organization and are trained in computer techniques by the machine manufacturer or by the training and program coordination group. It is said that it is easier to teach the machine to someone who knows the data processing problem than it is to teach the problem to someone who knows the machine. Thus these people are frequently drawn from the areas of the organization that are to be mechanized, although people possessing a wide variety of backgrounds (including accountants, engineers, mathematicians, industrial engineers, and trainees just out of college) have been used. Aptitude tests are available which can be used to screen out people who probably do not have the logical and abstract reasoning ability to perform these functions.

The belief that it is easier to teach programming to someone who knows the job than to teach the job to someone who knows programming has likely led some organizations into the trap of minimizing the importance of experience and technical ability in this area. It is highly desirable that there be a competent, experienced nucleus at the start (perhaps people brought in from outside the company), around which a technically competent group can be developed, and which at the same time will provide the experience that prevents the group from having to learn everything by repeating the common mistakes.

In some organizations the systems development and programming functions are performed entirely within the sections for which the data processing is to be done, with the people involved being drawn from these areas, and trained by the data processing organization, but never actually leaving their own areas and becoming a part of the electronic data processing group. This approach is not likely to lead to the development of an integrated system.

In other organizations these people are attached to the electronic data processing organization while the systems development and programming is being done, and are returned to their parental organizations at the completion of the project. Frequently the teams are made up of one or two people from the central data processing organization and one or two people from the area to be served. In other organizations the entire job is done by professional systems analysts and programmers permanently attached to the electronic data processing organization.

Because skill and experience in systems development and programming are highly desirable to produce efficient results, it appears desirable to have professional members of the data processing organization on each team. On the other hand, because of their knowledge of the application to be mechanized and because of their established relationships with the people working in these areas, it may be helpful to include on the team one or more people from the area to be mechanized. Thus, teams made up of both types of people may have the advantages of both without the limitations of either.

Program Maintenance

Even after a machine program has been written and debugged, and the conversion made to computer processing, the systems analysis and programming job has not been fully completed. A data processing system must be dynamic rather than static. The programs must be kept up to date and must be revised whenever changes are made in the input, output, processing, or the equipment used. This is the function of the program maintenance group, and a surprising amount of this type of work must be done in a data processing organization.

The program maintenance group is usually divided into teams, each of which maintains a group of related programs. Thus, each group is always familiar with the programs for which it is responsible, so that when changes are necessary they can be made without undue confusion. Upon completion of a major project in the systems development and programming group, one or more members of the development team may be transferred to the program maintenance section to maintain these programs.

Machine Procedures

Since, for many data processing applications, punched card equipment is superior to computers—and for other areas a combination of punched card equipment and computers is desirable—most organizations that have computers also use a substantial amount of punched card equipment. The machine procedures group develops punched card procedures and wires the more complicated control panels for the punched card machines. With the installation of a "glamorous" computer, there is a tendency to neglect this area, but the quality of both the systems analysis and the programming of punched card equipment may be crucial in determining the efficiency of the entire system.

DATA PROCESSING OPERATIONS

The production work of mechanized data processing takes place in the data processing operations section. In a large-scale installation more than a hundred people may be employed in the preparation of input material, the operation of punched card machines, auxiliary equipment, and the computer. Supervision of production may be complicated by the fact that partial or complete second- or third-shift operations are common.

Data Origination and Control

Whenever a mechanized data processing facility becomes loaded to the point that the machines are being efficiently utilized, scheduling and priority questions begin to arise. When expensive equipment is involved, it is particularly important that the gathering of input data, key punching, auxiliary equipment operations, electronic data processing runs, and report preparation mesh together smoothly so that deadlines can be met and costs can be minimized. This problem is further complicated because the data processing load fluctuates with the volume of transactions, report deadlines tend to be concentrated at the end of accounting periods, and special one-time reports are frequently required.

If the equipment is to be operated efficiently and the output reports are to be prepared on time, each operation must be precisely scheduled so that the machines are not idle while waiting for input information. Yet enough flexibility must be allowed so that occasional machine breakdowns do not cause report deadlines to be extended. The manager of data processing operations is, of course, responsible for such scheduling. However, because of the importance of timely input data, scheduling is often grouped with the input and customer relations area and performed under data origination and control.

The attitude of the rest of the organization toward centralized data processing is so important that it is desirable to give special attention to the customer relations function. All contacts with these customers, including the scheduling of input and deadlines for reports, should be handled by a group that is talented in human relations and interested in providing good service to the organization. If this is not done, both programmers and machine operators are likely to be plagued by complaining customers—to the detriment of the proper performance of their primary functions. Moreover, since some of the best technical people may be less than expert in human relations, the relationships between the customer and the data processing organization may deteriorate.

As was discussed in Chapter 9, the control of accuracy is an important consideration in the design and operation of mechanized data processing systems. Since many accuracy problems are caused by erroneous input information, and since the establishment of proper controls originates with the input, the functions of editing and control are grouped with the preparation of input and contact with customers. This function must also be coordinated with the internal and external auditors of the organization.

Input Preparation

The efficiency of a mechanized data processing system is especially sensitive to the effectiveness with which input information is prepared for machine processing. Ideally, the information should be recorded in processable form with a minimum of manual processing and as near to the source of the information as possible. Input may be placed in machine-processable form by automatic recording in punched cards or paper tape, by mark sensing, prepunching, key punching, remote input units, and so forth.

Key punching and other input preparation functions are similar to normal clerical functions, such as typing, and are usually performed by women. Since a substantial number of key punch operators may be involved (from 30 to 60 in a large organization), there is no reason why it should not be supervised as a separate section of the organization.

Occasionally, the function of data preparation will be decentralized to the location in which the data arise. In these situations, several key punches may be located in and supervised by the user organizations. This has the advantage of pinpointing the responsibility for the accuracy of input data, and can be a satisfactory method of organization if it is not a symptom of a function-oriented rather than an integrated data processing system.

Punched Card Operations

As was mentioned previously, a substantial amount of punched card equipment may be used in an organization that has a computer. Relatively large numbers of machine operators may be involved in the operation of this equipment. Although these jobs do not require creative ability, they require manual dexterity and an ability to accurately follow predetermined procedures.

The supervision and scheduling of a punched card installation is a complex job, so the skills of the supervisor of these activities are similar to those of a job-shop foreman. In the organization chart shown in Figure 15–1, the creative functions of punched-card procedure design and control-panel wiring are performed under systems development and programming.

EDP Operations

It would appear that the operation of a computer is strictly a button-pushing job—and, theoretically, this should be true—but its effective operation is heavily dependent upon the skill of the console operator. In the first place, the computer console is composed of a complex set of switches and buttons which must be pressed in a specified sequence. Mistakes in operating these switches can completely foul up computer processing. Moreover, emergencies due to incomplete or erroneous input information, machine malfunctioning, or inadequately written or debugged programs occur with discouraging frequency. Since use of this equipment may cost several hundred dollars per hour, the console operator should be capable of handling such emergencies expeditiously. Thus, considerable analytic ability, and coolness under pressure—combined with manual dexterity—are required of a good console operator.

As was indicated in Chapter 8, a considerable amount of effort has been devoted to the development of systems that make computer operation more automatic and routine, and less demanding for the operator. And an essential part of the documentation of a program is a set of detailed instructions that specify how the operator should handle each emergency that can occur. Effort should also be devoted to building checks into all programs that will reduce the number of emergencies requiring operator intervention; and every program should have a standard restart procedure for getting under way again after any interruption.

There is some question of how much the console operator should know about programming. If he understands programming, he can handle complex emergencies with which he could not otherwise cope. On the other hand, internal control is strengthened if he does not know programming, for he cannot modify the program for fraudulent purposes. With adequate documentation, well-designed programs, and a good operating system, it is not necessary that the operator be familiar with programming.

In addition to the operation of the console, magnetic tape reels must be mounted and removed in the proper sequence. This function is usually performed by assistants, who may also operate card-to-tape, tape-to-card, and tape printer equipment.

Detailed records of emergencies and the steps that were taken to correct them must be maintained for adequate control of accuracy; otherwise it may be impossible to determine whether mistakes in console operation have introduced errors. Also, detailed records of production time, idle time, machine downtime, and so forth must be maintained for analysis purposes so that realistic schedules can be established and proper performance maintained. Some machines have been equipped with a real-time clock that can be interrogated by the program to enable the operating system to automatically gather usage statistics.

Tape Librarian

To assure that the correct programs and the proper input and output tapes are used at all times, most installations include a tape librarian who maintains records of tape usage and who controls and issues the required tapes. It is her responsibility to see that tapes are not released for reuse until the information they contain is no longer required, and that worn-out tapes are retired when they begin to cause excessive machine errors.

Cost Accounting

How the costs of data processing are distributed within the organization has an important influence on the relationship between the data processing center and the rest of the organization. There are two major methods of charging costs, each of which has certain advantages and disadvantages.

It is possible to consider the data processing department as an overhead cost and to distribute it to other departments in the same way as general overhead. This type of costing might be desirable when developing an integrated data processing system, for it permits mechanization of data processing areas without regard to their individual efficiency in order to promote the efficiency of the entire system. On the other hand, this type of costing may lead to mechanizing areas of data processing which should never be mechanized, because a manager can thereby transfer his data processing costs into overhead for the entire organization.

The usual method of assigning data processing costs is to distribute all (or part) of them according to the machine-hours used on the various applications. This method of costing tends to insure that the areas are efficiently mechanized, for the managers involved can directly compare the cost of the mechanized system with the cost of the system currently used to decide whether or not to change. On the other hand, it may be more difficult to achieve an integrated system under this costing method, for, to increase the efficiency of the entire system, it is frequently desirable to mechanize areas which, considered by themselves, are inefficient.

EXERCISES

15.1 What are the abilities required for a good manager of data processing? Why is each of these qualities important? Where can such a man be obtained?

15.2 Why are data processing operations separated from systems development and programming?

15.3 What is the best way to decide whether or not to acquire a computer?

15.4 What changes would be desirable in Figure 15–1 if only punched card equipment were used?

15.5 What changes would be desirable in Figure 15–1 if only small-scale electronic data processing machines were to be used in connection with punched cards?

15.6 What changes would be required in the data processing organization if small computers were employed at several locations—rather than centralized operations in one installation?

15.7 What changes would be required in the data processing organization for a real-time on-line system that incorporates remote input-output terminals?

15.8 It is possible to decentralize systems analysis and programming among the user organizations. What problems might arise if this were done? What advantages might be obtained through this approach?

SUPPLEMENTAL READINGS

CANNING, RICHARD G. *Installing Electronic Data Processing Systems.* New York: John Wiley & Sons, Inc., 1957.

    This little book, based on the presentation of a case study, discusses the process of installing and using a large-scale electronic data processing system. Chapters 2 and 3 include discussions of the organizational changes involved and of the personnel required. Appendix 2 presents the desirable characteristics for people filling various jobs in the data processing organization.

Data Processing Manning Survey. Published by the Systems and Procedures Association, and reprinted in *Datamation,* Vol. 4, No. 2 (March-April, 1958), pp. 31–33.

    Presents the results of a survey of data processing job descriptions, titles, and pay ranges in the New York City area.

GALLAGHER, JAMES D. *Management Information Systems and the Computer.* New York: American Management Association, 1961.

Section 2 has a discussion of the internal organization of the data processing group, with illustrations of organization charts of large companies.

Performance Analysis of Data Processing Services (Form E20–8110–1). International Business Machines Corporation, White Plains, N.Y. (1963).

Discusses methods for measuring and controlling costs and efficiency in the operations area of a data processing organization.

Use of Electronic Data-Processing Equipment. Hearings before the Subcommittee on Census and Government Statistics of the Committee on Post Office and Civil Service (House of Representatives, 86th Congress). Washington, D.C.: U.S. Government Printing Office, June 5, 1959.

Includes reports on government requirements for data processing specialists, salary scales, and the selection and training of people. Pages 100–120 contain interesting comments on selection and training, including opinions about the use of aptitude tests.

16 PROBLEMS INVOLVED IN INTRODUCING A COMPUTER

ALTHOUGH there are many potential advantages in the use of electronic data processing, the introduction of an electronic computer into an organization also introduces important and complex problems. The computer does not automatically solve problems: it is only a tool and someone must devise a way to use it in a particular application. But before we can get around to solving the problems for which we obtained the computer, it is necessary to face many problems that the computer itself creates.

As was discussed in previous chapters, the data processing system of an organization is of almost unimaginable complexity. The introduction of a computer usually involves widespread changes in this complex system. Moreover, the data processing system is inextricably interrelated with the entire organization, so that changes in the data processing system may have an extreme impact upon the performance of the organization.

Indeed, the potential benefit of the computer may be directly proportional to the disturbance that its introduction creates, for the use of the computer should open possibilities that are not attainable with less powerful processing capabilities. To take advantage of these new possibilities widespread (and difficult) changes must usually be made. Thus a computer that introduces no problems is unlikely to produce significant results.

This chapter discusses some of the most important problems that arise with the introduction of a computer. Our objective is to present the problems, not to present solutions. The solutions will be different, depending upon the particular circumstances, and in some cases there may be no solutions. The important thing, however, is that these problems be faced by management before their symptoms jeopardize the success of the new data processing system.

HUMAN PROBLEMS

One of the major problems of our era is that of overcoming the economic and sociological difficulties occasioned by automation. This problem, of course, is not limited to computers or paperwork mechanization; it is much broader, involving the replacement of human effort by machines in production, transportation, communications, marketing, and data processing. Historically, this process of replacement of man by machines has often created widespread sociological and economic problems. The introduction of the first automatic looms in England created vast unemployment; mechanization in the coal mining industry has profoundly affected both the worker and the economics of the industry; and mechanization on the American farm is vastly increasing the productivity of the farm worker, but at the same time destroying the traditional "family" farming operation.

In the long run, almost everyone agrees that automation will contribute to a vastly improved standard of living. In the short run, however, automation may cause some vexing unemployment problems.

First, our labor force is growing rapidly, so new jobs must be created at a rapid rate just to keep even. Thus automation can cause trouble merely by slowing down employment's rate of growth. Secondly, there is a structural problem. Although automation may actually create more and better jobs than it destroys, the person who is replaced may not be suited by ability or training for any of the jobs created, or the jobs created may be located far away.

Data processing automation is psychologically different from the mere replacement of human muscles by machines, for it seems to be intrinsically degrading to our sense of human worth to replace brainpower by machines. Historically, the office worker has been well insulated from the hazards of layoffs or replacement, but in recent recessions thousands of clerical workers were released by such companies as Chrysler and U.S. Steel, and, because computers have made them unnecessary most of them will never be replaced.

Labor Union Reactions

Although they are aware of the many problems associated with automation, some top American labor leaders have publicly welcomed the opportunities it affords, at the same time attempting to concentrate public attention upon management and governmental responsibility for helping solve the resulting problems of dislocation. CIO president Philip Murray once said:

I do not know of a single solitary instance where a great technological gain has taken place in the United States of America that has actually thrown people out of work. I do not know of it, I am not aware of it, because the industrial revolution that has taken place in the United States in the past 25 years has brought into the employment field an additional 20 million people.[1]

And Walter Reuther, as president of the CIO, said in testimony before a congressional subcommittee:

First of all, we fully realize that the potential benefits of automation are great, if properly handled. If only a fraction of what technologists promise for the future is true, within a very few years automation can and should make possible a four-day work-week, longer vacation periods, opportunities for earlier retirement, as well as a vast increase in our material standards of living.

At the same time, automation can bring freedom from the monotonous drudgery of many jobs in which the worker today is no more than a servant of the machine. It can free workers from routine, repetitious tasks which the new machines can be taught to do, and give to the workers who toil at those tasks the opportunity of developing higher skills.[2]

Despite this attitude, use of the electronic computer has presented problems to organized labor. Wallace Webber, president of Local 889 of the United Auto Workers, a white-collar local that represents office workers in Chrysler auto plants, stated:

Three years ago Local 889 had 5,000 members. Now we have 4,000, and the loss mostly is due to the inroads of automation in offices.

. . . In the long run, this [the increasing use of computers] may eliminate half our jobs.[3]

Actually, relatively few office workers are unionized, so the introduction of computers may present organized labor with an important opportunity to organize these workers by exploiting the fear, uncertainty, and changes in status that accompany office automation.

The Effect of Computers on Total Employment

Although many people are aware that automation has many and widespread effects upon our economy, we do not yet know very much

---

[1] Quoted by Robert C. Tait (Statement before the Subcommittee on Economic Stabilization of the Joint Committee on the Economic Report, 84th Congress) from hearings published under the title "Automation and Technological Change," pp. 204–5.

[2] Walter P. Reuther, *ibid.*, p. 101.

[3] "Office Automation Hits UAW," *Business Week*, April 9, 1960, p. 58.

about this impact. We do not yet know how fast American industry is automating. We do not know how to balance the job-creating and job-destroying aspects of automation to arrive at a net result. Nor do we know whether the jobs left after automation are interesting and challenging, and thus uplifting in human values; or whether the remaining jobs are dull, repetitious, and degrading to the human intellect.[4]

Many limited studies of the employment changes induced by computers have been published. For example, a Bureau of Labor Statistics study of 20 large-scale data processing installations in industry showed that computers had not reduced the total number of office employees but had, instead, reduced the rate of growth of this type of employment.[5] Although instances can be cited where large numbers of clerical workers have been replaced by computers, in the main these organizations have been so large that their ordinary growth in other areas has overcome this reduction so that total clerical employment in most such organizations has not been significantly reduced. *So far,* the major impact of computers on total clerical employment has been to slow its rate of growth.

This slowdown is indicated by the growth rate figures for all clerical jobs:

1950 to 1960 *Average Yearly* *Gain*	*Gain in 1962*	*Gain in 1963*
2.81%	2.6%	0.9%

There is abundant evidence that automation—and its accompanying efficiencies—is primarily responsible for the slower growth rate in office employment.[6]

Of course, there is another side to the coin, for computers also create new jobs. In December, 1956, at the dedication of the hundredth IBM 700 series computer, IBM vice president L. H. La Motte said:

Inside of a decade we expect there will be close to 10,000 stored program computers installed. This means that somewhere around 150,000 to 200,000 people will have to be trained to use the machines. It isn't very often that an entirely new profession of such size is established.[7]

---

[4] See "A $5-million Search for Answers," *Business Week,* July 4, 1964, pp. 84–86.

[5] *Adjustments to the Introduction of Office Automation.* U.S. Department of Labor, Bureau of Labor Statistics, Bulletin 1276, 1960.

[6] This quotation and the figures appear in a note in the periodical *Computers and Automation,* July, 1964, p. 11, which is based on the report "Office Automation" by T. Stanton in the *Wall Street Journal,* May 5, 1964.

[7] *Computing News,* Vol. 5, No. 94 (February 1, 1957).

Apparently, Mr. La Motte was right in the ball park, for in 1964 there were about 156,000 analysts, programmers, and operators working with computers, and it was estimated that more than twice as many people would be required for such positions in 1970.[8]

Effects on the Individual

Although the impact of computers on total employment in the economy is of great importance, the manager of a firm installing a computer must carefully consider what may happen to the *individual* when the computer is introduced. There are a number of studies to guide us here. A Bureau of Labor Statistics study (cited above) found that within one year about one-third of the clerical workers in affected areas had been reassigned to other positions. Total clerical employment in the affected areas had been reduced by about 25 percent, and about 90 percent of the employees affected were in jobs involving posting, checking and maintaining records, filing, computing, tabulating, key punching, and related machine operations.

An early study by the Department of Labor on the effect of a Univac installation at a large insurance company reveals a typical displacement pattern.[9] Of the 198 persons formerly required to perform the functions taken over by the computer, only 85 were expected to remain after the computer was completely installed. Table 16–1 shows what happened to the 106 persons who, at the time of the study, had been displaced.

This same study indicated that the insurance company required 20 new jobs associated with the actual operation of the computer, and 9 new jobs in systems and procedures work. Although the total number of jobs in the affected section was drastically reduced, the average salary of the remaining 85 employees was $4,200 per year, compared to the previous average of $3,700 per year. This rise in average salary is partially accounted for by a slight amount of upgrading into more responsible positions and a wholesale elimination of lower-paying jobs. The major effect of this computer was to allow a reduction of 92 women's jobs, paying from $250 to $283 per month, while the total number of men employed in the section actually increased.

---

[8] Dick H. Brandon, "The Computer Personnel Revolution," *Computers and Automation,* August, 1964, pp. 22–25.

[9] K. G. Van Auken, Jr., "The Introduction of an Electronic Computer in a Large Insurance Company" (Printed as an appendix to the testimony of James P. Mitchell, Secretary of Labor, before the Subcommittee on Economic Stabilization of the 84th Congress on October 24, 1955; and included in "Automation and Technological Change," pp. 290–300) .

TABLE 16–1

Distribution of Releases from Division	Men	Women	Total
Transferred to other jobs within the division...............7		65	72
Transferred to jobs in other divisions.......................2		13	15
Retired...		1	1
Resigned (14 marriages, 2 jobs in another company, 2 moved to other areas).......................................		18	18
Total...9		97	106

Source: "Automation and Technological Change" (Hearings before the Subcommittee on Economic Stabilization, 84th Congress), p. 296.

What happens to the workers who are displaced by computers? Evidently, relatively few people have been laid off as the result of their jobs being taken over by the computer. Most of the workers replaced by the electronic data processing machine are apparently performing work that requires minimum skills, and consequently drawing minimum pay. These positions are usually filled by young women who plan to work a few years before marriage. Because of the high demand for this type of worker, because of the relative ease with which they can be transferred to other unskilled jobs within the company, and because of the rapid turnover, relatively few difficulties have arisen in this area. Since it takes months to install and convert to a computer system, these workers can usually be eliminated during this period by the "A and P method": attrition and pregnancy.

Thus, for this class of worker, the burden is transferred from the current office force to the young person with minimal training just entering the work force. This policy of "firing by not hiring," or what John Diebold calls "obituary accounting," solves the personnel problem for the company involved, but it still contributes to general unemployment.

One should not get the impression from this discussion that no significant displacement problems are involved in installing a computer, for the older workers or lower-level supervisors—who have achieved a certain amount of seniority but whose experience is no longer required—frequently present difficult and heartrending problems. These workers may have served long and faithfully, yet their experience and skills may not be readily transferable to other jobs of similar level, and they may be rather inflexible and difficult to retrain. Ameliorating the difficulties of these people can be difficult, time-consuming, and sometimes baffling.

Aside from jobs eliminated, many other jobs may be substantially changed. And here there are two possibilities: (1) The computer may take over the dull, routine part of the job, allowing the worker to concentrate his abilities on the creative and challenging aspects, or (2) The computer may take over the interesting parts of the work, leaving only the boring, repetitive labor such as the preparation of input information. Undoubtedly, both situations arise in practice, so it is difficult to generalize without knowledge of the specific situation.

Morale Problems

Despite everything that can be done to reduce its impact upon the individual, we must face the fact that the introduction of an electronic computer into an organization can and must affect the jobs of some of the workers. And—human nature being what it is—the introduction of a computer may injure the morale of people who actually will not otherwise be affected by the machine.

When rumors that management is considering using a "giant brain" begin to spread through the office, an accompanying fear for their job security is likely to spread among clerical workers. In addition, there is a natural tendency to resent and fear any changes that may occur in the job itself (quite apart from the fear of actual unemployment). People do not like to change, especially when they are faced with the possibility of changes caused by a thing so unknown and mysterious as a "giant brain."

One of the most critical factors affecting the success or failure of an electronic data processing system is the attitude of employees, throughout the organization, toward the machine. As we have seen, the machines are totally dependent upon humans for the provision of accurate input at the proper time, as well as for the planning and design of adequate programs. Resentment by employees during the system's design and analysis stage, which might cause them to withhold or falsify information concerning the job to be done, can vastly increase the difficulties involved. After the machine is installed, production schedules can be completely disrupted by tardy data, and the machine procedures can be badly snarled by a relatively low proportion of erroneous or missing data.

As an illustration of problems that can arise, let us consider the installation of an early model large-scale computer at Detroit Edison. Although this company established a policy that no employee would be laid off as a result of the installation, this did not completely solve the problem.

Detroit Edison recognized it would have problems obtaining the cooperation of those employees directly related to the processing that was to be converted to the computer, so a program was developed to educate these employees and to encourage them to help in the conversion. This proved quite successful, for this group of people was willing to make personal sacrifices to insure the success of the installation.

However, a sizable group, primarily concerned with customer relations, were also significantly affected. Because they were only indirectly related to the new system, these people were overlooked and did not fully participate in the employee education and orientation program. During the conversion, serious problems were caused by the attitude of these people and their resentment of the machine and the changes it caused. In the words of Mr. Elliott, director of Central Data Processing for Detroit Edison:

> This resentment resulted in accusations, the magnification of errors, and frictions between the less oriented employees contacting the customers and the more oriented employees maintaining the accounts. It also resulted in much challenging of procedures, which had been approved by their own superiors in this indirect area of responsibility.
>
> This became quite serious. People were talking about "this 705 system." Feelings became so intense that top management people began to be quite concerned about the adequacy of the new system. Just after the first of this year, our President decided that the whole matter should be looked into. Consequently, outside consultants were hired to evaluate the system. Of course, it is quite a letdown after you've gone through a change of this magnitude to have it questioned as to adequacy.[10]

The consultants reported that Detroit Edison's procedures were sound and that the conversion involved no more than the normally expected number of errors. The installation ultimately was successful, yet the human relations problems almost caused disaster.

Experience has indicated that, with proper planning, employee dislocation and morale problems can be substantially reduced. This, of course, requires that management be concerned with the effects of the machine upon its employees, and that it devote much thought to the retraining, selection, and communications problems involved. Most dislocation problems can be ameliorated if management, sincerely believing that the company employees are among its most valuable resources, actively concerns itself with employee welfare. Under such conditions, the psychological problems are also mini-

---

[10] J. D. Elliott, "EDP—Its Impact on Jobs, Procedures and People," *Journal of Industrial Engineering*, Vol. IX, No. 5 (September–October, 1958), pp. 407–10.

mized and can usually be taken care of by a properly planned and well-timed employee educational program.

There has been, and will undoubtedly continue to be, a lively debate among professional managers over the basic responsibilities of the manager. One can argue that in a competitive economy the manager makes his highest contribution to society by making profit maximization his major objective. Others support the position that the manager's responsibility to society is to "fairly" allocate the rewards of the enterprise among the customers, the community, the stockholders, and the employees. Different managers and different companies should and do have their own philosophies in this matter, and these philosophies and the realities of competition will determine the company's policy towards its employees. But it should be recognized that these policies and attitudes will influence the human problems involved in introducing a computer.

Company policy will, to a large extent, determine the effects that the use of an electronic data processing machine will have on employees. Company policy toward employees, as well as the overall pattern of labor relations, should have been determined long before a computer is installed. When the use of a computer is first seriously considered, and *before* rumors have a chance to start, both the policy and the effects of the machine should be explained to all employees who may be affected.

Mr. Wesley S. Bagby describes a seemingly successful program in this area:

At Pacific Mutual we established a comprehensive program to orient our employees on the subject of electronic data processing . . . at the same time that we decided to make a full-scale feasibility survey. A member of top management told *all* employees why the study was being made, what we thought it might lead to, and how they would be affected. He emphasized that any jobs eliminated would be the repetitive, monotonous, primarily clerical tasks. He promised that, if the study justified acquiring a machine, each employee would have a chance to qualify for the upgraded jobs which would be created by it. Perhaps most important of all, he assured each employee that even if his or her job were eliminated, the employee would be retained and relocated in suitable work at no reduction in salary.

We kept our staff informed of the progress of our studies and—when a decision was reached—of our reasons for installing a system. We told them of every major step in our long-range plans for converting our ordinary insurance record-keeping activities of manual and punched-card to tape-processing methods. Educational material on electronics was a regular feature in our house organ, and a series of lecture courses was made available for those interested.[11]

It should be noted, however, that those closely associated with electronic data processing have tended to ignore the existence of morale problems, and have therefore failed miserably in solving them. For example, in one company on the West Coast (where a study was made) the following situation was found:

Many workers have already been transferred, demoted, or dismissed. Interviews with some of the survivors, now in jobs preparing data for a computer, disclosed unanimous discontent with the monotony, routine, and pressure involved. Yet, when asked for his view of employee reaction to the innovations, [the] EDP manager asserted in all sincerity that they all "just love" the changes. Moreover, he maintained, they are "thrilled with the challenge of automation."[12]

ORGANIZATIONAL PROBLEMS

An organization should be designed to meet the requirements of the job to be done. Under manual methods, those parts of the organization devoted to data processing are organized in conformance with the capabilities and limitations of people. The tasks to be done are broken down into simple steps, so that the processing is accomplished by passing batches of work from one specialized section to another. Because of the poor accuracy of human processing, however, elaborate systems of control and duplication of efforts are built up to insure accurate results. To a large extent, the organizational structure is dictated by the problems associated with supervising groups of people.

Data processing has traditionally been a decentralized operation— a portion of the work of each department within an organization is concerned with data processing. Certain areas (such as production) may do relatively little data processing while other areas (such as payroll) are almost exclusively concerned with it.

When an electronic data processing system is used, a large part of the work may be removed from its previous organizational location and centralized for machine processing. One of the major advantages

---

[11] Wesley S. Bagby, "The Human Side of Electronics," in *Proceedings of the Second Annual AMA Electronics Conference: Pioneering in Electronic Data Processing, Special Report No. 9,* February 27–29, 1956, and published by the American Management Association.

[12] Reported by Ida Russakoff Hoos, "When the Computer Takes Over the Office," *Harvard Business Review,* Vol. 38, No. 4 (July–August, 1960), pp. 102–12.

of electronic data processing is the integration of this work into a single system, thereby avoiding the duplication and wasted effort inherent in a manual system. Therefore, it is often necessary to make widespread organizational changes to use these new machines effectively. The work of certain sections of the organization may be completely taken over by the machine, while other sections should perhaps be reorganized to parallel the changed functions of the group.

One of the most common complaints against electronic data-processing machines is that management has been unable to replace the number of people it had expected to replace. This condition is partially attributable to the difficulties associated with modifying an organizational structure which evolved through the years, and which, in the process, became so entrenched as to be almost unassailable.

Any change in organization involves matters of individual prestige among the managers of the affected areas. Some influential managers may vigorously oppose the trimming of their clerical forces, ignoring the fact that the work no longer exists. Furthermore, each individual worker may perform many different clerical operations, some of which may not be readily accomplished by a machine. For example, a computer at present cannot calm an irate customer, type a letter, or expedite an order. When a relatively small portion of the entire job is taken over by a computer, it is likely that the worker affected may still find himself busy eight hours a day doing that part which is left —and be supported in this position by his supervisor.

Sometimes these changes provoke a serious power struggle within management. Typically, the "old guard" tends to defend the status quo, while the "young turks" see attractive advantages that may result from such changes. It is not unheard of for the computer to become a pawn in an out-and-out power struggle between opposing factions within the organization.

The more effective the utilization of the electronic data processing system, the greater the effect is likely to be on the organization as a whole. The machines have not yet exhibited their full impact on organizational structures because few truly integrated data processing systems have been developed to date. However, as more powerful machines are produced, and as we learn more and more about utilizing their capabilities, the machines will be more thoroughly integrated into total management information systems and become operating rather than mere record keeping systems. This thought is expressed by Mr. M. J. Kami as follows:

We believe that in the long-range future, data processing equipment will have to help in the actual operations of the business; that it will be used for direct assistance to the people operating or running the different parts of the company, including management at the top, who must consider the whole operation. In the system of the future there are certainly going to be people—foremen, credit managers, and salesmen, even vice presidents. Therefore, the system of the future—"integrated data processing system" if you prefer the term—will have on its periphery communicating or talking centers with the various operating departments of the business.

The emphasis will be on the use of the system in operations. For example, the foreman, by putting into the system through his communicating or talking center [the] information about his work in process, or the work which has been completed, will use the central equipment to assist him in deciding what to do next. . . .

To give another example, the credit manager will be able to interrogate the system and get back necessary information about the standing of his customers' accounts to show whether credit should be extended or denied. The salesman will be able to interrogate the system in order to find whether goods are in stock and what delivery dates may be given, and so on.[13]

No one knows for certain what the organizational implications of the data processing system of the future will be. However, experience indicates that it is absolutely necessary for management to understand that organizational problems are involved and be willing and able to make the required changes. This is another reason why the use of a computer should be a top-management consideration: without the support of top management, the organizational changes required to effectively utilize a computer cannot be made.

Centralization versus Decentralization

What will be the effect of the computer on the tendency toward decentralized management? One of the major factors motivating decentralized management has been the communication and data processing bottlenecks that have hindered centralized management in making the required decisions at the proper time. The solution has been to decentralize the decision function to the lowest possible place in the organization. However, the use of the computer, combined with the technique of management by exception, may break the bottleneck of time and information and thus remove some of the basic motivation for decentralization. The use of electronic data

---

[13] M. J. Kami, "Long-Range Data Processing Problems," from mimeographed copy of a talk given at an IBM Seminar at Endicott, N.Y., August 6, 1957.

processing machines may tend to reverse the trend toward decentralization of management by making it less necessary.

The use of a large-scale electronic computer undoubtedly requires a high volume of repetitious processing. Thus, in many organizations, it is necessary to centralize data processing to obtain the volume necessary to make such equipment economically feasible. The question then arises: Can we centralize data processing and still maintain decentralization of management?

In the first place, the importance of this question may be reduced by the use of smaller computers that can process information almost as efficiently as the large machines without requiring such large volume. Equipment exists that makes it possible to decentralize data processing without overwhelming losses in machine efficiency. Second, there are two facets to decentralization. One facet is concerned with geographical decentralization: the location of facilities at widely scattered geographical points. The other aspect is the decentralization of management authority and responsibility, which is independent of actual geographical location.

As discussed in Chapter 13, modern communications advances have significantly reduced the time and distance problems involved in the communication of information. Thus, it is possible to centralize data processing in a geographically decentralized organization, and it should make little difference to a manager whether his data processing is done by a computer in the next room or thousands of miles away.

Indeed, some profess to envision data processing with a centralized computer as a powerful influence for furthering decentralized management, for the use of a centralized data processing system to assist top management in the evaluation and control of decentralized management may eliminate one of the major drawbacks of decentralization.

Sylvania Electric Products Corporation has constructed an electronic data processing center at Camillus, New York. Sylvania is decentralized, both in terms of geographical location and management philosophy, and so has leased a wire communications network which links the data processing center to Sylvania locations in 61 cities and towns throughout the entire United States. According to Leon C. Guest, Jr., controller:

It is our plan eventually to have all record-keeping relating to the engineering, manufacturing, and distribution, as well as administrative effort, maintained at the Data Processing Center. The Center will obtain pertinent information from all areas of the company, summarize such information, and present it in the most usable form to the management responsible for each operation.

The Data Processing Center, therefore, will become strictly a service department whose responsibility it is to gather information from the operating divisions, and to transmit that information at the earliest possible moment to the individual who must make the operating decision based on the information so provided in the form most helpful to him.[14]

There are two approaches in considering centralized data processing for decentralized managers. One approach asserts that if a manager is given the authority and responsibility to make operating decisions, it is only logical that he be given the authority to determine the information that he will use in his decision making process and how this information will be processed and presented. This approach entails an expensive burden of system analysis and design, for a separate system must be designed and programmed for each manager. Also, it is unlikely to produce anything even resembling an integrated system.

The other approach gives the decentralized manager the authority and responsibility for operating decisions within the structure of a uniform management information system. Here top management has much tighter control of decentralized management, for company policy is reflected in the information system, and the information system also provides higher management with feedback information concerning performance of the decentralized manager. Thus, in a sense, this approach represents a partial recentralization of power.

Although it is possible to utilize computers effectively and still maintain decentralized management, it appears that the effect of the computer is to reverse the trend toward decentralization. This consensus is expressed by Whisler and Shultz as follows:

Often a policy of decentralization has been pursued because of the overwhelming complexity of large business operations and the need to react rapidly to new information as it becomes available. While business may be expected to become ever more complex, the new developments should deal with the information problem in heroic fashion. Under these pressures, significant changes in organization structure seem inevitable. Seminar participants were perhaps in closer agreement on this point than on any other discussed: that the pressures for change generated by the introduction of the new technology are in the direction of centralization of decision making, of control, and of co-ordination.[15]

---

[14] Leon C. Guest, Jr., "Centralized Data Processing for Decentralized Management," *Systems Magazine*, Vol. XX, No. 5 (September–October, 1956) .

[15] George P. Shultz and Thomas L. Whisler, *Management Organization and the Computer* (Glencoe, Ill.: Free Press of Glencoe, Inc., 1960) , p. 30.

Location of Data Processing Function

The position of the data processing function within the organization is of fundamental importance. In the first place, this position reflects the attitude of management towards the data processing function. If viewed as a necessary evil or a burdensome overhead, it is almost impossible for data processing to make positive contributions. On the other hand, data processing may be a creative force if viewed, according to the feedback concept, as a necessary and important contributor to the management control process. Data processing may be conceived as a fragmented, every-man-for-himself operation, or as an overall system designed to serve the needs of the entire organization. These various viewpoints are reflected in the organizational location of data processing and in the quality of the personnel assigned to the management of the function.

To make its maximum contribution to the management control process, data processing must be approached from the system-wide viewpoint. Thus the data processing function must be assigned sufficient authority to enable a system-wide approach to be taken. This is not to imply that the data processing function must dominate the organization; however, it is almost impossible to provide an integrated data processing system on the basis of a "service bureau" operation in which the data processing function is provided with specified input information and required to produce specified results. It is necessary that the data processing function have sufficient power within the organization to force the compromises necessary to provide an integrated system. (Incidentally, the possession of this power to force compromises does not imply that it should be used indiscriminately, for management leadership is frequently more effective in the attainment of the desired result; but the mere existence of the power makes leadership more effective.)

Most data processing centers are located in the finance area under the controller or chief accountant. Among the reasons for this location are: (1) The first interest in using computers in the organization arose among people in this area; (2) This is the traditional location of the punched card data processing installation; (3) Many of the most easily mechanized data processing applications occur in the accounting area; and (4) The functions of the controller cut across all areas of the organization.

It appears likely that the major potential for the use of computers lies outside the traditional accounting area. Because of the difficulties associated with crossing departmental lines, and the natural tendency of employees to be interested primarily in the areas of direct concern to their immediate superior, the location of a data processing center in the finance area may tend to limit the opportunities to utilize the equipment effectively.

In a number of companies which have been most successful in using computers the data processing function has been grouped with industrial engineering, operations research, and other activities with an organization-wide orientation to form an administrative services or management services unit. Reporting to a vice president or some other high officer of the company, this type of organization not only provides a company-wide viewpoint and sufficient power to make it effective, it also brings together many of the technical and management skills required to design and implement an effective management information system.

The organizational location that is required to provide conditions favorable to the development of an integrated data processing system differs from one company to another, depending upon many factors. In general, it appears desirable to place the manager of the data processing function near the level of the operating managers who would otherwise dictate the results required.

The proper location of the data processing center within an organization is not easy to determine but it may be extremely crucial to the successful use of a computer. Or, to put it another way, if a computer is limited by its organizational location to a piecemeal approach to data processing, it is not likely to achieve outstanding results. (The internal organization and staffing of an electronic data processing center were discussed in Chapter 15.)

INSTALLATION AND CONVERSION PROBLEMS

The overall process of deciding to acquire an electronic data processing machine, preparing for its arrival, and conversion of data processing operations to the machine involves a tremendous amount of time, money, and planning—as well as a continuous stream of assorted emergencies. In the following section, some of the problems and considerations involved in this process will be outlined.

The Decision to Buy

How do we answer the question: Should we obtain an electronic data processing machine? There are many ways of obtaining an answer, ranging from the situation in which the president of a company orders the machine because it is the popular thing to do, to systems studies involving several years and hundreds of thousands of dollars. None of them have been outstandingly successful because this is usually the *wrong question*. The pertinent question is: What type of management information system should this organization have?

A method for obtaining an answer to this question was presented in Chapter 14. It is obvious that this approach requires that the organization invest time, money, and talent not only in making a study, but in developing the capability for making this study. It is necessary to obtain and train the necessary systems analysts, to provide them with leadership, and to provide the required support and participation of management.

As the result of a systems analysis and design effort, both the objectives of the information system and the tools needed to implement it should be specified. These tools may or may not include a computer, but if a computer is required the organization should then know why it is needed, what it is to do, and what machine best suits the needs. In evaluating a proposed new system, management must consider the human and organizational problems involved in changing to the new system, as well as the more tangible costs of systems design, programming, and equipment.

There is a great temptation to try to obtain a quick answer to the question: Do we need a computer? But experience has shown that a quick answer may also be a wrong answer. There is an old saying concerning quick answers to complex questions: If you want it bad, you'll get it bad!

But more importantly, even if the organization actually needs a computer it is in no position to use one until it can decide what it wants to do with it, and then what type of computer is required. Again, there is a temptation to order a computer that seems suitable and then worry about putting it to work. Needless to say, this approach does not usually lead to outstanding success.

Preparing for the Machine

When a computer is placed on order, the manufacturer will usually quote a delivery time between one and two years from the date of the order. Although this may seem an unreasonably long time to wait, even if the basic system design has been completed the machine may well arrive before adequate preparations have been completed for its use.

One of the first problems to be faced is that of selecting and training a staff of systems analysts and programmers. Most of these highly skilled people must be obtained from *within* the organization and trained in schools conducted by the equipment manufacturer. The word "trained" is used rather loosely here—the manufacturers' schools provide only a "kindergarten" training. Most of the programmer's competence will be acquired by experience, so it is wise to expect a relatively low-quality product from these people for several months after they have been "trained."

As was mentioned in Chapter 14, the implementation of the basic system design involves a considerable amount of work. The detailed design must be completed, including flowcharting, detailed run breakdowns, forms layout and design, and manual procedures write-ups. Then detailed block diagrams must be prepared for each machine run, and programs must be written and debugged. Most computer manufacturers provide facilities for checking out programs on a similar machine before your machine is installed. So that productive use can be made of the equipment when it arrives, all of this should be completed (at least for a substantial portion of the system) before the machine arrives.

Physical Problems

One problem that has caused many headaches has been that of providing the physical environment required by the machines. Although most such machines are transistorized, it is usually necessary to provide a source of well-regulated and disturbance-free power, along with careful temperature, humidity, and dust control. The floors of the building may have to be strengthened to support the weight of the various units, and channels may be required under the floor in which to run cables that connect the components together. A machine room layout must be devised which will fit the various equipment components into the area provided, and in an arrangement that will allow efficient operation of the machine. The layout should also provide an aesthetically pleasing and intellectually satisfying view of the equipment to visitors (ranging from high school classes and employees' families to delegations of vice presidents), while at the same time not exceeding the restrictions of the machine manufacturer concerning cable lengths.

Thus substantial building modifications may be required to install a computer. One might think that these physical preparations could be easily completed in the one to two years available, but it is frequently a nip and tuck battle to complete them before the arrival of the machine, and sometimes installations are significantly delayed because remodeling is behind schedule. On the other hand, unforeseen difficulties can force the manufacturer to delay the equipment for a few weeks (or months) or the customer may encounter programming delays. When these three factors interact, the resulting uncertainty can be quite nerve-racking.

Conversion Problems

Before any major processing can start, it is often necessary to convert large files of information from written or punched card records onto magnetic tape. The difficulties that can be involved in this conversion are almost unbelievable. An incredible amount of inaccuracy and nonuniformity can exist in a punched card file. Manual files are likely to be incomplete, inaccurate, inconsistent, and to have unbelievable numbers of unexpected and unexplained deviations from their supposed format. The job of placing these files in a form in which they can be successfully machine-processed often involves thousands of man-hours and hundreds of machine-hours for its completion. It is reported that file conversion and "purification" cost a large insurance company around $12 million.[16]

As discussed in Chapter 9, the process of converting an application to the data processing machine usually involves running the application in parallel; that is, processing in the normal way and through the use of the computer at the same time, and comparing the results to detect inaccuracies in the program. The number of processing cycles which must be overlapped ranges from 2 to 3 (if one is lucky) to 20 or 30. Occasionally, an application will be run in parallel for several processing cycles, then converted completely to the electronic data processing machine, and, several cycles later, situations will arise that force the application to be taken off the computer and returned to the previous processing method.

During the conversion period the processing must be performed in two different ways, which may involve originating information in two different forms. Thus substantial pressure may be placed upon people outside the mechanized data processing organization at a time when they aren't too happy with the situation anyway. The difficulties that arise are therefore magnified in importance, and emergencies may become commonplace.

The above discussion may indicate that the process of converting

---

[16] "Special Report on Computers," *Business Week,* June 21, 1958, p. 77.

to electronic data processing involves difficult administrative and planning problems. The process extends over a long period of time during which training, systems analysis, programming, debugging, conversion, and production may all be going on simultaneously. As was discussed in Chapter 9, the amount of time required for any of these steps in a specific application is quite difficult to predict, so planning and setting of schedules is complicated. Moreover, considerable time pressure is exerted by the desire to get some use out of the expensive equipment that is available. Effective administration of this process is of extreme importance.

Several approaches that attempt to minimize the conversion problems have been devised and applied. One of the most popular of these approaches is to take over areas which have already been mechanized by punched cards. This minimizes the conversion difficulties, for punched card mechanization forces the reorganization of procedures and the isolation and standardization of exceptions that are required when converting to a computer. However, for procedures in which punched cards can be efficiently used, most of the benefits of mechanization have already been attained, and it may be difficult for the computer to compete with the cost of punched card processing. In other words, the major potential for the computer lies in areas where it is impossible to efficiently mechanize through the use of punched card equipment.

Another approach which minimizes the disruptions in the organization outside of the data processing center is that of making the data processing group a "service bureau" which takes over the data processing without changing the form or content of the input information or the output reports. Then the user is not required to make major adjustments when the computer is installed, and he should not be concerned with whether the processing is actually accomplished by a computer or by other means. This approach is likely to insure mediocrity. Not only may it preclude the efficient utilization of the computer, but it also is almost certain to prevent the attainment of any major improvements in the management information system. In general, it is simply a tacit admission that the data processing center does not have sufficient support from top management to enable it to be normally successful.

The only realistic approach to minimizing installation and conversion problems seems to be that of providing excellent administrative leadership and allowing sufficient time for thorough preparation *before* the machine arrives, combined with the assignment of sufficient numbers of qualified personnel to the task of studying data processing problems and developing procedures for using the machine to solve them.

If the organization has not utilized punched cards, it may be advisable to first install punched card machines and use them to gain some of the benefits of (and a great deal of experience in) mechanized processing before considering the installation of an electronic data processing system. The proper use of punched card data processing is an excellent training ground for the development of systems analysis and procedures personnel, as well as for educating the entire organization concerning the advantages and limitations associated with the mechanization of data processing.

This does not imply that a computer should necessarily be staffed exclusively by people from an existing punched card installation, for one of the most pressing problems associated with punched card installations has been that the people involved did not have the basic ability required to effectively use punched cards.

Pattern of Costs

One of the more interesting and difficult questions to be answered when deciding on an electronic data processing machine is: What will it cost? If the use of an electronic computer is being seriously considered in an organization, this question should probably be phrased: What will it save?

This question is seldom answered with any degree of accuracy when one is trying to decide whether or not to order a machine. As a matter of fact, it is an extremely difficult question to answer *after* the machine has been successfully installed and is actually making savings: many organizations who are using the machines do not know accurately how much (if anything) they are saving.

In the first place, it is difficult to precisely determine the true costs of data processing under a manual system. Second, during the time in which a data processing machine is being installed, the job to be accomplished may change radically in terms of the volume involved or the results obtained. Third, it is difficult to place a monetary value on such intangible factors as increased accuracy, more comprehensive information, and faster results. The evaluation of these intangible benefits is of utmost importance, for they often provide the major impetus for introducing electronic data processing systems.

However, it should again be emphasized that these intangible benefits are not automatically obtained as a by-product of the use of an electronic data processing machine. They must be deliberately sought through concentrated attention to management's need for higher-quality information and by devoting the best available brain power to the task of devising systems which provide the desired information.

Most of the electronic data processing machines available may be obtained on a rental basis, or may be purchased outright from the manufacturer. If the machine is purchased, two additional alternatives arise: Maintenance may be provided by the manufacturer through a maintenance contract, or it may be provided by hiring or training one's own maintenance personnel. Such factors as equipment obsolescence, interest rates and availability of money, the ratio of the purchase price to the rental price, the number of hours per day of planned usage, and the tax position of the organization are involved in deciding whether to rent or buy the equipment.

Much work has been done on the question of rental versus buying of capital equipment, and most of it is applicable in considering electronic data processing machines. Incidentally, computer programs have been devised that thoroughly analyze many factors and prepare reports showing the rate of return on investment for various useful lives.[17] Thus, by estimating the life of the equipment and comparing the corresponding rate of return with the rate provided by alternate investment opportunities, it is possible to decide whether it is best to rent or to buy the equipment.

Although the absolute magnitude of the costs or savings involved in the use of a computer will vary from installation to installation (and is quite difficult to determine precisely), the overall cost pattern has been established. For a typical *large-scale* installation, Figure 16–1 presents a framework in which to view the various components of cost, along with their relative magnitudes and their general time of occurrence. The horizontal axis of this diagram represents time and is marked in units of one year. Quantities upward on the graph represent costs in thousands of dollars per month, while quantities downward represent similar savings.

The cost of the systems study to determine whether or not to order the machine is shown on the first six months of this diagram. After the machine is ordered, the costs of training, systems analysis, and programming gradually rise to a total of around $12,000 per month. The total amount of this type of work before installation may vary

---

[17] See *A Rent or Buy Analysis with the IBM 650 Card System* in Supplemental Readings at the end of this chapter.

from 15 to 30 man-years, at an average cost of $10,000 to $12,000 per man-year.

Site preparation costs, which are incurred over a period of approximately one year before the arrival of the machine, range from a minimum of around $50,000 to a maximum of around $350,000. The cost of file conversion depends on the type of applications that are

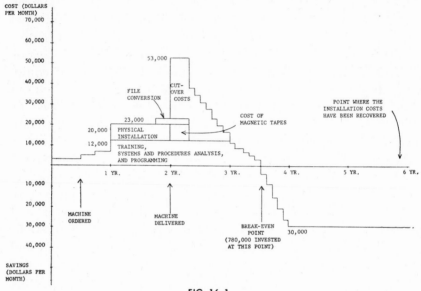

FIG. 16–1

Typical Cost Pattern

being placed on the machine and the previous status of the files involved. Most installations require several hundred reels of magnetic tape at a cost of around $40 per reel.

Since this diagram is based on the assumption that the machine is being rented, when the machine arrives the total monthly cost will immediately jump by the amount of the machine rental, which is assumed to be around $30,000 per month in this illustration. For a period of a few months, very little productive work is accomplished, but from then on, as programs are debugged and parallel operation is suspended, more and more productive work will be assumed by the equipment, and costs will fall until eventually the costs of data processing should return to the level that existed before the machine was considered back at year zero. On the diagram, this break-even point is reached three and one-half years after the start of the feasibility study, or one and one-half years after the machine was installed.

Of course, in addition to costs we must also consider any concrete benefits and savings attributable to the new data processing system, such as reduced inventories or production costs. As conversion continues, total benefits may increase and costs decline to where the new system shows a substantial profit. In this illustration it is assumed that the machine will produce a profit of $360,000 per year (or $30,000 per month) when it is fully utilized. However, at the break-even point, around $780,000 had been invested in systems analysis, programming, physical installation, file conversion, magnetic tapes, and unutilized machine rental. At $30,000 per month, it will take over two years after the break-even point to recover this $780,000. From this point on, then, a profit of $30,000 per month is received.

Let us emphasize again that this diagram represents only a conceptual pattern. Both the magnitude of costs and savings, as well as the time factors, will vary widely from organization to organization. For example, some organizations have been able to reach the break-even point within a year after the machine was installed, while others have been installed for several years without ever reaching the break-even point—and without any indications that they will ever be profitable. The monthly profit attained, which drastically affects the time necessary to recover installation costs, ranges from a substantial loss to around $100,000 per month.

It should be noted that equipment developments are rapidly affecting the costs of mechanized processing. In the first place, a wider range of equipment is being developed, so that the volume of processing required to use a computer is being reduced, and thus machines are available to efficiently satisfy a broader range of data processing requirements. Secondly, machine developments are continuously lowering the unit cost of processing. It is conservatively estimated that the machine costs of a unit of processing have been cut in half about every two or three years, and this progress is likely to continue in the future. Thus the range of potentially profitable applications of electronic data processing is continuously expanding.

SUMMARY

The introduction of a computer into an organization also introduces significant problems. These problems are usually greater for installations that aspire to the greatest potential benefit, for many of the problems are a result of radical changes in the fundamental information gathering and processing system of the organization.

Some of the most important problems are involved with people and their reactions to change. These problems can be minimized if they are recognized and taken into consideration from the start of the process. The effectiveness of the use of a computer frequently depends upon the solution of organizational problems which may prevent the use of a systems-wide approach to data processing.

Selection and training of people, detailed development of the new system, programming, installation of the machine, and conversion to the new system present complex administrative problems. These problems are difficult enough in the absence of the human and organizational problems mentioned above, but the combination can be overwhelming. Needless to say, administrative skill of the highest order is required for success.

In short, the introduction of a computer system is an illustration of widespread and drastic change, and presents all of the management problems associated with such change. Top management support and participation is required to accomplish such revolutionary change, for basic objectives and policies are involved, and problems are involved at all levels of the organization. Although the neglect of these problems does not automatically doom an installation to complete failure, solutions must be found if the installation is to be more than mediocre.

EXERCISES

16.1 Discuss the effect of the introduction of a computer upon the clerical workers in the organization. Is this effect desirable? If not, how can it be ameliorated?

16.2 What are the relationships between centralization of data processing and management decentralization?

16.3 Discuss the problems that are involved in the process of changing from manual methods to electronic data processing equipment. If you were in charge of such a conversion what would you do to reduce these problems?

16.4 Prepare a dynamic cost diagram similar to Figure 16–1 for a typical basic MAC installation. How does your diagram differ from the diagram in Figure 16–1?

16.5 Why is top-management participation necessary for the effective utilization of electronic data processing equipment? Is middle-management participation also required? Why?

16.6 In what respects does the impact of office automation upon the workers differ from the effect of factory automation?

16.7 When deciding between renting and purchasing a computer, it is necessary to estimate the useful life of the machine. What factors influence this useful life?

16.8 Read and analyze The Jiffy Manufacturing Case (Appendix A). Answer the questions at the end of this case.

SUPPLEMENTAL READINGS

Adjustments to the Introduction of Office Automation (Bulletin 1276). Washington, D.C.: U.S. Department of Labor, Bureau of Labor Statistics, 1960.

Presents the results of a study of the effect of installing large-scale computers in 20 offices in industry.

A Rent or Buy Analysis with the IBM 650 Card System (Form E 20–4040). International Business Machines Corporation, New York, 1959.

Presents a description of the formulas used in the 650 program for using the present value method to determine whether to rent or buy capital equipment.

Automation and Technological Change. Hearings before the Congressional Subcommittee on Economic Stabilization of the Joint Committee on the Economic Report, October, 1955. Washington, D.C.: U.S. Government Printing Office, 1955.

A report of hearings on the general impact of automation upon employment and productivity. These hearings include testimony by John Diebold, Ralph J. Cordiner, James P. Mitchell, Walter P. Reuther and many others, and contain a wealth of information on the status of automation at that time and its potential impact on the economy.

BAGBY, WESLEY S. "The Human Side of Electronics," *Proceedings of the Second Annual AMA Electronics Conference: Pioneering in Electronic Data Processing; Special Report No. 9.* The American Management Association, 1956.

An excellent presentation of the human problems involved in the installation of a computer.

BUCKINGHAM, WALTER. "The Human Side of Automation," *Business Horizons,* Vol. 3, No. 1 (Spring, 1960), pp. 19–28.

A general discussion of the impact of automation on the worker, much of which is applicable to office automation.

CANNING, RICHARD G. *Installing Electronic Data Processing Systems.* New York: John Wiley & Sons, Inc., 1957.

Through use of an illustration involving a single company, this book concentrates on the problems involved in preparing for and installing an electronic data processing system.

CRAIG, HAROLD F. *Administering a Conversion to Electronic Accounting.* Boston: Harvard University Graduate School of Business Administration, 1955.

This is a detailed case study describing the conversion of an insurance company to punched card accounting. It emphasizes administrative, human, and organizational problems involved in the conversion.

ELLIOTT, J. D. "EDP—Its Impact on Jobs, Procedures and People," *The Journal of Industrial Engineering,* Vol. IX, No. 5 (September-October, 1958), pp. 407–10.

This is an unusually frank discussion of the problems involved in installing a computer by the director of Central Data Processing of the Detroit Edison Company.

HOOS, IDA R. *Automation in the Office.* Washington, D.C.: Public Affairs Press, 1961.

A study of the impact of the computer on the occupational structure of the clerical labor force, on the persons and groups affected, and on the organizational structure.

Impact of Office Automation in the Internal Revenue Service (Bulletin 1364). Washington, D.C.: U.S. Department of Labor, Bureau of Labor Statistics, July, 1963.

Reports on the impact on personnel of the introduction of a large-scale computer for processing taxpayer records and auditing returns at the regional center in Atlanta, Georgia.

MCISAAC, GEORGE S. "How to Practice What We Preach in Making Business Changes," *Business Horizons,* Summer, 1963, pp. 29–36.

Discusses experiences in introducing computers as examples of the management techniques that facilitate or inhibit success in making drastic changes in organizations.

POSTLEY, JOHN A. *Computers and People.* New York: McGraw-Hill Book Co., Inc., 1960.

Chapter 8 discusses some of the effects of introducing a computer into an organization.

SHULTZ, G. P., AND WHISLER, T. L. *Management Organization and the Computer.* Glencoe, Ill.: Free Press of Glencoe, 1960.

This book is essentially the report of a conference held to discuss the impact of the computer on management and the organization. It presents the experiences of five companies that have made some progress toward implementing management information systems. These presentations are preceded by some excellent papers by the editors and other well known authorities.

Use of Electronic Data-Processing Equipment. Hearings before the Subcommittee on Census and Government Statistics of the Committee on Post Office and Civil Service, House of Representatives, June 5, 1959. Washington, D.C.: U.S. Government Printing Office, 1959.

This is a report of the use of electronic data processing equipment in the federal government. It emphasizes the personnel selection, training, and relocation problems involved.

WALLACE, FRANK. *Appraising the Economics of Electronic Computers.* New York: Controllership Foundation, 1956.

This book is concerned with the techniques that can be used to decide whether or not to install electronic data processing equipment.

WEBER, C. E. "Change in Managerial Manpower with Mechanization of Data-Processing," *Journal of Business,* Vol. 32, No. 2 (April, 1959), pp. 151–63.

Discusses several instances of changes in manpower because of the use of computers, with emphasis on shifts in the proportion of management to clerical workers.

17 INFORMATION TECHNOLOGY AND MANAGEMENT

TO ANYONE who has had the experience of observing a large number of electronic data processing installations it is obvious that we are a long way from realizing the full potential of this powerful new tool. For example, McKinsey and Company studied more than 300 computer installations in 27 manufacturing companies which had either been recommended by computer manufacturers or publicized as outstanding examples of the use of computers. The results of this thorough year-long study indicated that only 9 of these 27 companies were achieving results that justified the cost of their computers.[1]

Despite this rather spotty record of success, to the author's knowledge only one or two companies have reconverted from computer data processing to the previous system—and have returned the computer to the manufacturer. In fact, computers continue to be installed at an ever-increasing rate. Their potential benefits are so obvious and portend such revolutionary possibilities for improved management control that almost everyone is convinced that the problems associated with their use must be overcome. Therefore, in the first portion of this chapter we will consider some of the major pitfalls that have led to failure in the use of computers. This is only the negative side of an exciting group of developments, however.

The phrase Information Technology has been used for the amalgamation of computers with management science, operations research, systems analysis, simulation, etc. But Information Technology, as discussed in this chapter, represents more than a group of techniques; rather, its basic emphasis is upon improving organizational performance through a process of organizational research and

---

[1] See "Only One Out of Three Pays for Itself," *Business Week*, April 13, 1963, pp. 152–56.

development. Finally, at the end of this chapter we will consider the potential impact of Information Technology upon the manager of the future.

COMMON PITFALLS

The poor record of success in using computers is not due to poor machine performance for, in general, the computers have performed according to their specifications. This is not to imply that the proper machine for the job was always obtained, or even that a suitable machine for certain jobs has even existed, but only that since the late 1950s most machines have been as fast and reliable as the manufacturer claimed.

It is safe to say that no computer available today will *assure* success, or is there likely to be such a machine in the future. On the other hand, under the proper circumstances almost any machine obtainable from a reputable manufacturer can be utilized successfully.

As was discussed in Chapter 16, a number of problems must be solved to effectively utilize a computer. Usually, both human relations and organizational problems must be faced, and administrative ability may be taxed to the utmost by the overall complexity of the changes necessary.

Piecemeal Approach

It is readily apparent that one does not often achieve spectacular improvements by merely inserting a powerful computer in the place of humans and less powerful machines without revising the overall system. That which is relatively efficient in a manual system may be quite difficult to produce with computers, while very desirable information that is too costly to produce through a manual system may be efficiently produced by a computer. Moreover, because of the characteristics of humans, it is difficult to centralize manual processing, thus manual systems are not likely to be well integrated. Unfortunately, most manual systems have just grown, they were not designed.

Processing on a computer must usually be more centralized than with manual processing, but the potential benefits of this centralization are not achieved unless the system is redesigned so that it becomes truly integrated. To build an integrated system it is necessary to make changes in input, processing, and output, and to reassess the fundamental information requirements of the organization.

One characteristic of most of the disappointing electronic data processing installations is the lack of a systems approach. Actually, this is probably a symptom rather than the fundamental problem, for usually no one sets out to create a fractured system. A piecemeal approach usually results from not specifying as an objective the achievement of an integrated system, or from organizational problems, or from a lack of sufficient management participation in the planning and installation.

Also, a careful distinction must be made between objectives and tactics. In view of the immense problems involved in merely converting to computer processing, it may not be desirable to attempt to completely redesign the data processing structure of the organization when the computer is installed. Thus it may be rational to adopt the tactic of achieving an integrated system through a two-stage process: First, install the computer with only the system changes that are necessary and convenient; Secondly, when the conversion has been accomplished, redesign the system, utilizing the knowledge obtained in the first step.

This tactic does not necessarily insure success, nor does it always lead to failure. But in many of the failures it is obvious that the first step was attempted without realizing that step two would also be necessary. The most depressing characteristic of these failures is the realization that management has given up the struggle to attain an effective system.

Lack of Objectives

One of the most apparent characteristics of the failures is that many of them have suffered from a lack of objectives from their very inception. The futility of such situations is expressed in *Alice in Wonderland* in the well known conversation between Alice and the Cheshire Cat.

> "Cheshire-puss," she began, rather timidly—"Would you tell me which way I ought to go from here?"
> "That depends a good deal on where you want to get to," said the cat.
> "I don't much care where . . . ," said Alice.
> "Then it doesn't matter which way you go," said the cat.[2]

A computer is a challenging and an extremely glamorous piece of equipment, and, in a number of cases, has been obtained primarily because someone "just wanted" a computer. Obtaining an electronic

---

[2] **Lewis** Carroll, *Alice's Adventures in Wonderland.*

computer is a relatively easy objective, but it does not necessarily lead to the attainment of anything worthwhile. In the absence of rational objectives, it may well lead to considerable unpleasantness.

Although one would think that a mistake of this nature would seldom occur, the indications are that even today there is still a strong tendency in this direction. For example, an extremely high percentage of feasibility studies result in the ordering of a computer. It is not difficult to justify the use of a computer if the persons preparing the justification want one, for rough estimates of present and future costs can easily be manipulated to prove almost anything. Frequently, the persons preparing the estimates have emotional, prestige, and financial interests in obtaining a computer.

As was mentioned previously, a lack of objectives almost inevitably results in a piecemeal approach to the mechanization of data processing, for to approach the use of a computer on a system-wide basis it is necessary to have the improvement of the entire data processing system as a major objective.

It was emphasized in Chapter 16 that both organizational and human relations problems can lead to failure in the use of electronic data processing. Perhaps the major blame for the widespread adoption of the piecemeal approach must be placed upon these problems, for in many organizations, because of organizational problems and personal empires, it is impossible to implement a systems approach.

Inadequate Technical Capability

As has been repeatedly pointed out, the computer is merely a tool which must be creatively used if it is to provide valuable results. Consider the most spectacular triumphs of the computer, described in Chapter 1. Whether it be in science, engineering, automatic control, management science, or data processing, it is apparent that each achievement of a computer should actually be credited to someone who analyzed a problem that did not at first appear to be suitable for solution by use of a computer, and then devised a way to use the capabilities of the computer to solve that problem. Very seldom does a routine, straightforward approach lead to spectacular results. Perhaps one of the major advantages of the use of the computer is that the analysis of exceptionally creative people can be substituted for the performance of the average clerk.

There is no doubt that designing and implementing a system that uses a computer successfully requires a much higher order of analytical skills than those required of the ordinary clerk who processes data. Even those who supervise clerical data processing may be incapable of designing a good computerized system.

Although the computer provides the opportunity for spectacular success, it also presents the possibility of equally spectacular failure, so there is no place for the person with mediocre capabilities. When we talk of the need for "people," we do not mean just "bodies." It is much better to have five *excellent* people than 50 *average* people. And this is true of everyone involved: the manager of the installation, the systems analyst, the programmer, and even the console operators.

Lack of Management Participation

In Chapters 15 and 16, the administrative problems involved in the installation and use of a computer have been discussed. If these problems are not solved, this failure can easily lead to failure in the use of the equipment. It is often said that it is impossible to successfully install a computer without the support of top management, and this statement is obviously true. However, it is likely that it has frequently been misinterpreted. It does not merely mean that top management must *want* a computer—it is easy to want a computer, and it is equally easy to *not* want a computer later on when the problems involved begin to arise. Top management must understand the implications involved in the use of the computer before the word "support" achieves its proper meaning in the statement.

In this text a number of problem areas have been pointed out, any one or a combination of which can lead to failure. These problems have not been highlighted to provide guideposts by which one can achieve failure with a minimum of delay: there is no need for such assistance. The concern is with making effective use of electronic data processing, and such success is not likely to occur unless management has been forewarned concerning these problems before a computer is installed. Thus, one ingredient of success appears to be an understanding by management of the role of data processing in the organization and of the capabilities and limitations of the computer as a tool for this processing.

Another important factor in success must be a widespread participation by all levels of management in the design of the data processing system. A systems analyst, no matter how competent, cannot set the objectives of the entire organization or of its separate parts. This is the job of management. No systems analyst can be trusted to redesign the organization to conform to a computer. A systems analyst cannot set policy, he must incorporate management policy into the system. And no systems analyst can specify what information is to be used to make specified decisions; management must participate in the specification of systems requirements. The McKinsey and Company study, mentioned above, found that:

> In companies where computer operation has paid off handsomely, management men rather than technicians made the key decisions. They insisted on thorough planning to integrate the computer into operations, even if the operations had to be rebuilt to suit the computer, and they kept a running check on the results. A technician, no matter how expert he may be on computers, can't make decisions in the over-all frame of reference.
>
> Thus, where management takes the view that the subject is too occult to be mastered by anyone except the technician, a computer system is likely to be merely superimposed on an existing operation, or perhaps used largely to develop pet theories of the expert.[3]

All of the above requires widespread concern by management. Either the information system of an organization is of importance to the success of the organization, or it is not. If it is not important, there is not likely to be sufficient reason to seriously consider a computer. If data processing is vitally important to effective management control, then the concern and attention of management in the design of the system is imperative, whether a computer is used or not.

ORGANIZATIONAL RESEARCH AND DEVELOPMENT

We have come to recognize that, even with the active participation of management, it is not easy to design an effective management information system, for we do not yet know enough about organizations and how and why they work. Thus, many leading companies are beginning to realize their need for a continuous program of research and development whose objective is improved performance of the organization.

There is little doubt that there is tremendous potential for better organizational performance. The McKinsey and Company study indicated that, for those nine companies that had used computers successfully, their success had been reflected in million-dollar differences in net income between companies in the same industry.[4] And

---

[3] "Only One Out of Three Pays for Itself," *op. cit.*, p. 156.

[4] See "New Tool, New World," *Business Week*, February 29, 1964, p. 71.

our present success in improving performance through redesign of the organizational system may prove to be minimal—a drop in the bucket—as we learn more about the characteristics of such complex systems.

When we are concerned with the performance of a complex system, two levels of understanding are important. First, we need an understanding of the cause-and-effect relationships that govern the performance of the micro components of the system. Then we must achieve an understanding of the interrelationships between these components and how they interact to determine the performance of the overall system.

Historically, science has been concerned with obtaining an understanding of cause-and-effect relationships. Recently, we have begun to apply the knowledge and concepts of science to organizational and management-decision problems. The words *operations research, management science, and quantitative business analysis* all refer to the application of the scientific method and mathematical, statistical, and computer technology in organizational research and development.

It is possible to trace the history of the use of the scientific method to solve management and organizational problems back through Frederick W. Taylor and Thomas A. Edison to ancient Greece and the contributions of Archimedes to the defense of Syracuse. However, not until World War II, when teams of scientists were formed into operations research groups to study the problems associated with the use of new weapons systems, did the idea that the scientific method could be applied to the complex problems associated with the management of organizations begin to achieve widespread acceptance.[5] Thus the development of this approach parallels the use of the electronic computer, and the two are in fact closely interrelated.

The Scientific Method

That the fruits of science are useful cannot be seriously disputed in this technological age. Yet many practical men say "Give me facts, not theories." These men simply do not understand what science is all about, for the very essence of science is theory, or hypothesis, or model. And theory is actually a part of science that is useful to the practical man for theory presents the cause-and-effect relationships that the practical man uses to solve problems and design complex

---

[5] For a history of these developments see F. N. Trefethen, "A History of Operations Research," *Operations Research for Management* (J. F. McCloskey and F. N. Trefethen [eds.]) (Baltimore: The Johns Hopkins Press, 1954).

mechanisms. Of course, the theory of the scientist is different from the theory of the layman in that the scientist, as a part of his use of the *scientific method,* subjects his theories to rigorous testing.

Basically, the scientific method consists of three steps: (1) observation, (2) formulation of a theory or hypothesis explaining the result observed, and (3) testing of the hypothesis to determine whether or not it adequately explains the situation observed. These three steps are repeated over and over as long as flaws can be found.

It should be noted that the testing is of fundamental importance, for much of the progress of science is motivated by the discovery that the presently accepted law or theory is inadequate, and much of the faith that we have in science is justified by this rigorous testing. Note also that this simple, three-step process does not attempt to explain the creativity of science, nor does it describe the process by which the scientist creates his theories.

Model Building

In order to understand complex systems we frequently attempt to construct a model of the situation. A suitable model should possess certain characteristics of the reality it represents, without necessarily being identical with this reality. For example, a small-scale model may be tested in a wind tunnel in designing an airplane; a contour map may be used when designing a highway; an electrical network may be used to model the flows of fluid through a pipeline network; a computer program may be used to model the voting population of the nation on election night; and a system of differential equations may represent the dynamic characteristics of an airplane wing as it passes through the sound barrier. Even a written or verbal description of a problem or situation is a model.

In all of these illustrations, the model is an abstraction of reality, not reality itself. The model often expresses our understanding of some important characteristic of reality, and thus is frequently the same as the theory or hypothesis in the scientific method. One important characteristic of a model is that it allows us to *test* our understanding by manipulating it, observing its behavior, and comparing this with our observations of the real world. Thus, the concept of a model is of great importance in the area of organizational research and development.

Mathematical Models

The more complicated the problems and the systems with which we wish to deal, the more desirable it is to utilize formal, manipulable models instead of imprecise, non-manipulable verbal models. A mathematical model is a system of equations which in numeric form expresses the relationship between the factors that control the situation and the results obtained.

For example, let C represent the fixed costs of production, V the variable cost per unit produced, P the selling price per unit, and N the number of units produced (and sold). Then the revenue from sales is $P \cdot N$, and the cost of sales is $C + V \cdot N$. A mathematical model for profit is therefore:

$$\text{Profit} = P \cdot N - [C + V \cdot N]$$

In such a model P, N, C and V represent *variables,* quantities whose value may change or be changed.

Examples of Mathematical Models

Mathematical models are of great importance in organizational research and development. Before discussing their advantages and limitations, we will briefly describe some of the basic classes of models that have had significant practical applications or that have contributed important concepts to our understanding of important organizational problems.

Applications of *mathematical programming* are concerned with the allocation of resources so as to maximize profit (or minimize cost) where there are restrictions on how the resources may be used. In *linear programming,* the objective to be maximized (or minimized) is a *linear* function of the variables, and the restrictions can be expressed as *linear* equations or inequalities. Linear programming has been used to minimize the cost of transporting goods from factories to warehouses by determining which warehouses to service from each factory so as to meet the requirements at each warehouse while not exceeding the capacity of each factory. Linear programming has also been used for determining how to blend gasoline—or cattle feed—so as to meet the specified requirements of the resulting mixtures at the lowest cost; the best way to level production; the optimal use of plant capacity; the best choice of advertising media; the optimal scheduling of airline flight crews; and the minimization of trim losses in the manufacture of paper (to name but a few).

Dynamic programming is concerned with the determination of policies for the allocation of resources over time so as to maximize return. Such problems are encountered in various phases of logistics, in multistage investment programs, and in the study of optimal purchasing policies.

Queuing or *waiting line* models are concerned with situations in which facilities are provided to service customers whose arrival time has random characteristics. For example, how many checkout lanes should be provided in a supermarket? How many trunk lines should be provided in a telephone exchange? How many machine repairmen should be hired for a machine shop? All of these problems require a balancing of the cost of providing the service against the cost of customers waiting for this service.

The business manager is a gambler, whether he likes it or not (and whether he will admit it or not) , for he must make decisions that will be affected by future events which he cannot predict with certainty. The theory of *probability* makes it possible to incorporate uncertainty into models and thus to cope with situations in which uncertainty is inherent. Classical *statistics* is concerned with the application of probability concepts in the collecting and analyzing of data so as to reduce uncertainty. And modern *decision theory* provides a framework for combining a person's intuitive feeling for the probabilities with sampling, and with the costs of a wrong decision, so as to determine how much to spend on additional information before making a decision.

Game theory is concerned with competitive problems in which the outcome of an action depends not only upon what *you* do but also upon the actions of one or more competitors. Obviously, such situations are important and ubiquitous, so it is unfortunate that the theory of games has been able to determine solutions for *very few* practical problems. Game theory nevertheless contributes to our understanding of the source of the difficulties involved in such problems, and it also contributes a number of *concepts* that are most important in analyzing such situations.

Advantages and Limitations of Mathematical Models

The first advantage in the use of mathematical models is that they force one to ask the right questions. What are the important variables in this situation? What are the relationships between these variables? (Mathematical models must be quantitative: we must be concerned with numbers and measurement. Thus, the use of mathematical models does not allow hazy generalization; it forces one to be explicit and to face the problem squarely.)

Secondly, a mathematical model is manipulable. For example, in the simple profit model described above we started with:

$$\text{Profit} = P \cdot N - [C + V \cdot N]$$

With a little manipulation we can place this in the form:

$$\text{Profit} = (P - V)N - C$$

And, setting profit equal to zero, we can manipulate a bit more to find the "break-even" point:

$$N = \frac{C}{P - V}$$

Another important advantage of mathematical models is illustrated in Figure 17–1. We have a real-world problem which we

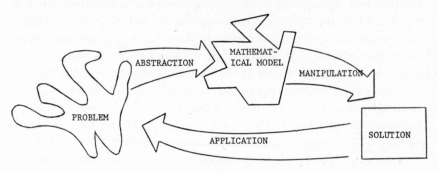

FIG. 17–1
Use of Mathematical Model

represent by a mathematical model. Then we can apply logical reasonings developed through the efforts of thousands of mathematicians over hundreds of years, to obtain a *solution* to the mathematical model, which can then be applied as a solution to the real-world problem.

This solution may be an answer to the specific problem. If, for example, we are using linear programming to blend gasoline, it will specify the amount of each component that should be used in the mixture. On the other hand, the solution may be in the form of a *decision rule,* a formula that can be used to decide what to do under a variety of conditions.

For example, the simple economic lot-size formula:

$$Q = \sqrt{\frac{2C_1 R}{C_2}}$$

specifies the optimum size Q of an order, given the total yearly requirements R, the cost C_1 of preparing an order, and the cost C_2 of carrying a unit in inventory for a year.[6]

---

[6] Note that this formula is based upon a number of restrictive assumptions which may or may not hold in a given situation.

There are some limitations, however, on the use of mathematical models. Consider Figure 17–1. The real-world problem is represented by a mathematical model. A solution to the model is derived by using the logical and manipulative power developed throughout the history of mathematics, and then this solution is applied as the solution to the real-world problem. The major weakness in this procedure is that although we can be almost certain it is a correct solution to the mathematical problem, it is a good solution to the "real" problem only if the mathematical model is a *faithful representation* of the real-world problem.

Thus, the use of a mathematical model is not magic, for a mathematical solution to a problem can be only as good as its translation into mathematics. This implies that the manager must participate in this translating process, for the manager is the one who should best understand the problem, and he bears the responsibility for using the solution.

Let us emphasize, however, that a model does not have to accurately represent the real world in order to be *useful,* remembering that the model is the theory (in the scientific method) that is subject to test. If the model represents only management's *beliefs* about the real-world problem, then the discovery that the model does not correspond to the real world indicates that these beliefs about the real world are inconsistent or inaccurate. In organizational research and development this type of knowledge is of great importance, for it triggers a search for better understanding!

Another limitation on the use of mathematical models is that as the problem becomes more complex, so does the difficulty of expressing the relationships in mathematical form. And the difficulty of solving the model also increases. In fact, even after applying the totality of mathematical knowledge and the power of the electronic computer, there are many mathematical problems that we simply cannot solve. Thus the model-builder may face a dilemma: on the one hand he must devise a mathematical model which faithfully represents the real-world problem (and is therefore complicated); on the other hand he must make the model simple enough that a solution *can* be obtained.

In summary, mathematical models provide tremendous insights when they are used properly. When the situation can be modeled with sufficient precision for the results to be useful (and when the model can also be solved), mathematical models are of great value. However, these characteristics must lead one to observe that mathematical models are likely to be most applicable to the individual components of a complex system rather than to the system itself.

SIMULATION MODELS

When a system is too complex to be represented by a mathematical model, or when it is impossible to solve the mathematical model, a *simulation* model may be considered. (Of course, mathematical models simulate the real world, so there may be some confusion between them and what we will refer to as *simulations*.) A simulation is distinguished from a mathematical model by the fact that:

1. A simulation is dynamic; time is an essential variable, and

2. A simulation model is not solved; it is operated over time and its performance can be observed.

Simulation models are frequently constructed to represent complex systems by creating mathematical models for the system components and linking these component models together to account for the interrelationships between these various components. An electronic computer may be used to progress step by step through short intervals of time, pausing at the end of each interval to compute the interactions between components. Thus it is possible to obtain a history of the performance of the system under specified conditions. By repeating the same process under other conditions, it is possible to compare results and decide which alternative is most desirable.

Thus we are able to experiment with changes in the organization, or with various decision rules, without actually affecting the day-to-day operations of the organization under study. For the first time, organizations can be studied in the laboratory under controlled conditions, and changes can be made and alternatives tested at relatively small cost.

As shown in Figure 17–1, to use a mathematical model we must build a model of the real world; then we derive a mathematical solution to the model, and apply this solution to the real-world problem. As shown in Figure 17–2, a simulation model is used in a different way. Rather than solve the model, we can only experiment with the simulation model and evaluate its performance under various conditions.

It is safe to say that simulation is the most significant technique yet devised for organizational research and development. And now, before discussing its advantages and limitations, we will describe some simulation models that provide concrete illustrations of the rather abstract concepts we have been discussing.

Job-Shop Simulation[7]

A job shop is a production facility that is composed of a number of different types of machines. A given part is produced by performing various operations on these machines in the required sequence. A punched card installation is an illustration of a job shop.

An important function in the operation of a job shop is that of "dispatching," determining what job or order to process next on each machine. This decision has an important bearing on the performance of the shop in terms of the level of in-process inventory, the percent

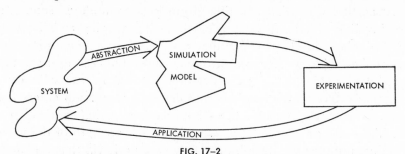

FIG. 17–2
Use of Simulation Model

of orders completed on time, the percent of utilization of the equipment, and other measures of effectiveness. Dispatching presents a complex problem because as soon as the shop load approaches a substantial percentage of its theoretical capacity, conflicts arise in which two or more jobs are waiting for a single machine, while other machines may be idle.

Although it appears that a simple enumeration of the possible schedules should suffice to solve this problem, the number of possible combinations is so astronomically large that the fastest electronic computer in existence could not evaluate them all within the time available. Further, no mathematical model that produces a practical shortcut has yet been devised for determining optimal schedules.

This problem may be considered as a complex queueing or waiting line problem that involves both series and parallel service facilities. The queues consist of jobs that are waiting for an operation to be performed by a particular machine. Simulation techniques

---

[7] This illustration is adapted from E. W. Martin's "Simulation in Organizational Research," *Business Horizons*, Fall, 1959.

have been applied to these queueing problems to test decision rules for deciding which waiting job to perform next on each machine.[8] If rules for operating a shop more efficiently can be devised, then these decision rules can be applied by a computer in an automatic production control system.

A job-shop simulation usually involves the use of an electronic computer with an input of a sequence of jobs, each of which is to be released to the shop at a certain time. Each job is represented by such information as the job number, the sequence of operations to be performed, the standard machine time for each operation, the due date for completion of the job, the value of the job, and any other information that is to be used in the decision rules being tested.

Associated with each machine group in the simulated shop is a waiting line of jobs to be processed. By progressing step by step through short intervals of simulated time, and by examining the status of each job and machine group at the end of each interval, the computer is able to apply the decision rules to be tested in each situation where an operation is completed or a new job enters the shop. During this process the computer can gather statistics on machine utilization, idle time, overtime, average length of the waiting line, number of late jobs, and any other criteria that can help evaluate the various alternatives being tested.

A "clock" is associated with each machine group, indicating the simulated time at which that machine will be free. Figure 17–3 shows a simplified sequence of steps that the computer goes through to simulate each time cycle. (For simplicity, this block diagram omits the considerations involved in entering new jobs into the shop.)

In block 1, the clock showing the earliest time of completion is selected, indicating that the machine associated with it will be the next to complete an operation. If this is the last operation on the job, a card is punched with statistics about that job. If other operations are to be performed on the job, blocks 4, 5 and 6 either assign the job to the required machine, if it is available, or place the job in its proper position in the queue of jobs waiting for the required machine group.

The processing for the particular time period on that job is then completed, so, through blocks 8, 9 and 10, the computer can assign a

---

[8] Much of the pioneering work in this area has been done by Allen J. Rowe of the General Electric Company. See his article, "Computer Simulation Applied to Job Shop Scheduling," in *Report of the System Simulation Symposium* (held in New York City May 16–17, 1957), published by the American Institute of Industrial Engineers.

job to the machine that was made available by the original completion of an operation in block 1. The process is repeated by selecting the next lowest clock, indicating the next event of importance, and so on.

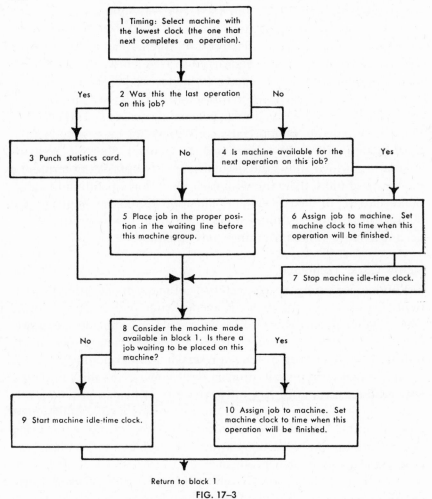

Return to block 1

FIG. 17–3

Computer Simulation of Time Cycles

Source: A simplified version of the block diagram on page 8 of R. W. Conway, B. M. Johnson, and W. L. Maxwell, "The Cornell Research Simulator," mimeographed research report of the Department of Industrial and Engineering Administration, Cornell University, October 1, 1958.

The major interest in this process may be focused on block 5, for in the process of assigning a job to a place in line any priority rule or procedure may be used. Thus, many such rules may be tested to discover the one that provides the highest efficiency in the operation of the shop. Furthermore, by altering the number and types of machines available—as well as by altering the rules for releasing jobs to the shop and assigning due dates—the results obtained under various combinations of circumstances may be investigated. A generalized job-shop simulator program, designed to simulate any job shop, has been written for the IBM 704 computer.[9]

A great variety of simulations are concerned with flows of units through complex, logical networks of queues; and this type of simulation is so important, and arises so frequently, that two automatic programming systems have been devised to make it easy to program and run such simulations on various computers. The SIMSCRIPT language[10] is similar in general concept to FORTRAN, but it is designed to be especially convenient for expressing simulation models. IBM has developed a General Purpose Systems Simulator,[11] which allows the simulation to be expressed in terms of a standardized block diagram, with each block corresponding to an action occurring in the real system. These programming languages are of great importance; without them, simulation programming would be much more time-consuming and expensive.

Monte Carlo Technique

Random variations are characteristic of many organizational situations. For example, although the average time between breakdowns may be known, machines require emergency maintenance at unpredictable intervals. Customer orders and deliveries, the weather, results from advertising and from research and development, absenteeism, even occurrences of coronary occlusions, all exhibit unpredictable random variations. Not only are random fluctuations *characteristic* of the process, in many situations this unpredictable randomness is so essential that the common simplifying technique of using average values simply "assumes away" the problem, for, without the randomness, there is no problem.

There are two basic ways in which this randomness can be introduced into a simulation. The first of these is to use historical data as an input to the system. For example, in job-shop simulation the orders entered into the shop could be obtained from a "typical" period of the shop's history. Similarly, histories of time between

---

[9] See "Job Shop Simulation Application," distributed in mimeographed form by the IBM Math and Applications Department, Data Processing Division, White Plains, New York.

[10] See H. M. Markowitz, B. Hausner, and H. W. Karr, *SIMSCRIPT, A Simulation Programming Language* (Englewood Cliffs, N.J.: Prentice-Hall, Inc., 1963).

[11] See IBM's *General Purpose Systems Simulator II* (Form B20–6346).

machine breakdowns, customer orders, and the weather might be used as input to introduce random variation into simulations.

However, there are times when historical data of this type are not available, or too expensive to collect, or inconvenient to enter into the computer or to store in memory. At other times we wish to investigate how a system might react to changed characteristics or patterns of these random occurrences. For example, what would be the effect of introducing more reliable equipment? Or what would happen if our average demand were to increase by 50 percent next year? Whenever it is inconvenient to use past history, it is still possible to produce synthetic data, with the desired characteristics of randomness, by use of the Monte Carlo technique.

We will illustrate the Monte Carlo technique by reference to the job-shop simulation discussed above. When a job is placed on a machine, the simulation must determine how long it will take to process the job. The standard operation time used for planning purposes is only an average time, whereas the actual operation may take significantly more or less time than the average time. In a real shop, the standard time can be used for planning purposes, but the actual time consumed by an operation is not known until *after* the operation is completed. Thus in blocks 6 and 10 of Figure 17–3 it is necessary to involve random variations in the determination of how long it will take to complete a particular operation on the machine involved.

Consider how this problem in simulation might be handled by use of the Monte Carlo technique. Each time an operation is scheduled on a machine, we wish to determine an actual operation time that is based on the standard time but also involves the variation which occurs in actual practice. If R represents the ratio of actual time to standard time, then actual time can be found by multiplying standard time (which is known) by R. Thus, to utilize the Monte Carlo technique in handling this variation from standard time, a statistical distribution of R is used. In the absence of theoretical considerations, it is possible to approximate this distribution by analyzing past experience. Assuming that there are 200 observations of scheduled time and actual time, a histogram of the number of occurrences of each ratio (Figure 17–4) can be plotted.

The histogram can be transferred into a frequency distribution by dividing each of the graphed values by the number of observations (200, in this case) and converting to a percentage to obtain the experimental probability of each ratio (Figure 17–5).

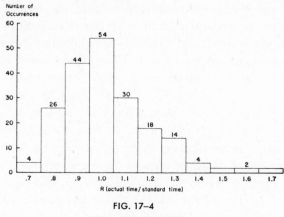

FIG. 17–4

Time Distribution

Table 17–1 may then be constructed from this information, so that the table intervals corresponding to each value of R are equal to the percentage probability associated with that R value. Since the ratio .7 has a probability of 2 percent, we assign the two numbers 00 and 01 to the ratio 0.7. The ratio .8 has a probability of 13 percent, so we assign the thirteen numbers 02 through 14 to the ratio 0.8, and so on, to obtain the rest of this table.

To use the Monte Carlo technique to simulate random fluctuations, it is necessary only to have access to a random sequence of two-digit numbers (Table 17–2), each of which may be used with

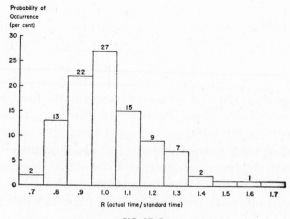

FIG. 17–5

Frequency Distribution

Table 17–1 to determine a specific ratio of actual time to scheduled time.[12]

For example, starting with column 2 in Table 17–2 and reading

Random Number	Ratio
0–1	0.7
2–14	0.8
15–36	0.9
37–63	1.0
64–78	1.1
79–87	1.2
88–94	1.3
95–96	1.4
97	1.5
98	1.6
99	1.7

TABLE 17–1

Monte Carlo Technique

down, the first number is 73. Reference to Table 17–1 shows that R is 1.1, so the actual time is 1.1 times the standard time. The next number is 20 and R is 0.9, so the actual time would be 0.9 times the standard time.

36	73	18	13	03	15	36	19
42	20	51	14	94	53	12	79
98	49	11	59	16	27	09	37
50	84	01	16	74	33	90	85
71	73	94	89	29	95	58	63
55	42	81	98	35	37	28	07
28	51	33	52	23	54	75	05
01	12	42	27	48	49	91	72
26	38	86	34	16	96	84	68
36	00	04	38	92	89	06	26

Source: *Produced by the author by a squaring method.*

TABLE 17–2

Random Numbers

By continuing to draw random numbers for use with Table 17–1 to determine the corresponding value of R, a pseudo-history can be accumulated that in the long run will have the same statistical characteristics as the sample from which Figure 17–4 was derived,

---

[12] Random digits may be obtained from some chance device, such as spinning a perfectly balanced wheel with equally spaced digits or by reference to published tables of random digits (which are also available in punched card form). Alternatively, suitable random digits may be generated by the computer itself by using one of several mathematical techniques that produce sequences of digits that satisfy all tests of randomness.

while the individual occurrences that comprise this pseudo-experience are characteristically random. A pseudo-experience derived in this way from the use of Table 17–1 and a sequence of 200 random numbers is graphed in Figure 17–6. Although there is a marked similarity in appearance between Figures 17–4 and 17–6, they are by no means identical. This should not be surprising, for the distribution of any other sample of 200 actual observations should not be expected to be identical to the first sample.

When a machine time is required in the job-shop simulation of blocks 6 or 10 of Figure 17–3, the next number in Table 17–2 would

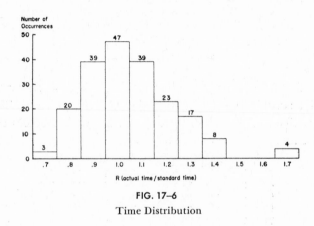

FIG. 17–6

Time Distribution

be used with Table 17–1 to determine a value of R that would be multiplied by the standard time to obtain the actual time required.

In any situation in which random variations are of importance, the Monte Carlo technique can be utilized in the simulation to provide suitable random occurrences. This technique is frequently used in several places in a single simulation.

Inventory Simulation

Some of the simpler but most widely used simulations are those designed to study and experiment with various approaches to inventory management. A wide variety of mathematical models has been devised to represent various types of inventory problems. Each mathematical model corresponds to a specific set of assumptions as to the patterns of demand, what happens when stock is entirely depleted, the characteristics of replenishment lead time, and the costs that must be considered. Despite the many models, it is unlikely that the assumptions of any of these models are exactly satisfied by the actual inventory situation.

This lack of suitable models for most situations, combined with the difficulty of measuring the costs to be considered (such as the cost of being out of stock), make inventory simulation an attractive tool. A typical inventory simulation[13] allows one to experiment by varying each of the following factors:

1. Method of forecasting demand,
2. Method of setting order points,
3. How order quantities are established,
4. How out-of-stock situations are handled,
5. Whether joint-item or single-item replenishment methods are used,
6. How frequently stock records are reviewed to determine if action should be taken,
7. The characteristics of replenishment lead times,
8. Whether over-age stock should be purged, and if so, when.

In order to use this simulator it is only necessary to select a method for handling each of the above factors. Then the simulation can be run, using historical demand data (or synthetic data generated by the Monte Carlo method), and a report prepared showing performance under the specified conditions. Information reported for each item may include the average inventory level, the number of replenishment orders placed, the replenishment ordering costs, the number of demands, the percent of orders that are routinely filled, the total units of demand, the percent of the total units demanded that were routinely filled (called the service percentage), percentage filled from backorder, average time orders were held in backorder, average age of items issued, total over-age removals, on-hand stock, on-order stock, backordered stock, and information on the effectiveness of the forecasting procedure.

This information can be used to evaluate the performance of the tested method of managing the inventory. Perhaps the average inventory is too high, so it might be desirable to try decreasing the safety stock and reviewing the stock records more frequently. By experimenting with such changes it is possible to arrive at improved approaches to managing this inventory. Since both customer service and inventory carrying costs are of great importance to most organizations, better management of inventories may pay handsome dividends. And when inventory record keeping is to be mechanized by

---

[13] See *Inventory Management Simulation for Manufacturing Industries* (Form E20–8063), International Business Machines Corporation. White Plains, N.Y., 1961.

means of a computer, it is necessary to evaluate the methods to be incorporated into the computer program in order to determine the impact upon the service level and average inventory. Thus, this type of simulation has been most useful in systems analysis and design studies.

Industrial Dynamics

One of the pioneers among those who view organizations as complex systems is Professor Jay W. Forrester of M.I.T. who developed his Industrial Dynamics approach after having helped design the SAGE air defense system. Professor Forrester views a business organization as interrelated flows of materials, money, information, manpower, and capital equipment.[14] Management attempts to optimize the performance of the organization by means of policies and decisions that act as valves to regulate these flows. Industrial Dynamics is the name that has been given to the attempt to obtain an understanding of the effects on organizational performance of the interrelationships between organization structure, management policy and decision rules, and the flows of materials, manpower, information, money, and capital equipment.

As the first step in an extended program of research, an electronic computer was used to simulate the flows of information and goods between customers and the factory in a durable goods manufacturing organization. This distribution system involved inventories at the three levels of factory warehouse, distributor, and retailer. The time lags in the flows of information and goods between customers and retailers, retailers and distributors, distributors and factory warehouse, and the lags involved in changing factory production levels were included in the simulation model, along with inventory control and reordering decision rules at each of the levels involved.

Use of this simulation model indicated that under certain seemingly innocuous combinations of decision policies and delays, relatively minor random fluctuations in customer demand can be amplified to produce serious oscillations in factory production and inventory. By augmenting this model to include the effects of advertising, it was shown that the policy of setting advertising budgets as a percentage of sales can be an important cause of severe fluctuations in the production level required rather than a stabilizing influence.

---

[14] Much of this discussion is adapted from E. W. Martin's "Simulation in Organizational Research," *Business Horizons*, Fall, 1959. For further information see J. W. Forrester, *Industrial Dynamics* (New York: John Wiley & Sons, Inc.) , 1961.

The inclusion in the model of a limitation on factory capacity indicated that, even with sales that never reached more than 90 percent of capacity, it might appear that a substantial amount of additional capacity was required, thus leading management to wasteful overexpansion of facilities.

Of course, the objective of an industrial dynamics simulation is to provide the basis for redesigning the organization to obtain better performance. At least one company has been reported to have used this approach with some success, and several others are experimenting with industrial dynamics.[15]

The industrial dynamics group at M.I.T. devised and implemented the DYNAMO programming language for use in running simulations on the computer. This system compiles and runs very rapidly, requiring but a few seconds on an IBM 7094 computer to produce several years of history. Incidentally, one of the outputs of the DYNAMO simulation is a graphical print-out of the values of variables that are of interest.

The industrial dynamics approach to simulation differs from approaches that can be handled by SIMSCRIPT and the General Purpose Systems Simulator because the former must be expressed in terms of "levels" and "rates," while these latter simulations are concerned with discrete elements. It remains to be seen whether or not the industrial dynamics abstraction will be widely successful in improving the performance of organizations, but there is no question that Forrester has developed significant insights for our understanding of the role of management in designing organizational systems.

Other Large Simulations

As long ago as 1954, United Airlines started work on an extremely ambitious simulation of its aircraft maintenance facilities. This simulation has been of significant value in helping management find an optimum combination of such factors as the number of mechanics to have available, overtime policies, hangar facilities, the number of reserve airplanes in the system, schedule and ground times, and the management of the basic maintenance program.

Several other leading organizations are in the process of developing giant simulations of all or part of their organizational systems. When completed, these simulations will be used to test alternative policies and possible organizational changes designed to improve

---

[15] See "New Way to Spot Company Troubles," *Business Week*, November 4, 1961, pp. 158–64.

organizational performance. (There is, however, very little *specific* information available about what these organizations are doing, for not only are such models designed to provide competitive advantages, they also incorporate the very essence of top management policy and philosophy. Thus, such models must be classified Top Secret, for if a businessman were able to obtain the simulation model of a competing firm he might gain a tremendous competitive advantage through his ability to anticipate reactions to his actions.)

In addition to the simulations of the organizations mentioned above, there are a number of simulations of general organizations that are being used for research into organization theory.[16]

Advantages and Limitations of Simulation

The major advantage of simulation models is that they make possible things that were heretofore impossible. Without simulation, the only way to evaluate proposed changes in a complex system is to make the changes and see what happens. In organizational systems this trial-and-error process is both difficult and expensive. It is also hazardous, because systems which involve people may react to *experimental* changes in different ways than they might react to permanent changes: implementation and human relations problems tend to distort the results of such experiments. Thus simulation models are of great importance in systems design because they allow the systems designer (1) to be sure that he understands the existing system and (2) to experiment with proposed new systems.

However, we should note that simulation is by no means an easy solution to all problems. First, complex systems require complex models, and it is difficult, time-consuming, and expensive to construct large, complex, simulation models. Secondly, it may be difficult to decide whether the simulation is an adequate representation of the real system, and it may also be hard to decide what to change when the simulation is inadequate. Finally, as we have noted, a simulation is not solved; it is, instead, used for experimentation. Usually a number of different variables can be changed, and the resulting combinations of alternatives may turn out to require a very large number of experiments. And there is still no assurance that a solution of the problem will be found.

---

[16] For examples, see Charles P. Bonini, *Simulation of Information and Decision Systems in the Firm* (Englewood Cliffs, N.J.: Prentice-Hall, Inc., 1963). Also see R. C. Sprowls and M. Asimow, "A Computer Simulated Business Firm," *Management Control Systems* (D. Malcolm and A. J. Rowe [eds.]) (New York: John Wiley & Sons, Inc., 1960).

Despite these problems, simulation is undoubtedly the most important tool yet devised for organizational research and development. In the area of management decision making, simulation provides the opportunity to predict the consequences of changes in operating policies as well as to experiment with changes in the structure of the organization. In the area of data processing, the use of simulation may lead to better answers to the fundamental question: What information should be provided? When? And to whom?

It seems likely that over the next 20 years simulation will be used to discover principles of organization in areas where today we do not even suspect that causal relationships exist. This will not come about immediately, for our first simulations are but crude representations of reality. However, their inadequacies serve to concentrate our attention on the areas where we lack understanding, and we will be able to construct more and more accurate simulations based on improved understanding.

HEURISTIC SIMULATION

It is impossible to conclude a discussion of computer simulation without mentioning the important research area of simulating human thought processes. As was mentioned in Chapter 1, some success has been achieved in using the computer to solve certain "ill-structured" problems. Computer programs exist that prove mathematical theorems, play checkers, design electric motors, balance assembly lines, and select investment portfolios. And all of these accomplishments are achieved by simulating (to some degree) the way humans attempt to solve these problems.

A problem is said to be well-structured if there is a simple definite objective to be obtained, if the variables that control the attainment of this objective are known and measurable, if the relationships between these variables and the objective are known, and if a computational procedure exists for determining the values of the variables that optimize the objective. A problem is ill-structured to the extent that it does not satisfy these same conditions.

For example, there may be several objectives that are poorly defined and partially conflicting. The variables that control the situation may not be known, or may not be measurable, or their relationship to the objectives may be indefinite. Or there may be no practical computational procedure that can be used to solve the problem. In other words, a well-structured problem is one that can be solved by means of a mathematical model. An ill-structured problem is one that we do not understand well enough to solve with a mathematical model.

Many important management problems are ill-structured and are not likely to become well-structured in the near future. Despite this fact, managers are solving such problems every day. People have the ability to act rationally in these messy and difficult circumstances. They may not always arrive at a perfect or even a satisfactory solution, but they are able to cope with most of these problems intelligently.

On the other hand, everything that we have learned about computers and how they are programmed indicates that they are only useful for solving well-structured problems. As we have said over and over, computers can perform arithmetic, make simple logical choices, and follow explicit directions, but they have no intuition or judgment; and if an unanticipated situation comes up, the computer has no power of its own to determine what to do.

Meaning of Heuristic

Heuristic is a rather difficult word to define. Webster's Collegiate Dictionary defines it as "serving to discover or to stimulate investigation." In its technical sense, heuristic is frequently associated with the simulation of human problem-solving techniques by means of computers. The process of solving a problem may be conceptualized as being similar to finding one's way through a maze and arriving at a solution. Each decision point in this maze corresponds to a set of alternative steps that can be taken next in the problem solving process. The human problem-solver wanders through this maze, taking wrong turns and retracing his steps, but eventually he will probably "muddle through" to a solution.

Humans, moreover, manage to find their way through this maze in a remarkably effective manner—a way that is superior to chance. In other words, when a human problem-solver makes a choice of how to proceed, the probability is pretty good that this choice will lead to a solution. In fact, the human seldom considers all the alternatives, but the few that come to his mind have a high probability of leading to success. The problem in using computers heuristically, then, is that of instructing the machine to make good choices in such a searching process.

This leads us to a more technical meaning of the word. A heuristic is any principle or device (that can be programmed) that contributes to *reducing* (or *reduction*) in the search for a solution. Note that a heuristic need not be foolproof; it may eliminate some or all paths leading to a solution, but, like similar human choices, it should contribute to the selection of paths that have a high probability of leading to a solution. In fact, several heuristics have been discovered by asking good human problem-solvers to think out loud while solving problems and analyzing the resulting tape recorded histories of their paths through the problem solving maze.

For example, planning is a useful heuristic. In planning, we devise a set of subgoals that break a large problem down into a series of smaller problems. Another heuristic is that of working backwards from the goal to the existing situation. And still another heuristic is comparing that which we need with what we have, detecting similarities, and attempting to reduce the differences.

Problem solving has been observed to be a highly recursive process. Describing the process used by a person to prove a theorem in Euclidian geometry, H. A. Simon says:

. . . the subject compares the theorem to be proved with some theorems he knows—he looks for similarities and differences. These suggest subproblems, whose solution may contribute to the solution of the main problem: "I have to prove two triangles are congruent. Are any pairs of sides equal? Can I prove some pairs of sides are equal?" Subproblems may, in turn, generate new subproblems, until he comes to a problem he can solve directly. Then he climbs back up to the next level of problems above. He gradually begins to assemble results that look as though they will contribute to the solution of the whole problem. He persists as he gets warmer, backs off to another direction of search when he finds a particular trail getting cooler.[17]

In current examples of heuristic programs a limited number of these general heuristics are combined with remembered specific information (such as theorems previously proved). The logical question is whether recursive use of such modest powers can actually lead to solutions of complex ill-structured problems. Considerable evidence has been gathered to make a case for an affirmative answer.

List-processing Languages

Significant developments in programming languages have been a by-product of experimenting with heuristic simulations. Since recursive symbol manipulations with complex logical structure are not

[17] Herbert A. Simon, *The New Science of Management Decision* (New York: Harper & Bros., 1960), p. 23.

conveniently programmed in the standard mathematical or data processing languages—such as FORTRAN and COBOL—special *list-processing* languages have been devised. In Information Processing Language V (IPL–V) the basic unit of data is a *list*, which is an ordered set of computer words containing symbols.[18] This language provides convenient means for adding items to the beginning or the end of a list, for inserting or deleting items from a list, and for generating new lists. Since the items in a list may be the names of other lists, these structures may be quite complex.

Another interesting feature of IPL–V is the use of push-down pop-up stacks for storing symbols. These stacks are similar to a cafeteria well for holding plates: when a plate is put on top of the stack, it pushes the others down; and as a plate is removed, the next one pops up.

Finally, this language includes provision for recursive processes which make it possible for a subroutine to execute itself as it moves from one subproblem level to a lower subproblem level.

List-processing programming languages may have a substantial impact upon the development of machines—as well as on data processing programming languages. Since data processing consists mainly of symbol manipulation and complex logic, it is likely that the new concepts in list-processing languages may turn out to be extremely valuable in data processing, particularly as we begin to implement more complex information systems (which may even include heuristic decision processes).

There is no doubt that heuristic simulation is an important approach for understanding human problem-solving behavior. And similar simulations are leading to a better understanding of other psychological and physiological phenomena. Also, there are several examples of the use of heuristic techniques to solve specific ill-structured problems for which the heuristic approach is superior to the results achieved by human problem-solvers. Theoretically, it appears that if the impressive power of the computer to pursue complex but well defined alternatives can be combined with the heuristic capabilities of humans, we should be able to attain extremely impressive problem-solving abilities.[19]

---

[18] For further descriptions of this language, see Allen Newell's *Information Processing Language—V Manual* (Englewood Cliffs, N.J.: Prentice-Hall, Inc., 1961).

[19] As was mentioned in Chapter 13, another approach to obtaining this combination of machine and human abilities is that of providing convenient means for human-machine *interaction* in problem solving. See Edward Fredkin, "The Time Sharing of Computers," *Computers and Automation*, November, 1963, pp. 12–20.

It is difficult to predict how far we will be able to go in this direction. At present our results are highly specific; that is, a different heuristic approach is required for each type of problem. Our ability to devise means of solving wider classes of problems is yet to be demonstrated. If we devise such means, the results could be truly revolutionary, for then the replacement of human thought (and much of management) would become a matter of economics: Which is more economical, a man or a machine?

COMPUTERS AND ORGANIZATIONAL RESEARCH AND DEVELOPMENT

As mentioned in Chapter 1, perhaps the greatest influence of the computer has been on management attitudes. The glamor of computers, and their cost, and hard-headed experience have combined to convince management leaders that it is necessary to adopt a systems viewpoint toward data processing. And this step has brought us up to the even higher viewpoint of visualizing the organization as a system. If we can see the organization as a *complex* system, we must reach the conclusion that one of management's most important responsibilities is to make sure that this system is as effective as possible.

Since everyone admits that we do not know enough about organizational systems to be able to really design them well, management's attitude toward organizational research and development (perhaps called Systems Analysis, Management Science, or Operations Research) is becoming more favorable. Several organizations, in fact, are making substantial investments in such activities in the expectation of receiving valuable competitive advantages.

At the same time that it stimulated management interest in organizational research and development, the computer also provided a breakthrough capability for coping with hitherto unmanageable problems. By reducing the costs of computation by a factor of at least 10,000, and the time required by a factor of about 10,000,000, the computer has made it feasible to solve large mathematical models. And, without the computer, effective simulation of large systems would be unthinkable.

Note, however, that it is not absolutely necessary to have a computer in the organization to be able to do effective organizational research and development. The model-building activities consume most of the time and effort in such research, so the portion for which the computer is required is but a relatively small part of the total, and a service bureau computer facility is usually quite suitable for solving mathematical models or running simulations. However, installation of a computer frequently brings into the organization a number of people who are interested in model-building activities, and it may also (as mentioned above) influence the management climate toward organizational "R and D."

Organizational R and D has a great impact on the use of computers. There is no question but that a computer used to duplicate a manual system is likely to be less than spectacularly successful. Securing the full potential of the computer usually depends upon radical restructuring of the data processing system, and probably upon substantial changes in the organizational system. And as we progress into the relatively new area of real-time systems, in which computers are linked together by communications networks, the need for creative systems analysis and design grows even greater. Only with substantial time, money, and talent investments in organizational research and development is it possible to take maximum advantage of the characteristics of modern equipment.

IMPACT ON MANAGEMENT

Electronic computers and the associated information technology is having, and will continue to have, a growing impact upon management and managers at all levels. Many managers and educators are very concerned about this impact. John F. Mee has said:

> Many a manager fears that he is engaged in a career race that will end in a photofinish between his retirement and his obsolescence for his job.[20]

Professor Mee has also stated that he thinks *he* will make it, but that his may well be the last generation to do so! And the new generation of managers heartily agrees.

> We'll never really be able to put computers to work until we get a whole new generation up there! *Business Week* reporters picked up that kind of comment, or agreement with it, from employees in almost every industry from retailing to heavy chemical production.[21]

In the remaining portion of this chapter we will consider the influence of information technology upon the jobs of management, the likely changes in management structure, and, finally, those man-

---

[20] John F. Mee, *Advanced Management*, September, 1961.
[21] Quoted from "New Tool. New World," *Business Week*, February 29, 1964, p. 82.

agement qualities which will become more important because of information technology.

Changes in Management Jobs

It appears that middle and top management will be affected quite differently by the growth of information technology. Let us consider middle management first. It is apparent that just as they replace large numbers of clerks, the widespread use of computers will also reduce the needs for middle-management supervision of those clerks that remain. As we have previously mentioned, providing for these displaced supervisors can be a difficult problem. And this problem may grow in significance as we mechanize more and more thoroughly. For example, direct entry of information by remote devices or by character readers is not yet widespread, but as it grows it will reduce the need for key punch operators and others who prepare data, and, consequently, will reduce or eliminate the need for their supervisors.

It is apparent that middle management will spend less time on winnowing information, separating the interesting and important from the trivial. Likewise, the computer will be used to perform analyses that are currently done by middle managers' simulating computers. Thus much of the dull, repetitious portions of the typical middle manager's job will be eliminated by the computer.

Furthermore, some of the direct control activities previously performed by low-middle managers will be programmed as decision rules. For example, inventory ordering and production scheduling decisions are currently being made by computers. There is a question as to how far this "programming" can be carried. Obviously, we can only program what we can understand, but what we understand is changing under the impact of organizational research and development.

How about judgmental decisions; can the computer take these over? Some authorities apparently believe that we will make impressive gains in converting ill-structured problems, that are now solved by judgment, into well-structured problems that can be handled by computers. And there are many who believe that the computer will compete with people not only by doing such work more economically, but also by doing it better.

There is an interesting research study that is pertinent to this question. You may be familiar with the Litkenhous predictions of the outcomes of future football games. These predictions are made by means of a secret formula which uses only the past scores of all teams, and no other information. Jesse G. Harris, Jr., performed a set of experiments in which he contrasted the predictive ability of the Litkenhous formula[22] against predictions made by Litkenhous himself, by a sportswriter, and by several football coaches whose teams were involved. These persons could look at the predictions of the formula and, by judgment, combine any extra knowledge they might have of physical condition, motivation, relative strength, or other factors to make their own predictions. Not one of the human predictors could do any better than the formula, and some did substantially worse.

On the basis of the above, it appears that information technology may significantly encroach upon the jobs of middle management. However, there will always be a need for managers who can motivate and handle people and who have the drive to push things through to a successful conclusion. And there will obviously be increased opportunities for information technologists at the middle management level.

It appears likely that top management will also be affected, although perhaps not so significantly as middle management. In the future, faster, more comprehensive information will be available to top management. Therefore it appears likely that top management will take back some of the everyday control which is now delegated to middle management. Some authorities foresee the gap between top and middle management as widening significantly, with top management taking over some of the more challenging and creative tasks of middle management.

Top management will, of course, retain the crucial responsibility for formulating the objectives and policies of the organization. In the future, as now, a major concern of top management will be with the overall "personality" of the firm. In this connection, as information technology grows in importance, top management will be forced to face the growing problem expressed by Sydney J. Harris:

> The real danger of our technological age is not so much that machines will begin to think like men, but that men will begin to think like machines.[23]

Two important concerns are expressed here. First, there is the danger that formal analysis will tend to stifle individual creativity,

---

[22] Jesse G. Harris, Jr., "Judgemental versus Mathematical Prediction," *Behavioral Science,* October, 1963, pp. 324–35.

[23] Sydney J. Harris, Publishers' Newspaper Syndicate (quoted in *Readers Digest*).

and that models, decision rules, and computer programs may tend to become unassailable and unchangeable. This may well lead to disaster, for when we cease the search for better understanding and better ways of coping with the environment, the new, creative system of today will become the obsolete, inadequate straightjacket of tomorrow.

And the second implication concerns some moral ramifications of information technology. Top management should be aware of the difficulty of incorporating concepts of morality and concern for human values into models, decision rules, and computer programs, because these concepts are hard to define precisely and may be virtually impossible to measure. Therefore top management must be vigilant in insisting that the organization serve human purposes by humane means.

Changes in Management Structure[24]

It appears, as we have seen, that there will be relatively fewer middle management line jobs, and that the middle manager will be further removed from top management. Also, the number of middle management levels will likely be reduced.

The reduction in the ranks of line managers will come as the result of the increasing number of information technology specialists. Since the specialists will have to adopt an organization-wide viewpoint, and since they must interact with top management, it is likely that these staff activities will be concentrated at the top instead of being decentralized throughout the organization.

Finally, the systems approach to organizations has tended to break down traditional departmental lines and to restructure the organization into fewer sub-units. There is a growing tendency toward integrating activities around functions without introducing artificial organizational barriers that are no longer required after the information system is integrated.

Management Qualities That Will Be Emphasized

First let's make it plain that the outstanding manager of today would likely be outstanding tomorrow as well, for today's outstanding manager must possess a wide variety of characteristics (intelligence, judgment, leadership ability, and analytical ability) that will

---

[24] Many of these ideas are derived from George P. Shultz and Thomas L. Whisler, *Management Organization and the Computer* (Glencoe, Ill.: Free Press of Glencoe, 1960).

be essential in the future. But it is also likely that the relative importance of certain characteristics will gradually change under the influence of the growth of information technology.

In the process we have outlined, the computer will take over much of the data processing screening and analysis which now takes up a good deal of management time. The manager will have less "busy-work," but, on the other hand, will be expected to be more analytical and creative. When problems are isolated by the information system, there will be a premium on the manager's ability to solve these problems and less emphasis on his ability to screen through mountains of data to detect them.

Of course we recognize by now that the real secret of the electronic computer lies in its program, which can capture the analysis of the creative individual and apply his analysis to individual situations. Thus, those managers who specialize in information technology will find that there will be a premium upon training in analytical disciplines and upon creativity in applying these techniques. And there will also be a premium upon the ability to communicate with top management (in both directions), for the man who cannot communicate will likely solve the wrong problem or devise a solution that will not be used.

On the other hand, the manager in the organization of the future must be able to communicate effectively with the various types of information technologists. As Martin Shubik has said:[25]

The alphabet and reading were necessary for the first industrial revolution. Some mathematical literacy is necessary for the second industrial revolution which is now under way.

Thus, it is widely recognized that the educational background for future management must include familiarity with concepts (such as mathematics) that are useful for understanding information technology (and information technologists).

Because of the growing gap between middle managers and top managers, these questions arise: Where will the top managers of tomorrow come from? Will they be able to work up through the thinned ranks of middle management? Will special training programs be required to bridge the gap between middle management and top management? Can simulation techniques be used to give middle management experience which will be helpful in top management positions?

---

[25] In a discussion at a meeting in Chicago on May 2, 1964, sponsored by the Committee on the Undergraduate Program in Mathematics of the Mathematical Association of America.

Gilbert Burck has pointed out that, because they had rigorous logical training and were forced to take a company-wide view of problems, legal and financial specialists have supplied a large part of the top management talent for the past forty years.

The higher order of systems and computer people should be in an even better position to know about the business than lawyers and treasurers were. They not only will have to understand the company's operating techniques and its relationships with the outside world, they will have to take both an analytical and a creative attitude toward them. . . . Although the ranks of computer-systems men contain a lot of men who seem "bloodless" and excessively engrossed in the technicalities of their indubitably fascinating business, some have already ascended to high management posts. The law of averages and their own intellectual growth should take care of others. The computerized world will be an oyster for the young man with brains, judgement, personality, education, ambition—and a good knowledge of computers.[26]

Let us attempt to summarize the message of this book in a single paragraph. The electronic computer and its associated information technology present a tremendous opportunity to the organization that is prepared to use them intelligently. On the other hand, it is apparent that the use of an electronic computer is not a panacea for poor management. As a matter of fact, excellent management is required to utilize an electronic computer successfully, and the management attributes emphasized by the computer are already of great importance to management success. Thus, the use of a computer is likely to make poor management more apparent, and good management even better.

EXERCISES

17.1   Discuss the reasons why it is difficult to implement the systems approach to data processing.

17.2   What are the major reasons that contribute to failure in the use of computers?

17.3   Why is the quality of people so important to the success of electronic data processing?

17.4   Why is it necessary to have top-management support to successfully install a computer?

17.5   Why is it necessary to have the participation of all levels of management to utilize electronic data processing effectively?

17.6   What is organizational Research and Development?

17.7   What is a mathematical model?

---

[26] Gilbert Burck, "Management Will Never Be the Same Again," *Fortune*, April, 1964, p. 204.

17.8 What is a simulation model? Distinguish between a simulation model and a mathematical model.

17.9 What is heuristic problem solving? What is its relation to computers and their use?

17.10 Discuss the advantages and disadvantages of a model-building approach to organizational Research and Development.

17.11 Discuss the relationships between organizational Research and Development and the use of computers.

17.12 What is information technology, and what long-range impact is it likely to have upon management?

17.13 What is likely to be the effect upon an individual manager of the installation of a computer in his organization?

SUPPLEMENTAL READINGS

BROSS, IRWIN D. J. *Design for Decision.* New York: The Macmillan Company, 1957.

A presentation for the intelligent layman of the major ideas of modern statistical decision theory.

BURCK, GILBERT. "Management Will Never Be the Same Again," *Fortune,* August, 1964, p. 124.

This article explores the impact of the computer and information technology upon management and the organization.

DEARDEN, JOHN. "Can Management Information Be Automated?" *Harvard Business Review,* March-April, 1964, pp. 128–35.

This article asserts that some of the thinking about the impact of the computer on top management is erroneous, for the major impact will be on operating information—which (he asserts) should be kept away from top management.

FORRESTER, JAY W. *Industrial Dynamics.* New York: John Wiley & Sons, Inc., 1961.

In addition to describing the philosophy and techniques of Industrial Dynamics, this book contains a gold mine of model-building philosophy. The introduction, Chapters 1–4, and Chapter 13 are especially helpful.

GAUMNITZ, R. K., AND BROWNLEE, O. H. "Mathematics for Decision Makers," *Harvard Business Review,* May-June, 1956, pp. 48–56.

Presents the importance of mathematics in decision making and some of the implications for the future.

LEAVITT, H. J., AND WHISLER, T. L. "Management in the 1980's," *Harvard Business Review,* November-December, 1958, pp. 41–48.

A very significant article that discusses the implications for the future of the growing importance of information technology.

MILLER, D. W., AND STARR, M. K. *Executive Decisions and Operations Research.* Englewood Cliffs, N.J.: Prentice-Hall, Inc., 1960.

An introduction to the philosophy of model-building, with illustrations from many areas of business.

Morris, William T. *Management Science in Action.* Homewood, Ill.: Richard D. Irwin, Inc., 1963.

An excellent presentation of the impact of management science on management. A good discussion of the difficulties inherent in using management science.

Shultz, G. P., and Whisler, T. L. *Management Organization and the Computer.* Glencoe, Ill.: Free Press of Glencoe, 1960.

This book is the result of a conference and includes the papers presented and the discussions of the papers. It is a must for those interested in the management and organizational implications of information technology.

Simon, Herbert A. *The New Science of Management Decision.* New York: Harper & Bros.: 1960.

This significant little book is concerned with the impact of management science and information technology upon management and organizations. It includes a lucid discussion of heuristic problem solving by one of the pioneers in this area.

APPENDIX

A THE JIFFY
MANUFACTURING CASE

THE JIFFY MANUFACTURING COMPANY is a rapidly growing Midwestern company that makes and markets a very seasonal group of products. During the first week of each of the four major selling seasons it is crucial that this company quickly detect and rapidly react to trends of consumer preference. The faster they can detect "hot" items and get them into accelerated production, the more profit they can make.

Under the leadership of Mr. Edward J. Sampson, president, Jiffy Manufacturing last year made a profit after taxes of $1,527,000 on net sales of $35,304,000. The company owns its factory and an office building, and has a second office building under construction that will be occupied next year. Jiffy employs around 3,000 people.

GROWTH OF DATA PROCESSING FACILITIES

About 20 years ago the sales manager, Mr. Cecil Harrison, decided that he needed a small punched card installation to produce rapid and accurate sales analysis figures that would aid in quickly spotting seasonal sales trends. He persuaded Mr. Sampson to allow him to acquire such equipment, and he hired young Harry Burton, who had worked with punched card equipment, to run the installation. Over the years this installation was quite satisfactory to Mr. Harrison. Harry Burton was ingenious in working with the machines, and he was able to develop procedures to prepare the reports that Mr. Harrison wanted; he was also flexible enough to be able to run flash reports to answer special questions when they arose.

Since sales activities were seasonal, Burton had much idle machine time between peaks, and, being an accommodating fellow, he began to perform a number of jobs for the controller. However, as this load grew, conflicts arose between the demands of the controller and the peak loads of the sales analysis. Extremely loyal to Mr. Harrison, Burton usually resolved these conflicts by delaying the controller's work, and finally, about five years ago, the controller, Mr. Lloyd Kramer, decided to get his own equipment and establish his own data processing installation.

The controller's installation grew rather rapidly, and about two years ago Mr. Richard Edmonds, a salesman for a large computer company, was hired as senior systems analyst, and a small punched-card-oriented data processing computer was installed. Edmonds is an adequate systems man, and supervises the efforts of two other recently hred young systems analyst trainees.

COMPUTER PROPOSED

A few months ago Kramer and Edmonds decided that their growing needs justified the acquisition of a small magnetic-tape data processing computer and suggested to Mr. Sampson that such a machine be obtained. After investigating a number of small computers, they narrowed their consideration to two machines, each of which appeared to be suitable for their needs for the next three to five years.

These two machines (hereafter called Machine A and Machine B) were particularly appealing because Jiffy Manufacturing Company could rent or buy either of them for approximately 50 percent less than their new price; they were only two years old and in perfect condition. Although the machines were manufactured by different companies, and were quite dissimilar internally, each could write magnetic tape that the other could read.

Both were building-block machines that could be expanded as required in the future, but it was thought likely that any additional components added would be at the full price. Machine B was considered to be more powerful than Machine A, but it also cost more; and Machine A had better service facilities and backup computers available in the immediate area.

When the fact that they were considering a larger computer became known throughout the company, several men approached Mr. Sampson and suggested that the company consider the establishment of a centralized data processing facility to serve the needs of the entire organization, rather than have several equipment installations. Mr. H. N. Meyer, director of planning, was particularly concerned because, with two separate systems, the data he needed for special studies were difficult to assemble and process if parts of it came from several sources. Also, Mr. Earl Miller, production manager, was upset because he felt that his data processing needs were not being provided for and would not be adequately served by either the existent or the planned installations.

COMMITTEE FORMED

Mr. Sampson was convinced that computers are here to stay and that Jiffy Manufacturing needed more powerful data processing equipment, especially in view of the projected growth of the company. He asked Harrison, Kramer, Miller, and Meyer to meet as a committee (with Meyer as chairman) to study the problem and to recommend whether or not a centralized data processing facility should be established.

As this committee met and discussed the problem, it became apparent that there was an undercurrent of distrust between Kramer and Harrison, probably dating back to their difficulties when they shared the same punched card installation. Both agreed that they needed additional equipment, but neither appeared willing to make extensive use of equipment that was administered by the other.

There was a further problem of location. The logical place to locate a data processing facility was in the new building just then being completed. But the controller's people were being transferred to the new building, and the sales organization was to stay in the old building.

The committee meetings were long and frequently explosive, with Meyer and Miller trying to convince Kramer and Harrison of the logic of a single installation to serve all the needs of the company. Kramer's attitude was: "Why should I give up something that is now running satisfactorily?" And Harrison appeared convinced that he could obtain little good from an installation that was under Kramer's control or located in the new building.

COMMITTEE REPORT

About the only thing the committee could agree upon was that they preferred Machine A to Machine B. Otherwise, they "agreed to disagree," with Meyer and Miller submitting one set of recommendations and (paradoxically) Harrison and Kramer submitting another.

The reports submitted to Mr. Sampson, attached as Exhibits I, II and III, speak for themselves.

EXHIBIT I

To: *President Edward J. Sampson*   From: *H. N. Meyer, Chairman of Committee to Study Data Processing Needs*

The Committee to Study Data Processing Needs wishes to submit the attached report which contains recommendations concerning the place of data processing in the Jiffy Manufacturing Company. In transmitting the report I should like to comment briefly upon a divergence of views which represents a basic policy question upon which the committee is unable to reach unanimity.

All members of the committee are in full agreement that we have an imperative need for compatibility of data, cooperation among administrative offices which are producers and consumers of data, and the extension and amplification of the reporting and analyzing of data. The committee is also in agreement that additional data processing equipment is needed to accomplish these objectives.

Some members of the committee feel that these aims can best be accomplished through the establishment of a centralized data processing center which would remove much of the autonomy of the present two data processing installations and would integrate them into one combined installation. The director of this installation and his superior would have the responsibility of establishing priorities for data processing jobs (running payrolls, printing sales reports, etc.) and for determining the nature and timetable for new data processing services to be performed by the data processing center.

Other members of the committee feel that the autonomy of the present data processing installations should be preserved and that additional data processing equipment should (1) be assigned to one unit to be shared by the other, or (2) be added to both installations. These views are attached to the committee report as position statements of the persons involved.

The committee believes that the alternative plans which are worthy of consideration are:

1. Establishment of the data processing center staffed and equipped as described in the attached report.
2. Acquiring Machine A and placing it in the controller's installation with the understanding that the sales department, production department, planning group and others may use it when it is free.
3. Allocation of Machine A to the sales department installation and authorization for the controller to acquire Machine B.

EXHIBIT II

To: *President Edward J. Sampson*

In an earlier document it was reported that this committee endorsed in principle the establishment of a centralized data processing center. The committee has continued to work on the problems attendant to the implementation of this proposal, and the members of the committee whose names are signed below wish to make additional recommendations.

1. The undersigned reaffirm our endorsement of a centralized data processing center and recommend that such a unit be established as soon as it is feasible. We further recommend that the tabulating unit now operated by the sales department retain its autonomy for the present and utilize central data processing facilities for operations that require computer capabilities. We anticipate that the sales department will convert its record keeping operations to the tape system as rapidly as possible and that economies of staff and machine rental in its tabulating division will result as the conversion proceeds.

2. We recommend the installation in the centralized data processing center of Machine A with four magnetic tape units. We believe that this equipment is the logical first move in meeting our present data processing needs and can be expanded as necessary to meet our needs for the next three to five years.

3. Fundamental to the effective utilization of the recommended installation is adequate systems analysis and programming support which must be provided in the budget of the data processing center. We recommend that the staff of the center include not only a director and programmer-operators from existing personnel within the company, but also recommend that additional systems analysts-programmers be added to the center staff. We estimate that a minimum of three systems analysts-programmers would be needed to convert present programs to Machine A and to convert the record keeping in the sales department to tape at a rate sufficient to provide for efficient utilization of the computer upon its arrival.

4. We recommend that the data processing center be located in the new office building. As data processing needs grow and as new computer equipment becomes available, the location of the center may need to be reexamined; but for the present we believe that this is the optimum location for the installation.

5. Consideration has been given to the location of the data processing center in the organizational structure of the company. Because of the service functions and the shared availability of the facilities, we believe it would be unfair to impose the burden of impartial administering of computer availability and decision making concerning new systems upon

either of the major users of the center facilities. We feel that the center should be administered by an office which has personnel acquainted with the potentialities and limitations of data processing equipment, and one which is in a position to see data processing needs in the framework of overall company operation, but we have no specific recommendation for the organizational location.

6. Recognizing that the data processing applications currently under way and those which might well be added in the near future are of such complexity that the ability of a single office to make decisions concerning priorities might be severely taxed, we recommend that an Advisory Committee to the Data Processing Center be established. This committee, which might be similar in composition to the Committee to Study Data Processing Needs, would be charged with the responsibility of assisting the Center in evaluating equipment needs, for assigning priorities for systems design of new data processing applications, and for production runs.

(*signed*)   H. N. Meyer
Earl Miller

EXHIBIT III

To: *President Edward J. Sampson*

The undersigned members of the Committee to Study Data Processing Needs wish to submit the following comments and recommendations. We have attempted to keep in mind the discussions, exchange of information, and other pertinent data acquired as members of the committee in arriving at our recommendations. It is to be recognized that the committee meetings have resulted in considerable differences of opinion between members as to the physical and organizational location of data processing within the company.

It is with this in mind that we have examined the possibility of establishing two administrative processing centers: one for the sales area and another for the financial area. One reaction to this has been that it results in excessive cost to the company. If the long-range view is taken, however, the two installations may prove to be more economical and efficient than a single operating unit. It is well established that the Jiffy Manufacturing Company will continue to grow in the next few years at a very rapid pace, and Machine A, considered for a single center, no doubt will become inadequate within a three- to four-year period. At this time bigger and more powerful equipment will be required. Depending on the hardware available at that time, it is possible that complete reprogramming may be necessary.

If one looks at the cost of establishing a data processing center in the controller's office, with the 50 percent discounts offered either Machine A or Machine B can easily be justified. The controller's office has made a cost analysis in this respect, and, through the acquisition of Machine B, the total monthly expense—projected over a period of ten years—would be $2,867 per month. This cost can easily be justified by direct comparison to the cost of the basic card system installed in the office. Furthermore, it has been stated that the sales department and others have enough data processing needs to justify Machine A. If these premises are valid, it would certainly appear that we should take a long-range view and acquire equipment that will be adequate to handle the projected growth in the next eight to ten years.

The attached cost comparison chart (Table A–1) estimates the cumulative rental or purchase cost of computers for data processing during the next ten years. At present, we are in the rather enviable position of being able to rent Machine A at a 50 percent discount and to purchase Machine B on a five-year basis at more than a 50 percent discount. The cost comparison chart indicates the advantage of obtaining and retaining these two particular machines at these advantageous prices. We believe that similarly attractive deals for such machines may not be available again in the foreseeable future.

One major advantage of having two machines is that double input and output capacity is provided. Normally, this input-output is the limiting factor on data processing rather than the internal computer capacity of the machine. Another point in favor of the purchase of a computer is that the General Accounting Office has recently been urging federal departments to purchase rather than rent; they feel it is possible and entirely practical now that the computers we are discussing are completely transistorized and have an extremely small amount of down time.

Possibly of even greater importance than the cost factor is that of direct administrative control, the capacity to make decisions, and the absence of diametrically opposed viewpoints that would occur in operating a single data processing installation. About the only location within the company structure where a single data processing center could be effectively administered is directly under the President's office. This, of course, may not be at all feasible or within the realm of possibility. Any other placement of this single center has, in our committee meetings, been objectionable to one or the other of the two major users. Therefore, the establishment of two data processing centers would eliminate unnecessary negotiation and arbitration in order to arrive at fair and just decisions.

We recommend the establishment of two data processing centers, one for the sales department and another for the controller's department. An attempt should be made, in both of these installations, to consider and discuss systems approaches which may affect the other's operations. The standardization of systems work in the two data processing installations should be coordinated by a steering committee composed of interested representatives from all areas of the company. We feel that the Director of Planning should be represented on this committee to insure compatible and integrated systems development for the entire company. Obvi-

TABLE A–1

Equipment Cost Comparison of Computers

	1st Year	2d Year	3d Year	4th Year	5th Year	6th Year	7th Year	8th Year	9th Year	10th Year	Average Cost per month
One Computer (starting with Machine A)	$43,200	$43,200	$ 56,800*	$ 56,800	$ 91,400†	$ 91,400	$ 91,400	$120,000	$120,000‡	$120,000	$6,952
Released equipment	–38,400	–38,400	–38,400	–38,400	–38,400	–38,400	–38,400	–38,400	–38,400	–38,400	–3,200
Cost of additional equipment	$ 4,800	$ 4,800	$ 18,400	$ 18,400	$ 53,000	$ 53,000	$ 53,000	$ 81,600	$ 81,600	$ 81,600	$3,752
Cumulative Cost	$ 4,800	$ 9,600	$ 28,000	$ 46,400	$ 99,400	$152,400	$205,400	$287,000	$368,600	$450,200	
Two computers:											
Machine B	$58,500	$58,500	$ 58,500	$ 58,500	$ 58,500§	$ 10,300	$ 10,300	$ 10,300	$ 10,300	$ 10,300	$2,867
Machine A	35,000	35,000	35,000	35,000	35,000	35,000	35,000	35,000	35,000	35,000	2,917
Total	$93,500	$93,500	$ 93,500	$ 93,500	$ 93,500	$ 45,300	$ 45,300	$ 45,300	$ 45,300	$ 45,300	$5,784
Released equipment	–49,200	–49,200	–49,200	–49,200	–49,200	–49,200	–49,200	–49,200	–49,200	–49,200	–4,100
Cost of additional equipment	$44,300	$44,300	$ 44,300	$ 44,300	$ 44,300	$ –3,900	$ –3,900	$ –3,900	$ –3,900	$ –3,900	$1,684
Cumulative Cost	$44,300	$88,600	$132,900	$177,200	$221,500	$217,600	$213,700	$209,800	$205,900	$202,000	

* Add cost of high-speed tape units ($1,140 per month).
† Add fast printer and faster arithmetic unit ($2,884 per month).
‡ Replace Machine A with Machine C, which is faster but has program compatibility with Machine A.
§ Machine B has been paid for; maintenance costs will be $10,300 per year.

ously, all output magnetic tape should be in a common form which is usable on both computers. This is possible with the installation of the suggested machines.

It is our hope that the above viewpoint will be seriously considered in order to expedite more effective data processing within the Jiffy Manufacturing Company.

(*signed*)   Cecil Harrison

Lloyd Kramer

Questions for Discussion

1. Analyze and evaluate the proposal submitted by Harrison and Kramer.
2. What problems should Mr. Sampson consider in deciding what to do?
3. What should Mr. Sampson do?

B

BINARY NOTATION
AND ARITHMETIC

TO PROVIDE as fast an arithmetic unit as possible for a given cost, many scientific computers operate on numbers expressed in binary notation. The usual notation for writing numbers is called decimal notation, and the value of a digit is based upon the position in which the digit occurs. In the number 957, the 9 does not really represent the number 9, it represents 9 times 100. Likewise, the 5 represents 5 times 10. Thus, 957 is actually $9 \times (10)^2 + 5 \times (10) + 7$. You must know the position in which a digit appears in the number to properly interpret its meaning. Each time we move one position to the left the value of that position is multiplied by 10, thus progressing from the units position to the tens position to the hundreds position to the thousands position, and so on.

Numbers may be written in several ways. For example, twenty-seven may be written as 27 in decimal notation or as XXVII in Roman numerals. In the usual positional notation discussed above, the number ten is called the *base* of the notation. Ten is used as the base of our notation because we happen to have ten fingers. However, any other number could be used, and in different civilizations both twenty and sixty have been used. Mathematically, it might be more convenient to use twelve instead of ten, for dozens would be easier to express, and fewer fractions would have repeating decimal equivalents (such as $\frac{1}{3} = .3333 \ldots$).

To express numbers in a notation with n as the base, single digits for each number from zero to $n-1$ are required. Thus, in the decimal system, the digits 0, 1, 2, 3, 4, 5, 6, 7, 8, and 9 are required. If twelve were used as the base, two extra symbols would be required to represent ten and eleven. Thus, we might denote ten by τ and eleven by ϵ providing the digits 0, 1, 2, 3, 4, 5, 6, 7, 8, 9, τ, ϵ. Then, in base twelve, 10 would represent twelve, 11 would represent thirteen, 1_T would represent twenty-two, 1_ϵ would represent twenty-three, and 20 would represent twenty-four.

In the binary system of notation the number two is used in place of ten as the base of the positional notation. Since only the digits less than the base number are required, in binary notation we use only the digits 0 and 1, and each number is expressed as a string of zero's and one's. For example, the number five is written in binary notation as 101, $1 \times (2)^2 + 0 \times (2) + 1$, while the number 100 written in binary becomes 1100100, $1 \times (2)^6 + 1 \times (2)^5 + 0 \times (2)^4 + 0 \times (2)^3 + 1 \times (2)^2 + 0 \times (2) + 0$.

Binary to Decimal Conversion

Given any binary number, it is easy to translate it into decimal form by the following process: Start with the right-most digit. If this is a 1, write it down. Then, working toward the left, the next position represents 2, the next 4, the next 8, and so on, doubling each time. Whenever a one is encountered, write down the corresponding positional value. At the conclusion of this process, add them all up. For example, for the binary number 1101001011101 we would have:

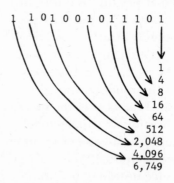

Decimal to Binary Conversion

The process of translating a number from decimal notation into binary is a bit more complicated. One method involves dividing the decimal number by 2 and recording the remainder, then dividing the quotient by 2 and recording the remainder, and continuing this process (as illustrated below for the number 6,749 [start at the top and work down]) :

Remainder

2	6749	
2	3374	1
2	1687	0
2	843	1
2	421	1
2	210	1
2	105	0
2	52	1
2	26	0
2	13	0
2	6	1
2	3	0
2	1	1
	0	1

Then, reading the remainder column from the bottom, 6,749 is represented as 1101001011101 in binary notation.

Binary Calculations

If one can forget what he knows of decimal arithmetic, binary arithmetic is extremely simple. The addition and multiplication tables, involving only the digits zero and one, are shown below:

Addition
$0 + 0 = 0$
$0 + 1 = 1$
$1 + 1 = 10$

Multiplication
$0 \times 0 = 0$
$0 \times 1 = 0$
$1 \times 1 = 1$

Addition takes place digit by digit, starting from the right. For example, consider eleven plus seven in binary notation:

$$
\begin{array}{r}
1011 \\
+111 \\
\end{array}
$$

Starting at the right, $1 + 1 = 10$, so we put down the zero and carry 1.

$$
\begin{array}{r}
1 \\
1011 \\
111 \\
\hline
0 \\
\end{array}
$$

Then $1 + 1 = 10$, and $10 + 1 = 11$, so we put down 1 and carry 1.

$$\begin{array}{r} 1 \\ 1011 \\ 111 \\ \hline 10 \end{array}$$

At this point $1 + 0 = 1$, and $1 + 1 = 10$, so we put down zero and carry 1.

$$\begin{array}{r} 1 \\ 1011 \\ 111 \\ \hline 010 \end{array}$$

Finally, $1 + 1 = 10$, so we obtain:

$$\begin{array}{r} 1011 \\ 111 \\ \hline 10010 \end{array}$$

To check, in decimal notation the binary number 10010 becomes eighteen, which is eleven plus seven.

Suppose we wish to multiply 1011 by 101:

$$\begin{array}{r} 1011 \\ \times 101 \end{array}$$

The multiplication is easy, since we merely multiply by 0 and 1 to obtain partial products, as shown below:

$$\begin{array}{r} 1011 \\ 101 \\ \hline 1011 \\ 10110 \end{array}$$

To complete the multiplication we must add these partial products to obtain 110111. As a check, 1011 is eleven and 101 is five, while 110111 is fifty-five.

Octal Notation

Octal notation, using eight as the base, is convenient for interpreting binary numbers. Since eight is close to ten, it is relatively easy to convert our thinking to the use of octal notation. Also, by dividing the digits into groups of three, binary numbers may be converted to octal notation. Thus, those who use binary machines frequently program in octal notation, and desk calculators which calculate in octal notation are available for their use.

To convert the binary number 1101001011101 (which is 6,749 in decimal notation) to octal, we separate the digits into groups of three, starting at the right: (1) (101) (001) (011) (101). Then, interpreting each group as binary representation of a single digit, we produce the octal number 15135. As a check, inserting the powers of eight, this number represents $1(8)^4 + 5(8)^3 + 1(8)^2 + 3(8) + 5$, which is $1(4,096) + 5(512) + 1(64) + 3(8) + 5 = 4,096 + 2,560 + 64 + 24 + 5 = 6,749$.

C

FLOATING DECIMAL
REPRESENTATION

ANY NUMBER can be placed in a standard form with the decimal point in a specified position and the actual location of the decimal point indicated by multiplying by a suitable power of 10. In this notation, negative exponents (which indicate division by the corresponding power of 10 move the decimal place to the left, while positive exponents move it to the right, as shown below.

$$
\begin{aligned}
.0000125 &= .125 \times 10^{-4} \\
.000125 &= .125 \times 10^{-3} \\
.00125 &= .125 \times 10^{-2} \\
.0125 &= .125 \times 10^{-1} \\
.125 &= .125 \times 10^{0} \\
1.25 &= .125 \times 10^{1} \\
12.5 &= .125 \times 10^{2} \\
125 &= .125 \times 10^{3} \\
1250 &= .125 \times 10^{4} \\
12500 &= .125 \times 10^{5}
\end{aligned}
$$

Numbers expressed in the above standard form, in which a power of 10 is multiplied by a number with the decimal point to the left of the first non-zero digit, are said to be in floating decimal notation. Arithmetic operations may be performed with floating decimal numbers by using rules that produce the result in floating decimal form.

For multiplication and division, these rules are simple. For example, to multiply $.125 \times 10^{4}$ by $.200 \times 10^{-2}$ we multiply $.125 \times .200 = .0250$ and $10^{4} \times 10^{-2} = 10^{2}$ to obtain the answer $.025 \times 10^{2}$. However, because the decimal point is not to the left of the first non-zero digit, we must move it to the right and adjust the exponent to obtain $.25 \times 10^{1}$. As a check, $.125 \times 10^{4} = 1250$,

.200 × 10^{-2} = .002, and .25 × 10^1 = 2.5. Since 1250 × .002 = 2.5, the results are correct.

The major advantage of floating decimal notation is in division, which can be set up so there is no danger of quotient overflow since both numbers have the same relative magnitude except for the exponents. As an example of division, consider .625 × 10^{-7} divided by .125 × 10^6. Since .625 ÷ .125 is 5 and 10^{-7} ÷ 10^6 is 10^{-13}, the result is 5. × 10^{-13}, which must be adjusted to obtain .5 × 10^{-12}.

Addition and subtraction are more complicated in floating decimal notation because the decimal points must be lined up (by making their exponents the same) before these operations can be performed. For example, .625 × 10^{-3} + .125 × 10^{-4} can be expressed:

$$\begin{array}{r} .6250 \times 10^{-3} \\ .0125 \times 10^{-3} \\ \hline .6375 \times 10^{-3} \end{array}$$

Whenever the exponents are widely different, this adjustment requires much shifting.

Arithmetic units of computers may be constructed to compute directly with numbers in floating decimal form, and automatic programming techniques (floating decimal subroutines) may be used to compute with these numbers. Computing in floating decimal form makes programming of complex computational problems much easier, for it is not necessary for the programmer to keep track of the decimal point and program the shifts required by the computations. On the other hand, the programmer may have little knowledge of how many figures are significant in results computed by means of floating decimal arithmetic.

Most scientific computers have instructions available (as standard or optional features) that compute with floating point numbers. Because of the shifting involved, floating point addition and subtraction are slower than the corresponding fixed point instructions, but floating point multiplication and division are usually faster than the fixed point operations.

Both the number and the exponent are usually stored in the same word. Since the number itself and the exponent both have signs which may be different, in decimal machines the notation is modified by adding 50 to the exponent, so that exponents from −50 to +49 may be expressed by the positive numbers 00 through 99. There is no uniformity in floating decimal notation among various computers and automatic programming systems, but one notation places the number (up to 8 digits) in the first 8 positions of the word and the modified exponent in the right-most 2 positions. In such a machine the number $-125,000,000,000$ (which is $-.12500000 \times 10^{12}$) would be stored as $1250000062-$, while the number $+.0000000125$ (which is $+.12500000 \times 10^{-7}$) would be stored as $1250000043+$.

Input and output may be in floating decimal form, or conversion back and forth between fixed and floating notation may be programmed. The programmer must know which locations contain floating point numbers and which contain fixed point numbers, for erroneous results are produced by computing with fixed point numbers by means of floating point instructions, or vice versa.

D INDEX OF MAC INSTRUCTIONS

Instruction	Abbreviation	Code	Page
Long Right Shift	LRS	30	146
Long Shift and Round	LSR	31	146
Multiply	MPY	19	143
Punch Card	PCD	71	140
Print	PRT	72	140
Read Card	RCD	70	138
Read Disk	RDD	79	371
Read Magnetic Tape	RMT	73	314
Receive	RCV	67	326
Reset Add to A Register	RAA	65	133
Reset Add to Index Register 1	RA1	02	192
Reset Add to Index Register 2	RA2	03	192
Reset Add to Index Register 3	RA3	04	192
Reset and Subtract from A Register	RSA	66	135
Reset and Subtract from Index Register 1	RS1	08	192
Reset and Subtract from Index Register 2	RS2	09	192
Reset and Subtract from Index Register 3	RS3	10	192
Rewind Tape	RWT	77	315
Seek	SEK	78	371
Store A Register	STA	20	134
Store Index Register 1	ST1	21	192
Store Index Register 2	ST2	22	192
Store Index Register 3	ST3	23	192
Store M Register	STM	24	136
Subtract from A Register	SUA	16	136
Subtract from Index Register 1	SU1	11	192
Subtract from Index Register 2	SU2	12	192
Subtract from Index Register 3	SU3	13	192
Tape Back Space	TBS	75	314
Transmit	TSM	68	326
Write Check	WCK	81	372
Write Disk	WRD	80	371
Write End-of-File Tape	WET	76	315
Write Magnetic Tape	WMT	74	314

INDEX

This book has been set on the Linotype in 11 point Baskerville, leaded 2 points, and 10 point Baskerville, leaded 1 point. Chapter numbers are in Spartan Heavy and chapter titles are in Spartan Medium. The size of the type page is 27 by 46½ picas.